DIRECTIONS IN DEVELOPMENT

Reversing the Spiral
The Population, Agriculture, and Environment Nexus in Sub-Saharan Africa

Kevin M. Cleaver
Götz A. Schreiber

The World Bank
Washington, D.C.

Cover photo: World Bank Photo Library (R. Witlin).

Library of Congress Cataloging-in-Publication Data
Cleaver, Kevin M.
    Reversing the spiral : the population, agriculture, and
environment nexus in Sub-Saharan Africa / Kevin M. Cleaver and Götz
A. Schreiber.
        p. cm. — (Directions in development)
    Includes bibliographical references
    ISBN 0-8213-2769-0
    1. Human ecology—Africa, Sub-Saharan. 2. Agriculture and state—
Africa, Sub-Saharan. 3. Agriculture—Environmental aspects—
Africa, Sub-Saharan. 4. Africa, Sub-Saharan—Economic
conditions—1960- 5. Africa, Sub-Saharan—Environmental conditions.
    6. Africa, Sub-Saharan—Social conditions—1960- I. Schreiber,
Götz A., 1944- II. Title. III. Series: Directions in
development (Washington, D.C.)
GF701.C54   1994

Contents

Text Figures

Text Tables

Appendix Tables

Foreword

Over the past thirty years, most of Sub-Saharan Africa has seen rapid population growth, poor agricultural performance, and increasing environmental degradation. Why do these problems seem so intractable? Are they connected? Do they reinforce each other? If so, what are the critical links? *Reversing the Spiral* tests the hypothesis that these phenomena are strongly interrelated. The finding — that this nexus is very much at work in Sub-Saharan Africa — tells us that the design of development efforts must come to reflect this reality.

Key links are found in traditional crop and livestock production methods, land tenure systems, women's responsibilities, traditional family planning mechanisms, and methods of forest resource utilization. Traditional systems and practices, well suited to people's survival needs when population densities were low, were able to evolve in response to slow population growth. But with the acceleration of population growth in the 1950s, traditional ways came under increasing strain resulting in the triad of problems addressed here.

Solutions are complex. Effective responses have not been forthcoming from international and donor communities, except on a very limited scale in a few places. This study assesses successful and failed interventions. With that base it recommends concrete and implementable strategies to intensify agriculture, increase demand for smaller families, reform land tenure practices, conserve the environment, and address the special problems of women. An important message is the need for Africans themselves to lead the process and for empowered farmers to manage their own development.

Understanding that the major African dilemma described in this book resulted from a nexus of problems enables a nexus of solutions. The hope is that the message of *Reversing the Spiral* — by stimulating and informing policies and investments of governments, NGOs, and donors and by engaging African leadership — will effect the recovery of food security, natural resources, and health in Africa.

Several country-specific population, agriculture, and environment nexus studies have been initiated to deepen this work and are referred to in this book. The *Supplement to Reversing the Spiral,* a detailed statistical analysis supporting the argument of the book, has been published as a companion to this volume. Inputs to the study came from World Bank staff, the FAO, the Caisse Française de Développement, the French government's Ministry of Cooperation, USAID, the Swedish International Development Authority, the German KfW, the British ODA, IFPRI, SPAAR, the World Wildlife Fund, the World Resources Institute, the Global Coalition for Africa, and a large number of African officials and academics.

E. V. K. Jaycox
Vice President, Africa Region
The World Bank

Acknowledgments

This study has benefited from considerable input from a number of our colleagues both within and outside the World Bank. Roland Michelitsch conducted much of the statistical analysis summarized in the *Supplement* to this volume. Sandy Gain, Pushpa Schwartz, and S. Yalamanchili contributed statistical material.

An initial report setting out the hypotheses to be studied was the subject of a seminar held at the World Bank in June 1990, chaired by Michel Petit. Subsequently, seminars were held with the Country Departments of the Africa Region of the World Bank. A formal review in the World Bank of an initial draft report in December 1991 was chaired by Michel Petit. Drafts have been presented to representatives of African governments and development agencies as well as of nongovernmental organizations at the West and Central African Rain Forest Conservation Conference in Abidjan in October 1990, to academic fora organized by Montclair State College in New Jersey in November 1990 and by the Harvard Center for Population and Development Studies in March 1992, to an international conference on population issues in Africa organized by the Government of France in September 1991, to staff of USAID on several occasions between July 1990 and August 1993, to officials of the Caisse Française de Développement in Paris in January 1992, and to staff of the Federal Ministry for Economic Cooperation (BMZ), Kreditanstalt für Wiederaufbau (KfW) and Gesellschaft für Technische Zusammenarbeit (GTZ) in Frankfurt in April 1993. Members of the World Bank Africa Region's Thematic Team on the Population, Agriculture, and Environment Nexus have also provided comments and suggestions. These various inputs and reviews, and additional research stimulated by the comments and suggestions received, have resulted in the present study.

Special thanks for support, comments, suggestions, and contributions are due to: E. V. K. Jaycox, Robert McNamara, Ismail Serageldin, Caio Koch-Weser, Michel Petit, Anand Seth, Steve O'Brien, Ishrat Z. Husain, Michael Gillette, Pierre Landell-Mills, Fred Sai, Dunstan Wai, Ishrat Husain, John Peberdy, Dennis Mahar, Leif Christoffersen, François Falloux, John English, Susan Cochrane, Althea Hill, Harry Walters, Agi

Kiss, François Wencélius, Joanne Salop, Jean Doyen, Cynthia Cook, Willem Floor, Mary Dyson, Elizabeth Morris-Hughes, Julia Clones, Paul Shaw, John Spears, Moctar Touré, Phillippe Caquard, Montague Yudelman, Allen Kelley, Michael Paolisso, Larry Stifel, P. C. Mohan, Dixie Barlow, and Deirdre T. Murphy, and staff of the FAO and the Caisse Française de Développement.

Finally, the comments and suggestions of four anonymous reviewers have been most useful and are acknowledged with particular gratitude.

Acronyms and Abbreviations

ADB	African Development Bank	IPM	integrated pest management
AIDS	Acquired Immune Deficiency Syndrome	ITTO	International Tropical Timber Organization
CFCs	chlorofluorocarbons	ITCZ	InterTropical Convection Zone
cm	centimeter		
CMR	child mortality rate	IUCN	World Conservation Union (formerly International Union for Conservation of Nature)
CNN	cloud condensation nuclei		
CPR	contraceptive prevalence rate		
DHS	demographic and health survey	kcal	kilocalorie
		km	kilometer
FAO	Food and Agriculture Organization of the United Nations	LPG	liquefied petroleum gas
		MCH	maternal and child health
		mm	millimeter
FHH	female-headed household	NARS	National Agricultural Research System
FP	family planning		
GEF	Global Environmental Facility	NGO	nongovernmental organization
GIS	Geographic Information System	NRR	net reproduction rate
		SPAAR	Special Program for African Agricultural Research
ha	hectare		
HYV	higher-yielding variety	SSA	Sub-Saharan Africa
IARCs	International Agricultural Research Centers	STDs	sexually transmitted diseases
IBRD	International Bank for Reconstruction and Development	TFR	total fertility rate
		UNDP	United Nations Development Programme
IDA	International Development Association	UNEP	United Nations Environment Programme
IEC	information, education, and communication	WFS	World Fertility Survey
		WMO	World Meteorological Organization
IITA	International Institute of Tropical Agriculture	WRI	World Resources Institute
IMR	infant mortality rate		

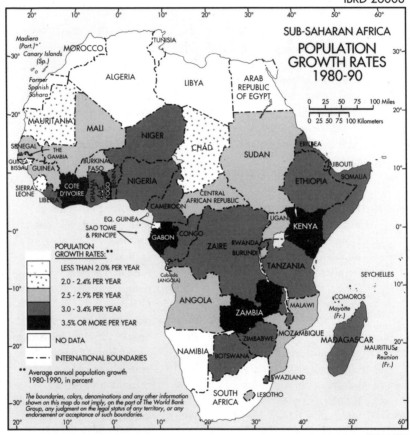

SUB-SAHARAN AFRICA
POPULATION GROWTH RATES 1980-90

POPULATION GROWTH RATES:**

LESS THAN 2.0% PER YEAR

2.0 - 2.4% PER YEAR

2.5 - 2.9% PER YEAR

3.0 - 3.4% PER YEAR

3.5% OR MORE PER YEAR

NO DATA

INTERNATIONAL BOUNDARIES

** Average annual population growth 1980-1990, in percent

The boundaries, colors, denominations and any other information shown on this map do not imply, on the part of The World Bank Group, any judgment on the legal status of any territory, or any endorsement or acceptance of such boundaries.

JULY 1994

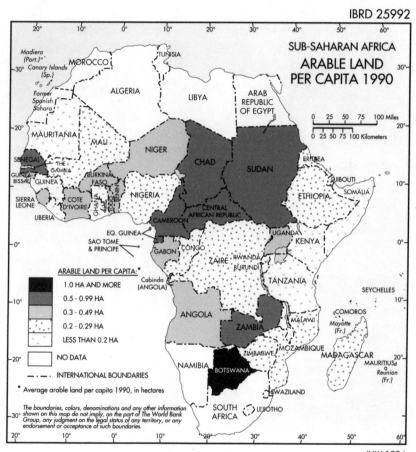

IBRD 25992

SUB-SAHARAN AFRICA
**ARABLE LAND
PER CAPITA 1990**

0	25 50 75 100 Miles
0	25 50 75 100 Kilometers

ARABLE LAND PER CAPITA:*

■ 1.0 HA AND MORE

■ 0.5 - 0.99 HA

▨ 0.3 - 0.49 HA

⬚ 0.2 - 0.29 HA

☐ LESS THAN 0.2 HA

☐ NO DATA

— · — INTERNATIONAL BOUNDARIES

* Average arable land per capita 1990, in hectares

The boundaries, colors, denominations and any other information shown on this map do not imply, on the part of The World Bank Group, any judgment on the legal status of any territory, or any endorsement or acceptance of such boundaries.

JULY 1994

1
Introduction

Over the past thirty years, most of Sub-Saharan Africa (SSA) has experienced very rapid population growth, sluggish agricultural growth, and severe environmental degradation. Increasing concern over these vexing problems and the apparent failure of past efforts to reverse these trends led the authors to take a fresh look at the available research findings and operational experience. The objective was not to compile and address all of the agricultural, environmental, and demographic issues facing Africa or simply to juxtapose these three sets of problems. It was to gain a better understanding of the underlying causes and to test the hypothesis that these three phenomena are interlinked in a strongly synergistic and mutually reinforcing manner.

The need to survive — individually and as a species — affects human fertility decisions. It also determines people's interactions with their environment, because they derive their livelihood and ensure their survival from the natural resources available and accessible to them. Rural livelihood systems in SSA are essentially agricultural, and agriculture is the main link between people and their environment. Through agricultural activities people seek to husband the available soil, water, and biological resources so as to "harvest" a livelihood for themselves. Such harvesting should be limited to the yield sustainable from the available stock of resources in perpetuity so as to ensure human survival over successive generations. Improvements in technology can increase the sustainable yields or reduce the resource stock required. Population growth should thus be matched or surpassed by productivity increases so as to safeguard the dynamic equilibrium between the stock of resources and the human population depending on it for survival. Over the past thirty years, this has not been the case in most of Sub-Saharan Africa.

This study's findings confirm the hypothesis of strong synergies and causality chains linking rapid population growth, degradation of the

1

environmental resource base, and poor agricultural production performance. Traditional African crop and livestock production methods, traditional methods of obtaining woodfuels and building materials, traditional land tenure systems and land use arrangements, and traditional gender roles in rural production and household maintenance systems were well suited to survival needs on a fragile environmental resource endowment when population densities were low and populations growing slowly. But the persistence of these traditional arrangements and practices, under severe stress from rapid population growth in the past thirty to forty years, is causing severe degradation of natural resources which, in turn, contributes further to agricultural stagnation.

Rapid population growth is the principal factor that has triggered and continues to stimulate the downward spiral in environmental resource degradation, contributing to agricultural stagnation and, in turn, impeding the onset of the demographic transition. The traditional land use, agricultural production, wood harvesting, and gender-specific labor allocation practices have not evolved and adapted rapidly enough on most of the continent to the dramatically intensifying pressure of more people on finite stocks of natural resources.

Many other factors also have a detrimental impact on agriculture and the environment. These include civil wars, poor rural infrastructure, lack of private investment in agricultural marketing and processing, and ineffective agricultural support services. Inappropriate price, exchange rate, and fiscal policies pursued by many governments have reduced the profitability and increased the risk of market-oriented agriculture, prevented significant gains in agricultural productivity, and contributed to the persistence of rural poverty.

A necessary condition for overcoming the problems of agricultural stagnation and environmental degradation will be, therefore, appropriate policy improvements along the lines suggested in the 1989 World Bank report on Sub-Saharan Africa's longer-term development prospects (World Bank 1989d). These policy changes will be instrumental in making intensive and market-oriented agriculture profitable — thus facilitating the economic growth in rural areas necessary to create an economic surplus usable for environmental resource conservation and to provide the economic basis for the demographic transition to lower population fertility rates. That this can occur has been demonstrated in a few places in Africa that pursued good economic and agricultural policy, invested in agriculture and natural resource conservation, and provided complementary supporting services to the rural population. This study provides evidence for both the causes of the problem and its solution.

The Three Basic Concerns

Population Growth

Sub-Saharan Africa lags behind other regions in its demographic transition. The total fertility rate (TFR) — the total number of children the average woman has in a lifetime — for SSA as a whole has remained at about 6.5 for the past twenty-five years, while it has declined to about 4 in all developing countries taken together. As life expectancy in Sub-Saharan Africa has risen from an average of forty-three years in 1965 to fifty-one years at present, population growth has accelerated from an average of 2.7 percent per annum for 1965–1980 to about 3.0 percent per year at present. Recent surveys appear to signal, however, that several countries — notably, Botswana, Kenya, and Zimbabwe — are at a critical demographic turning point. This study discusses the factors that have contributed to the beginning of the demographic transition in these countries.

Agricultural Performance

Agricultural production in Sub-Saharan Africa increased at about 2.0 percent per annum between 1965 and 1980 and at about 1.8 percent annually during the 1980s (Table A-9). Average per capita food production has declined in many countries, per capita calorie consumption has stagnated at very low levels, and roughly 100 million people in Sub-Saharan Africa are food insecure. Food imports increased by about 185 percent between 1974 and 1990, food aid by 295 percent. But the food gap (requirements minus production) — filled by food imports, or by many people going with less than what they need — has been widening. The average African consumes only about 87 percent of the calories needed for a healthy and productive life (Table A-10). But as with population growth, a few African countries are doing much better, with agricultural growth rates in the 3.0 to 4.5 percent per annum range in recent years (Nigeria, Botswana, Kenya, Tanzania, Burkina Faso, and Benin). The policies of these countries help show the way forward.

Environmental Degradation

Sub-Saharan Africa's forest cover, estimated at 679 million ha in 1980, has been diminishing at a rate of about 2.9 million ha per annum, and the rate of deforestation has been increasing (Table A-19). As much as half of SSA's farmland is affected by soil degradation and erosion, and up to 80 percent of its pasture and range areas show signs of degradation. Degraded soils lose their fertility and water absorption and retention capacity, with adverse effects on vegetative growth. Deforestation has significant negative effects on local and regional rainfall and hydrological systems. The widespread destruction of vegetative cover has been a major factor in prolonging the period of below long-term average rainfall in the Sahel in the 1970s and 1980s. It also is a major cause of the rapid increase in the accumulation of carbon dioxide (CO_2) and nitrous oxide (N_2O), two greenhouse gases, in the atmosphere. Massive biomass burning in Sub-Saharan Africa (savanna burning and slash-and-burn farming) contributes vast quantities of CO_2 and other trace gases to the global atmosphere. Acid deposition is higher in the Congo Basin and in Côte d'Ivoire than in the Amazon or in the eastern United States and is largely caused by direct emissions from biomass burning and by subsequent photochemical reactions in the resulting smoke and gas plumes. Tropical forests are considerably more sensitive than temperate forests to foliar damage from acid rain. Soil fertility is reduced through progressive acidification. Acid deposition also poses a serious risk to amphibians and insects that have aquatic life cycle stages; the risk extends further to plants that depend on such insects for pollination.

Unlike the situation of population growth and agriculture, there are few environmental success stories in Africa, although there remain large parts of Central Africa that are little touched. In looking closely, however, places can be found, such as Machakos District in Kenya, where environmental improvements have occurred along with rapidly expanding population. Good agricultural and economic policy, and investment in social services and infrastructure, are found to be the critical ingredients to such success (English and others 1993; Tiffen and others 1994). These positive experiences form the empirical basis for an action program to overcome the downward spiral elsewhere, which is discussed below.

Key Elements of the "Nexus"

Shifting Cultivation and Transhumant Pastoralism

Shifting or long-fallow cultivation and transhumant pastoralism have been appropriate under conditions of slow population growth, abundant land, limited capital, and limited technical know-how. The ecological and economic systems were in equilibrium. The key to maintaining this equilibrium was mobility. People shifted to a different location when soil fertility declined or forage was depleted. This allowed the fertility of the land to be reconstituted through natural vegetative growth and decay. For field cropping, this typically involved farming a piece of land for two to four years, then leaving it fallow for as long as fifteen to twenty-five years. Herders' mobility generally involved a far greater geographic range, but a far shorter temporal cycle, dictated by the seasonal availability of water and forage.

As long as land was abundant, more land could be gradually brought into the farming cycle to accommodate the slowly growing populations. Where population density increased slowly, the traditional extensive agricultural production systems gradually evolved into more intensive, and eventually permanent, systems which included soil conservation, fertility management, various forms of agroforestry, and the integration of livestock into farming systems. This has happened, for instance, in the Eastern African highlands, in Rwanda, and in the more densely settled areas of northern Nigeria.

But in most of Sub-Saharan Africa the scope for further expansion of cropland has drastically narrowed. Large areas of forests, wetlands, river valley bottoms, and grassland savanna have already been converted to farmland. This can be seen particularly in most of West Africa and in traditional grazing areas of eastern and southern Africa. On average, per capita arable land actually cultivated declined from 0.5 ha per person in 1965 to slightly less than 0.3 ha/person in 1990 (Table A-18). In many areas, rural people are increasingly compelled to remain on the same parcel of land, yet they continue to use their traditional production techniques. Soil fertility and structure deteriorate rapidly where fallow periods are too short and traditional cultivation methods continue to be used. As a result, crop yields decline and soils erode. In most areas, population growth has been so rapid that the reduction of arable land per farmer and the associated soil degradation have greatly outpaced the countervailing innovation and adjustment by farmers. When farming is no longer viable, people migrate to establish new farms on land previously not used for farming — in semiarid areas and in tropical forests where soil and climatic conditions are poorly suited to annual cropping. Migrants bring with them the knowledge of only those farming techniques they practiced in the areas they left, and these are often detrimental to their new environment.

In some countries, land continues to be more abundant in relation to current population. But in some of these land-abundant countries, much of the land is under tropical forests which need to be preserved. In most of Africa, rapid population growth is pushing settlers to extend farming and grazing into areas that are agroecologically unsuited to these forms of land use.

One of the conditions that stimulated Asian farmers to adopt "green revolution" technology — the abundance of labor relative to cultivable land — is increasingly emerging in parts of SSA (see, for instance, Pingali and others 1987, Lele and Stone 1989). But institutions and individuals have not been able to adapt quickly enough in the face of very rapid population growth. Slow technological innovation because of ineffective agricultural research and extension systems is only part of the reason. The poor transport infrastructure throughout most of SSA severely blunts farmers' incentives to switch from subsistence to market production and from extensive to intensive farming. Inappropriate agricultural marketing and pricing as well as fiscal and exchange rate policies have reduced the profitability of market-oriented agriculture, prevented significant gains in agricultural productivity, and contributed to the persistence of rural poverty. Poorly conceived and implemented agricultural projects have not helped. The lack of agricultural intensification in most of Africa has meant that expanding rural populations must depend on increasing the cropped area, to the detriment in many cases of natural resource sustainability.

Women's Time and Their Role in Agriculture and Rural Production Systems

The widespread prevalence of gender-specific (gender-sequential and/or gender-segregated) roles and responsibilities in rural production systems may be a major factor contributing to agricultural stagnation and environmental degradation and even to the persistence of high fertility rates. In many areas, women have primary or sole responsibility for food crop production, and they usually manage separate fields for this purpose. Women also tend to have significant obligations concerning labor to be performed on men's fields and with postharvest processing activities.

Given women's triple roles — child bearing/rearing, family and household maintenance, and production/income-earning activities — the pressures on their time continue to intensify. With increasing deforestation, combined with growing populations requiring more fuelwood, fuelwood has become scarcer. Women must walk farther to fetch it — or reduce the number of hot meals prepared. Increasing populations put greater pressure on available water resources, while environmental degradation reduces the availability and accessibility of water. Women must walk farther to fetch water, and get their daughters to help them. Throughout much of rural Sub-Saharan Africa, women also are the primary means of porterage. In the absence of adequate rural transport infrastructure and of means of transport other than human porterage, women spend substantial time headloading not only water and fuelwood, but farm produce and other commodities to and from their homes.

As growing numbers of men leave the farms to work in towns and cities, women are increasingly taking on primary responsibility for farm operations — while their recourse to adult male labor is diminishing. About 70 percent of Congo's farms are today managed by women, for example, and in Ghana more farmers are women than men. Moreover, the expansion of higher-input cash cropping under male control tends to increase demands on female labor for traditional female activities such as weeding and harvesting. In Zambia, women in farm households headed by males contribute more hours daily than men to farm work (8.5 hours versus 7.4 hours) and nonagricultural tasks (5 hours versus 1.1 hours). At the same time, women are traditionally confronted with severe restrictions on access to land and capital. These restrictive attitudes persist and today are reflected in limited access to extension advice; to productive land; to institutional credit; and to improved production, processing, and transport technology. In Botswana, a 1984 study found women contributing almost 70 percent of the value of crop production, but receiving the benefit of less than 15 percent of national agricultural outlays. These constraints, combined with intensifying pressures on women's time, severely impede productivity improvements and intensification of women's farming operations. Most women farmers have little choice but to continue practicing traditional low-input, low-productivity farming which, with sharply shortened fallow periods, is neither environmentally sustainable nor viable in terms of longer-term agricultural productivity. The severe pressure on women's time also retards progress in cash crop production controlled by men that depends on significant female labor input at critical times.

The heavy pressure on women's time also has implications for infant and child welfare and, hence, infant and child mortality — with significant repercussions on fertility aspirations and attitudes toward family planning. More contentious is the hypothesis that the multiple work burdens and the heavy time pressure on women may be a contributing causal element behind the persistent high population fertility rates. Additional labor is often the only factor of production that women can easily add, or are able or even compelled to add, in order to meet their multiple and increasing production and household management responsibilities. The combination of traditional attitudes and constraints with greatly increasing workloads of women may thus be part of the explanation for the continuing extraordinarily high fertility rate in SSA, now about 6.5 children per woman on average (compared to less than 4 in other developing countries).

There are, of course, many other factors that contribute to these high fertility rates. Traditional attitudes that favor numerous offspring, particularly sons, play an important part. Polygamy and the widespread

practice of women marrying considerably older men are both phenomena that tend to increase women's economic and social dependency on
sons and, hence, their willingness to bear many children. High infant
and child mortality rates, resulting, among other things, from poor
nutrition and poor maternal and child health care, are potent induce-
ments to maintaining high fertility rates. The relative importance of
these and other factors has not been established, and may never be.
Nevertheless, the severe and increasing pressure on women's time and
the significant gender-based constraints faced by women in their pursuit
of both traditional and nontraditional farming activities may be preventing the emergence of women's *demand* for fewer children and thereby
contribute to the persistence of high fertility rates.

Land Tenure Systems

Customary land tenure systems provide considerable security of tenure
on land brought into the farming cycle (clearing, cropping, fallowing,
reclearing) through customary rules of community land ownership and
allocation of use rights to members of the community. In most cases, the
tenurial security enjoyed by members of the community is sufficient to
induce investment in land. Outsiders, or *strangers* (i.e., nonmembers of
the community) may obtain use rights of various types, but in many
cases with considerably less long-term security. As long as populations
increased only slowly and the demand for land use rights by migrants
from other communities remained modest, traditional systems were
able to accommodate the emerging need to move towards de facto
permanence of land rights assigned to community members (Magrath
1989; Migot-Adholla and others 1991).

There are, however, other aspects of traditional land tenure systems
that have not adjusted rapidly enough to changing economic conditions.
In most traditional systems, for instance, the individual users' ability to
transfer land use rights is subject to significant constraints — due to
customary norms and/or the absence of effective administrative and
legal mechanisms. Tree tenure arrangements are often distinctly separate from land use rights pertaining to the cultivation of annual crops
and can result in serious conflict. Much common property land —
forests, wetlands, and range lands — has become de facto open-access
land and has been converted to farming, often with significant negative
environmental consequences. In many areas where traditional land
rights systems provided for overlapping and complementary uses by
sedentary farmers and transhumant herders, the development of valley
bottoms into permanent cropland has created major constraints on the
mobility of herders, with negative implications for environmental integ-

rity. Increasing population pressure and agroenvironmental problems are inducing considerable rural-rural migration. Since migrants often come with conflicting traditions of land allocation and land use, *strangers'* tenurial rights and their implications for land resource conservation are of increasing concern. These various pressures are causing traditional land tenure systems to break down, reducing tenurial security.

Most governments and external aid agencies have mistakenly believed that traditional tenure systems provide inadequate tenurial security and that these systems are not conducive to the introduction of modern agricultural technology and market-oriented agriculture. They also witnessed the erosion in customary laws and practices regulating land use that occurred as a result of significant rural-rural migration, changes in social values and customs, and ambiguities created by the overlaying of "modern" land administration systems over traditional ones. In many instances, this led to the emergence of de facto open-access systems that are not conducive to resource conservation or to private investment in soil fertility maintenance and land improvement.

Many governments have responded by nationalizing the ownership of land — and then allowing customary rules to guide the use of some land, while allocating other land to private investors and public projects. Often, the well connected have used their influence to wrest land from its customary owner-occupants. The result has been reduced, rather than improved, tenurial security. In most cases, this has accelerated the breakdown in customary land management and the creation of open-access conditions, especially in forest and range areas. In open-access conditions, settlement and exploitation by anyone are permitted and environmental degradation is invariably rapid. Where governments allocated individual land titles — as in Kenya, Zimbabwe, and Côte d'Ivoire — this generally ignored the prior existence of customary tenure arrangements, and more often than not, the actual results have differed considerably from the stated intent. Local community and individual land resource management has been discouraged, while political and economic elites have succeeded in alienating the land from its traditional owners and users. This has skewed land distribution and intensified the exploitation of land resources for private short-term gain.

Forest and Woodland Exploitation

The heavy dependency on wood for fuel and building material has combined with rapid population growth to contribute to accelerating forest and woodland destruction. This is particularly severe around major urban centers where it has led to the appearance of concentric rings of deforestation. Fuelwood has generally been considered a free good, taken largely from land to which everyone has the right of access. This has impeded the development of efficient markets for fuelwood. Urban woodfuel prices reflect primarily transport costs, not the cost of producing trees, and there will be no incentive to plant trees for fuelwood production until transport costs to urban markets become high enough to justify periurban planting. This is beginning to happen around some cities and in very densely populated areas, but the scale of such planting is very inadequate. Alternative fuels, such as kerosene or liquefied petroleum gas (LPG), are more costly to obtain and not available in open-access conditions, and are therefore not replacing woodfuels in significant quantities.

Commercial logging has significantly contributed to deforestation. Although directly responsible for no more than 20 percent of forest destruction in SSA as a whole, it has been considerably more destructive in some countries, such as Côte d'Ivoire. Moreover, logging usually leads to a second phase of forest destruction: logging roads provide access for settlers who accelerate and expand the process of deforestation that the loggers have begun. Logging concessions rarely take into account the traditional land and forest use rights of forest dwellers. These rights, once eroded, are disregarded by new settlers penetrating along the logging roads.

The degradation and destruction of forests and woodlands accelerate soil degradation and erosion, eliminate wildlife habitat, lead to loss of biodiversity, and have severe implications for local and regional climates and hydrological regimes. Deteriorating climatic and hydrological conditions negatively affect agriculture. The worsening fuelwood situation forces women and children to walk farther and spend more time to collect fuelwood. Closely related, and increasingly of concern, is the fact that animal dung and crop residues are being used as fuels. Under conditions of shortening fallows, characteristic of much of SSA, the economic utility of dung and crop residues is far greater when they are used to maintain soil fertility. People also must walk farther and/or pay more for building materials and the many important nonwood forest products they depend upon for medicinal purposes, home consumption, and traditional crafts and industries. For forest dwelling people, forest destruction threatens not only their lifestyles and livelihood systems, but their very survival.

Population Growth Revisited: Feedback from the Nexus

Agricultural stagnation and environmental degradation probably inhibit the demographic transition because they retard economic development, which is the driving force behind this transition. The extraordinarily high fertility rates prevailing in Sub-Saharan Africa are the result of many factors. The fundamental problem is low *demand* for smaller families. In many societies, becoming a parent is a precondition for becoming a socially recognized adult. Fertility enhances female and male status, while infertility can result in severe anxiety and, particularly for women, can be socially and economically devastating. Such widespread phenomena as polygyny and women marrying considerably older men tend to increase women's eventual economic and social dependence on sons and hence their willingness to bear many children.

Infant and child nutrition and mortality are affected by the availability of safe potable water and by the number of nutritious and warm meals provided. Where environmental degradation reduces the availability and accessibility of water and fuelwood, there is a negative impact on infant and child mortality and hence a positive impact on parental demand for more children. Where girls are kept out of school to help with domestic tasks, including water and fuelwood fetching, there are strong negative repercussions for their fertility preferences and their ability to make knowledgeable decisions about family planning once they reach childbearing age.

The preference for many children is also linked to economic considerations. In many communal land tenure systems, the amount of land allotted for farming to a family by the community (through its head or its *chef de terre*) is a function of the family's ability to clear and cultivate land. With hired labor in most settings being rare (although labor pooling for certain tasks is not uncommon), it is family size or, more correctly, family labor that determines land allotment. This is also true in open-access systems where the size of holding equals land cleared and cultivated. This counteracts efforts to simulate demand for fewer children. Moreover, as long as there is (or is perceived to be) as yet unfarmed and unclaimed land available, there is no incentive for individuals to manage their land more intensively or to limit their family size so they can bequeath a viable farm to their offspring.

Elements of an Action Plan

The appropriate policy response and action program to address these problems are not easily brought into focus. Many of the most immediately attractive remedies have been tried and have failed. For example, individual land titling — intended to clarify resource ownership, prevent further degradation of common property regimes into de facto open-access situations, and improve tenurial security — has been tried in several countries and has been beset by significant problems. Similarly, efforts to introduce "modern" agricultural tecnology in the form of higher-yielding varieties, chemical fertilizer, and farm mechanization have not met with great response from farmers. Soil conservation and forest protection efforts have had little success outside relatively small areas. And efforts to slow population growth through programs based primarily on the supply of family planning services and the distribution of contraceptives have not been successful in most SSA countries.

Enough is known already to incorporate the recommendations made here in projects and policy. The main actions that can be defined are as follows:

- Promote demand for smaller families and family planning based on cultural and agricultural/economic incentives, rather than simply on the supply of family planning services.

- Create farmer demand for "sustainable" agricultural technology, partly through appropriate research and extension, partly by the elimination of open-access land tenure conditions, partly by the policy-created artificial scarcity of farmland, and necessarily through agricultural policy reform of the kind identified in *Sub-Saharan Africa: From Crisis to Sustainable Growth* (World Bank 1989d), which will make farming less risky and more profitable.

- Pursue measures necessary to create a market for fuelwood. This will require mainly land tenure reform, extension advice on agroforestry, and fuelwood plantations.

- Ensure that agricultural services and education serve women, in order to stimulate reduced demand for children, improve women's farming practices, and reduce the work burden in water and fuelwood gathering. This will save women's time for family management and food production and nonagricultural income-generating activities.

- Reduce forest and wildland degradation by land tenure reform, agricultural intensification, infrastructure policy, migration policy, and population policy.

- Create environmental action plans to focus on agricultural and population causes of environmental degradation.

- Formulate urban policies that have links to population, agriculture, and the environment (as safety valves for population increase and market generators for agriculture and fuelwood products).

- Make greater use of spatial plans incorporating the above elements for specific localities.

- Encourage community and individual management of implementation. This is crucial and can be induced by affirming community and individual ownership of land and water resources and stimulated by fiscal and pricing incentives, allocation of public funds for community initiatives, adjustment of external assistance in support of local action, reorientation of public support services to back local initiatives, and training of community leaders.

Several SSA countries have begun to implement various elements of this action plan. Over twenty national environmental action plans are under preparation. Macroeconomic and agricultural policy reforms are underway in over half the African countries, although with mixed success. A few countries have successful family planning programs, and others are developing promising programs. Agricultural research and extension systems are beginning to place more weight on "sustainable" technology and responsiveness to varying farmer demand. A very few countries have brought much of this together and obtained positive synergies between agricultural growth, environmental protection, and reduction in fertility rates. Kenya, Uganda, Tanzania, Botswana, and Mauritius are examples. Others, such as Ghana and Zimbabwe, are moving in the right direction. Major deficiencies remain in rural health care and education (particularly female education), rural infrastructure, participation of local communities in development efforts, forest and conservation policy, land tenure reform, urbanization policy, and family planning programs.

Conclusions

Past efforts have, on the whole, failed to reverse the direction of the downward spiral that is driven by the synergetic forces of this nexus. Part of the explanation appears to be that these efforts have been pursued too narrowly along traditional sectoral lines — matching established institutional arrangements and traditional academic disciplines — while crucial cross-sectoral linkages and synergies have been ignored. At the same time, primary emphasis in most sectoral development efforts has generally been placed on the supply side, i.e., on efforts to develop and deliver technology and services. Far more emphasis needs to be given to promoting effective *demand* for environmentally benign technologies that intensify farming, for family planning services, and for resource conservation. The synergies inherent in the nexus provide considerable potential in this regard. Addressing these issues requires appropriate cross-sectoral analysis and the development of action programs that cover the linkages and synergies among sectors. These programs should focus on price incentives, trade and fiscal policies, public investments, and asset ownership (such as land) as tools to promote sustainable resource management. To facilitate efficient implementation, action should, however, be defined within single sectors.

In analytical work that should precede the formulation of action plans and developmental interventions, far greater attention needs to be paid to the social organization of production and consumption, of decisionmaking and resource allocation, and of access to resources and services. These systems and structures can be very complex and often differ substantially among communities. This implies the need to use relevant "units of analysis." Terms such as "household," the "family," and the "family farm" may not be appropriate if they are simply taken to convey concepts of social and economic arrangements familiar to twentieth-century industrial economies. Many societies are characterized by complex resource allocation and pooling arrangements for both production and consumption purposes, based on lineage, kinship, gender, and age groups. It is imperative to be cognizant of these arrangements, to analyze the impact of development interventions on individuals in this context, and to design development efforts such that traditional groups can implement and manage them. Gender issues are particularly critical, especially in terms of gender-specific divisions of responsibilities, tasks, and budgets, as well as in terms of access to resources, information, and markets. Interventions and incentives do not necessarily work in the same direction or with the same intensity for men and women.

Work in Progress and Follow-Up

To help answer some of the questions that remain and to adapt the analysis to the situation of specific countries, a follow-up to this study was begun in 1993. It included the preparation of "nexus" studies in Côte d'Ivoire, Ethiopia, Malawi, Nigeria, Rwanda, and the Sahelian countries as a group. These studies confirm the findings of the general study but provide evidence of variation in the way in which the various factors interact. In addition, concurrent monitoring is underway regarding the progress of preparation and implementation of national environmental action plans and of national population programs. The mechanism for the former is the "Club of Dublin," consisting of representatives of African governments and donor agencies. The institutional mechanism for deepening the population agenda for Sub-Saharan Africa and for monitoring its progress is the African Population Advisory Committee, with similar membership. It is intended that a similar African Agricultural Advisory Committee, managed by prominent Africans, will also be established. Finally, the donors have agreed to focus on nexus issues as part of the donor coordination effort entitled the "Special Program for Africa."

2
Agricultural Stagnation and Environmental Degradation

Agricultural Stagnation, Population Growth, and Food Security

Over the past twenty-five years, agricultural production in Sub-Saharan Africa rose by only about 2.0 percent a year, while aggregate population growth averaged about 2.8 percent per year (Tables A-2 and A-9).[1] Per capita food production has declined in most countries of the continent (Table A-10). Cereal imports increased by 3.9 percent per year between 1974 and 1990, food aid by 7.0 percent per year. But the food gap (requirements minus production) — filled by imports, or by many people going with less than what they need — is widening. In the early 1980s, about 100 million people in Sub-Saharan Africa were unable to secure sufficient food to ensure an adequate level of nutrition for themselves, and average food consumption per capita declined during the 1970s and 1980s in seventeen of the thirty-six SSA countries for which data are available (Table A-10).[2] In years of poor harvests the numbers affected have been much larger. Severe food shortages were exceptional in the 1960s, but are no longer so. Famines in several countries in the 1980s were graphic indications of natural calamity, as well as of civil disruption, in the region. On average, officially estimated per capita food intake in Sub-Saharan Africa in the late 1980s, at 2,027 calories per day, was below the 1965 level and significantly lower than in other parts of the developing world. The average in India, for example, is 2,238 calories daily per person. The average African consumes only about 87 percent of the calories needed for a healthy and productive life.

The available data show no acceleration of aggregate agricultural growth in the 1980s. It has, in fact, been slightly below the longer-term average of 2.0 percent a year recorded for the past three decades (Table A-9). (It was higher than 2.0 percent in the 1960s and much lower in the 1970s.) This poor performance is also evident in the decline of agricul-

16

tural export earnings. Export volumes and values have declined for almost all SSA countries from 1980 to 1990 (Table A-13), with volume declining at 2.7 percent per year on average. There are notable exceptions. Exports of tea and horticultural products from Kenya, cocoa from Côte d'Ivoire, and cotton from several West African countries have grown substantially in volume. But the success stories are few.

Projections, based on present trends, are disturbing. Aggregate population growth has accelerated to over 3.1 percent a year (Table A-2). Projections based on current trends in fertility and mortality rates (including the impact of AIDS) indicate only a slight deceleration in aggregate population growth through the year 2000. The total fertility rate (TFR) for Sub-Saharan Africa as a whole has declined only marginally from 6.6 from in 1965 to 6.4 at present (Table A-2). By contrast, the average TFR for all the world's low-income countries declined from 6.3 in 1965 to 4.0 in 1987. During the same period, the crude death rate in Sub-Saharan Africa fell from 23 to 16 (Table A-3). In countries with a high incidence of AIDS, death rates will rise, but nowhere is population growth expected to fall below 2 percent per annum by the year 2000, even under worst case AIDS scenarios currently considered plausible.[3] Unless efforts to reduce TFRs succeed (or mortality rates rise dramatically due to currently unanticipated AIDS developments), population growth rates will decline very little.

Table 6.1 (p. 99) shows the implications of these trends for Sub-Saharan Africa's future food gap. In 1990, Sub-Saharan Africa's 474 million people produced about 90 million metric tons of maize equivalent of food. With 100 million tons of aggregate consumption, there was a gap of 10 million tons met by imports. At currently projected growth rates, Sub-Saharan Africa's population will total about 1,184 million and its food production will reach about 163 million tons of maize equivalent in 2020. Even with no change in average per capita consumption, aggregate requirements will be about 250 million tons. The 87 million ton food gap would be almost nine times today's gap and equivalent to about one-fourth of the present annual production of cereals in the United States. Food aid varied between 4 million and 7 million tons of cereals per year in the 1980s and could not conceivably increase sufficiently to fill this gap. Without significant per capita growth in agricultural production it is difficult to imagine sufficient overall economic growth that would generate the resources needed to finance food imports of this magnitude — or, for that matter, to maintain educational and health services and infrastructure facilities.

These disturbing trends will not continue indefinitely. What is at issue is how they will eventually be overcome. Will the strong synergies and the dynamics of these trends lead to human and environmental degradation and ultimately to widespread starvation? Or will these trends be overcome through voluntary, but determined, action to reduce population growth and promote sustainable agricultural development and growth?

The Deteriorating Natural Resource Base and Ecological Environment

Much of Sub-Saharan Africa's natural resource base and ecological environment is deteriorating. If present trends continue, this deterioration will accelerate. The most pressing problem is the high rate of loss of vegetative cover — mainly the result of deforestation and the conversion of savanna to cropland — which in turn leads to loss of soil fertility and soil erosion. Global and regional climatic changes and deviations from longer-term average conditions are also causal factors — but human impact on the environment in Sub-Saharan Africa may itself be an important element contributing to these climatic changes.

Deforestation

In much of Sub-Saharan Africa, deforestation is a major problem — with significant local, national, and global consequences. Forests provide a multitude of products and serve many functions, including essential environmental ones. With deforestation, these are lost. Forests and woodlands are cleared for farming and logged for fuelwood, logs, and pulp wood. Data on forest resources and rates of extraction and clearing are imperfect, as are data on most of Africa's environmental resources, but information is continually improving and reliable enough to suggest the scale of the problem. In 1980, there were about 646 million hectares of forests and woodlands in Sub-Saharan Africa. A 1980 FAO/UNEP study estimated that 3.7 million hectares of tropical Africa's forests and open woodlands were being cleared each year by farmers and loggers (Lanly 1982). More recent estimates suggest that close to 2.9 million hectares were lost each year during the 1980s (Table A-19), mainly through conversion to farm land, but the rate of deforestation may be accelerating as the aggregate area still under forests continues to shrink. Reforestation during the 1980s amounted to 133,000 hectares per year, only about 5 percent of the area lost each year to deforestation (Table A-19).

Aggregate data obviously obscure important differences among regions and countries. Deforestation has been particularly rapid in West Africa, with East Africa and southern Africa also suffering substantial losses in forest cover. Large tracts of tropical forest still remain, especially in Zaïre, Gabon, Congo, the Central African Republic, and Cameroon. It would take many years for Central Africa's forests to be completely destroyed, but the process has started. In most of East Africa and southern Africa, as well as in the West African coastal countries, the process is far advanced.

Degradation and destruction of forests have a severe impact on wildlife habitat and biodiversity, with potentially irreversible losses of animal and plant life. The World Conservation Union (IUCN) and the World Resources Institute (WRI) estimate that 64 percent of original wildlife habitat in Sub-Saharan Africa has already been lost (Table A-22). The main causes are deforestation, conversion of wildlands to agricultural uses, and other human activity. Excessive harvesting, poaching, and illegal trade also take a heavy toll on many species. Degradation of tropical moist forests has a particularly negative impact on biodiversity by destroying plant and animal life that may exist nowhere else in the world.

As forests and woodlands are destroyed, people must walk farther or pay more for fuelwood, construction materials, and other forest products. Woodfuels are the staple source of household energy in Africa, and many agroprocessing and rural artisanal and semi-industrial activities also use woodfuels.[4] Fuelwood deficits are severe in the Sahel, in the savanna regions of West, Central and East Africa and in the arid areas of southern Africa (Table A-21). They impose particular hardships on

---

Box 2-1   The Threat to African Wildlife

The World Resources Institute (WRI) has compiled estimates of the number of threatened species in Africa (WRI 1992:304–309). Examples include the following (see also Tables A-23 and A-24):

- Eighteen of the 226 known species of mammals in Côte d'Ivoire are threatened with extinction, and seventy of the 3,660 known plant species are rare and threatened;
- Zaïre has the most known species of mammals in Africa, and twenty-two of these 409 are threatened;
- Fifty-three of Madagascar's 105 known mammal species and twenty-eight of its 250 known species of birds are threatened;
- In Chad, eighteen of the 131 known species of mammals are threatened;
- In Kenya, fifteen of the 314 known mammal species are threatened, and 144 of the 6,500 known species of plants are rare and threatened; and
- Of South Africa's roughly 23,000 plant species, 1,145 are listed as rare and threatened.

women who are usually responsible for household fuel provision. As fuelwood becomes scarce, women (and children) have to spend more time collecting it from more distant sources and eventually begin to substitute crop residues and manure which would otherwise be used to maintain soil fertility.

The loss of future wood for the forest industry will be another important cost of continuing deforestation. In the period 1985–1987, the six largest African timber exporters (Cameroon, Congo, Côte d'Ivoire, Gabon, Ghana, and Liberia) exported US$500–600 million worth of timber annually. Without significant afforestation, the potential for future export earnings will be lost as forests disappear.

Forests also provide a wide variety of nonwood products for local populations. Many are used particularly by women to meet subsistence needs or to generate cash income, and various wild plant and animal food sources are especially important in times of stress (FAO 1989; 1990a). A recent FAO publication lists ninety-four different forest and farm tree foods as being commonly used in West Africa (FAO 1990a:102–103); thirty forest species are listed as being commonly used for fodder (FAO 1990a:113). Women often possess much specialized knowledge in this regard (Molnar and Schreiber 1989); in Sierra Leone, women listed thirty-one different products they gather from bushes and trees near their villages (Hoskins 1989:43). Traditional medicine throughout Sub-Saharan Africa is highly dependent on a variety of forest plants.[5] As forests are degraded and destroyed, these resources are no longer available and/or accessible to the local populations.

Deforestation also has a particularly severe impact on forest dwellers, such as the pygmies, threatening not only their traditional lifestyles, but their very survival (Bailey, Bahuchet and Hewlett 1992; Dyson 1992; Peterson 1992; Winterbottom 1992).

Box 2-2   Nonwood Forest Products Gathered by Women in Brakna, Mauritania

The wide variety of nonwood forest products utilized by women is illustrated by the arid region of Brakna in Mauritania:

- *Foods and livestock feed:* Gums, fruits, leaves and grasses, chemicals from plants for preserving butter, couscous seasonings, a wild grain (*aze*) used as animal feed;
- *Medicines, cosmetics, dyes, etc.:* Medicinal plants, henna and pods for cosmetic purposes, incense plants;
- *Utensils, handicrafts, etc.:* Fronds, grasses, dyes, leather tannins, floor mats (Smale 1985).

Soil Degradation and Erosion

Much of Sub-Saharan Africa is highly vulnerable to soil degradation and erosion. Such land degradation is often, more dramatically but somewhat loosely, referred to as "desertification": the process of sustained deterioration of the biological productivity of land. It is manifested in such phenomena as soil erosion, soil structure deterioration, compaction, reduction in organic matter and nutrient content, and salinization. The vulnerability of much of Sub-Saharan Africa to land degradation is due to factors such as soil characteristics, intense soil drying in the dry seasons, severely erosive seasonal rainfall in many areas, wind erosion in drier areas, and low-resource farming with inadequate soil conservation measures. The Soil Reference and Information Centre in Wageningen, Netherlands, has recently published estimates of the extent and severity of land degradation in Africa. Its data indicate that about 321 million hectares (14.4 percent of the total vegetated land surface) are moderately, severely, or extremely degraded and a further 174 million hectares are lightly degraded (Oldeman and others 1990).[6] Most of this is in the West African Sahelo-Sudanian Zone, in Sudan, Ethiopia, Somalia, and Kenya, as well as in southern Africa, but parts of many other countries (such as the northern areas of many West African coastal countries) are also affected.

Sizeable areas used for cropping in low-rainfall regions are subject to soil degradation and soil fertility loss. Topsoil losses even on gently sloping cropland have been reported to range from 25 tons to 250 tons per hectare annually from Niger to Madagascar and from Ethiopia to

---

Box 2-3   Soil Erosion and Degradation: The Data Problem

Despite their pervasiveness, the extent and impact of the degradation, erosion, and desertification of Africa's soils are not easy to assess. Reliable data on which to base national, regional, and continental estimates are scarce. Soil erosion rates are difficult to calculate, and published data on degradation and erosion are highly location-specific and often of doubtful reliability, because of poor measurement techniques. They are also subject to considerable misinterpretation, especially when field data are extrapolated to develop aggregate estimates for entire watersheds, regions, or countries. Moreover, most research on the relationship between soil degradation and erosion and soil productivity has been carried out in temperate zones (notably the United States), but there are vast differences in this relationship throughout the world as also in the resilience of land systems and the rate of new soil formation (Seckler 1987; Stocking 1987).

Zimbabwe (Table A-26). These rates translate into losses of between 2 mm and 2 cm of topsoil annually. Moreover, there is location-specific evidence that erosion is accelerating. A study of Tanzania's Shinyanga region, utilizing the fact that trees and bushes can be dated to determine changes in ground surface height over time, found that soil erosion during the first sixty years of the current century averaged about 1.4 t/ha/year; twenty to thirty years ago it was 10.5 t/ha/year; and during the past two decades it has averaged 22.4 t/ha/year (Stocking 1987:56–57).

The agronomic relevance of such data is difficult to assess, however, without information on new soil formation and total topsoil remaining. Topsoil depth should be at least 15 cm for most annual plants, with an additional 35 cm of subsoil beneath to provide sufficient rooting depth (but optimal rooting depth obviously differs among crops). In temperate climates the natural rate of soil formation on nonagricultural land is about 0.8 mm per year, but it may be three times this much in the humid tropics (Seckler 1987:91); these rates are likely to be higher on well-managed and lower on poorly managed farm land. Nevertheless, given the poor fertility characteristics of most African soils and the prevailing low-input farming practices, topsoil losses in the middle and upper ranges of the magnitudes reported will cause rapid productivity declines.

Soil erosion is usually accompanied by other aspects of soil degradation, such as deteriorating soil structure, reduced moisture retention capacity, soil nutrient depletion, and reduction in soil fauna and flora. A major study undertaken in the late 1970s estimated that, with unchecked soil degradation and erosion and no change in farming technology, the productivity of land in Africa would decline at an average rate of 1 percent per year between 1975 and 2000 (Higgins and others 1982:23–25). In Zimbabwe, nitrogen and phosphorus losses attributable to erosion on arable land were estimated to be about three times the amount of fertilizer used in the 1984/85 crop year; compensating for this nutrient loss through fertilizer applications would have cost US$1,500 million — or US$35 per hectare of arable land (FAO 1990b).

Much soil eroded from uplands and slopes is deposited in the bottomlands along river courses. But these deposits are deficient in organic material and poorly structured, require good tillage, and are usually too heavy for hoe cultivation or traditional plows. Access to more efficient agricultural technology (machinery for land preparation, drainage to prevent waterlogging, etc.) has made it increasingly possible for land-hungry farmers to extend cultivation into these areas — but with often deleterious consequences for riverine ecosystems and for pastoralists (see below).

Box 2-4   Extent and Economic Cost of Soil Erosion in Mali

Soil erosion on cultivated land in Mali has been estimated to range from a low of 1 t/ha/year in the arid north to a high of 31 t/ha/year in parts of the more densely settled and intensively cultivated south of the country. Given the enormous difficulties involved in quantifying the effect of soil degradation and soil loss on farm productivity, the researchers had to work with a range of values for the critical parameters that define this link. The associated crop yield reductions were estimated to range between 2 and 10 percent per year for the country as a whole. The present value (using conservative parameters of a ten-year time horizon and a 10 percent discount rate) of current and future net farm income forgone as a result of one year's soil loss was estimated to fall between 4 and 16 percent of agricultural GDP (Bishop and Allen 1989).

Rangeland Degradation and Desertification

About 25 million of the world's estimated 40 million nomadic and transhumant pastoralists live in Africa (Bass 1990). Between 1963 and 1983, according to FAO estimates, the number of cattle increased by 74 percent in Sudano-Sahelian Africa, by 65 percent in humid and sub-humid West Africa, and by 61 percent in southern Africa (FAO 1986). At the same time, the extent and quality of the rangeland declined. Cultivators moved into the best grazing areas and converted them to cropland; the traditional use rights of pastoralists, and particularly of transhumant herders, were ignored or overridden, and their herds were increasingly forced to more marginal land which is rapidly degraded by overgrazing. The increasing cultivation of valley bottoms has further compounded the problem: it restricts pastoralists' ability to move their herds there and to use these lands as migration routes during the dry season, thus forcing them to remain on degrading rangelands and around permanent water points. Restrictions on the movement of pastoralists across national boundaries have had similar effects.

The issue is not simply one of too many animals relative to the available grazing areas. Long periods of below-normal rainfall and severe droughts have accelerated the degradation of rangelands, and past efforts to address the problem of water supplies for pastoralists have often compounded, rather than ameliorated, the problems. Deep wells have been sunk to ensure water supplies during the dry season, but with free access to these wells, the number of animals congregating around them far exceeds the carrying capacity of the surrounding rangeland,

causing rapid deterioration. Desertification has tended to spread out-
ward from these areas of excessive and prolonged animal concentration.

Water Resource Depletion and Degradation

In large parts of Sub-Saharan Africa, water is the critical limiting
resource, not merely in terms of agricultural production, but in the
broader context of the population-agriculture-environment nexus as
such. "Accelerating water scarcity may well influence the time of population stabilization — for example, by significantly influencing birth
rates, death rates, migration patterns, or all of these variables" (Falkenmark 1991:81). Unfortunately, many countries do not yet have adequate
basic data to assess their water availability,[7] but conflicts over competing
demands on scarce resources are becoming increasingly evident. The
potential for such conflicts rises rapidly with population growth and
economic development. At the rates of population growth currently
projected, water availability per capita will decline to half of its present
levels in almost all SSA countries within twenty-five years. A recent
macrolevel assessment suggests that ten countries in Sub-Saharan Africa
will face severe water stress situations by the turn of the century:
Mauritania, Niger, Somalia, Kenya, Burundi, Rwanda, Malawi,
Zimbabwe, Namibia, and Lesotho. By the year 2025, eleven more will
have joined this list: Mauritania, Senegal, The Gambia, Burkina Faso,
Togo, Benin, Nigeria, Ethiopia, Uganda, Tanzania, and Mozambique
(Falkenmark 1991:83–85).

Rivers, streams, lakes, swamps, and coastal waters are important
resources. They provide critical economic goods and services and per-
form vital ecological functions. They need to be protected and prudently
utilized, but many are seriously affected by sedimentation, siltation,
agrochemical runoff, industrial pollution, and inefficient utilization.
Pollution from domestic sources has become a concern around many
large cities and in countless rural areas where lack of safe potable water
is a major health issue. Such problems are increasingly serious in many
parts of Sub-Saharan Africa, although quantitative information is particularly poor in this respect. The causes include soil erosion, deforestation, destruction of protective shoreline vegetation, indiscriminate
drainage, encroachment for farming, poorly conceived irrigation development, and lack of environmental regulations and enforcement on
industrial activities. Many irrigation and hydropower schemes that
involve damming and diverting rivers have adversely affected the flora
and fauna of the downstream floodplains, the wildlife and livestock
carrying capacity of the floodplain grasslands, the extent and productivity of wetlands and riverine forests, and the productivity and sus-

tainability of downstream fishing and of farming based on traditional recession irrigation. Large impoundments also imply large evaporation losses. Other problems include coastal erosion, saltwater intrusion into aquifers in coastal areas, and destruction of coastal wetlands critical for birds and marine life. Problems have also been encountered with the spread of water-related diseases around water impoundments and irrigation schemes where water remains standing in fields and canals.

Groundwater resources have also come under pressure, especially in the arid and semiarid regions. In some areas, groundwater reserves are being drawn down for irrigation much faster than they can be replenished. Deforestation, soil degradation and erosion, and poor on-farm soil and water management all increase surface runoff (causing erosion) and reduce the amount of rainfall that infiltrates the soil and eventually percolates into underground aquifers. Prolonged periods of below-average rainfall and unusually frequent and severe droughts have, of course, greatly exacerbated this problem (Table A-25).

Drinking water in rural areas is the most pressing concern, but water scarcity is also a severe constraint on livestock and home garden production in many parts of arid and semiarid Africa and even in many subhumid regions. During the dry season, rivers, streams and springs in many areas of Sub-Saharan Africa run dry, and women often have to go very far to obtain meager quantities of water, which is often of very poor quality. As groundwater tables recede due to reduced rainfall and reduced rain infiltration into the soil and into subsurface aquifers, wells dry up and must be dug deeper or abandoned.

Environmental Degradation and Climatic Change

The consequences of environmental degradation are profound. Most alarming is the possible negative impact on rainfall, although direct causality is difficult to establish. Extensive meteorological monitoring and research suggest increasing aridity throughout the Sahel during the 1970s and 1980s. Figure 2-1, which depicts annual rainfall deviation from the 1900–1987 long-term average, is telling. It shows that the Sahel has always experienced wide variations in annual rainfall, but also that rainfall has been consistently and significantly below the long-term average every year from 1970 to 1987 (Jayne, Day, and Dregne 1989). There have also been significant declines in average rainfall in the coastal countries along the Gulf of Guinea and in eastern Africa.[8]

Climatologists' hypotheses to explain rainfall decline in Sub-Saharan Africa's drier regions include long-term climatic cycles as well as changes in ocean surface temperatures and in wind patterns over Africa brought on by changes in global atmospheric temperatures. The causes

Figure 2-1 Departures in Rainfall from the Long-Term Average for the Sahel Zone, 1900–1987

(percent)

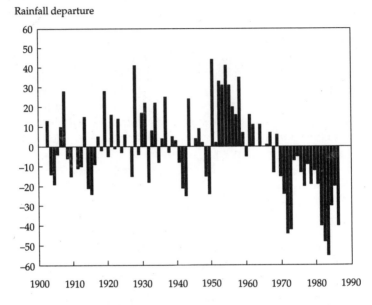

Source: Jayne, Day, and Dregne 1989, p. 5.

of Sahelian drought may still be poorly understood, but a broad consensus is emerging that they are related to large-scale patterns of atmospheric circulation — specifically to the reduced northward extension over Africa of the InterTropical Convergence Zone (ITCZ), the band of wet weather that surrounds the globe where the trade winds from the southern and northern hemispheres converge (Odhiambo 1991:79). These ITCZ extensions, in turn, are affected by cyclical changes in ocean surface temperatures.

There is increasing agreement that land surface changes — which include changes in albedo, evapotranspiration, soil moisture, surface temperature and roughness, and dust generation — can prolong and intensify Sahelian drought by reinforcing the atmospheric conditions which initially reduce rainfall (Nicholson 1989:53–54). Evidence is accumulating which strongly suggests that the widespread and severe changes in land surface characteristics in West and Central Africa caused by human activity have disrupted the normal cycle of the ITCZ extension over Sahelian Africa, causing the prolonged decline in rainfall from the long-term average.

Box 2-5   Is the Sahara Expanding Southward?

Satellite imagery now allows scientists to monitor the latitudinal movement of the southern edges of the Sahara (and of the other North African
deserts contiguous with it), running from southern Mauritania to mid-
Sudan. These data are available only since 1980, so that longer-term trends
cannot be inferred from them. The Sahara expanded southward in the first
four years for which these data are available (1980 to 1984), when there
was a serious drought. As a result, it was about 1.3 million km^2 (or 15
percent) larger in 1984, when the drought was most severe, than in 1980.
Although rainfall since 1984 has remained significantly below the mean
for 1900–1987, it has not again been as low as in 1984. The Sahara has
therefore receded in size from its 1984 peak, but not back to what it covered
in 1980 (Tucker and others 1991).

Changes in the land surface are partly caused by reduced rainfall itself,
but human activity, notably deforestation and removal of vegetative
cover on rangeland and cropland, has a considerable impact. If the
massive generation of smoke and atmospheric gases caused by biomass
burning is considered, as it should be, as an additional change in "surface" conditions over much of West Africa, it is difficult not to conclude
that growing human populations have an impact on climatic change.
Indeed, there is increasing concern about the effect of biomass burning
of the enormous scale represented by African forest and grassland fires
on the behavior and properties of clouds.[9]

Tropical forests are extremely important for recycling water between
the Earth's surface and the atmosphere, and their disappearance has
serious consequences for regional and global climate. They are highly
efficient in returning rainwater to the atmosphere in the form of water
vapor, which forms new clouds and leads to subsequent rainfall.
Rainforest regions thus store enormous quantities of water not only in
the soil and biomass, but also in the atmosphere above them. When
tropical forests disappear, water runs off quickly and much of it flows
into the sea. This not only affects local and regional hydrological cycles,
but also has potentially serious effects on climate. An important mechanism for the redistribution of heat is the atmosphere's ability to store
energy in the form of water vapor and to release this energy again when
vapor condenses into cloud droplets. If less water is available for this
process, heat absorbed at the ground has to be removed by other means
such as radiation and dry convection, leading to higher surface temperatures and to changes in the vertical distribution of heat (Andreae and
Goldammer 1992:88).

Deforestation is also a major cause of the rapid increase in the accumulation in the atmosphere of carbon dioxide (CO_2) and nitrous oxide (N_2O), two of the heat-trapping greenhouse gases that cause global warming (MacNeill and others 1991:11–13). Deforestation has been estimated to account for about one-quarter of worldwide net CO_2 emissions into the atmosphere (Andreae 1991:276); the remainder comes from the combustion of fossil fuels (most of which occurs, of course, in the industrialized countries of the northern hemisphere, in the countries of the former Soviet Union, and in China).

Burning of forests and grasslands causes enormous atmospheric pollution with both regional and global implications. Burning of biomass (forests, grasslands, agricultural wastes, fuelwood, etc.) worldwide is responsible for about one-third of global emissions of carbon aerosols into the atmosphere. Africa accounts for over 42 percent of tropical and almost 37 percent of global biomass burning annually and contributes more to gas and smoke emissions from biomass burning than any other region of the world (Andreae 1991:272; Andreae and Goldammer 1992:82). The destruction of tropical rainforests through burning directly contributes to the greenhouse effect, because the CO_2 released (up to 600 tons of dry matter per hectare) is not recaptured rapidly enough by regrowth on the same site of grasses or crops (ranging from 5 tons to 50 tons of dry matter per hectare). About 31 percent of annual burning of tropical forest biomass worldwide occurs in Africa, 46 percent in South and Central America and 22 percent in Asia (Andreae 1991:272–273).

About 90 percent of biomass burning in Africa is accounted for by the annual dry-season burning of savanna and grasslands — to clear them for farming, to stimulate grass growth and control pests and shrub growth, or to facilitate hunting. About one-third of total worldwide emissions from biomass burning is due, thus, to savanna burning in Africa. Unlike deforestation, however, savanna burning does not contribute significantly to the greenhouse effect, because the CO_2 released by the burning is recaptured into new savanna vegetation during the next annual growth cycle. But due to its geographic and temporal concentration, African biomass burning results in regional atmospheric pollution levels that are comparable to, and at times exceed, those in industrialized countries.

Acid deposition is higher in the Congo Basin and in Côte d'Ivoire than in the Amazon Region or in the eastern United States and is largely caused by direct emissions from biomass burning and by subsequent photochemical reactions in the resulting smoke and gas plumes. High levels of acid deposition have a negative effect on plant health and on fish and other aquatic organisms. Due to the longer average leaf life in the tropics, tropical forests are considerably more sensitive to foliar damage than temperate forests. Acid deposition also poses a serious risk to amphibians and insects that have aquatic life-cycle stages and depend on rain water collected in plants and mosses and between dead leaves. This risk extends further to the many plants that depend on such insects for pollination. There is also an effect of soil degradation through progressive acidification and associated problems such as leaching of aluminum, manganese and other cations, interference with nitrogen cycling, and the disturbance of microbial processes in the soil (Andreae and Goldammer 1992:88–89).

Environmental Degradation and Agricultural Stagnation

Soil degradation and erosion (excepting the often dramatic gully erosion that occurs where surface runoff is concentrated) are insidious processes, not readily apparent to farmers until the effects are severe and irreversible with the means traditionally available. They deplete the soil of nutrients, diminish its moisture retention capacity, and reduce the depth of the rooting zone for annual crops. These effects exacerbate the impact of drought. Farmers and pastoralists in the semiarid regions of Sub-Saharan Africa have always had to cope with drought, and they relied on effective adjustment mechanisms. But when drought extends over several successive years, as was the case in the 1970s and early 1980s, the problems become extremely serious.

The problems were compounded by the fact that the main traditional coping and adjustment mechanisms — shifting cultivation with long-duration fallows, and pastoralists' mobility — had become severely constrained. In the Sahel, for instance, rainfall during the 1950s and 1960s, when populations began to grow rapidly, was well above the long-term average almost every year. As a result, cultivation had been expanded into traditional rangelands, making both cultivators and pastoralists more vulnerable to drought. Range and pasture areas were reduced in size and the mobility of transhumant pastoralists was increasingly restricted. At the same time, a growing share of total cropland was in marginal areas, and changes in farming practices (for example, shorter fallows, reduction of multivariety seeding and intercropping, displacement of traditional drought-tolerant varieties) rendered farmers increasingly more vulnerable to climatic risk (as well as to plant pests and diseases).

As vegetative degradation and desertification proceed, the livestock carrying capacity of pastures and rangelands declines. Crop yields decline as the result of soil degradation and erosion on cropland. Available data on average cereal and root crop yields show decreases in many countries — despite significant investments in agriculture (Tables A-11 and A-12). Site-specific information confirms the problem in many countries.[10] The data suggest that environmental degradation, accelerated by population pressures, is part of the cause of Sub-Saharan Africa's slow rate of agricultural and economic development — through its negative impact on soil fertility, rainfall, water availability, and the supply of fuelwood and other forest products. Exacerbating this are a frequently poor agricultural policy environment, low use of productivity-enhancing agricultural inputs, and the generally low productivity of rural labor — attributable in large measure to low health and nutritional status and low educational attainment levels of the rural population.

Notes

1. Statistical information on agricultural performance, as on most other aspects of social and economic development, is difficult to obtain and tends to be of poor quality. This study draws on what is generally considered to be the best available statistical information (see the Statistical Appendix for data and sources).

2. The data on which estimates of food availability and consumption are based (such as crop acreage, yields, livestock production, processing and storage losses) are of poor quality in most African countries. Increasingly, it is also recognized that noncultivated plants and "bushmeat" contribute far more to many Africans' diets, particularly in poor crop years, than has been captured in official statistics. Nevertheless, few observers are as skeptical of the general picture of serious food deficits as Svedberg (1991).

3. Demographic modeling of the potential impact of AIDS is extremely difficult. Some simulations suggest that AIDS may reduce the population growth rate of SSA as a whole by as much as 0.5 to 1.0 percentage points in the early decades of the 21st century — through drastically higher mortality rates. But higher mortality rates may delay fertility declines.

4. UNDP/World Bank (1992), Tables 14-8 through 14-1, provides country-specific data on energy consumption, including consumption of fuelwood.

5. The InterAfrican Committee on Medicinal Plants and African Tropical Medicine and the Scientific, Technical and Research Commission of the OAU have published a pharmacopeia of African medicinal plants of proven efficacy, *African Pharmacopeia* (1985), and several African countries have established research institutes focusing on traditional medicine and the sources and effects of the active ingredients in medicines administered by traditional healers (DeJong 1991).

6. WRI/IIED estimates are even higher, suggesting that more than 80 percent of Sub-Saharan Africa's productive drylands, some 660 million hectares, are affected by "desertification" (Table A-27).

7. The *Sub-Saharan Africa Hydrological Assessment* attempts to meet this need by assisting countries to develop a reliable hydrological data base (see Chapter 10, note 1).

8. In Côte d'Ivoire, where deforestation has been the most rapid, mean annual rainfall declined significantly during the 1970s and 1980s (World Bank 1989a).

Rainfall in Senegal decreased by 2.2 percent a year in the 1970s and 1980s, and there was a sharp decrease in rainfall in northern Nigeria and Cameroon (Lele 1989c; Lele and Stone 1989). Rainfall also declined dramatically throughout Ethiopia during that period (World Bank 1987a).

9. Cloud droplets form around aerosol particles, called cloud condensation nuclei (CCN). Biomass burning generates and releases into the atmosphere vast amounts of pyrogenic aerosol particles, which are very effective as CCN. The more CCN in the atmosphere, the more droplets form, resulting in smaller droplet size with a given amount of available water. Clouds composed of smaller droplets are lighter in color, reflect more sunlight back into space, and are less likely to produce rain. Since clouds are a major regulatory and control mechanism for the Earth's heat balance, large-scale modifications in cloud properties have a strong impact on global climate. The increasing abundance of CCN is, therefore, likely to have potentially critical impact on precipitation efficiency — compounding the changes in hydrological cycles in the tropics caused by land surface changes such as deforestation (Andreae and Goldammer 1992:87–88).

10. See, for example, Barnes 1990a and 1990b; Bishop and Allen 1989; Elliot 1986; Falloux and Mukendi 1988; Gorse and Steeds 1987; FAO/IBRD Cooperative Programme 1991; Lal and Okigbo 1990; Matlon 1990; de Montalembert and Clement 1983; Mortimore 1989a and 1989b; Nelson 1988; Stocking 1987.

3
The Demographic Dimension

The Lagging Demographic Transition

Sub-Saharan Africa lags behind other regions in its demographic transition. The total fertility rate (TFR) for SSA as a whole has remained virtually unchanged at about 6.4 to 6.6 for the past twenty-five years (Table A-2). This is significantly higher than in other countries with similar levels of income, life expectancy, female education, and contraceptive prevalence. In a number of countries of Sub-Saharan Africa fertility in fact has risen (in large part due to significant success in treating diseases that cause infertility), while it has declined elsewhere in the developing world.

Recent statistics, collected through nationally representative sample surveys carried out between 1986 and 1989 under the Demographic and Health Surveys (DHS) Program,[1] appear to signal, however, that several countries are at or near a critical demographic turning point (Table A-8).[2] In Botswana, the TFR fell from 6.9 in the mid-1960s to 4.7 in 1989, and in Zimbabwe it dropped from 8.0 to 5.3 over the same period. In Kenya, the TFR declined from 8.2 in 1977/78 to 7.7 in 1984 and to 6.5 in 1989 (Kelley and Nobbe 1990:33.). Encouraging, too, are the data from Nigeria which indicate a TFR of 5.7 in 1990, compared with 6.9 in 1965. In Côte d'Ivoire, Ghana, Mozambique, and Sudan, fertility also appears to have begun a secular decline (Table A-2).[3]

Life expectancy in Sub-Saharan Africa has risen from an average of 43 years in 1965 to 51 years in 1990 (Table A-1). In eighteen countries, average life expectancy today is 53 years or more. Mainly due to the decline in mortality rates, population growth has accelerated from an average of 2.7 percent a year for 1965–1980 to about 3.1 percent a year at present (Table A-2). And, given the age structure of SSA populations, the momentum for continued growth is already built in. Even if the TFR were to drop immediately to the replacement level of 2.2 births per woman, it would take almost a hundred years before the population would cease growing. By then it would be 80 to 100 percent larger than it is today.

Figure 3-1 Total Population of Sub-Saharan Africa, 1960–1990

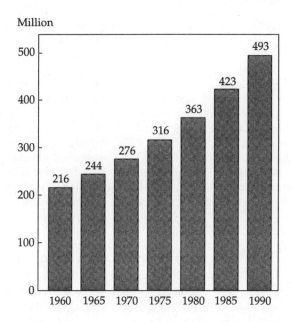

The high fertility rates, and the marriage, reproductive, and contraceptive behavior patterns that underlie these, arise in part from the fact
that most women live in rural areas and have little or no education, few
opportunities outside their traditional roles, and limited legal rights.
Childbearing enhances their status, and most women marry and begin
having children early and continue to have them throughout their
fecund years. But the comparative lack of urbanization and education
does not explain everything: data available from the World Fertility
Survey (WFS) for 1978–1982 indicate that urban and rural, educated and
uneducated women in Sub-Saharan Africa have and want more children
than their counterparts elsewhere.[4]

Women in Sub-Saharan Africa marry early: WFS data for the early
1980s show that, on average, 40 percent of all women aged 15–19 and 75
percent of those age 20–24 were or had been married (Cochrane and
Farid 1989). Early female marriage increases the number of fecund years
a women spends in union and therefore tends to exert upward pressure
on the TFR. Even urban women in Sub-Saharan Africa marry earlier than
rural women in North Africa and Asia (Cochrane and Farid 1989).

Contraceptive use in Sub-Saharan Africa is far below that in other
regions (Tables A-5 and A-6). It is associated primarily with the desire

---

Box 3-1   Population Projections for Sub-Saharan Africa

Recent World Bank projections assume that the TFR for Sub-Saharan Africa (including South Africa) will decline from 6.5 percent in the period 1985–1990 to about 3.25 percent by 2030. This implies average annual population growth rates of just over 3 percent in the 1990s, 2.9 percent in the following decade, and close to 2.6 percent in the decade thereafter. In this scenario, the SSA population would exceed 1,000 million by the year 2012. By the turn of the present century, SSA would be second only to Asia in terms of total population. Aggregate population growth will remain above 2 percent per year at least until 2025, by which time the population of Sub-Saharan Africa, at 1,378 million, would be 2.6 times that of today. The net reproduction rate (NRR) will decline to 1 only by 2060. And Sub-Saharan Africa would reach a hypothetical stationary population of over 3,100 million only some time after the year 2150 (Stephens and others 1991).

---

for child spacing and only secondarily with the wish to limit family size (Table A-6). Use of efficient contraceptive methods generally increases with urbanization.[5] Low contraceptive use is due in part to poor knowledge. There are wide differences among countries, but on average, only about half of all women in SSA had, by the early 1980s, heard of a way (either efficient or inefficient) to prevent pregnancy. This compared with rates of 85 to 95 percent in other regions (Cochrane and Farid 1989). By the late 1980s, the DHS surveys showed measurable increases in the percentage of women who had knowledge of modern contraceptive methods: in ten of the twelve SSA countries surveyed and for which data are available so far, between 64 and 98 percent of currently married women aged 15–49 knew of at least one modern contraceptive method (the exceptions were Mali and Nigeria, with only 29 percent and 41 percent, respectively). The DHS data on contraceptive prevalence rates (CPRs) indicate, however, the difficult task ahead: only between 1 and 6 percent of these married women were currently using a modern contraceptive method, and the percentage of married women using any contraceptive method ranged only between 3 and 13 percent. The exceptions, with significantly higher CPRs, are Botswana, Kenya, and Zimbabwe (Table A-8).

Among all groups of women, desired fertility is far higher in Sub-Saharan Africa than elsewhere. However, the WFS data analyzed by Cochrane and Farid also showed that: (a) younger women desire fewer children than do older women; (b) urban women want fewer children than do rural women (although urban residence has not yet become a strong fertility depressant — the rural-urban differentials being smaller

---

**Box 3-2   Contraceptive Prevalence Among Women:
Sub-Saharan Africa vs. Other Regions**

Data for the early 1980s indicate that the percentage of women in Sub-
Saharan Africa who had "ever used" any contraceptive methods varied
widely — from 2 percent in Mauritania to 74 percent in Côte d'Ivoire. The
average for the ten SSA countries covered in the World Fertility Survey
(WFS) was 26 percent, compared with 40 percent in both North Africa and
Asia and 62 percent in Latin America. The regional comparison revealed
far greater differences when only "efficient" methods were considered:
only 6 percent of women in SSA had ever used these, compared with 32 to
50 percent of women in other regions.

Based on reported "current users," contraceptive prevalence in SSA was
very low indeed, of both efficient and inefficient methods. In six of the ten SSA
countries surveyed, fewer than 1 percent of all women were current users
of modern methods. The difference between "currently using" and "ever
used" was much greater in SSA than elsewhere, probably reflecting the
comparatively much greater use in SSA of contraceptive practices for birth
spacing, rather than for limiting family size (Cochrane and Farid 1989).

---

in SSA than in other regions); and (c) educated women want far fewer
children than do uneducated ones.

In Sub-Saharan Africa, as elsewhere, women's education affects fertility preferences, use of modern contraceptive methods, and fertility.
Cochrane and Farid found that:

- There are considerable differences in desired family size among
  countries (see also Table A-8), but with increasing maternal education there is both a decline and a clear convergence across countries.

- Current use of any contraceptive method was only 4 percent among
  the least educated (compared with 19 to 34 percent in other regions), but 19 percent among the most educated (compared with
  43 to 56 percent in the other regions).

- Although current use of contraceptive practices among the most
  educated women in Sub-Saharan Africa was only about the same
  as among the least educated in North Africa and well below the
  least educated in Asia and Latin America, even this low rate was
  sufficient to lower the TFR to about 5 for women with seven or more
  years of schooling.

Fertility rises with a few years of schooling, but then declines (as in
other regions). But the effect of maternal education on fertility has been
less pronounced, to date, in Sub-Saharan Africa than elsewhere.

The very high infant and child mortality rates (Table A-3) prevent achieving desired, or target, fertility levels — and this helps explain the low CPRs (Tables A-5 and A-6). Contraceptive use increases as the number of living children increases. Although infant and child mortality have declined over the past two decades (in some countries substantially), they remain much higher than in other regions (albeit with considerable differences among countries).[6] Higher child survival rates reduce the need to replace children who have died or to have more children to insure against the likelihood of future deaths. Infant mortality rates are well below the SSA average of 107 in Botswana (36), Kenya (67), and Zimbabwe (48). The same is true for child mortality rates, where the SSA average is 177: Botswana (40), Kenya (105), and Zimbabwe (57). In each of these countries, the TFR has begun to show a decline, signalling the onset of the demographic transition (Table A-8).

Infant mortality is highest in rural areas, and children born to young mothers are at greater risk. Infant mortality is also higher for first-born children and for those born seventh or later. Children's survival chances are greater if the interval from the previous pregnancy is longer (maternal attrition, lower risk of low birth weight, maternal attention). Infant and child mortality decrease consistently with the mothers' education. Urban-rural differences in infant and child mortality are significant and somewhat larger in Sub-Saharan Africa than in other regions.

Prolonged and near universal breastfeeding has been the main factor keeping fertility below a biological maximum in most SSA countries. The duration of breastfeeding is generally shorter in urban than in rural areas, but it does not decline as rapidly with mother's educational levels as in other regions. The most educated women in Sub-Saharan Africa breastfeed considerably longer than those in Latin America and Asia. Breastfeeding has important positive effects on child health — and, indirectly, via reduced infant mortality, on fertility decisions. It also affects birth spacing — and thereby maternal health, infant health, and fertility. In this respect, postpartum infecundity is far more important in Sub-Saharan Africa than elsewhere, accounting for 59 percent of the reduction in fertility from the biological maximum. On average, fertility in SSA is only 67 percent of what it would be in the absence of breastfeeding.

Nevertheless, fertility patterns do not seem to be fully explained by the proximate determinants of marriage, postpartum infecundity (breastfeeding), and contraceptive use. Abortion, sterility, subfecundity, and spousal separation appear to suppress the "maximum" fertility below that observed in other regions. This suggests the need for more research on other determinants of fertility to understand current levels and probable future trends (Cochrane and Farid 1989).

Figure 3-2   Infant Mortality Rate, 1960–1990

Per 1,000 live births

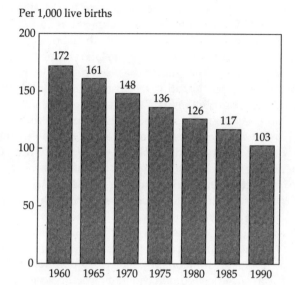

Note: For 42 countries in Sub-Saharan Africa.

Fertility and Agriculture: Part of the Nexus?

Fertility is highest in rural areas — reflecting economic and sociocultural factors which affect fertility aspirations. Traditional lineage and kinship systems, gender roles, and intergenerational relations contain strong pronatalist forces, and women's fertility usually is a major determinant of their status. Extended families, where the costs of high fertility are only partly borne by the couple making the fertility decision, tend to encourage high fertility. In most of rural SSA, labor is not readily available for hire and must be mobilized from within the household or through social or kinship arrangements specific to the community. For men, polygamy (or polygyny) is a widely practiced way of securing the labor of women and their children — but even women may welcome co-wives as co-workers (e.g., Netting 1993:89). Polygamous men generally have more children than monogamous men, while women in polygamous marriages tend to have fewer children than those in monogamous marriages (Bongaarts and others 1990:135–136).

Women may recognize far more readily than men the costs of high fertility to their own and their children's health. This may be particularly prevalent in polygamous unions where each woman is responsible for her own children. The costs of children are lower to men than to women, yet the value of child labor may be higher to the mothers than to the fathers — except in communities where fathers have and assert priority rights to their children's labor. For women, the labor of their children is often the only means of securing adequate labor to cope with their many responsibilities. (In many communities, women try to ease their peak labor constraints by participating in various forms of kinship- or community-based work group and labor exchange arrangements.) As water and woodfuels become more scarce and the time required to obtain them increases, the need increases for children to help with the mothers' growing workload associated with these survival activities. Child labor is also increasingly needed to compensate for declining male labor in food crop production, particularly in poor families that cannot hire wage labor. This may contribute to the persistence of high fertility rates.[7] In much of SSA, men and women cultivate different crops on separate plots, and women's farming systems depend heavily on female and child labor. Most women marry at an early age and often considerably older men. Coupled with the high rates of divorce/separation and the fact that in most African societies women can gain access to critical assets (such as land) and public services only through male relatives, this may increase women's willingness to bear many children so as to have sons to turn to when husbands leave or die. The desired number of children is considerably higher among rural women in Sub-Saharan Africa than among their counterparts in any other region of the world. And in no other region of the world do women play as significant a role in agriculture as in Sub-Saharan Africa.

The characteristics of most traditional land tenure systems may also bear upon fertility decisions — but more research is needed to establish this link. Where access to land for farming is granted to all members of a community, this may be a disincentive to fertility control. Where the amount of land allocated is based on the ability to cultivate it, this ability — under the low-resource farming conditions prevailing in most of Sub-Saharan Africa — is primarily determined by the ability to mobilize labor. In most cases, this means family labor — more specifically, female and child labor. Indeed, a number of field studies report this to be an important incentive to increase family size through such means as polygamy and pressure on women to have many children.

Among groups with matrilineal descent and inheritance traditions, further complications may arise because land use rights are not passed on from fathers to their children, but to uterine relatives (in most cases males). This weakens the link between land availability and land resource management on the one hand and demand for fewer children on the other. It also weakens men's incentives to invest in maintaining the fertility of the land they farm.[8] Fathers may see little point in preserving farm land in good condition beyond their own lifetime or in having few children so as to pass on a viable farm unit to each of them. Women, conversely, may face social pressure to bear many children so as to increase the number of future claimants to land resources who belong to their lineage.

The implication derived from the above is that most rural Africans attach high economic value to having large numbers of children. Larger families appear to fare better economically than small families. Children contribute labor in cropping, livestock tending, fishing, water and fuel-wood fetching, and child rearing. The available evidence, although imperfect, suggests that high demand for children may be partly the result of the historic abundance of land and the shortage of labor, combined with high infant, child, and overall mortality rates and high food insecurity. Maintaining high fertility is the rational response of people who seek to ensure adequate family labor and the survival of children who would support them in old age. For men in particular, polygyny makes good sense in this situation because it increases the supply of female and child labor and improves the prospects for security in old age. The widespread practice of payment of a bride price (instead of the woman's family providing a dowry) reflects this reality where women are wanted for their labor and their ability to bear many children. Early female marriage, common in Africa, also increases the prospects for multiple childbirths.

Various other trends also tend to keep the TFRs high. As forest resources, water availability, and soil fertility decline, farmers and pastoralists obtain less product per hectare. The main resource available to them to increase production is family labor, which permits increasing the extent of the land farmed. It also makes it easier to diversify the sources of family income with more seasonal or full-time off-farm employment. Hence, agricultural stagnation and environmental degradation, in resource-poor situations characteristic of most of Sub-Saharan Africa, provide an economic incentive — and often a survival strategy — to maintain large families. These factors also provide an incentive to keep children out of school to work on the parental farm or with the family's livestock.

This situation is exacerbated by the specific and important responsibilities placed on women in most farming systems of Sub-Saharan Africa. Women are often responsible for food cropping, and almost always for fuelwood and water provision (Chapter 5). As soil fertility declines and distances to fuelwood and water sources increase, many rural women are faced with the situation that the only resource that can be increased to meet the increasing need for labor is child labor. More labor substitutes for reduced soil fertility and compensates for the greater difficulty in obtaining fuel and water. This then completes a vicious circle in which population growth, combined with traditional farming practices, contributes to environmental degradation, in turn contributing to further agricultural stagnation and to the persistence of high rates of population growth.

These hypotheses are consistent with statistical tests (see the Appendix to Chapter 3) which show that, other things being equal, TFRs are highest in those SSA countries that have the most cultivated land per capita. Similarly, TFRs are highest in countries with the highest infant mortality rates, lowest level of female education, lowest urbanization, and greatest degree of land degradation. This suggests that demand for children as well as TFRs will decline over time — even without an active population policy — as population density on cultivated land increases, and if female school enrollment rates rise, infant mortality declines, urbanization increases, and environmental degradation is minimized.

However, changes in these determinants of the demand for children are coming about only slowly. Analysis of available cross-country data suggests a considerable degree of inertia in fertility rates as well as the presence of many other factors that influence fertility rates but for which data are not available. Cultural elements appear to be very important. Commenting on the findings obtained from the analysis of the WFS data collected in the late 1970s and early 1980s, one of the program leaders stated that the onset of the demographic transition "appears to be determined more by ill-understood cultural factors than by any objectively ascertainable development indicators" (Gille 1985:279). These cultural determinants are likely to change only slowly, even though many of the factors that help shape culture are changing. Fertility rates will decline, but only slowly, and only if infant mortality declines and environmental degradation is arrested. But progress in these two critical areas is occurring too slowly to compensate for the enormous difference between the current rates of growth of population and of agricultural production.

Nonetheless, rising population pressure on cultivated land, declining infant mortality rates and improvements in female education are stimulating demand for family planning services. Much of this demand remains, at present, unmet (Table A-6).

Notes

1. The DHS Program, a follow-up to the World Fertility Survey (WFS), is a nine-year program to assist developing countries in implementing fifty-nine demographic and health surveys.

2. The TFR has declined most dramatically in Mauritius, falling from 4.8 in the mid-1960s to 1.9 by 1990 (Table A-2).

3. Detailed analysis of the DHS data is still in progress, and this study could therefore not yet draw fully on the information collected under the DHS Program. Note also that the data in Table A-2, which represent the "best estimates" currently available in the World Bank's demographic statistical data base, do not in all cases fully reflect the most recent survey findings obtained under the DHS Program.

4. Under the WFS, national surveys were undertaken in the late 1970s and early 1980s. Using these data, Cochrane and Farid (1989) carried out a comparative analysis to ascertain similarities and differences in fertility and underlying causal factors between SSA and other regions; when they undertook this study, WFS data were available for ten SSA countries.

5. Interestingly, when efficient and inefficient methods were considered together, urban use was higher than rural use in only three of the ten countries for which WFS data were available (Lesotho, Nigeria, Sudan). Traditional practices of fertility control, such as breastfeeding, might have been abandoned in the course of modernization, while modern methods were not yet adopted widely enough to offset this. This explanation is frequently given for the small differentials in fertility across socioeconomic groups, but the available data on breastfeeding practices in Sub-Saharan Africa do not support this conjecture. Breastfeeding does not decline rapidly with increasing education (Cochrane and Farid 1989).

6. The differential is higher in the case of child mortality, due to high mortality in the second and third years of life, following weaning. Toddler and child mortality rates are two to three times greater in SSA than in Latin America and Asia. Toddler and child mortality at all levels of mother's education are higher than in other regions (Cochrane and Farid 1989; see also Table A-3).

7. This is suggested, though not necessarily proved, by the statistical analysis summarized in the Appendix to Chapter 3.

8. Among the matrilineal Akan in Ghana, for example, it is frequently observed that a son employed in an urban job is very reluctant to have remittances he sends to his father invested in improving the father's farm ventures because these investments will, upon the father's death, benefit the son's maternal uncles or cousins, rather than himself.

Appendix to Chapter 3

Statistical Analysis to Explain Intercountry Variations in Total Fertility Rates

The available data, for thirty-eight countries, were used to test a number of the country-level findings concerning the determinants of high TFRs. A first set of tests was undertaken using cross-country data, looking at relationships in the variation of variables across countries. The results were consistent with the analysis presented in Chapter 3, but questions remained concerning the robustness of the results and the statistical fit. A second set of tests was therefore carried out on a much larger set of data which included both time series and cross-country data. The results are reported here, along with any differences with the findings from the first set of tests. The results of both sets of tests are highly consistent. (The data and the methodology used are discussed in the Supplement to this volume.)

For these tests, TFRs are hypothesized to be related to the independent variables as follows: positively to infant mortality (the higher the expected loss of infants, the more births are desired to ensure sufficient survivors); negatively to female school enrollment (better educated women want fewer children); negatively to food security (the greater the food security, the lower the need for children to provide farm labor); positively to cultivable land per person (the more cultivated land per person, the greater the need for family labor to work it); positively to the rate of deforestation (the higher the rate of deforestation, the greater the need for child labor to help fetch wood and water); and negatively to urbanization (urbanization lowers the TFR).

These hypotheses are tested by means of statistical regression with the TFR as the dependent variable. The independent variables are all lagged one year. The lag structure is arbitrary; several were tried, but the statistical fit did not improve. The Supplement presents results of tests for combinations of different countries and different data. Only the sign of the coefficient, the range of t-statistics and the range of significance levels in the various tests are reported below. Since the methodology used does not permit the value of the coefficient to be readily interpreted, it is not reported.

Independent Variables	Coefficient	t-statistic	2-Tail Significance Test
Infant mortality rate	positive	4.6–4.9	0.0%
Female school enrollment rate	negative	2.3–2.8	0.6–2.2%
Calorie supply as % of requirement	positive	0.9–1.4	17–38%
Hectares cultivated per person	positive	2.0–4.7	0.0–4.5%
Rate of deforestation	positive	0.2–1.3	21–82%
Degree of urbanization	negative	1.9–2.9	0.4–6.4%

Adjusted R squared = 0.44 to 0.46

The coefficients for female school enrollment, area cultivated per person, infant mortality, and the degree of urbanization are statistically significant at above the 90 percent level, with a 2-tail significance test of 10 percent or less. (The 2-tail significance test indicates the probability of the coefficient actually being zero. Hence, a 2-tail test of 2.2 percent for the rate of female school enrollment indicates a 2.2 percent probability that the coefficient is zero — or a 97.8 percent probability that it is not zero.) Although the relationship between deforestation and the TFR is positive, as hypothesized, the statistical tests do not suggest significance. The coefficient for calorie supply has the wrong sign and is insignificant.

In the tests with single-year cross-country data, the results were essentially the same, except that deforestation was also significantly related to the TFR, and the coefficient for calorie supply was positive, as hypothesized, but insignificant.

These findings suggest that the TFR is lower as female primary school enrollment is higher. The greater the area cultivated per person, the higher the TFR. The higher the infant mortality rate, the higher the TFR. The greater the rate of urbanization, the lower the TFR. The positive association between the rate of deforestation and the TFR has ambiguous significance. This may be because the rate of deforestation is a poor proxy for the rate of degradation of the rural environment which includes soil and water degradation. Or the hypothesis itself may be incorrect. If further analysis establishes the significance of this relationship, it suggests that greater demand for child labor is associated with environmental deterioration (more labor needed to obtain wood and water and to produce food as the productivity of farm land declines due to deforestation). The relationship between nutrition and the TFR is even more ambiguous, and the hypothesis could not be supported statistically. At very low levels of nutrition, improving calorie intake may increase fertility and, hence, the TFR. Or there may be no relationship. Better data are needed to resolve this.

4

The Nexus of Population Growth, Agricultural Stagnation, and Environmental Degradation

The Main Linkages

The preceding chapter cited evidence suggesting that agricultural stagnation and environmental degradation, combined with customary land tenure systems and the traditional roles of rural women, may contribute to maintaining high fertility rates. These systems and practices appear to create demand for child labor as a means to ensure family survival. The difficulties faced in analyzing these relationships are rooted in the multiplicity of factors that affect the rate of population growth, environmental degradation, and the pace and direction of agricultural development in Sub-Saharan Africa. In addition, there are important variations across countries. This chapter pursues the analysis of multiple and synergetic links between rapid population growth, poor agricultural performance, and environmental degradation. The role of women in rural production systems, a major link in this nexus, is discussed separately in Chapter 5.

The complexity of these linkages and the seeming ambiguity of the analysis result primarily from Boserup's finding that agricultural intensification occurs as population density on agricultural land increases (Boserup 1965). Others have published more recent material confirming the applicability of the Boserup hypothesis to many developing country situations, including in Sub-Saharan Africa (for example, Binswanger and Pingali 1984, 1988; Pingali, Bigot and Binswanger 1987; Lele and Stone 1989). It should not be surprising that this phenomenon has been observed so widely. Farmers are unlikely to have an incentive to intensify their agricultural production (i.e., to generate more output per unit land area) unless there is a constraint on land. If there is no land constraint, and land is free or very cheap, it makes sense from the

---

Box 4-1   Ukara Island, Lake Victoria (Tanzania):
Agricultural Intensification under Population Pressure

An extreme example of agricultural intensification under population pressure is that of Ukara island in Lake Victoria. Faced with considerable population pressure and soils of low fertility, the island's inhabitants, the Kara (or Wakara), had developed, prior to European contact, a highly refined intensive farming system, which included erosion control, crop rotation with intercropping and green manuring with legumes, fodder cultivation, stabling of cattle, and fertilizing of fields (farmyard manure, leaf manure, household ash). The tenure system was based on private property, with inheritance and sale of land. The system has, however, reached its limits. The island's population has numbered about 16,000 since the beginning of the century; population density is about 500 per km^2, and the average family holding amounts to 1 hectare of arable land. There has been little, if any, population growth, whereas there has been substantial population growth in the rest of the Lake area where shifting cultivation is still practiced. Excess population moves to the mainland, where labor-intensive techniques are quickly abandoned because the returns to labor are far higher with the extensive systems still possible on the mainland (Ludwig 1968; Kocher 1973; Ruthenberg 1980:158–160; Netting 1993:52–53).

---

farmer's perspective to extend the use of land and minimize the use of other inputs, including capital and labor. Shifting cultivation and pastoral livestock raising are perhaps the best illustrations of this situation. They have predominated in most of Sub-Saharan Africa.

Consistent with Boserup's findings, these customary extensive farming and livestock systems change when populations become more dense. This can be seen in the Kenya highlands, Burundi, Rwanda, the Kivu Plateau in eastern Zaïre, and in parts of Nigeria. In Rwanda in particular, intensive traditional agricultural systems exist, brought about by the scarcity of land relative to the population dependent on it. In most of Sub-Saharan Africa, however, land has been abundant until recently, and in some countries it still is.

Traditional crop production and animal husbandry methods, traditional land tenure systems and land use practices, traditional methods of obtaining woodfuels and building materials, and traditional responsibilities of women in rural production and household maintenance worked well and could evolve slowly when population densities were low and populations were growing only slowly. The hypothesis is that rapidly increasing population pressure in the past twenty to thirty years has, in most of Sub-Saharan Africa, overwhelmed the only slowly evolv-

---

Box 4-2   The Kofyar in Nigeria:
Extensive Farming When the Land Frontier Opens

The Kofyar initially lived as subsistence farmers on the Jos Plateau in north-central Nigeria. As population density on the escarpment increased, they intensified their farming system, with increasing reliance on agroforestry, terracing, and manuring. When population growth on the plateau outpaced the ability of their farming system to sustain the increased numbers, the Kofyar obtained permission from tribes in the Benue River plains to clear low-land forests and farm there. The migrants abandoned the intensive farming techniques they had practiced on the plateau and adopted instead an extensive forest-fallow farming system focused on cash cropping and market-oriented animal production. The subsistence farms on the Jos Plateau had averaged about 1.5 acres, while the new farms in the cleared forests were 4 to 5 times that size (Netting 1968; Stone 1984). However, over a period of about thirty years, as population density in the newly developed lowlands increased, the settlers gradually intensified their farming methods again (Netting 1993).

---

ing rural traditions of farming, livestock raising, fuelwood provision, land allocation and utilization, and gender-specific responsibilities in household maintenance and rural production systems. This has led to an accelerated degradation of natural resources. And this in turn has contributed to the low rate of growth of agriculture. In those few places where agricultural intensification has occurred most rapidly, there has been very little, if any, degradation of natural resources.

The complexity of these multiple interrelationships is further increased by interaction with the economic policy environment characterizing many African countries since the mid-1960s. Exchange rate, tax, trade, and agricultural price policies in many African countries have often combined to render agriculture unprofitable. The mechanisms for developing and transmitting improved agricultural technology are severely inadequate throughout Sub-Saharan Africa. Excessive government control of agricultural marketing and processing has either squeezed out the private sector or forced it to operate clandestinely, yet public sector marketing and processing enterprises have performed poorly. Farmers have not usually been permitted to associate freely in farmer-managed cooperatives, nor to market freely their products. Throughout Sub-Saharan Africa, this lack of empowerment of farmers has discouraged them from investing. To break out of the trap of rapid population growth, low agricultural growth, and environmental degradation, these policy constraints must be overcome. The World Bank's 1989 long-term perspective study on Sub-Saharan Africa suggested how this might be done (World Bank 1989d). *Reversing the Spiral* contends that measures will also be needed to overcome the constraints imposed by increasing population pressure on traditional cultivation, fuel provision, and tenure systems, and by the roles customarily assigned to women in rural societies. Appropriate policy reforms will make the more rapid evolution of these traditional systems easier.

Traditional Crop Cultivation and Livestock Husbandry Methods

For centuries, shifting cultivation and transhumant pastoralism have been, under the prevailing agroecological conditions and factor endowments, appropriate systems for people throughout most of Sub-Saharan Africa to derive their livelihood, in a sustainable manner, from the natural resource endowment of their environment. The ecological and economic systems were in equilibrium. The key to maintaining this equilibrium was mobility. People shifted to a different location when soil fertility declined or forage was depleted, allowing the fertility of the land to be reconstituted through the natural processes of vegetative growth and decay. For field cropping in forest- and bush-fallow systems, this typically involved cultivation periods of two to four years, land then being left fallow for as long as fifteen to twenty-five years. Transhumant herders' mobility generally involved a far greater geographic range, but a far shorter temporal cycle. They would move their herds on extended migratory patterns as dictated by the seasonal availability of water and forage and in most cases repeat the same cycle in one or sometimes two years.

These mobile systems of shifting and long-fallow cultivation and pastoral transhumance were suitable because of low population density, abundant land, limited capital and technology, and often difficult agroclimatic conditions. As long as population growth was slow and land was available, the additional people could be accommodated by gradually taking more land into the farming cycle and establishing new settlements on previously uncropped land. Adjustments, including gradual intensification of farming, were made as and when they became necessary, but the pace of adjustment required was slow because population growth was slow. Intercropping in Rwanda, for example, was an indigenous adaptation of this type, necessitated because shifting cultivation became increasingly constrained by rising population density.

In the absence of sufficiently rapid and widespread technological change, population growth has led to the expansion of the area under cultivation. This has involved mainly the conversion of large areas of forests, wetlands, river valley bottoms, and grassland savanna to crop-

---

Box 4-3   Land Requirements for *Chitemene* Cultivation in Zambia

The suitability of land for *chitemene* cultivation in Zambia depends, among other things, on the density of woody vegetation available for cutting and on the land's regeneration capability. At the present levels of fram technology and productivity, a person completely dependent on *chitemene* requires for survival one hectare under cultivation each year (Stølen 1983:31–32; Vedeld 1983:98–100). If 50 percent of the land in an area is suitable for *chitemene* and the regeneration cycle is twenty-five years, the aggregate land requirement for long-term ecological sustainability of the system is 50 ha per person. In a village of 200 people, requiring a total area of 100 km^2 to sustain *chitemene* farming, individual fields would be as far as 5.1 km from the village — assuming the village land forms a perfect circle and the village is located in its center.

This simple arithmetic also shows that traditional farming and land use practices, combined with constraints on the time people can afford to spend walking to and from their fields each day, limits the size of farm settlements. Some people eventually migrate to establish new villages in virgin forest land once the situation in their home village becomes too difficult.

---

land. Since 1965, the area farmed in SSA has increased by over 21 million hectares (Table A-17). Much of this has taken place on ecologically fragile and agriculturally marginal land, which is not suitable for sustained farming and eventually abandoned in an advanced state of degradation. Forested land has declined by about 65 million hectares since 1965 (Table A-17). But land available to expand cultivation has become increasingly scarce in most of Sub-Saharan Africa, drastically narrowing the scope for further expansion. Most farming systems in SSA are, in fact, not land surplus systems, but land-extensive systems (Eicher 1984a:455). Over the past twenty-five years, crop acreage has expanded by only 0.7 percent annually, and the population pressure on cropped land has increased sharply. On average, per capita arable land in Sub-Saharan Africa declined from 0.5 hectares per person in 1965 to 0.4 ha/person in 1980 and to less than 0.3 ha/person in 1990. For comparison, between 1965 and 1990 crop acreage declined from 0.6 ha/person to 0.4 ha/person in China and from 0.3 ha/person to 0.2 ha/person in India (Table A-18).

Because of agroclimatic and soil characteristics, the potential productive land endowment per capita in most of Sub-Saharan Africa is even poorer than these simple acreage statistics suggest. Niger, for example, is more densely populated than India or Bangladesh if account is taken of the extremely poor quality of its agricultural resource endowment.

Figure 4-1 Population Pressure on Cropland in Sub-Saharan Africa, 1961–1987
(total and rural population per hectare of cropland)

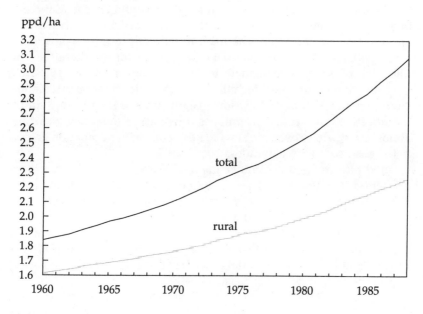

Nigeria and Senegal are more densely populated than the Philippines. And Mali, Burkina Faso, and The Gambia are twice as densely settled as Indonesia (Binswanger and Pingali 1987; Matlon 1990).

There is considerable diversity among countries, but everywhere fallow periods are shortening as populations increase and the land frontier recedes. In many areas, from Mauritania to Lesotho, fallow periods are not sufficiently long anymore to restore soil fertility. Increasingly, farmers are compelled to remain on the same parcel of land — yet they change their farming methods only very slowly.

These people face a critical dilemma: a central element of their traditional farming system — the ability to shift around on the land — is being eliminated by population pressure, yet they continue to use the other elements of their customary production systems. Where fallow periods are too short, or nonexistent, and where traditional cultivation techniques continue to be used, soil fertility deteriorates and soils are not conserved. Wind and water erosion, soil nutrient depletion, acidity, and deteriorating soil structure become common and increasingly severe. As a result, crop yields decline, forcing farmers to expand production along the already receding land frontier. This expansion occurs first within the vicinity of their settlements — on more steeply sloping land and in nearby forest, wetland and range areas. As this option becomes increasingly limited, people migrate to establish new farms, often in semiarid areas and in tropical forests where soil and climatic conditions are poorly suited to the cultivation of annual crops and yields are therefore low. The migrants bring with them the techniques they practiced in the areas they abandoned, and these techniques are often detrimental to their new environment. Although they soon begin to experiment with simple modifications in farming techniques, this indigenous adjustment has almost everywhere been too slow to keep pace with population growth in the past two to three decades.

Good pasture land is diminishing as the most productive tracts are converted to cultivation. The mobility of pastoralists' herds is further reduced as settlers increasingly cultivate bottomlands previously available to herders during their dry season migration. The concentration of increasing numbers of livestock on smaller areas destroys pasture vegetation, further reducing their carrying capacity and contributing to range degradation and eventual desertification (Gorse and Steeds 1987; Falloux and Mukendi 1988; Nelson 1988).

Diminishing forest and woodland resources provide less fuelwood and other forest products, many of which are of considerable importance for rural livelihood and survival systems. Similarly, surface and groundwater resources are increasingly affected by the drastic alterations in land uses and vegetative cover. The effects of the worsening fuelwood and water scarcity are most directly felt by some of the most vulnerable: women and children. More time and effort are required to obtain these vital commodities. Or people must manage with less of them. One consequence of reduced woodfuel supplies is the increasing use of dung and crop by-products as fuels. This reduces their availability as farming system inputs to maintain soil fertility. Similar effects result from diminished availability of, and access to, water for household and home garden use: health and sanitation standards deteriorate, and home garden productivity declines.

These problems are gravest in parts of the Sahel and of mountainous East Africa and in the dry belt stretching from the coast of Angola through southern Mozambique. There are other countries where land appears to be more abundant in relation to their current populations. These countries lie in Central Africa, humid West Africa, and southern Africa. However, much of the potentially arable land in Central and humid West Africa is under tropical forest. To preserve biodiversity, maintain rainfall, and preserve the humid climate on which its tropical agriculture is based, much of this area should not be cultivated. Instead, the humid forests need to be preserved. This land has not been cultivated so far because it is poorly suited to cultivation (except possibly of certain tree crops). Soils in Africa's rain forest zones are typically low in nutrients and of high acidity. Yet even in these more land-abundant countries, the problem that is the focus of this study can already be observed. An expanding population depending on agriculture and livestock is moving into the tropical forest areas, extending crop production and grazing into areas that are agroecologically unsuited to these forms of land use.

No analysis is available that quantifies the impact of environmental degradation caused by more people practicing traditional shifting cultivation and transhumant and pastoral livestock raising. It has therefore not been possible to separate the contribution of this phenomenon to poor agricultural performance in Sub-Saharan Africa from that of the policy problems identified earlier. There appears to be little doubt, however, that these policy deficiencies have slowed the evolution of ancestral systems into systems more sustainable with higher population density. (A statistical test of this hypothesis is summarized in the Appendix to Chapter 4.)

Land and Tree Tenure Systems and the Nexus

Critics of traditional tenure systems in Sub-Saharan Africa argue that these constrain agricultural productivity and cause environmental degradation — because land resources are not privately owned, but are either common property of a community, clan, or ethnic group or are open-access resources owned by no one. They further argue that users of such resources have no incentive to limit their consumption thereof because they cannot be certain that other users will similarly limit theirs. Lacking secure property rights, individuals are dissuaded from adopting long-term conservation, investment and production strategies. There are two possible solutions, it is argued, to this problem: (a) establishing firm rules, with enforceable sanctions, which limit individual use of the resource for the common good; or (b) individualization/privatization of resource ownership and tenure, and registration of individual titles. In the critics' view, rapidly rising population pressure makes effective common ownership regulation increasingly more difficult. Based on the "tragedy of the commons" argument, they urge that land be placed in individual private ownership.

Opponents of tenure individualization focus on its alleged negative impact on land distribution and social equity. Evaluations of tenure reform in Kenya and Botswana are cited as showing that individualization of land tenure has led to land grabbing, concentration of land

---

Box 4-4 Examples of Indigenous Land Tenure Systems

In **The Gambia**, each village has an identifiable land area that is administered by the village headman. Any compound can clear unclaimed land
outside the village jurisdiction and claim it for the village. Land is passed
on through the male lineage. Women obtain land for farming mainly from
their husbands, but also receive some from their parents. Men cultivate
groundnut, millet, and sorghum; women grow rice and vegetables. Maize
is grown by both men and women. Women help with millet and sorghum
harvesting and are beginning to grow some groundnuts. Seasonal migrants from other parts of the country or from Senegal (*strange farmers*) can
obtain land for cropping in return for working several days each week on
the fields of the compound head; they return to their own villages at the
end of the cropping season (Norem and others 1988:303–304).

In **Tanzania**, land was traditionally controlled and allocated by patriar-
chal clan leaders to heads of households or extended families. Today, all
land is owned by the state, and the "Village Act" requires that each
member of the village, male or female, be assigned separate plots to
cultivate specific crops that are designated in the village bylaws. It is
reported to be widespread practice for land to be allocated to male household heads, who in turn assign plots to their wives, sons, and daughters.
Often, vestiges of the traditional system remain, and the original users,
usually males, retain some right over land even if it is currently lying fallow
(Mtoi 1988:346).

Among the Bemba in **Zambia**, landholdings are semipermanent. Local
chiefs allocate land according to farmers' ability to cultivate (dependent
especially on the availability of draft power). Tenure is based, thus, on
customary rights allocated by local chiefs and secured through clearing
and continuous use of particular plots. Land use rights are passed on
through the matrilineal kinship system. Farm sizes are large, averaging
close to 100 hectares, but only about 5 percent of the farm is actually
cultivated at any given time under the land-extensive traditional farming
system (Hudgens 1988:373–387; Sutherland 1988:389–406).

---

ownership, de facto expropriation of women, landlessness, and increasing marginalization.

Reality is far more complex. There is a wide diversity of farming
systems in Sub-Saharan Africa, determined by differences in population
density, agroecological conditions, sociopolitical organization, lineage
and descent definitions, inheritance and residence patterns, agricultural
technology, and degree of commercialization. The correspondingly
wide range of seemingly different land tenure systems is therefore not
surprising. There are, however, important similarities among most of

them. Most define land rights, particularly ownership rights, for groups. Individual or family use rights rest on customs recognized by the group. The group, not the individual, owns the land — although there is no formal recording or land titling. An individual's entitlement to the land is transitory, although in most cases lineages enjoy continuous use rights over specific parcels. As fallow periods become shorter and cultivation of plots becomes more continuous, land is increasingly retained by families, households, or individuals and transferred or bequeathed under prevailing customary rules (Migot-Adholla and others 1991; Netting 1993:157–164). There is, thus, gradual institutional change in response to rising population pressure, and this change accompanies and facilitates the evolution and intensification of agricultural production.

Customary tenure systems involve important intricacies. Ownership, management responsibility, and use rights are often not identical. Use rights to different products from the same piece of land may be vested with different individuals or groups. Pastoralists and sedentary farmers may coexist on the same land, with farmers having cultivation rights and pastoralists grazing rights after crops are harvested. On the same plot of land, the right to the products of trees and the right to plant annual crops may be quite distinct and vested in different individuals or groups (see below).

Where, under customary tenure systems, usufruct rights are acquired simply by clearing land, the incentive has been strong for settlers to move into previously uncultivated forest or savanna areas and to clear the land quickly in order to strengthen their claims and weaken those of other potential (even current) users. In Mali, for instance, many farmers plow far more land than they intend to crop in order to establish and protect their land use rights for the future. (Plowing without establishing crops renders the land even more vulnerable to erosion than if it were cropped.) Even under government-sponsored land development schemes, the ability to *clear*, rather than to develop, the land is often a key determinant of eligibility.[1] This extends cultivation to marginal lands, is environmentally detrimental, and imposes costs on the previous users — often pastoralists or traditional forest dwellers.

As fallow periods shorten or valley bottoms are taken under cultivation, land rights of farmers tend to take precedence over those of herders, who are then forced to remain on more marginal and more rapidly degrading rangeland. Where sedentary farmers and transhumant herders have coexisted in symbiotic land use systems, the incorporation of livestock activities into settlers' farming systems also tends to cause difficulties for the pastoralists, who are then compelled to keep their herds increasingly on pasture land alone. As a result, soil fertility declines more rapidly on such rangeland (Gorse and Steeds 1987; Stocking

Box 4-5   Land Tenure and Gender Roles in Farm Production among the Fula and Mandinga in Guinea-Bissau

Among the Fula and Mandinga in Guinea-Bissau, land is communally owned by the resident clans of the village and is allocated by the male clan elders to the individual compounds. The male compound heads then allocate land to the individuals within their compounds. Use rights can be granted on a collective or individual basis. Men and women, married or not, can obtain use rights to individual plots and have the right to dispose of the harvest from these.

Collective fields remain under the control of the compound head, who is responsible for maintaining the collective granary, and work on collective fields has priority over work on individual plots.

Grasslands around the settlements are farmed exclusively by men, in a grass-fallow rotation of four-to-eight-year cycles, with sorghum, millet, fonio, cassava, groundnuts, and cotton. Male collective fields must be planted with subsistence crops (millet, sorghum) for home consumption. Male cash crops (groundnuts, cotton, cassava) are grown only on males' individual plots. Upland forest areas are used, with men and women working together, in long-cycle slash-and-burn shifting cultivation to grow upland rice, millet, maize, and tubers.

River valley land with sufficient moisture is utilized and controlled exclusively by women; they make all planting decisions and have the right to distribute and/or sell the product from their individual fields. Female collective and individual fields are always located in the valley bottoms and are used for rice cultivation. The clans' senior women allocate this land to the individual compounds, and the senior woman of each compound is responsible for the compound's collective fields and allocates individual plots to the compound's women. The senior women also hold the rights to the oil palms in the valley bottoms.

All women receive from the village elders rights to water and land for gardens where they grow vegetables; they have the right to dispose of the produce of their garden.

Some men grow cassava, cocoyam (taro), maize, sweet potato, and beans in their own gardens (Lifton 1991:1–19).

1987; Falloux and Mukendi 1988; Nelson 1988; Mortimore 1989a and 1989b).

In many customary tenure systems, land for farming is assigned to eligible claimants on the basis of their ability to clear it and to establish field crops. In others, bush or forest fallows tend to revert to communal authority and can be reassigned to another claimant. The shortening of fallows may therefore also be the result of the cultivator's attempt to safeguard his or her rights to the plot. Because land is becoming scarce, shortened fallows may also be caused by someone else moving in too soon after the previous cultivator has left the plot to natural regeneration.

Understanding the complexities of local tenure systems is especially important for comprehending the incentive system that applies to agroforestry activities. It also often helps explain deforestation. Tree tenure may be distinctly different from land tenure.[2] One person or group may have rights to the land, while others have rights to the trees on it, or to certain products from certain trees at certain times. In northern Sudan, for instance, a tree and its fruits may belong in shares to the owner of the land, the person who provided the seedling, and the owner of the waterwheel that irrigates the land (Gregersen and others 1989:156). In some systems, tree clearing may be the only way to establish uncontested usufruct rights for cultivation. Elsewhere, tree planting may be regarded as laying claim to land. In many areas, diverse arrangements concerning rights in trees are common and of considerable relevance to those deciding whether to plant trees — and which trees.

Tree tenure issues are particularly critical where deforestation is severe and the fuelwood crisis pressing, but also where tree crops have potential for environmentally sustainable and profitable agricultural development. In some countries, because all forest land is owned by the state, people may fear that if they plant trees their land will revert to the government. In parts of the Sahel, people have been unwilling to plant certain trees because these are on the forest department's protected list,

---

Box 4-6   Tree Tenure Rights

Tenure rights in to trees comprise a variety of specific rights, primarily those of creation (i.e., planting), use, and disposal.

- Use rights include: (a) gathering rights — for example, the right to gather or lop dead branches for fuelwood, to gather things growing on a tree (such as fungus or insects), or to gather tree products from under the tree, such as fallen leaves or fruit; (b) use of the standing tree — such as hanging honey barrels in it; (c) cutting parts or all of a living tree — for livestock fodder or building material, for instance; (d) harvesting produce.
- Disposal rights comprise the right: (a) to destroy (by uprooting or felling individual trees) or to clear a section of forest; (b) to lend; (c) to lease, mortgage, or pledge; (d) to bequeath; and (e) to sell (Gregersen and others 1989:155–157).

and to cut or prune them would require going through tedious procedures to prove they own the land and planted the trees and to obtain cutting permits (Timberlake 1986).

A recent study in Ghana, Kenya, and Rwanda found that customary land tenure systems do not appear to be insecure (Migot-Adholla and others 1991). Many farmers enjoy transfer rights on their lands — although these rights may be subject to approval by family or lineage members. Women's tenurial security is generally far less certain than that of men (see Chapter 5), but the opposite may be the case in some matrilineal-matrilocal societies. To the extent that the social system sanctions transactions in land, such transactions are sufficiently recognized. Traditional tenure systems continue to evolve, and many have over time accommodated increasing degrees of individual ownership and management control. Rapid population growth and growing commercialization of agriculture increasingly necessitate investing in land management and improvement, hastening the individualization of land rights (Migot-Adholla and others 1989).[3] In many cases, private rights to land have become virtually exclusive, although they fall short of outright ownership. Other members of the community may have secondary concurrent or sequential rights that permit, for instance, fuelwood collection or livestock grazing. Inheritance has emerged as the most significant form of acquisition of agricultural land in traditional rural society, and rights to such land are very secure; nevertheless, security of tenure is strengthened by continuous occupation and cultivation. Restrictions on the sale of inheritable land may still apply in some systems (as in the northern Mossi Plateau in Burkina Faso), but in others land has been sold for half a century or more and can be mortgaged and leased (as in the Hausa areas of southern Niger and northern Nigeria). Purchases are becoming an increasingly important means of acquiring land. This is occurring in Kenya, with its history of land registration and government intervention in land matters, but also in Ghana and Rwanda, where governments have been less active in providing and enforcing a well-defined legal framework for land transactions (Migot-Adholla and others 1989).

Problems arise as traditional tenure systems begin to impose constraints on evolving agricultural production systems and on the adoption of technological change. Unfortunately, most African governments and external aid agencies have mistakenly believed that traditional community ownership of land did not provide adequate tenurial security, and that it discouraged investment in the land. This perception arose largely from failure to understand fully the intricacies of customary tenure systems with their emphasis on various user rights and the often subtle, but important, differences among different communities' arrangements. A particularly important aspect of most, if not all, ancestral African land tenure systems — the concept of the inalienability of land — has been widely regarded as an obstacle to agricultural development: land markets did not readily develop, and individual land ownership was difficult to establish as collateral for institutional credit. (Of course, smallholders anywhere in the world are extremely reluctant to mortgage, and hence risk losing, their land.)

There has also been an erosion and breakdown in customary laws and rules governing sustainable use and management of land and other common property resources. This has occurred under the pressure of rapid population growth and has been exacerbated by large-scale migration in many countries and by changing social values and customs. Increasing commercialization of agriculture has induced changes in land use, farming systems, and cropping patterns. Inappropriate pricing signals arising from government interference in input and output markets have often hastened such changes into unsustainable directions. And central authorities have frequently undermined the capability of local decisionmaking bodies to manage their natural resource environment by imposing tight controls over local organizations, removing authority to central agencies, and creating new organizations that compete or conflict with traditional ones (Blaikie and Brookfield 1987; Gorse and Steeds 1987). In many areas, resources that were under effective communal management have, as a result, been converted into de facto open-access resources (e.g., Nekby 1990).

The response of many governments has been to nationalize land ownership, but then to allow customary law to guide the use of some land while allocating other land to private investors, political elites, and public projects. This has reduced, not increased, tenurial security. Investing in the land becomes risky for farmers, since governments can and do reallocate land to serve "national purposes." In many cases this accelerates the breakdown of customary land management systems and emergence of open-access conditions in which exploitation by anyone is permitted.

In much of the West African Sahelo-Sudanian Zone, for instance, pasture and even croplands are often treated as a free good under current policies. Wells have been sunk to permit access to ostensibly unexploited or underexploited rangeland, and settlers in less densely populated areas are not subject to any land use guidelines. In both cases, legal incentives would help by offering land rights in exchange for management responsibilities (Gorse and Steeds 1987). In most countries, forest land has been taken over by governments, overriding the rights of

---

Box 4-7   Common Property vs. Open-Access Regimes

There is much misunderstanding of the difference between common property and open-access regimes. Open-access resources are at great risk of over-exploitation, since they lack clearly defined ownership and use rights assignations as well as effective management. Common property systems, by contrast, are well-structured arrangements in which group size is known and enforced, management rules are developed, incentives exist for co-owners to adhere to the accepted arrangements, and sanctions work to ensure compliance. There is a set of agreements within the community over the rights to use of communal land resources by various members and/or subgroups of the community and by *strangers*, even in sparsely settled areas. Communal land really means not so much communally managed land, but land to which members of the community have rights, while outsiders do not or only under specific and tightly prescribed conditions (Repetto and Holmes 1983; Blaikie and Brookfield 1987; Bromley and Cernea 1989; Barnes 1990a).

---

indigenous populations. Though nominally controlled, these "protected" or "reserved" forests have become virtually open-access resources for large- and small-scale exploitation, because the responsible agencies have not been able to provide effective management.

Open-access systems, found especially in forest and range areas, result in rapid environmental destruction — a repetition of the process widely observed before the agricultural transformation in Europe and usually (albeit mistakenly) labeled "the tragedy of the commons." Open-access systems are not conducive to resource conservation or to investment in land. This problem was resolved in Europe largely by the allocation of land to individual owners who then had an incentive to invest in it, develop it, and conserve it.

As noted earlier, there may be a further problem in open-access systems, which may also be a problem of customary tenure systems. In most of rural Sub-Saharan Africa, access to nonfamily labor is limited. Hiring wage labor is rarely an option, simply because there is, as yet, no class of landless laborers, although population pressure is leading to the emergence of seasonal and migrant wage labor in many countries. More common in many communities is the pooling of labor for certain tasks, sometimes among gender and age mates within a village, more often among members of a larger kinship group. Granting access to land for farming to members of a community on the basis of their ability to cultivate it may therefore be a disincentive to control human fertility, because the ability to cultivate land is generally determined by the ability to mobilize family labor (e.g., Amankwah 1989:21). Field studies report this to be an important incentive to increase family size through polygamy and pressure on women to bear many children.

The "solution" often proposed to overcome these various problems is the allocation of individual land titles, through large-scale titling programs. But the experience with such programs has been poor. Individualized land titling in Kenya and Botswana has facilitated land grabbing, concentration of ownership, and concomitant landlessness. In Nigeria, large tracts for which members of the political and economic elite obtained occupancy certificates under the provisions of the 1978 Land Use Act have been rapidly cleared of vegetation with motorized equipment so as to preclude any possibility of smallholders remaining or becoming active on such land; this has been an effective way of eliminating potential contestants to land claimed under the provisions of the Act, but it has also been extremely abusive of the environment. Such land grabbing had been practiced by European colonists, and some of the new elites have used the same methods.

However, the problems in Kenya, Botswana, and Nigeria may be associated more with the problem of transition from traditional to modern tenure systems. The rights of customary land and tree owners were largely disregarded, and members of the political and economic elite too easily manipulated the legal and administrative systems to wrest land from its traditional owners. However, once obtained, individual land ownership does provide an incentive to develop and maintain the land. This can be witnessed in the intensive sustainable farming practiced by smallholders in the Kenyan highlands, by private landowners in Zimbabwe and Botswana, and on tree crop plantations in Côte d'Ivoire.

To avoid the problems associated with an unduly rapid move to private individual titling, or the even greater problems of nationalizing land ownership, it will be prudent to establish legal recognition and protection of customary tenure systems, combined with an effective and transparent mechanism to provide individual or group titles on demand and only with the agreement of the traditional landowners and users (such as pastoralists). Only a demand-driven process of individual land titling will be possible and advisable. However, as traditional land tenure systems break down, and to resolve existing problems in open-access systems, land titling will be necessary for agricultural growth, soil conservation, and forest protection.

Deforestation, Fuelwood, and the Nexus

In arid and semiarid areas, the need for woodfuel is a major cause of the reduction in tree cover. Excessive lopping and felling, combined with poor regeneration capability, have set in motion a downward trend that has been sharply accelerated by prolonged periods of drought and by increasing livestock pressure on young regrowth. In many areas woodfuel extraction considerably exceeds natural regrowth. Fuelwood shortages in fact limit the "carrying capacity" of arid and semiarid West Africa more than do low crop and livestock yields (Gorse and Steeds 1987:13,28).

Woodfuels are the staple source of household energy, with 90 percent of all households using them for cooking, the main end-use of energy in Sub-Saharan Africa (Barnes 1990a). Some agroprocessing and rural artisanal and semi-industrial activities (such as fish smoking, tobacco curing, shea nut processing, pottery, brick making, smithies, distilleries, beer brewing) also use considerable quantities of woodfuels. In Malawi, 100 kg of firewood are used to cure 3–12 kg of tobacco; in Côte d'Ivoire, 100 kg of wood are used to smoke 66 kg of fish (Dankelman and Davidson 1988). In many countries, woodfuels are used in industrial production as well (tanneries, cigarette and match production, breweries, tea factories). In the early 1980s, wood accounted for over three-fourths of total energy supply in thirteen of SSA's sixteen least developed countries (de Montalembert and Clement 1983). In urban areas, charcoal is partly replacing wood.

The fuelwood problem is a function primarily of population density and of agroclimatic and vegetation zone and is, therefore, very region- and location-specific. A 1983 FAO study (de Montalembert and Clement 1983) identified the regions where people faced acute fuelwood scarcity or deficits. Populations facing "acute scarcity" were defined as those in areas where energy requirements could not be met even by taking wood on a nonsustainable basis or by making use of animal waste. Populations facing a fuelwood "deficit" are those in areas where fuel needs were met by taking wood on a nonsustainable basis. The most vulnerable areas include the arid and semiarid zones south of the Sahara as well as eastern and southeastern Africa and the islands and mountainous regions. Fuelwood deficits were identified in the savanna regions of West, Central, and East Africa. The number of people affected by fuelwood shortages, already large, is expected to increase steadily:

- The arid regions face the most severe problem — with the woodfuel scarcity, rather than food production capability, imposing the more stringent limit on the land's carrying capacity.

- In the more densely populated savanna zone, only 25 to 50 percent of total fuelwood needs can be met from annual regrowth; conditions for tree regrowth are generally favorable, but rapid population growth is causing problems.

- In the less densely populated savanna, supply is still adequate for the resident population, but needs could rapidly outstrip supply in the absence of appropriate interventions.

- In Central Africa, with tropical forests and low population densities, woodfuel supplies are likely to be adequate well into the next century. However, increasing rates of cutting are contributing to deforestation and the resulting environmental problems.

- The coastal strip along the Gulf of Guinea has excellent conditions for tree growth, and tree plantations are widespread. Fuelwood supply is adequate, but this will change in the near future, especially around the large and rapidly growing urban concentrations.

- The densely populated highlands of eastern Africa already face woodfuel deficits. Reforestation efforts in Burundi and Rwanda, though rather successful, have been unable to keep pace with demand growth.

In 1980, eleven countries faced negative fuelwood supply-demand balances: Burkina Faso, Burundi, Chad, The Gambia, Kenya, Malawi, Niger, Rwanda, Swaziland, Tanzania, and Uganda (Table A-21). By the end of the century, Ethiopia, Madagascar, Mali, Nigeria, Senegal, Sierra Leone, Sudan, and Zimbabwe are expected to join this list. Since a significant switch to other fuels is not likely or possible in the short to medium term, population growth translates almost directly into a growth in demand for woodfuels (except to the extent that fuel efficiency is improved). Yet continued reliance on woodfuels is clearly threatened in many regions by unsustainable exploitation.

Over time, urbanization will facilitate a switch to nonwood fuels, but urban Africa still depends very heavily on wood. Woodfuels are the fuel of the poor, including the urban poor. In many cities, as much as 90 percent of all households use woodfuels for cooking. Fuelwood prices in urban areas are high and rising. In some cities spending on fuelwood now claims up to 20 percent of the income of poor households. Urban demand for woodfuels has been far more destructive of forest resources than rural fuelwood gathering, mainly because of inappropriate policies. Rapid urban growth has led to intense cutting of wood on a large scale around cities and along major roads. Wood is brought from considerable distances, charcoal from even farther, and there are steadily widening rings of deforestation around cities such as Ouagadougou, Dakar, and Niamey. Woodfuels are supplied to major cities in eastern Africa such as Mogadishu from as far as 500 km away.

Transport costs and trade margins account for most of the cost to urban consumers, and the cost of trucking woodfuels to urban markets is the main determinant of the distance from which woodfuels are brought. Where motor fuels are priced well below world market levels, as in Nigeria, the effect is to extend drastically the distances over which trucking of woodfuels to urban centers is profitable, and the impact even on distant forest resources is particularly severe. Woodfuel prices to "producers" (usually collectors or exploiters of forest resources, rather than actual producers) tend to be extremely low, often as low as 5 to 6 percent of the urban consumer price. This provides no incentive to produce fuelwood commercially. Given the wide spread between the stumpage price and the consumer price, higher stumpage fees, providing incentives for more-efficient harvesting and for fuelwood production, would have little impact on urban consumer prices (Barnes 1990a).

The commercialization of the urban fuelwood and charcoal economy has increased the utility of rural fuelwood sources: under subsistence conditions, local fuelwood resources were used only to meet local demand, but these resources can now also be exploited for sale outside. Limited and inelastic subsistence demand is replaced by limitless and elastic export demand (from the standpoint of the local economy), leading to much more rapid rates of exploitation than would be implied by local population growth alone (Repetto and Holmes 1983). The collection of fuelwood and its sale in urban/peri-urban areas by poor rural women, on their own account or under contract to commercial traders, is an obvious example.

As studies in Botswana, Malawi, Nigeria, and Tanzania have confirmed, woodfuel demand first increases with rising income and later declines with increasing substitution of kerosene, liquefied petroleum gas (LPG), and electricity. The potential for such interfuel substitution depends heavily on economic growth and on income distribution in cities where economies of scale can be realized in meeting demand for fuel from such alternative sources. It also depends on pricing policies and supply security at the consumer level (Barnes 1990a). To the extent that slow economic growth and rapid population growth prevent significant increases in average per capita incomes, demand for woodfuels will continue to increase about as rapidly as population growth. Moreover, even if aggregate economic growth can be accelerated, but is inequitable and leads to widening disparities in income distribution, this will impede the switch to nonwood fuels.

The brunt of the fuelwood crisis falls on women: they must manage household energy needs through fuel collection, preparation, and use. Men do not usually involve themselves in fuel provision for the household under subsistence conditions, but there are exceptions (as among the Muslim Hausa); they usually take over only when the fuel economy becomes commercialized. Children increasingly have to help their mothers with this task. Girls in particular have to help in fuelwood fetching, fuel preparation, cooking, and tending the fire. In Tanzania, girls help their mothers as soon as they can walk. In many parts of Africa it is not uncommon for mothers to take their daughters from school to help them gather fuel. Women (and children) have to walk increasingly farther and take more time to collect fuelwood. In parts of Sudan, the time needed to fetch fuelwood increased more than fourfold between the mid-1970s and the mid-1980s (Agarwal 1986). This time is diverted from other pressing tasks — including timely crop planting and weeding (thus depressing crop yields) and childcare (which is increasingly entrusted to school-age girls kept at home). When fuelwood sources were more abundant, fuel gathering could often be combined with other activities, such as walking home from school or from the market or field. With increasing scarcity, fewer sources, and longer distances, the loads carried become larger and heavier, more time is required, and the opportunity to combine wood fetching with other tasks is reduced.

Women very rarely have access to any labor-saving technology for their task — transport aids or efficient tools for cutting or felling. They carry heavy loads to reduce the number of trips required to provide fuel for their household (and often their nonfarm income-earning activity as well). They may headload as much as 35 kg (even though in many countries 20 kg is the maximum legally permissible headload for women) over distances of up to 10 km, often over difficult terrain. Carrying such heavy loads damages the spine, causing difficulties during pregnancy and childbirth, uses up substantial energy, and is a cause of frequent accidents.

Fuel scarcity leads to changes in nutritional patterns, especially to fewer meals being cooked or meals being cooked less well (Timberlake 1986:34). In parts of the Sahel, many families have gone from two to only one cooked meal per day (Agarwal 1986); others mix uncooked millet with water for a midday meal (Tinker 1987). A study in Rwanda found 62 percent of families cooking only once a day and 33 percent cooking even less often (Dankelman and Davidson 1988:71). Fuel shortages also induce shifts to foods that require less energy to cook, but may be nutritionally inferior. Women in Burkina Faso refused to use soybeans because of the long cooking time and greater fuel requirement compared with the traditional cowpeas (Hoskins 1979) — until they were taught to ferment the beans into soybean cake, which reduced the heating time from as much as twelve hours to one (Tinker 1987). Switching to raw or partially cooked food or to cold leftovers is becoming more common (Dankelman and Davidson 1988:71). The shortages of fuelwood, of food and of women's time combine into a serious nutritional and health problem. Partial cooking can cause significant health problems. Water purification requires boiling — not possible without fuel and time. Hot water to wash dishes, utensils, laundry, and children may be out of the question (Dankelman and Davidson 1988:71–72). The impact of nutrition and health problems on labor availability and productivity for farming and other income-generating activities is, of course, negative.

The intensifying fuelwood shortage has another important negative effect on rural women. Many of their nonfarm income-earning activities require fuelwood: food processing, beer brewing, fish smoking, pottery making, etc. Fuelwood scarcity therefore severely limits their opportunities to supplement their income through such activities. This is an increasingly critical issue in view of the widespread gender-separation of budgets and women's almost exclusive responsibility for child rearing (see Chapter 5).

Eventually, women have little choice but to switch to other fuels. Interfuel substitution in rural Sub-Saharan Africa usually means a switch to less efficient fuels — most commonly to crop by-products and residues and dung, which are far more valuable if recycled as inputs into the farming system to help maintain soil fertility. Many such fuels are less convenient than firewood or charcoal, requiring more tending and fire-feeding, generating more smoke and less heat, and so on. Cooking may take longer and require even more fuel than before.

Using crop by-products and dung as fuel also has significant negative effects on soil fertility, water retention, crop yields, and soil degradation and erosion. This is increasingly happening, for example, in areas such as the Ethiopian highlands and the northern part of the Sahelo-Sudanian Zone. In Ethiopia, an active urban market for animal dung has developed where fuelwood resources have become depleted (Anderson and Fishwick 1984). The importance of agricultural wastes and dung for fertility management in farming systems is particularly critical as fallows are shortened and recycling of crop waste and dung is essential in the move towards agricultural intensification. Under the agroecological conditions of much of Sub-Saharan Africa, this is extremely important: organic matter is quickly mineralized in the absence of shading tree canopies, and nutrients are leached rapidly from most soils. One study estimated that dung used as fuel in Ethiopia in 1983 would have increased the country's cereal output by 1–1.5 million tons if it had been used as fertilizer instead (Newcombe 1989:132).

There are many causes for the fuelwood problem, including the traditions of its use and the absence of alternative fuels. The major reason for the lack of success in introducing alternative fuels is that wood has been regarded in most of Sub-Saharan Africa as a free good, taken largely from land to which everyone has the right of access (open-access land). As a result, a market for fuelwood has not developed in many countries despite its increasing scarcity. Even where fuelwood scarcity and high transport costs have created a market, the "producer price" of wood has remained below its replacement value because most supplies come from open-access forests. Market prices do not include the environmental costs of heavy fuelwood extraction. Alternative energy sources, such as kerosene, LPG, and electricity are costly; their cost more closely reflects their scarcity value since they are not obtainable from open-access sources. Despite dwindling forests and wood supplies, other fuels are not substituted in significant quantities, because the price of fuelwood is lower than that of alternative fuels. Investments in kerosene, LPG, and electricity supply systems must be made more efficient to make them more price competitive with fuelwood. Fuelwood prices, conversely, need to be increased. Chapter 8 suggests how this may be accomplished.

Logging

Commercial logging also takes a heavy toll — in large part because of inappropriate logging policies and practices. Commercial logging by itself is responsible for only about 10 to 20 percent of forest destruction in Sub-Saharan Africa, but it has been considerably more destructive in some countries, such as Côte d'Ivoire. It is, in fact, probably not so much the quantity logged but rather the procedures used that is the chief cause of forest destruction.

Logging practices are rarely monitored or controlled, and abusive logging practices are so common that they have become the norm (Repetto 1988a; Spears 1988). Replanting is rare, because there is neither an incentive nor a requirement to do it. Concession agreements usually require neither replanting nor maintenance of concession areas as a forest. Most are also too short in duration to provide any inducement to the concessionaires to manage the concession areas for sustainable long-term multicycle production. Logging concessions are often awarded as a form of political patronage and abandoned once mined. Stumpage fees tend to be very low, further encouraging extensive and destructive logging (Grut, Gray and Egli 1991). In some cases, governments subsidize logging through tax and duty exemptions and through governmental financing of roads and infrastructure in forests. Subsidies provided to wood processing industries have the same effect. Areas closer to ports appear to be most abused, with high transport costs being probably the most important factor protecting inland forests against logging in parts of Central Africa.

There is widespread agreement that logging in tropical forests, as now practiced, is not consistent with the sustainability of rain forest ecosystems. It has been argued that logging itself, if properly undertaken, need not necessarily destroy the forests. However, recent surveys suggest that there are no sustained-yield forest management systems practiced on any sizeable scale in West and Central Africa (Goodland 1991:14; Besong and Wencélius 1992). Even selective logging for certain species and/or trees of certain size disrupts these fragile ecosystems with their multitude of highly specialized life forms and of intricate multiple symbiotic relationships so severely that they will not survive intact. Although less directly linked to the nexus, population growth will stimulate more logging, with its significantly negative impact on the environment. Through the environmental impact may come declines in rainfall, increases in water runoff and, hence, declines in agricultural yields (see Chapter 2).

Logging almost invariably leads to a second — and more damaging — phase of forest destruction. Logging roads provide access for land-hungry settlers into areas previously difficult to enter. Moving along and spreading out from the logging roads, landless or shifting cultivators rapidly take over logged-over forest areas, clear the remaining vegetation, and convert the land to agricultural uses — usually at very low levels of productivity. This accelerates and expands the process of deforestation begun by the logging companies. Logging concessionaires ordinarily acquire rights to log from governments, ignoring the long-standing customary land and forest rights of forest dwellers. These rights, once eroded, are not respected by new settlers penetrating along the logging roads.

In virtually all countries of Sub-Saharan Africa, the institutions charged with managing and protecting national forest resources tend to be very weak. Forest guards and rangers often have neither the operating resources nor the training to monitor what is happening in the forest. They are even less equipped and prepared to regulate logging companies, deal with poachers, assist forest dwellers, and prevent encroachment by land-hungry settlers. These institutional weaknesses are so grave that farmer encroachment and logging occur on a significant scale even in many national parks. Forest services have little capacity to plan, to levy taxes, to undertake land use surveys, or to deal with land use disputes in forests (Besong and Wencélius 1992).

The causes of the logging problem are related to those of the fuelwood problem. Forests have been widely regarded as reservoirs of free goods to be mined. Governments have shared in the bounty with private loggers through stumpage fees and taxes. However, once the forest disappears, the nontimber products and the environmental services it provides disappear with it. The forest is disappearing fast.

Notes

1. In Sudan, for example, the parastatal Mechanized Farming Corporation has been awarding fifteen-year leases only to people who clear 85 percent of their assigned holdings in three years (Southgate 1990).

2. See Raintree (1987) for a number of detailed tree tenure studies in Sub-Saharan Africa.

3. There are exceptions — still found, for example, in southeastern Nigeria or western Sudan — where individuals and families may be given access to an amount of land but not to a specific plot. In such systems, where use rights for cultivation of seasonal crops rotate each year or after several years, individuals may not be keen on making long-term investments in land improvement (Migot-Adholla and others 1989).

Appendix to Chapter 4

Statistical Analysis to Explain Intercountry Variations in Crop Yields

As in the case of the analysis of total fertility rates, two independent statistical investigations were undertaken to explain the cause of variation in yields per hectare of various crops, between countries and over time. (Both are described more fully in the Supplement.) Unfortunately, some of the relationships discussed in Chapter 4 could not be investigated due to lack of suitable data. However, limited testing may establish the plausibility of the hypotheses:

- Incidence of drought will significantly affect crop yields.
- Crop yields should be higher where population is growing most rapidly relative to cultivated land. People begin to intensify agriculture as cultivable area per person declines. Hence, statistical analysis should show an inverse relationship between area cultivated per person and crop yields (all other things being equal). However, the rate of growth in yields stimulated by declining availability of cultivable land per person will be significantly lower than the rate of population growth.
- Efforts to stimulate intensification (use of fertilizer, for example) will significantly accelerate the increase in crop yields beyond the growth rate stimulated by rising population density alone. This should be observed as higher yield growth rates in countries using more fertilizer (all other things being equal).

- Primary school education, of males and females, should facilitate farmer adoption of intensive farming techniques and therefore be associated with higher crop yields.
- Countries with more rapid degradation of their natural resource endowment, as reflected in higher rates of deforestation, should have lower crop yields, other things being equal.
- Countries with a policy environment more accommodating for profitable market-oriented farming should have higher crop yields than countries with less conducive policies.

Pooled Cross-Country Time Series Analysis

The pooled cross-country time series analysis investigated the determinants of crop yields for cereals as a whole, as well as separately for rice, maize, sorghum, wheat, and cassava. The independent variables were drought, the nominal protection coefficient (representing the adequacy of agricultural policy), primary education, and cultivated area per capita. The higher the nominal protection coefficient, the higher is the farmgate price of the commodity relative to the world price. This is a proxy for the quality of the agricultural policy environment.

In summary, the following results were obtained (see the Supplement for details):

- Crop yields are negatively related to drought: the coefficient on drought is negative for all crops and in all cases except for rice significant at the 10 percent level (this is the 2-tail significance test, meaning that there is a 90 percent probability that the coefficient is different from zero).
- Crop yields are positively related to good agricultural price policy: the coefficient on the nominal protection coefficient is positive and in the case of cereals and sorghum significant at the 10 percent level. It shows no impact on cassava yields, however; this makes sense because cassava is a subsistence crop which is least affected by price policy.
- Crop yields are positively related to primary education: the coefficient on primary education is positive, except for cassava and maize where it is highly insignificant. In the cases of rice and sorghum, it is significant at the 10 percent level.
- As hypothesized, yields are higher as the availability of cultivated land per capita declines: the coefficient on per capita land under annual and permanent crops is negative, except for cassava where it is highly insignificant. In the cases of rice and maize, it is significant at the 10 percent level. This means that for the crops which are most commercialized, the smaller the land holdings, the higher the yield (other things being equal).

- The results for cassava are strikingly different from those for the cereal crops. Neither the nominal protection coefficient, nor primary education, nor per capita farm size affect cassava yields. Cassava is a subsistence crop and rarely traded on international markets.

Single-Observation Cross-Country Analysis

A separate analysis was undertaken of the causes for variations in crop yields using a different data set with single observations for each country. The main drawback of this approach is that it eliminates the time dimension from the analysis and that there are fewer observations. On the other hand, it allows a larger number of independent variables to be included. This analysis tested the statistical relationship between cereal yields (averages for 1984–1986) as the dependent variable, using as independent variables: cultivated area per person (average 1965–1987), fertilizer use per hectare in 1987/88 (fertilizer use remained fairly stable in the 1980s), percentage of the school-age population in primary school (average 1965–1987), the rate of deforestation in the 1980s, and the general "appropriateness" of agricultural policy during the period 1980 to 1987. Except for the rate of deforestation, the values for each variable were converted to their natural logarithm and a regression equation was fit to these data; the coefficients reported below therefore represent elasticities. Policy appropriateness is represented by a dummy variable having the value 1 for countries where policy is judged to have been conducive to profitable agriculture, and 0 where it is judged to have been inappropriate. Of the thirty-eight countries considered, twenty-four were judged to have pursued inappropriate policies, fourteen appropriate. This rating of countries is consistent with the categorization by the World Bank; it is, however, highly subjective. The role of women in agriculture and the effect of the land tenure situation could not be quantified and therefore were not tested in their impact on yields.

The equation, with the dependent variable being average cereal yields in 1984/86 (natural logarithm), is as follows:

Independent Variable	Coefficient	t-statistic	2-Tail Significance Test
Constant	5.45	10.1	1%
Cultivated ha per person[a]	−0.33[b]	2.5	2%
Fertilizer use per ha[a]	0.10[b]	1.7	10%
Primary school enrollment rate[a]	0.17[b]	1.2	24%
Deforestation rate	−0.05	0.9	39%
Agricultural policy dummy	0.30	1.9	7%

Adjusted R squared = 0.45
F Statistic = 7.0

a. Converted to natural logarithm.
b. Represents elasticity.

The equation explains about 45 percent of the differences in cereal yields among the thirty-eight countries; this is not as good as the pooled time series cross-country equation.

Consistent with the hypotheses and with the results from the pooled time series cross-country data, the smaller the cultivated area per person, the higher are cereal yields, all other things being equal. The coefficient (0.3) is identical using the two sets of data. The statistical relationship is highly significant, with a t-statistic of 2.5, and with a 2-tail significance test of 2 percent (indicating only a 2 percent probability that the coefficient is actually zero). It suggests that the pressure to intensify farming mounts with increasing population density on cultivated land; it is true even when the use of fertilizer and other modern inputs, the policy environment and primary school enrollment rates are held constant. This reflects farmers' ability to respond to rising population density with simple technological innovations. But, also consistent with the hypotheses, the coefficient is less than 1, suggesting that a decline in cultivated area per person (due to population growth) will only stimulate people to intensify farming at a rate of about one-third that of population growth itself. Historically, this is what happened. Cropland expanded at a rate of less than 1 percent per year, and yields increased on average by slightly more than 1 per year, giving an agricultural output growth of only about 2 percent per year for SSA as a whole for the 1965–1990 period.

A 1 percent increase in fertilizer intensity is associated with a 0.1 percent increase in cereal yields. The coefficient is significant statistically (2-tail test of 10 percent, indicating a 90 percent probability that the coefficient is not zero). Since fertilizer use is extremely low in SSA (averaging 85 grams per ha in 1987/88, compared to China, for example, where it is 2,360 g/ha), there is vast scope for increasing its use. This is also true for other modern tools and inputs, with which fertilizer use is highly correlated; given this correlation, the fertilizer variable also picks up the effect of the use of other modern inputs. Growth rates of fertilizer use (and other modern inputs) of 10–15 percent per year during the next decade are feasible. This would stimulate growth of cereal yields, according to this equation, by 1.0–1.5 percent per year.

A 1 percent increase in the share of primary school-age children enrolled in school is associated with an 0.17 percent increase in cereal yields. The statistical relationship is weak, but when added to the evidence cited in the text and the significance of this variable in the pooled cross-country time series tests, it suggests that better overall educational attainment has a positive impact on farm productivity. This makes sense, since in most SSA countries the majority of the adult population works in agriculture and associated activities.

The dummy variable representing agricultural policy adequacy is statistically significant in explaining cereal yield variation among countries. A better policy environment is associated with higher yields, all other things being equal. This is consistent with the pooled cross-country time series analysis showing the significance of the nominal protection coefficient.

Consistent with the hypothesis, countries experiencing the most rapid deforestation have lower cereal yields, all other things being equal. But the statistical relationship shows no significance. The problem may be that deforestation is endogenous. The statistical tests summarized in Box 4A.2 suggest that deforestation itself is related to population density on cultivated land, intensity of fertilizer use, and agricultural policy. Therefore, when assessing the determinants of crop yields across countries, these other factors already pick up the impact of deforestation, thus leaving deforestation as such with a coefficient not significantly different from zero.

The above analysis also suggests the plausibility (though not the likelihood) of achieving 4 percent per year average growth of agriculture in SSA. This could occur from: more labor use per hectare facilitated by continued population growth (causing a 1 percent increase in annual output growth); 1.5 percent annual yield growth attributable to a 15 percent annual increase in the use of fertilizer (and of other modern inputs); and a rate of expansion in the cropped area of 0.5 percent per year. This gives a total output growth rate of 3.5 percent per year. An increase in the number of countries with appropriate agricultural policy and with primary school enrollment increasing at 2 percent per year should suffice to provide the additional 0.5 percent annual growth rate required to reach the postulated aggregate growth target. However, in the long run, as population growth slows, the scope for policy improvement narrows, and further expansion of cropped area becomes less feasible, sustaining 4 percent annual growth will become more difficult. It will depend increasingly on greater use of modern inputs and equipment, genetic improvements in crops and livestock, and improvements in people's educational attainment. Hence the importance of improved agricultural research and extension and of general education.

Appendix continues on the following page.

Statistical Analysis to Explain Intercountry Variations in the Rate of Deforestation

The analysis in Chapter 4 suggests that deforestation is related positively to population pressure on cultivated land (the smaller the cultivated area per person, the higher the rate of deforestation), the rate of population growth (the higher population growth rate, the higher the rate of deforestation due to land clearing and fuelwood provision), and policies favorable to agriculture (the more profitable agriculture and logging, the more rapid the clearing of forests). It is negatively related to the use of modern farm inputs such as fertilizer (the greater the use of modern farm inputs, the lower the need to clear more land for farming). Open-access land tenure situations were also hypothesized to stimulate deforestation, but this cannot be quantified.

To test these hypotheses, regression analysis was undertaken with the rate of deforestation as the dependent variable. Two separate data sets were used, as described for the analysis of crop yields (see the Supplement for details).

The nominal protection coefficient has no statistically significant relationship with deforestation, contrary to the hypothesis.

Using the data set with single observations per country, the dummy variable distinguishing countries with good agricultural policy (the variable has a value of 1) from those having poor policy (value 0) is nearly significant (2-tail test of 11 percent, or significance at the 89 percent level). The coefficient is positive, as hypothesized. The result is therefore ambiguous. Even if poor agricultural policy were to reduce the rate of conversion of forest to cropland, it would not be appropriate to pursue poor agricultural policy to conserve forest resources, because the objective of accelerating agricultural growth will override that of reducing the rate of deforestation in every country. However, this finding does suggest the need for mitigating actions to retard deforestation when agricultural policy is good. Land use planning will be important in this context.

The hypothesis that population pressure on cultivated area increases the rate of deforestation could not be confirmed. In the pooled cross-country time series analysis, the relationship is not statistically significant. In the simple cross-country sample, this variable had the expected negative coefficient (the smaller the cultivated area per person, the higher the rate of deforestation), but the significance level was very marginal (2-tail significance test of 15 percent). The result is therefore ambiguous and unconfirmed.

Drought proved to increase the rate of deforestation significantly.

As hypothesized, the use of modern farm inputs such as fertilizer is negatively related to the rate of deforestation. Intensifying agriculture slows the rate of deforestation. This is likely to be the most important policy available to deal with this problem.

5
The Role of Women in Rural Production Systems

A central aspect of the population-agriculture-environment nexus is the role of women:

- Bearing and rearing children, women directly influence both the size and the quality of the future stock of human resources.

- As household managers, women are the primary managers and users of a variety of natural resources, most notably fuelwood and water.

- As farmers, women are responsible for a very substantial share of food crop production and a variety of other agricultural activities, and their decisions and activities have a direct bearing on soil fertility and erosion, water infiltration and retention, and waste and by-product recycling.

Women's triple responsibility — childbearing and child rearing, household management, and production activities (most rural women in Sub-Saharan Africa also pursue nonfarm production and income-earning activities) — and the increasing pressures on their time and energy have important consequences for human resource development, agricultural productivity, and environmental sustainability. As their agricultural workload grows, women face rising pressures in their role as household managers, and their childbearing and childcare burden remains as heavy as ever. Legal, institutional, and technical developments have added further constraints on women (such as land titling, access to credit and extension, research orientation). The promotion of cash crops, mechanization, extension, and formal credit systems have mainly been directed at men. As men turn to nonfarm employment, women increasingly become the actual managers of the family farm. In many areas, 50 percent or more of all farms are managed by women — yet traditional and legal constraints remain severe. Fuelwood and water are becoming increasingly scarce, and more time is required to obtain them. (These pressures, coupled with women's often inferior health, education, and nutritional status, also render women poorly equipped to take advantage of emerging and better income-earning opportunities outside agriculture.) The intensifying time constraint means that women either reduce the time spent on certain tasks or depend increasingly on the labor of their children. This may be one of the factors explaining the persistence of high fertility rates.

Efforts to intensify agriculture, conserve natural resources, and reduce population growth will therefore have to be focused to a significant extent on women. These efforts will have to aim primarily at: reducing women's severe time constraints; lowering the barriers to women's access to land, credit, and extension advice; introducing technologies useable by and beneficial to women; and upgrading women's educational standards and skills.

The Female-Headed Household Syndrome

The female-headed household (FHH) is a widespread and increasing phenomenon in many parts of Sub-Saharan Africa. It has always been common in societies that practice polygyny and spousal separation of residences, or in which divorce has been easy and frequent. In some regions, where long-term or seasonal male out-migration is particularly prevalent,[1] female-headed households account for 50 percent or more of total rural households. This also means that an increasing number of smallholder farms are managed by women.

The concept of the female-headed household is often misunderstood or misinterpreted. It is not a static concept, but a life-cycle issue. African women may move in and out of being household head several times in the course of their lives (due to marriage, divorce, husband's death, remarriage, husband's out-migration, husband's return). Female-headed households are not simply a marginal group — remnants of "nuclear families" that have lost their male heads due to death, divorce, or migration. They are a common and economically and socially important reality with far-reaching implications for development policy. The great majority of women in Sub-Saharan Africa who reach adulthood are likely at one or more times throughout their adult lives to head a household that is without a resident adult male. One important implication is that all women must be reached with development assistance interventions.

Female-headed households differ from male-headed households (MHHs) most importantly in that most of them lack ready access to adult

---

Box 5-1 Women in Kenyan Smallholder Farming

According to the 1979 census, 33 percent of all rural smallholder households in Kenya were headed by women, with the highest percentages in Nyanzxa, Eastern, Western, and Central provinces. Data from Kakamega and Machakos districts show that even these high percentages do not fully represent the extent of de facto female-headed households. Surveys report that 55 and 47 percent, respectively, of the farms in these areas were in fact managed by women. Smallholder farm production is increasingly the responsibility of women. An estimated 96 percent of rural women work on the family farm; women provide three-fourths of the labor on smallholdings and actually manage about two-fifths of these smallholdings (World Bank 1989b).

A village survey in central Kenya found husbands absent in 70 percent of the households surveyed and the wives cultivating the entire holding. In the other 30 percent of households the wives cultivated their own plots within the holding. In the majority of cases, women made the decisions on crops to be grown and input purchases and use. Credit decisions were taken by the husbands or by both spouses jointly (Due 1988).

---

male labor. They are also usually underendowed in other important respects — notably in land, capital, farm equipment, and transport aids. Land farmed may be far less than land allocated or controlled, due to labor constraints and the lack of access to draft animals, farm machinery, and hired labor. Capital may or may not be a constraint, depending on the incidence, amount, and timing of remittances from absent husbands or other relatives.[2] For most FHHs, access to various public sector services is also severely limited, especially in the case of extension, institutional credit, and services delivered through formal cooperatives.

The differences between female- and male-headed households in access to key resources and markets have been well documented in case studies from Zambia, where the ownership of oxen is closely correlated to farm size, productivity, and profitability. In Lusaka Province, MHHs are far more likely than FHHs to own oxen; hence, the area that can be cultivated is larger in male-headed households. MHHs also have better access to other support services. In the Western Province, male-headed households are six times as likely as female-headed households to have oxen. The introduction of oxen into farming and of cash-earning opportunities have both essentially been limited to men, leading to significant differences between male- and female-headed households — a "feminization of poverty" (Sutherland 1988).

The Gender Division of Rural Labor and Farming Systems

Women are estimated to provide between 50 and 80 percent of all agricultural and agroprocessing labor in most countries of Sub-Saharan Africa — prompting Ester Boserup to write of Africa as "the region of female farming par excellence" (Boserup 1970). But this fact remains obscured by poor statistical data and flawed perceptions on the part of most policy makers. This has been called the "invisible women" syndrome.

The data problem is partly the result of inadequate definitions of "farm work" and partly due to flawed data-gathering procedures (such as unrepresentative reference time periods, wrong choice of respondents, etc.). In Malawi, as elsewhere in Sub-Saharan Africa, agricultural tasks are assigned by gender and are sensitive to seasonal variation. A 1970 ILO estimate reported 40 percent of the agricultural labor force to be women, but the 1972 Census, with only a one-week reference period, reported merely 12 percent of the labor force to be female; the 1977 Census, using a one-year reference period, reported 51.6 percent of the agricultural labor force to be women (Doorenbos and others 1988).

The gap between perceptions and reality regarding women's farm work is often very wide. In Zambia, women in male-headed farm households were found, to the surprise of male researchers, to contribute more time daily than the men to farm work (8.5 hours vs. 7.4 hours) as well as to nonagricultural tasks (5.0 hours vs. 1.1 hours) (Due 1988).

The gender division of labor (in farm and nonfarm production, processing, marketing, household maintenance, subsistence and survival activities, child rearing, etc.), its determinants, and changes over time are important for agricultural and poverty alleviation policies. This division of labor varies widely among cultures. It is also determined by characteristics of the household,[3] the individual, the farming system, the local natural resource base, the community, and the national economic and political system. Gender roles and responsibilities may undergo seasonal variations, due to farm production requirements, for example, or to seasonal male out-migration (Dixon-Mueller 1985:119–123). Gender roles in farming systems also change over time, in response to cultural, technological, political, commercial, ecological, demographic, and other factors.

Gender divisions of labor have implications, for instance, as regards the promotion of various crops, subsidization of certain inputs, targeting of research and extension, pricing, land tenure policies, etc. Shifts in cropping patterns will have different effects on labor required by genders. Control over returns affects incentives to work. Social norms need to be ascertained and considered to avoid mistakes. Three-fifths of respondents to a survey in Botswana considered selling crops (but not cattle) a job for women only; extension, credit, transport, and marketing interventions for crops would therefore need to focus on women to make sense (Dixon-Mueller 1985). In the eastern Uluguru Mountains of Tanzania, male involvement in such activities as fetching water and fuelwood or preparing meals is out of the question (Mtoi 1988:349); efforts to address the water and fuelwood problems in this region would therefore need to be directed at women.

The organization of farm labor and production responsibilities varies widely, but tends to be highly gender-specific. In some regions, men and women farm fields jointly, usually in a gender-sequential mode, but sometimes side by side. In other areas, a substantial portion of agricultural activities is gender-segregated: women grow their own crops on separate plots — but they are also required to work on the plots and crops owned/managed by their husbands. In much of Sub-Saharan Africa, men and women farm separate fields and grow different crops. Labor may be allocated by crop, by task, or both — men performing certain tasks on women's fields and women performing others on men's fields. In some areas, men may work fields communally with other men, or gender-based work parties carry out certain tasks jointly. Hired labor is important in some areas and for certain activities. Labor sharing is common in some regions, usually within lineages or communities and often along gender-specific lines. The introduction of commercial crops (which may be food crops intended for commercial marketing) or the commercialization of traditional crops often leads to changes in gender specificity of farming activities and responsibilities. Men tend to take on the market-oriented production, leaving women to cope with providing for the family's subsistence needs.

The gender-specific separation of farming responsibilities, with men and women producing different crops on separate plots, is often so explicit that there are two distinct gender-specific farming systems operating side by side. Details vary considerably among regions and sociocultural groups, but in most of these dualistic systems, and where markets have developed for farm products, women tend to be responsible for the production of food crops for home consumption, while men more often produce explicitly for the market. This has often been couched in the simple dichotomy: cash crops = men's crops, food crops = women's crops. In this extreme simplicity, this statement is clearly not valid. Although industrial and export crops often tend to be the domain of men, men also engage in substantial food production where food crops have good markets or where custom places the responsibility for producing the main staple on men. Where farming is generally subsistence oriented, men often produce the main staple on their fields (usually

---

Box 5-2   The Gender Division of Farm Labor

Among the Gulmantche in northern **Burkina Faso**, men traditionally cultivated and controlled the millet and cotton crops. When groundnuts were introduced as a cash crop in the 1940s to facilitate payment of taxes, women became the major producers of this crop. Men began to take up groundnut cultivation only in the 1970s when cotton cultivation became less remunerative (Hemmings-Gapihan 1982).

In the forest zone of southern **Ghana**, men used to clear land and fell trees; women planted, weeded, harvested, transported, and processed the crops. With the introduction of cocoa, men moved into pure cash cropping, leaving food crop cultivation for home consumption largely to women. Without male help, women often could no longer grow yams, the traditional staple, and switched to cassava, which requires less labor and can be left in the ground for up to two years to be harvested when needed. Today, most women grow plantains, maize, cocoyam, cassava, and vegetables; they also help the men, especially in headloading farm produce (Dey 1984b; Date-Bah 1985:214–216).

Farming systems research in Kilosa, **Tanzania**, showed women contributing about half the labor on major crops and more than that on minor crops and on all other household tasks. Women were particularly active in planting (56 percent), weeding and thinning (52 percent), and harvesting (58 percent); they also contributed significantly to activities widely assumed to be male domains, such as land preparation (46 percent). Women's labor input was particularly high in rice (67 percent) and beans (59 percent), followed by maize (48 percent), sorghum (40 percent), sunflower (39 percent), and cotton (39 percent). Men dominated the marketing of all crops, except of rice where women's contribution was 50 percent (Due 1988).

In **Zambia**'s Luapila Province, the labor division in farming varies with the farming system. In semipermanent fields, men prepare mounds for cassava and ridges for maize, while women plant, weed, and harvest. In *chitemene* fields, men (usually sons-in-law) lop branches, while women pile and burn them, seed, and harvest. Men dominate decisionmaking for cash crops, women are responsible for food crops (Sutherland 1988).

---

with considerable labor input from the women), while women grow a variety of supplemental food crops. Conversely, women do not necessarily limit their production activities to subsistence crops. Where market outlets exist and social customs permit, they not only sell part of their surplus (even if it is a temporary one and they have to purchase supplies in the market when the quantity stored at home is depleted), but they also produce a variety of "minor" crops for sale to pay for other household necessities.

Box 5-3 Women's Rights to Land in Some East African Tenure Systems

In **Kenya**, women traditionally did not inherit land, but their rights to use land belonging to a male relative were assured. Today, unless the land is registered in their own name, women's land use rights are threatened by land commercialization. Except in some areas with matrilineal traditions, women make up a minuscule percentage of registered landholders. Property rights after divorce or husband's death differ considerably among tribes, and customary laws are upheld in courts. Among the Luo, Kisii, and Masai, widows or divorced women may have to return to their native families, because wives have no property of their own. Kikuyu women are entitled to property acquired before marriage and to some share of property acquired with joint effort during marriage (Ventura-Dias 1985:172–173).

In the rice farming systems of **Madagascar**, the household is the basic unit of production and consumption, but men and women have differential access to resources and complementary labor roles. Traditionally, men controlled the usufruct rights to most land. These were inherited by their sons; daughters could inherit use rights if there was enough land. With rising population pressure, control over land has become tighter and more individualized, with rights akin to ownership although these may not be officially registered. Women do not generally have independent land rights, but grow food and cash crops on land allocated to them by their husbands. However, women may acquire direct ownership or usufruct rights in four ways: a women may purchase land; on divorce a woman has the right to one-third of any land bought during the marriage by the household (even though the husband may have controlled the funds and negotiated the purchase); widows may use their young sons' land to provide for their children; and widows and divorcees sometimes farm on a sharecropping basis (Dey 1984b).

In the matrilineal-matrilocal communities in **Malawi**'s Zomba District, women's tenurial security is very high, while that of men is low. Women tend to live in the settlements of their birth. They obtain plots from their mothers or grandmothers or from the village headman who has the formal right to allocate and reallocate land (a right increasingly rendered moot by the nonavailability of vacant land). Women do not lose their land after divorce, separation, or widowhood (Hirschmann and Vaughan 1983:89).

The male and female farming systems differ in many important respects. They have different primary objectives and distinctly different resource endowments. They face different incentive systems and different constraints. Risk perceptions and risk management strategies differ significantly, as do access to factor and product markets, to improved technology, to information, and to various support services. There also

---

Box 5-4   Women's Rights to Land in Some West African Tenure Systems

In **Ghana**, despite significant differences among ethnic groups, land generally belongs to the community and use rights are held by the lineage. Any member of the lineage, male or female, may occupy unappropriated communal land and thereby acquire usufruct rights to that land. For most practical purposes, this approximates ownership. In practice, lineage members seeking land to farm ask the lineage head to assign them a piece of land. Discrimination against women in this allocation process is widely reported: fewer women obtain land; women often get less fertile land; and women obtain smaller parcels. On low-fertility land, women can only grow cassava instead of yams, and with smaller holdings they cannot rotate among plots and must farm the same plot every year. Some women also farm on land they obtain as gifts from husbands or parents. In some patrilineal groups, such as the Krobo, women usually have no access to lineage land, unless they are unmarried, live in their parental home, and cultivate land allocated to them by their fathers. Agricultural commercialization has led to increasing commercialization of land, and land sales are now taking place. Various types of tenancies are the other major form of rural land alienation (Date-Bah 1985:221–222; see also Migot-Adhollah and others 1989, 1991).

Land ownership in **Sierra Leone** is communal. Women have access to communal land, but land clearing and plowing are too difficult for women who cannot afford hiring tractors or wage labor to do this work. They therefore work mainly on land owned by their husbands or other male kin or as laborers on other farms for payment in cash or kind. Men and women cooperate in farming: women are mainly active in planting, weeding, and harvesting, men in land clearing and tilling. Women also cultivate home gardens and grow groundnuts and cassava on abandoned rice fields; surplus production is sold. They sometimes grow cotton which they spin; the men sell the yarn or weave it for themselves or for the women. Rice is the main staple, and rice processing is the women's responsibility (Stevens 1985:285–286).

---

are important resource and commodity flows between the two systems. In most cases, the direction of these flows tends to be heavily biased in favor of the male systems. These factors all have implications for women's productivity, time and resource use, status, and fertility decisions, as well as for household-level food security and child welfare.

A major difference between the two farming systems concerns access to land. Where women have specific and gender-segregated crop production responsibilities (as distinct from participation in farming activities controlled by men), they require access to specific and distinct plots, and women's rights to land assume special importance. Although there are a number of exceptions, particularly in matrilineal communities with matrilocal residence systems (e.g., Hirschmann and Vaughan 1983:89), women's tenurial security is usually far weaker than that of men. Moreover, as men expand the scale of their farm operations in response to market incentives and by making more use of improved technology, they often reserve the better land for themselves, pushing women to marginal land. Krou women living near the Tai Forest in Côte d'Ivoire had to leave their own fields because of expanding coconut and oil palm plantations and increasing immigration of new settlers from the Sahel. They were forced to move into the forest where they farmed clearings left by loggers. In these areas, soils were not suitable for the cultivation of annual crops, and farming caused environmental damage (Bamba 1985).

Access to labor is another problem. Women's farming systems depend very heavily on female and child labor. Adult male labor may be available from husbands or other male relatives, but usually only for very limited and specific tasks. In many communities, women try to ease their peak labor constraints by participating in various forms of kinship- or community-based work group arrangements and labor exchanges. But in most settings, women's only resource to meet their production obligations in the face of multiple other demands on their time is their own labor and that of their children. This may contribute to the maintenance of high fertility rates.

For female-headed households, limited access to male labor is a particularly severe constraint. A serious consequence of the decline in available male labor can be observed in many forest- and bush-fallow cultivation systems. In Côte d'Ivoire, for instance, men are often late carrying out their traditional tasks of clearing, burning, and fencing women's upland rice fields; this results in late planting and reduced yields (Dey 1984b). In some countries, lack of male labor for clearing dense vegetation and women's inability to do it with the simple hand tools available to them is forcing women to continue cropping land that needs fallowing to recover. Since women can clear light secondary bush, fallow periods are also being reduced (Dey 1984b). In both cases, the result is accelerated degradation of such plots.

Another example of labor constraint faced by FHHs is the deterioration of the resource base in parts of Zambia where *chitemene* farming is the traditionally predominant form of land use and where adult male labor is increasingly scarce at the farm level. With mainly women, old people, and children as sources of labor, the traditional practice of climbing trees and lopping branches for burning on *chitemene* fields is being replaced by the felling of whole trees. This severely affects the regeneration capability of the available and accessible resource base (Vedeld 1983:98–99). Moreover, the long distances between village and fields and the rising pressure on women's time are forcing people to shorten drastically the fallow period on their fields, cutting it from the traditional twenty-five years to as little as ten years (Stølen 1983:32–33). Although millet is preferred in the diet in Zambia, the nutritionally inferior cassava has increasingly replaced it as the main staple because millet production is constrained by labor scarcity. Millet is now used mainly for brewing beer to generate cash income. Most people's *nshima* now consists of about 70 percent cassava meal and 30 percent millet meal.

Among the Balanta Brassa in Guinea-Bissau, the growing outmigration of men has similar effects. Women face ever more direct responsibility for the traditional irrigated rice cultivation in saltwater swamps (*bolanhas*), but increasingly lack access to sufficient adult male labor to maintain the complex dike and canal systems that form the basis of this production system. At the same time, changes in hydrology, due to prolonged drought and upstream dam construction, are increasing the salinity and reducing productivity in the *bolanhas*. As a result, the pressure on upland areas is rising, with negative consequences for the environment and the sustainability of the traditional farming systems (Lifton 1991).

Box 5-5   Gender, Farm Labor, and Market Access

In a village study in **Cameroon**, men were found to work an average of 32 hours per week, women over 64 hours per week. Domestic tasks took up 31 hrs/wk for women, 4 hrs/wk for men. Farm work averaged 12 hrs/wk for men and 26 hrs/wk for women. Men worked mainly on cocoa, but some also grew bananas and plantains for sale. Women produced mostly food crops, for home consumption and for sale — food sales being their main source of cash income. Men engaged in a far wider range of nonfarming activities than women, although trading in food, drinks, and cigarettes was a frequent secondary activity for women. Men's hourly returns from nonfarm activities were considerably higher than women's hourly returns from food crop production. Men helped their wives with some land clearing activities; women had to work on their husbands' plots when they were asked to do so.

When a road was opened through their village, women responded by more than doubling their time spent on growing food crops for marketing. Men responded by growing more bananas and plantains for sale to wholesalers and spending less time helping their wives grow food crops (Henn 1985).

Box 5-6 *Chitemene* **Farming in Zambia**

In the *chitemene* farming system of the Bemba in Zambia's Northern Province, crops are grown on cleared forest plots fertilized with ash obtained by burning tree branches collected from an area five to eight times the size of the cultivated field. Millet, groundnuts, and sorghum are grown for three years; then the plot is abandoned to regenerate. Men lop and fell trees and turn the soil. Men and women share in scaring birds away, harvesting, and building storage facilities. Women turn the soil, plant, weed, scare birds, harvest, and carry the produce home. They also cultivate pumpkins, sweet potatoes, and groundnuts. Men hunt, fish, and engage in interregional trade. Male out-migration became significant during the colonial era and caused gradual changes in the farming system. Since women could not easily lop trees, ash fertilization was reduced; where they tried to maintain the system, they cut down entire trees, but this inhibited regeneration. Cassava was introduced in the 1950s after a locust attack had caused severe food shortages. Traditionally, women had access to land, but with the rising emphasis on cash cropping of maize, cotton, sunflower, tobacco, and groundnuts, men increasingly used the better land themselves and became less willing to allot good land to women for food cropping. Maize is eaten on the cob for a few months and is not significant in the diet; pounding meal takes too much time, and the crop is largely sold. Sweet potatoes are no longer grown in significant amounts. Neither is sorghum, due to the time-consuming task of scaring birds away. Male out-migration continues and is still significant. The use of oxen has helped make up for declining male labor availability, but does not reduce the time needed for sowing, weeding, and harvesting, which are women's tasks (Tembo and Phiri 1988).

Since women more often lack the means to invest in agricultural intensification and soil conservation, farms managed by women are likely to be particularly constrained as regards possibilities for increasing productivity and particularly susceptible to resource degradation. Where farm machinery is available to the household or family, it is not necessarily available to the women; if it is, then rarely at the critical time. Since women cannot afford to take any risk with the family's food security, they proceed instead with the traditional tools available to them, depending on their children (and sometimes other women in their village or kinship group) to provide the needed labor.

In most SSA farming systems, women also provide significant labor input on the men's fields. Polygamy allows men to command more labor (that of wives and children) and thereby extend their farm size. Under most customary tenure systems, land is assigned on the basis of ability to cultivate. Hence, more wives increase the capability to cultivate and the amount of land that can be controlled. In fact, women often welcome an additional wife, because the husband is no longer solely dependent on a single wife and because a co-wife facilitates other methods of coping with survival needs. As men expand their farming operations, their demands on women's labor (for planting, weeding, harvesting, crop transporting and processing) increase.

Project interventions have often exacerbated the problem for women. Under a project in Cameroon, for example, men obtained land, water, seeds, and training to produce rice; women, on the other hand, were expected to carry out their traditional tasks in the men's rice fields in addition to cultivating sorghum on their own plots for family subsistence (Dankelman and Davidson 1988:13). A project among the Tiv in central Nigeria had similarly assymetrical impact on men's and women's workloads and incomes. Project design assumed the operation of a joint-family farm — although men and women traditionally have distinct labor roles and control of specific crops: men control millet, rice, benniseed, and melons; women yam, cassava, maize, sorghum, and cowpeas. Intended to raise productivity for all food and cash crops, the project had an uneven impact on male and female labor requirements. Annual agricultural labor input increased by 17 percent for women, compared with 6 percent for men. Moreover, male labor requirements were distributed more evenly throughout the year, while much of the additional need for female labor was concentrated in October-December, adding a new major labor bottleneck. The gender-specificity of farming responsibilities and income control also meant that serious conflicts arose for both men and women at times of peak labor demand — tradeoffs having to be considered between working on one's own crops or on those controlled by the other gender (Burfisher and Horenstein 1985).

The Separation of Budgets

In most Sub-Saharan societies, men and women also maintain separate budgets, and there are intricate, but well-established conventions concerning their respective sources of income and the responsibilities that are to be met from such income. Husbands and wives may sell to each other, even lend to each other at considerable interest rates. The support men are obliged to provide to wives (and children) varies considerably among communities. So does the importance of the immediate and extended family and of the household and compound as resource pools and as production and consumption units.

In most cases, women depend heavily on their own, independent (cash or kind) income sources, from farming and nonfarm activities, to meet their responsibilities. This has major implications in terms of the

Box 5-7 Gender Roles among the Balanta Brassa in Guinea-Bissau

The farming system of the Balanta Brassa is based on irrigated rice cultivation in salt water *bolanhas* (swamp paddies), supplemented with upland cultivation of foodgrains, cassava, groundnuts, beans, and fruit trees, especially cashew. The men are responsible for providing rice, the main staple. Women are obliged to provide labor on their husbands' *bolanhas* and the ingredients for the sauce that is eaten with the rice.

Land is owned by the patrilineage, and its male head allocates land to the compounds. The male compound head determines the allocation of land to collective and individual uses. Men have collective and individual *bolanhas* and control the output from both. They also control most upland fields (*lugars*) which they prepare and seed; the women help with weeding and harvesting. Men carry out all the land preparation on fields intended for subsistence crops. They prepare the *bolanhas*, often utilizing age-group work teams. Young men, in work groups, clear new land and build the ridges. Maintaining dikes and canals, regulating the water flow, and desalinating the *bolanhas* with rainwater are done by adult males. Rice nurseries are prepared by each individual family: men prepare the land, women seed. Women are responsible for transplanting (men often help), weeding (men and particularly children will help), winnowing the threshed rice, and carrying it to the village. Rice harvesting and threshing are done by younger men.

Most men give their wives small *bolanhas* in the swamps' fringes as well as *lugars* to grow crops of their own. Women also have vegetable gardens. They cultivate these plots with the help of their daughters and foster daughters. For ridging, they may obtain the help of their husband or mobilize a work group by providing rice and other compensation.

Rice produced on the husband's *bolanhas* is owned by him, but the bulk is consumed by the family. Some is given in compensation for labor provided to the wives (for sale), some is traded for tobacco or other consumer goods, and any surplus is used to invest in livestock, preferably cattle. By contrast, crops from the women's fields and gardens are their personal property and may be sold by them. Women also produce ceramics, soap, palm oil and wine, salt, as well as dried, salted, and smoked fish. They collect cashew nuts and produce cashew wine for the market, catch shrimp and small fish, and collect molluscs. They earn income from trading and the sale of cashew wine, palm oil, fish, vegetables, and rice.

Spousal incomes are not pooled, and women can dispose of their income as they please. It is not unusual for women to have more disposable income than their husbands. Husbands are responsible for the survival of the family and, except in times of abundance, all products from the men's fields are kept for home use. Women's obligations are almost completely met through their labor on male fields. Women use their income primarily for their own and their children's personal needs, to compensate work parties, and to pay for ceremonies (Lifton 1991).

Box 5-8   Budget Separation in Different Communities in Guinea-Bissau

Among the Fula and Mandinga in Guinea-Bissau, men are responsible for ensuring an adequate supply of staple food for the family. The women are entitled to the produce and income from their own fields; they use it primarily to meet their own and their children's personal needs as well as to meet social obligations, but the husbands may take part of it. Among the Balanta Brassa, the men are responsible for filling the communal granary as well, women being required to provide labor to their husbands as well as the condiments that are eaten with the daily rice. Women, in fact, often have considerably more disposable income than the men, derived from farming and from artisanal and trading activities, and are free to decide upon its utilization. Papel women also have quite specific responsibilities concerning their financial and material contribution to household maintenance and consumption expenses. Husbands have some control over the utilization of their wives' income, which is derived mainly from the sale of agricultural produce, fish, and cashew and palm wine (Lifton 1991).

---

incentives faced by men and women with respect to investing labor and/or capital in specific farming activities or other ventures (including soil conservation and fuelwood production). Research from Kenya highlights this: "In female-headed households, weeding raised maize yields by 56 percent while in male-headed households, yields increased by only 15 percent....where women controlled the crop and the income from that crop, they did have the incentive to provide the necessary labor input for weeding which resulted in significant increases in yields" (Horenstein 1989:13). Case studies abound documenting intrafamily conflicts over the allocation of women's labor between fields and crops considered to be under their own control and those controlled by men.

Given the separation of farming systems and budgets, the benefits of improved technology and productivity in male farming do not always translate into improved welfare for women and children. Men often spend their additional income on further inputs for their own production activities or on personal consumption. In the Banfora region of Burkina Faso (as among the Mandinga in The Gambia and Senegal), women spend a significantly higher proportion of their income on food, medicine, clothing, and school fees for their children than do men. Men spend relatively large amounts for bicycles, beer, or additional wives (Dey 1984a:64). It is not uncommon for children's nutrition to deteriorate while watches, radios, and bicycles are acquired by the adult male household members (M. Carr 1985:125). With women responsible pri-

---

Box 5-9 Gender Separation of Budgets among the Wolof in Senegal

A Wolof man is responsible for providing his wife with housing and a bed, a hoe and sickle, and new articles of clothing on the feast of *Tabaski*, as well as for the payment of taxes and the main part of the bride-wealth for his sons. In addition, he buys salt and the rope and bucket for drawing water.

The woman is responsible for providing the herbs and relishes when it is her turn to cook, firewood, and about one-sixth of the bride-wealth of her sons. She also buys the pulley for drawing water and the medicines used by herself and her daughters.

A substantial part of household expenses is, thus, not borne by the women — nor are new expenses always their responsibility. For example, grain threshing is paid by the men, while grinding mills are paid for by the women. The cost of modern medicine is shared between husband and wife — the women looking after themselves and the girls, the men looking after the boys. However, medicines used by very young children are always bought by the women.

Nevertheless, women's household expenses are increasing. Due to rising population pressure, the area cultivated has increased and many useful trees and plants have disappeared or now only grow far away from the village. Many women now have to buy herbs and relishes they formerly gathered in the bush. They also buy ingredients not formerly sold in the shops (such as dried fish, tomato paste, onions, and sugar). Women buy soap and matches (in earlier times soap was made at home and the fire was left burning continuously). The Wolof woman also purchases household articles. Today, these are increasingly numerous and include not only handicrafts, but also imported items such as plates and glasses. Even if these articles are initially bought with the husband's brideprice, it is the wife who pays for replacements.

Similar arrangements for sharing household expenses have been reported among Senegal's Hausa, Mandinga, Bambara, and Fulani (Venema 1986:90–91).

---

marily for family food and maintenance, men often reduce their contribution to family and child maintenance costs (food, fuel, clothing, medical expenses, soap, etc.) as women's incomes rise (Henn 1988). A study of two villages in Malawi found the nutritional status of women and particularly of children to be better in the subsistence village than in the village with significant cash crop (tobacco) production. Although other factors might have played a role, women's greater labor input to men's tobacco production contributed to lower food crop production and reduced the time women had available for cooking. The income generated from tobacco production was not used to purchase more food to compensate for women's lower food production (Engberg and others 1988:99–100).

Where men and women have clearly defined complementary roles in providing for the family, men often have no obligation to take over any of their wives' responsibilities even when the wives may have become unable to fulfil these themselves. If women lose their independent income, due to changes in farming systems induced by development projects or market forces, they may not be able to meet their customary obligations. This is not only shameful and distressing to them, reducing their social status and respect, but the family, especially children, suffer: nutritional levels fall, cleanliness and personal hygiene may be affected (women spend a relatively large proportion of their money on soap), clothing may be less than adequate, and school attendance may decline (Dey 1984a).

Women, Food Security, and Nutrition

Poor nutrition is a function of many factors, including not only inadequate food availability, but also suboptimal food preparation and feeding practices, pressures on women's time, lack of essential micronutrients, and poor sanitation and water supplies. The way mothers feed children and treat diarrhea also matters, as do the manner in which household income is controlled and spent and the selection and preparation of food. These behaviors appear to be independent of income levels and are compounded by poor health. Until progress is made in lowering birthrates and increasing food availability, efforts to improve nutrition must focus primarily on family-centered interventions to modify feeding practices. Nutritional status can be improved at any level of food availability. Women are obviously the main audience for nutrition education programs, especially concerning the value of breastfeeding and young children's needs at weaning and beyond.

Food insecurity and malnutrition are, in large part, also a gender and generational issue. Even within the groups most prone to malnutrition (urban poor, landless laborers, subsistence farmers, nomadic populations), women and children tend to be the most affected: "... within households, women get less food than men in absolute terms as well as in terms of their own nutritional requirements" (Horenstein 1989:14, citing McGuire and Popkin 1990). Small children and lactating mothers are the most vulnerable groups, and malnutrition is probably the biggest single contributor to high child mortality.

At the household level, food security is directly influenced by agricultural performance. Many of those facing food insecurity are small farmers — often women — in isolated areas with high transport costs and little or no access to markets. In most of these cases, increased production of food and greater stability in availability are likely to be the only ways to provide food security. Women face multiple constraints in securing adequate food for their children and themselves. Foremost among them are those rooted in the gender separation of farming and family mainte-nance responsibilities. This highlights the need to redress the biases against women farmers in access to extension, credit, and technology. Reforms in rural credit policies and institutions to promote female access to credit would help increase women's productivity in agriculture and their income from trade. In addition, the increasing fuelwood scarcity and the difficulty obtaining adequate quantities of safe potable water have an effect on food preparation and feeding practices, with particu-larly serious consequences for small children.

Technology improvements are needed for processing and storing local foods. Shorter preparation time will become increasingly valued as urbanization proceeds and as women face more demands on their time. Grain varieties amenable to central processing and easier to transport need to be developed. Improvements in storage would reduce physical losses and improve the regularity of food supplies to local markets.

Farm Technology and Gender

The separation of budgets also affects women's access to technology. Women farmers often are, or perceive themselves to be, restricted to low-technology farming because they cannot afford purchased inputs. Lack of collateral (mainly of land title) to obtain credit is only one part of the problem. Ability — real or perceived — to service debt is the other. Risk aversion is often far stronger among women than men, partly because a woman usually bears prime, if not exclusive, responsibility for feeding and maintaining the children and herself.

Gender is an important aspect of the farm technology problem (non-adoption, slow adoption, low utilization). Technology transfer is often hindered when intrahousehold dynamics are not taken into account. In many cases, women will have to provide the additional labor required. Or they may be involved in the decision whether to adopt the proposed new technology or not. Failure to understand these factors or to consider who receives the benefits and who bears the costs, and who will pay for follow-up maintenance costs, can be fatal to efforts at introducing new technology.

In Zimbabwe, hybrid maize was introduced directly to women farm-ers and production has increased substantially. In contrast, a program in Tanzania to promote hybrid maize cultivation through extension and the distribution of subsidized seeds, fertilizers, and pesticides to men encountered resistance from women farmers who predominate in food crop production because it increased their workload without giving them concurrent control over the additional income. There was also some resistance among the women to the cultivation of pure stands of hybrid maize, since maize is customarily intercropped with beans or cassava. The latter represent a valuable complement to maize, and their reduced importance in the farming system could have negative nutritional consequences (Dey 1984a:54–55). In Ghana, women were reluctant to switch to a new hybrid maize variety because it had an unpleasant taste, was hard to prepare, was less resistant to insects and drought, required different storage methods, and needed fertilizers which women felt affected its taste (Dankelman and Davidson 1988:18).

Few of the farm technology improvements developed and introduced to date have been geared to, or even cognizant of, the needs and constraints of women. The provision of mechanized equipment, new seed varieties, fertilizers, and herbicides has largely been linked to the introduction or expansion of industrial/export crop production and has, thus, mainly gone to men. Female farmers have benefited little. In many cases, women have in fact been left worse off. The introduction of animal-drawn plows may help men farm more land and/or reduce the time needed for land preparation — but it does not help the women who then have to plant, weed, and harvest. In Sierra Leone, the introduction of tractors and plows eased men's workload in rice cultivation, but women's workload increased by 50 percent due to more weeding and harvesting (Dankelman and Davidson 1988:13). Women's time constraints and the low productivity of their labor are already critical constraints to production increases, both on their own and on their husbands' plots. Yet women have not, on any significant scale, gained access to technology that would increase their labor productivity.

The adoption of animal draft power in Sub-Saharan Africa is usually motivated by the men's desire to reduce (male) labor requirements and/or increase the acreage cultivated. A major multicountry study found that the additional area tends to be used to produce cash crops (such as cotton, groundnuts, and rice), while the area under subsistence crops usually remains unaffected by the introduction of animal draft power (Pingali and others 1987:101). This finding confirms, of course, that farming intensification and investments in technological advances are associated with commercialization and market access. It also confirms, however, the technological gap between male and female farming systems even within the same household. Men take up animal-powered

Box 5-10 The Impact of Gender-Specific Work and Family Maintenance Obligations on Technology Adoption and Farm Productivity

In the Mwea settlement scheme in **Kenya**, young (mostly nuclear, but sometimes polygamous) families were settled to cultivate irrigated rice. Rice fields were leased for life to male tenants, and small plots to grow traditional self-provisioning foods were lent to each household. This meant, in effect, that food plots were allocated to wives as long as they stayed with their husbands. In polygamous households each wife had use of such a plot. Although women were by tradition responsible for providing the family's food and had done so with small surpluses for sale from their food fields, the food plots in the new settlements were too small to ensure family food self-sufficiency. Project planners had simply assumed that part of the rice crop would be used for family maintenance.

This led to serious difficulties within the families and for the project. In addition to working their food plots, women shared in all rice cultivation tasks and did all the weeding — while the men had little to do on the rice fields between planting and harvesting and often left the settlement for several months. Many women, unhappy with their heavier workload and the lack of control over the returns from their additional labor on husbands' fields, exercised passive resistance to work on the rice fields and did only minimal weeding, especially when this competed with work on their own plots. They wanted to work their own plots as carefully as possible since they had full disposal rights over the produce from these plots. They also needed rice as well as cash to purchase additional food and other household necessities. The remuneration they received from their husbands, usually in the form of paddy, was insufficient; it was used to meet family food needs or sold to purchase preferred foods, leaving not enough cash to buy firewood, a critical necessity since there were no forests nearby from which fuelwood could be collected. A women was considered fortunate if her husband bought six months' supply of wood.

Community issues were discussed in tenant associations chaired by leading farmers appointed by project management — but these were not appropriate fora for women to voice their complaints. Action was taken only when project management became concerned over the unexpectedly low rice yields and when some women complained directly to management. It came in the form of better milk and firewood supplies, which ameliorated women's cash problems. But it did not touch on the new and unfavorable set of intrahousehold exchange relations created by the scheme (Palmer 1985a:18; FAO 1985:36–37).

plowing and expand their cash crop acreage and production, while women remain stuck with hoe cultivation on their subsistence plots (and are often required to provide more labor on the men's fields as well).

Farm machinery may be available to the household, but not necessarily to its women. If it is, then rarely at the right time. In Senegal, "farming equipment is used first in the fields of the household head, then on those of his younger brothers or sons, in order of priority based on age. Finally, the women have use of the machinery. Thus, women who wait for the use of seeders and hoes are late in planting and weeding, significantly reducing their yields" (Loose 1979). Household possession of improved equipment or technology does not necessarily result, therefore, in time saving for women or in productivity improvement in women's farming activities. And, as noted above, improved technology and productivity in male farming do not necessarily improve the welfare of women and children in the household.

Women's Time Use and Productivity

Overcoming agricultural stagnation and food insecurity hinges on increasing the productivity of farm labor in general and in the production of food crops in particular. In many parts of Sub-Saharan Africa, where subsistence agriculture is largely a female task or where male out-migration has led to significant feminization of farming, this means placing strong emphasis on increasing the labor productivity of women. And while this, in many ways, will require the same kind of measures that improve the productivity of male labor, it also requires far greater sensitivity in policy, program and project design to the different constraints and incentives faced by men and women in rural production systems. Efforts to increase rural women's labor productivity will achieve very little unless they take into account (a) the exact modalities of their involvement in agricultural and agroprocessing work and (b) the severe limitations imposed on such work by other time-consuming tasks — rearing children and managing households.

Rural women work not only in farming. In much of Sub-Saharan Africa, they dominate many of the rural nonfarm activities that grow most rapidly as rural economies undergo structural transformation — activities such as food processing and preparation, tailoring, trading, and many services. They also have major stakes in many of the declining rural nonfarm occupations — basket making, mat making, ceramics, and weaving. Women therefore are key actors in the transformation of Africa's rural economy. To facilitate their contribution to an accelerated rural transformation requires that governments and donors explicitly recognize their critical role (Haggblade and others 1989).

Increased female productivity contributes to economic development. It helps increase aggregate productivity in the economy, reduces the incidence and the negative welfare outcomes of poverty, reduces fertility levels, and increases household demand for health and education services. Increasing the returns to female labor raises aggregate family income, but also women's control over that income and, hence, the share of total "family income" spent on food, health care, and other basic needs. Increasing female productivity also increases the opportunity cost of childbearing and thereby strengthens the incentives for families to invest in women's health and education.

"The real rural energy crisis is women's time" (Tinker 1987). The single most binding constraint to increasing female productivity in farming, and in other income-earning activities, may well be women's lack of time — or rather the inordinate amount of time women spend every day on low-productivity tasks that are essential for family maintenance and survival. Easing this time constraint requires measures which reduce women's domestic work burden. The provision of water and woodfuel sources close to the home would be an important first step. Essential, too, is affordable and appropriate time-saving technology to reduce the drudgery of food processing and preparation, water collection, and fuel fetching and preparation.

To improve the productivity of women farmers, a variety of measures are needed; many, particularly those concerning agricultural extension services, are already being implemented in a number of countries. Far less has been done so far in other important areas. Researchers need to be far more cognizant of women's heavy involvement in farming and of their special needs, objectives, and constraints; important aspects in this context are species characteristics and processing requirements for new varieties. Women's rights to land and access to credit are two more areas in need of attention.

Improved tools and equipment are essential to improve the productivity of rural women. Many small "appropriate technology" projects supported by voluntary agencies have successfully introduced simple yet effective devices that are affordable, require little maintenance, and are easy to use. Equipment for milling, shelling, dehusking, initial conditioning and processing of crops, and conservation of seeds offers many benefits in terms of raising productivity and allowing farm women to spend more time on other tasks. Small carts, wheelbarrows, and bicycles could substantially reduce the drudgery and time required to transport produce and inputs on the farm and to markets. These innovations have been largely neglected outside programs and projects supported by nongovernmental organizations (NGOs). They deserve far more emphasis in research and extension programs as well as in endeavors to promote local artisans and small-scale industry. A transport project in Ghana, aided by the World Bank, is moving in this direction: it supports the local manufacture of bicycles, bicycle trailers, and wheelbarrows and, working with local NGOs, their acquisition by local women under a hire-purchase system linked with a labor-intensive road construction and maintenance and tree-planting program (World Bank 1990c).

Reaching rural women with technology improvements is not necessarily simple. Many well-intentioned, but unsuccessful, stove programs attest to that. An assessment in Ghana showed that technologies accepted have generally been those that improved upon or upgraded traditional techniques — because this tended to ensure social acceptability by not disrupting accustomed practices, tastes, beliefs, and taboos. Other important aspects of successful technology projects for women were the involvement of intended beneficiaries in the identification and development of improvements and the propagation of improved technology within a package comprising group formation, training and credit. Conversely, cultural taboos among certain groups, such as restrictions on women's participation in weaving and on women touching cattle, prevented the adoption of some technologies (Date-Bah 1985).

Box 5-11 Cassava Processing in Nigeria

In Nigeria, *gari* production from cassava involves a number of steps: peeling, washing, grating, bagging, pressing, fermentation, sieving, and roasting. For a typical 125 kg bag of *gari*, 200 tubers are needed, and the total time required for processing averages over 50 hours. Peeling (30 hours) and roasting (13.6 hours) are the most time-consuming tasks. With costs of Naira (₦) 24.5–30.1 per bag and gross revenues of ₦ 31.0–37.6 per bag, net revenue per bag of *gari* ranged from ₦ 3.24 to ₦ 10.60 in 1981–1982 – equivalent to ₦ 0.06–0.21 per hour of work. Women in the sample surveyed produced between four and twelve bags per year. Initial efforts to introduce mechanization into *gari* production were not very successful. Widespread adoption was reported only for mechanical graters — but they were all owned by men who could afford the investment. Women benefited only by having the drudgery of manual grating reduced (Adekanya 1985).

Box 5-12   Female-Targeted Technology Introduction

In northern **Togo**, men grow the staples (sorghum and millet), while women provide the vegetables, meat, seasoning, and sauces. Deforestation has sharply reduced the number of *dawa dawa* trees from which women collect wood and the seed that they boil into a condiment important in their diet. Child malnutrition is widespread. This led to an innovative and successful farming and family health project in **Togo, Mali,** and **Ghana,** supported by World Neighbors and Family Health Advisory Services. It used soybeans as the entry point, but differed from other soybean projects by introducing them not as a cash crop, but as a legume for making sauces. Hence, the men did not object when the women asked for small plots to grow soybeans. The project began with demonstration plots and cooking demonstrations, visits to soybean-growing villages, and workshops in women's homes. Initially used as a substitute for the increasingly scarce *dawa dawa* seed, soybeans gradually also came to be used in other dishes and for a high-protein porridge for children (Gubbels and Iddi 1986).

Successful attempts at introducing improved technology for women in Ghana included a low-cost high-productivity fish smoking oven that required only minor adjustments from traditional smoking methods, sun-drying racks for fish, and improved cassava processing technology.

Policy reforms that alleviate women's capital and labor constraints are more likely to increase food production than policies designed to attract men into food cropping (Henn 1988). Steps taken in Zimbabwe, for example, to improve women's access to services and production incentives helped increase small farm output from 6 percent of the national total in 1982 to over 40 percent by the mid-1980s; one such step was to eliminate the requirement for husbands' signatures on wives' credit papers (Due 1988).

Programs for promoting women's development encounter few ethical difficulties, but there is little evidence of rapid change in the role and status of women. Projects combining the provision of information and education about family planning with other activities directed at women's development have been successful; but most are small-scale efforts. A far more broad-based and sustained approach is needed. Women's education and technical training should be given priority. Women's organizations need to be fostered. And women's nonfarm and entrepreneurial skills must be upgraded to diversify the sources of family income.

Box 5-13   Technology, Women's Time, and Productivity in Cameroon

Hand-operated cornmills were introduced into Cameroon in 1958. By 1961, membership in the societies founded by women to own and operate these mills numbered 30,000. With the time thus saved, the women turned to a variety of community and individual projects. They built roads to their villages so that trucks could take out their produce; they piped water from small streams into storage tanks to provide water in the dry season; and they built meeting houses in central locations where they could hold classes throughout the year. They learned how to look after their children, to cook and make soap, to read and write, and to do simple arithmetic. They fenced in their farms and set up cooperative shops. Above all, they learned how to improve their farming techniques (Carr and Sandhu 1987, citing E. D'Kelly, *Aid and Self Help*, Charles Knight, London, 1973).

Notes

1. In Lesotho, about 60 percent of all males aged 20–44 are employed in South African mines (Plath and others 1987).

2. Men's remittances are often small, since they themselves are poorly remunerated, have to pay for their own food and lodging, may have taken a second wife, or prefer to retain their savings for major purchases of their own. Remittances tend to be used to purchase essential food supplies. Sometimes they are used to buy fertilizers and hire labor. Only rarely are remittances sufficient to permit investment in labor-saving machinery or livestock.

3. Household size; gender and age composition; resource endowment; differential gender access to resources, services, equipment, credit, information, employment, markets, etc.

6
A Framework for Action

A Continental Perspective

Successfully addressing the problems discussed in the previous chapters will require simultaneous efforts in three areas: (a) significantly, and as quickly as possible, reducing the rate of population growth through efforts that bring down the TFR; (b) changing farming systems and cultivation practices from extensive to intensive systems that incorporate adequate soil conservation and fertility management measures to ensure long-term sustainability; and (c) improving natural resource management so as to ensure that the natural resource base and agroecological environment remain intact. Essential to the achievement of these objectives will be addressing the special problems faced by rural women and the emerging land tenure constraints.

Some Basic Targets

These closely interlinked objectives can be expressed in a basic set of quantitative aggregate targets for each SSA country regarding desirable and achievable population growth rates, food consumption, agricultural growth, and environmental resource conservation (Table 6-2, pp. 106–107). Although they are, of necessity, only rough approximations, they illustrate the magnitude of the effort required — but also the payoff that will result if the challenge is successfully met.

To summarize, for Sub-Saharan Africa as a whole, agricultural production needs to grow at about 4 percent a year during the period 1990–2020. This, given the present weight of agriculture in Sub-Saharan economies, is the rate required to achieve aggregate economic growth of at least the same rate. Daily per capita calorie intake should be increased from its present average level of about 2,027 to about 2,400 by the year 2010. The share of the population that is "food insecure" should be reduced from the present 25 percent to zero as rapidly as possible.

Unfortunately, scrutiny of the various country situations suggests that it is more realistic to aim for a target reduction to 10 percent by 2010 and to 5 percent by 2020. For environmental reasons, the rate of deforestation needs to be sharply reduced from the present average annual rate of 0.5 percent of the total remaining forest area to about 0.35 percent per year. Loss of remaining wilderness areas should also be minimized: as an indication, approximately 23 percent of Sub-Saharan Africa's total land area should be maintained as wilderness (compared with about 27 percent today). To preserve wilderness and forest areas, cropped land can only be increased from 7.0 percent of Sub-Saharan Africa's total land area at present to about 8.3 percent in 2020. The arithmetic of these indicative agricultural, food security, and environmental objectives requires population growth to decline steadily from the present average annual rate of over 3.1 percent to 2.3 percent per year in the third decade of the next century. This will require lowering the average TFR by 50 percent between today and the year 2030.

Accelerating Agricultural Growth

The first requirement is to achieve sustained agricultural growth (more precisely, growth of agricultural value added) of 4 percent a year. This is the target set in the World Bank's 1989 long-term perspective study for Sub-Saharan Africa (World Bank 1989d). It would permit gradually improving food security and increasing rural incomes and foreign exchange earnings and savings. Slower agricultural growth would also compromise the minimum macroeconomic growth targets for Sub-Saharan Africa. Case I in Table 6-1 (p. 99) shows the staggering food import requirements if present population and agricultural growth trends were to continue. The food gap, even at the present low average per capita food consumption levels (about 202 kg/cap/year), would increase from 10 million tons maize equivalent at present to 24 million tons by the year 2000 and to 80 million tons twenty years later.

Without a reduction in aggregate population growth rates, even sustained food production gains of 4 percent annually would only represent an increase on a per capita basis of less than 1 percent a year. Even with unchanged average consumption per capita, and with interregional food trade completely liberalized to allow intra-African food movement from surplus to deficit countries, aggregate food import requirements would therefore decline only slowly and would be eliminated only in the year 2004 (Table 6-1, Case II).

Even in this scenario, average per capita availability of food would not increase. There would (in the absence of distributional changes) be no change in the percentage of those malnourished and facing food insecurity, but a substantial annual increase in their absolute number.

Table 6-1 Population and Food Security, 1990–2020

Scenarios	1990	2000	2010	2020
Case I				
Population (millions), with total fertility rate remaining at currently projected levels[a]	494	664	892	1,200
Food production (million tons of maize equivalent), at current trend growth rate of 2 percent a year)	90	110	134	163
Food consumption (million tons), with unchanged average per capita consumption[b]	100	134	181	243
Food gap (million tons)[c]	10	24	47	80
Case II				
Population (millions), as in Case I[a]	494	664	892	1,200
Food production (million tons), at 4 percent annual growth	90	133	197	292
Food requirement (million tons), as in Case I[b]	100	134	181	243
Food gap (million tons)	10	1	–16	–49
Case III				
Population (millions), with total fertility rate declining by 50 percent by 2030[d]	494	657	875	1,169
Food production (million tons), at 2 percent annual growth	90	133	197	292
Food requirement (million tons)[b]	100	133	177	237
Food gap (million tons)	10	23	43	74
Case IV				
Population (millions), with total fertility rate declining by 50 percent by 2030[d]	494	657	875	1,169
Food production (million tons), at 4 percent annual growth	90	133	197	292
Food requirement (million tons)[b]	100	133	177	237
Food gap (million tons)[c]	10	0	–20	–55
Case V				
Population (millions), with total fertility rate declining by 50 percent by 2030[d]	494	657	875	1,169
Food production (million tons), at 4 percent annual growth	90	133	197	292
Food requirement (million tons), with rising per capita consumption[e]	100	144	210	280
Food gap (million tons)	10	11	13	–12

a. Population growth at 3.0 percent per annum, as per Table A-2.

b. Average of 2027 calories per person per day.

c. Defined here as consumption requirement minus domestic production; in 1990, this equaled self-financed cereal imports plus food aid. Negative sign denotes production surplus.

d. Target.

e. Average per capita consumption rising to 2,200 calories per day by 2000, to 2,400 calories per day by 2010 and stabilizing at that level thereafter.

More than one-quarter of Sub-Saharan Africa's population was faced with food insecurity in 1980/81 (Table A-10), and the available aggregate statistics suggest a possible deterioration in this situation during the past decade. A scenario of unchanged average per capita food availability would imply, therefore, that over a quarter of all people in Sub-Saharan Africa would still be facing food insecurity twenty-five years from now.

The importance of making rapid progress in reducing population growth becomes even more apparent, when the closely related objectives of improving nutritional standards and food security are taken into consideration. Average daily calorie intake should be increased from its present very low level of 2,027 calories per person to about 2,200 by the end of the century and to 2,400 (the current average for the world's low-income countries) by the year 2010. This would imply raising per capita food availability from an average of 202 kg/year to about 232 kg/year over a fifteen-year period (Table 6-1, Case V). Since aggregate food consumption requirements would rise sharply, the food gap would remain at roughly its present level of about 10 million tons a year until 2010 and would not be closed until about the year 2015 — even with sustained growth in food production averaging 4 percent per year and a steady decline in the rate of population growth to 2.3 percent per year during the decade 2020–2030 (implying a continuous reduction, beginning immediately, of the TFR over the next thirty-five years to half its present level). The potential food surplus which might gradually emerge thereafter under the assumption of static average calorie intake would presumably not materialize because consumption levels would increase above the 2,400 cal/cap/day level that typifies present average conditions in the developing world.

It is clear, then, that — even with 4 percent annual growth in food production — the important objective of bringing the percentage of the population subject to food insecurity down to zero over the next twenty-five years cannot be achieved, at the aggregate level, unless fertility rates are reduced by 50 percent. In addition, this objective will not be attained unless the growth in agriculture is equitably distributed over the population, benefiting urban dwellers as well.

The technological change required to realize the agricultural growth target of 4 percent per year will need to be land-saving in most of Africa for environmental reasons and labor-using in order to absorb the growing rural population. With capital also scarce, the technological change being promoted must be carefully matched to farmers' capacity to finance investments. Incremental capital use will not be inconsistent with the objective of environmental sustainability. The present labor scarcity in much of Sub-Saharan Africa at the farm and household level, one of the driving forces behind the high fertility rates, will ease over time with population growth — rural-urban migration notwithstanding. More labor per unit of land will lead to intensification. But intensification also requires making labor more efficient by adding capital. Part of this will have to be private capital, for fertilizers, animal traction, better tools, and investments in land amelioration and conservation. Much of it, however, will need to be public capital for rural roads and markets, water supply, investment in education, etc.

To minimize the need for bringing more land under cultivation, the productivity of land will have to increase very rapidly. Clearly, the expansion of the land frontier cannot be halted immediately; in any case, in some countries there still are sizeable tracts of potentially productive cropland as yet unutilized — due partly to technological constraints at the farm level (such as heavy bottom soils that require plowing and possibly drainage), partly to difficult access (lack of roads). Allowing for a continuing expansion in total cultivated area at a rate of about 0.5 percent per year (from about 150 million ha in 1987 to about 180 million ha in 2020), land productivity will have to increase by 3.5 percent annually over the next twenty-five years. Realizing this will be an enormous challenge (see Box 6-1).

Were the rural labor force to continue to increase at an annual average rate of about 2.5 percent, meeting the target of 4 percent annual growth in agricultural production would require that labor productivity in agriculture increase by at least 1.6 percent annually. Indeed, since those entering the rural labor force in the coming fifteen years have already been born, the decline in fertility rates included in this set of indicative targets will have a significant impact on the growth of the rural labor force only in the outer years of the time horizon used here. If the targets are achieved for a continuous reduction in the average TFR to 50 percent of its current level by the year 2030 and, hence, for an average rate of population growth of 2.8 percent between 1990 and 2030, and if the urban population were to increase at an average annual rate of 4.5 percent due to continuing rural-urban migration, the average annual growth of the agricultural labor force is more likely to be around 2.0 percent for the period as a whole (higher in the first two decades, substantially lower thereafter). Labor productivity would therefore need to increase steadily over time so as to average about 2.0 percent per year. Given the very high proportion of women in the agricultural labor force and the current low productivity of female labor in farming, an appropriate emphasis on improving the productivity of female labor will pay significant dividends in this regard.

In the longer run, as the scope for policy improvement narrows, and with increasingly more stringent constraints on the possibilities for further expansion of cropped area, sustaining an agricultural growth

---

Box 6-1   Are Annual Cereal Yield Gains of 3.5 Percent Achievable?

The statistical analysis of the determinants of cereal yields, summarized in the Appendix to Chapter 4, can be used to test the plausibility of these projections. According to the equation given there, increased labor use per hectare, facilitated by the growth in the rural labor force of 2.0 percent per year, would generate 0.7 percent annual growth in cereal yields. Annual rates of increase in fertilizer use of 15 percent (and increases in the use of other modern inputs associated with rising fertilizer consumption) would generate cereal yield increases of 1.5 percent a year. An annual increase of 2 percent in primary school enrollments would lead to annual increases in cereal yields of 0.3 percent. And an end to deforestation (if not an actual increase in forested area) would at least eliminate this cause of declining crop yields. Together, this would give a growth in cereal yields of 2.5 percent per year.

Other factors — such as more countries adopting appropriate agricultural policy, continually improving policies in all countries, a steadily expanding reach of rural transport infrastructure, improvements in marketing arrangements — would have to provide the additional stimulus needed to achieve the postulated 3.5 percent growth rate. This is a difficult, but not impossible challenge to meet.

---

rate of 4 percent per year will become even more difficult. It will depend increasingly on intensification through greater use of modern inputs and equipment, diversification into higher-value crops, genetic improvements in crops and livestock, and general improvements in education of the population. Hence the importance of improved agricultural research, extension, and general education discussed in subsequent chapters.

Managing Forest Resources

The growing population of Sub-Saharan Africa will need more fuelwood, building materials, and other wood and nonwood forest products. Woodfuel demand will increase roughly at the rate of population growth. Efficiency gains in energy conversion and use and some interfuel substitution in urban areas will somewhat dampen the rate of demand growth, but meeting currently unmet demand in fuelwood-deficit regions would have the opposite effect. Demand for other wood products should probably increase more rapidly, to allow development of forest-based industries, especially rural industries. Although the implications of such rising demand on forest area requirements are very difficult to quantify for Sub-Saharan Africa as a whole, orders of magnitude can be delineated here.

In 1984–1986, an estimated 370 million m^3 of fuelwood and charcoal were extracted from Sub-Saharan Africa's forests and woodlands, much of it in a manner destructive to the forest resources (World Bank 1989d). This implies an average per capita consumption of about 0.87 m^3 per year and is consistent with the average per capita consumption estimates of about 0.5 m^3 per year in urban areas and about 1 m^3 per year in rural areas. With about 100 million urban and 322 million rural dwellers in 1985, aggregate consumption, using these average parameters, would have been on the order of 372 million m^3.

With aggregate population growth declining over the next four decades to a rate of 2.3 percent per annum (and, thus, averaging, about 2.8 percent per year over this period), Sub-Saharan Africa's total population in 2020 would be on the order of 1,169 million (Table 6-1). Successfully addressing the key nexus problems would help reduce the rate of rural-urban migration, and urban population growth could be slowed considerably below the rates experienced in the last three decades. If urban growth were to average 4.5 percent a year, the urban population in 2020 would total about 485 million (up from about 130 million at present). The rural population would rise to about 685 million by 2020, implying an average rate of increase of a little over 2.1 percent per year.

Properly managed fuelwood plantations may sustain yields, on average, of 4 m^3 annually per hectare in the savanna zones and about 10 m^3/ha/year in the forest zones. It may be assumed that the urban population in 2020 will be about evenly distributed between these two main climatic zones. With average fuelwood requirements for urban dwellers amounting to 0.5 m^3 per person per year (in view of gradually increasing interfuel substitution and improvements in fuel utilization efficiency), 30.3 million ha of fuelwood plantations would be needed in the savanna zones in 2020 and a further 12.1 million ha in the forest zones to meet urban woodfuel requirements entirely from managed plantations. Assuming a lag of ten years from planting to harvesting, these plantations would need to be established within the next fifteen years. This implies an annual rate of plantation establishment of more than 2.8 million ha every year, beginning immediately. Thereafter, further expansion in plantation acreage would need to match further growth in requirements (minus efficiency gains).

To the extent that transport facilities can be improved and the switch from fuelwood to charcoal and briquettes can be accelerated, more productive plantations in forest zones could meet some of the needs of urban populations in savanna zones, thereby reducing the overall acreage needed for fuelwood production. Moreover, many degraded and currently unproductive woodland areas could be reforested; hence, not all the acreage required for fuelwood production would need to be in addition to current forest and woodland areas.

Of course, much of the woodfuel for urban markets can and should come from managed forests, rather than plantations. Forests managed for sustainable woodfuel production could yield, say, an average of 1 m^3/ha/year in the Sahelian and Sudanian savanna, about 2 m^3/ha/year in the Guinea savanna areas and an average of 4 m^3/ha/year in the forest zone. Using an average sustainable yield estimate of 1.5 m^3/ha/year for forests in the savanna zones, 81 million ha of well-managed forests in the savanna zones, and 30 million ha in the forest zones could, theoretically, meet the woodfuel needs of the urban population in 2020. This would imply that about one-fifth of Sub-Saharan Africa's entire remaining forest area would need to be brought under effective management regimes with the aim of providing an adequate flow of woodfuels for the urban population on a sustainable basis. Since almost half of the remaining forest area is concentrated in a few countries in the Central African forest zone (Zaïre, Gabon, Congo, Central African Republic, Cameroon) and on Madagascar, the proposition of meeting urban needs from managed forests in the other countries means that a far greater proportion of the forest areas still remaining in these countries will need to be managed in a manner that would ensure sustainable woodfuel supply over the long run. This will be increasingly the case as forests and woodlands are converted to farmland and other uses.

Rural populations would need to meet their woodfuel needs increasingly through agroforestry activities. Rural requirements may average about 1.0 m^3 per person annually. If a ten-year-old tree yields, at felling, 0.2 m^3 of wood suitable as fuel, this would indicate a need for five trees per person per year — or fifty trees per person in a ten-year planting and harvesting cycle. For a ten-member household, about 500 trees would be needed — around the compound, on field boundaries, in windbreaks, in mixed tree-crop farming systems, and in village groves and woodlots.

Clearly, these numbers can merely provide a rough indication of the orders of magnitude involved in satisfying woodfuel needs. As discussed earlier, the various dimensions of the fuelwood issue are highly location- and region-specific and require, thus, careful attention at the national, regional, and local levels. Nevertheless, on balance, it is critical to bring about an immediate and drastic reduction in the rate of deforestation and to expand the area of productive managed forests, forest plantations, and tree farming to meet the vast needs for woodfuels and other wood products.

An attempt has been made to determine realistic targets for the major regions of Sub-Saharan Africa for the area under trees (Table 6-2). These targets reflect projected wood requirements, plantation and tree farming possibilities, and projections of required and feasible expansion in cropped areas. Realism suggests that deforestation cannot be stopped entirely. But it should be possible to lower the overall rate of deforestation from the present 0.5 percent per year to 0.35 percent per year. This means that the average annual rate of cropland expansion would have to be reduced from the present 0.7 percent to about 0.5 percent. These are realistic targets. But achieving them requires that forests used for wood production be managed efficiently, so that wood harvesting would suffice to meet the needs of populations growing at 2.8 percent a year and also satisfy essential environmental objectives linked to the environmental service functions performed by trees and forests.

The challenge posed by these targets is enormous — requiring a complete and rapid reversal of past trends, rather than merely an intensification of ongoing efforts, to accelerate along a growth path already attained. As indicated in the preceding chapters, the destruction of forest resources is the result of a variety of interlinked factors and forces. Achieving the target postulated here will be even more difficult than attaining that for agricultural production growth.

Conserving Wilderness Areas

To preserve biodiversity and the economic and social value of nonforest wilderness areas, these areas should not be allowed to decline very much

---

Box 6-2   What Will It Take to Arrest Deforestation?

The statistical analysis (see the Appendix to Chapter 4) suggests that a reduction in the area cultivated per person at the projected rate of 2 percent per year will stimulate further deforestation at a rate of 1.2 percent of the remaining forest area per year. Annual population growth of 2.8 percent will lead to deforestation at a rate of 1.5 percent per year. On the other hand, an increase in the intensity of fertilizer use of 15 percent per year will lead to a reduction in the rate of deforestation of 2.9 percent yearly. The aggregate effect would be an increase at a rate of 0.2 percent per year in land under trees. However, a policy environment conducive to agricultural growth will stimulate farmers to expand cultivation into areas currently forested. The effort to preserve existing forests and expand the area under trees will be lost, therefore, unless environmental action plans and land use plans are prepared and implemented which channel the expansion of farming away from forests and from areas that are to be reforested. The indicative targets shown in Table 6-2 imply, more realistically, continued reductions in the forest and woodland areas, but at much slower rates than those recorded at present.

from their present extent of about 27 percent of Sub-Saharan Africa's total land area (compared with 39 percent of the world's land area currently classified as wilderness areas). A reasonable target was derived by projecting forward the present rate of wilderness conversion to urban and infrastructure development and the postulated maximum expansion of cropped land. This means that wilderness area would decline to about 23 percent of Sub-Saharan Africa's total land area. This would allow a continuing modest expansion of cropland at an average annual rate of 0.5 percent over the next twenty-five years and an expansion of the area put to urban, infrastructural, and industrial uses at about 7.9 percent per year as per current trends.

Achieving this objective of wilderness conservation will be as difficult as achieving that for reducing the rate of deforestation — and for the same reasons. One difference, however, is that education appears to be successful in creating heightened awareness among local people of the value of wilderness areas. Improvements in the coverage and efficacy of basic education are therefore likely to help, as are agricultural intensification and reduced population growth. On the other hand, a policy environment conducive to agricultural development and growth will provide strong stimuli to farmers to encroach on wilderness areas in order to expand the area under cultivation (the effect is far stronger than in the case of deforestation, mainly because of the far greater ease of converting nonforested land to farming). This underscores the importance of: (a) land use plans and environmental action plans and of their effective implementation to prevent such a development, (b) effective policies and infrastructure development to channel population movement and cropland expansion into less sensitive areas, and (c) widespread farmer access to markets and to yield-increasing farm technology.

Summary

There are, of course, considerable country variations in what is necessary and attainable. In Table 6-2 the above indicative overall targets have been adjusted to each country's circumstances and potential. Nevertheless, these targets are extremely ambitious. They indicate the magnitude of the problems faced and the efforts required. The elements of an appropriate action plan outlined in the following chapters are, therefore, similarly ambitious. Reaching these targets will be possible only by focusing on the synergetic effects inherent in the linkages and causality chains of the population-agriculture-environment nexus. With rising agricultural productivity and outputs and growing incomes, population growth rates are likely to decline more rapidly. With agricultural intensification and decelerating population growth, environmental protection and resource conservation become more feasible. And preserving environmental integrity makes it easier to achieve sustainable agricultural growth.

If the objectives set out in the preceding paragraphs are attained, the vision of the future of Sub-Saharan Africa would be one with a more slowly growing population, and with the rural population increasing more slowly than the urban population. Significant gains in both land and labor productivity would permit the population to feed itself and to increase incomes, without expanding the area farmed beyond what is environmentally sustainable and without depleting and degrading the natural resource base. This would be accomplished through the widespread adoption of locally appropriate sustainable agricultural technology and resource management practices, increased land tenure security, and special efforts to improve the productivity of rural women and ease their time constraints. Reducing the rate of forest loss and preserving a substantial part of Sub-Saharan Africa's wilderness areas would permit preservation of biodiversity and wildlife and ensure the lifestyles and survival of indigenous forest dwellers. It would also ensure an adequate supply of fuelwood and wood for construction and local industry and of other forest products for consumption and income-generation purposes.

These various interventions would have a strongly positive synergistic effect — as the negative effects of the present situation are synergistically related. Improved agricultural incomes (especially in conjunction with improved education and health care) would further induce declining demand for children, in turn reducing the pressure on the environment and allowing for some environmental regeneration. This in turn should have a positive effect on agriculture.

Realizing this vision will be enormously difficult, requiring radical changes in governmental policy and a strong commitment to assisting Sub-Saharan Africa on the part of international community. African governments, external aid agencies, and African and international NGOs will all need to pursue this goal. Most important will be the effort of millions of Africans acting, individually and collaboratively, in their own self-interest. The major elements of an action program are described in the chapters that follow.

Some Country-Specific Targets and Implications

Aggregate targets for Sub-Saharan Africa as a whole obviously are of limited operational relevance for individual countries. But they provide a useful and compelling framework within which appropriate objectives and targets will need to be set at the country level. Policy and public investment decisions are made at the country level. Table 6-2 summa-

Table 6-2 Indicative Country Targets for Population Growth, Agricultural Growth, Food Security, and the Rural Environment

Country	Average annual population growth rates (percent)		Average annual agricultural production growth rates (percent)		Average daily per capita calorie consumption		Population food insecure (percent)[a]		Deforestation rates per year (percent)[b]		Total land under crops (percent)		Wilderness area as percentage of total area	
	1980–90	Target 2020–2025[c]	1980–90	Target 1990–2020	1988–89	Target 2010	1980–81	Target 2020	1980s	Target 1990–2020	1987	Target maximum 2020	Present	Target minimum 2020
Sub-Saharan Africa	3.1	2.05	2.1	4.0	2,027	2,400	25	5	-0.5	-0.35	7.0	8.3	27	23
Sahelian Countries														
Burkina Faso	2.6	2.12	3.3	4.0	2,002	2,400	32	5	-1.7	-0.6	11	22	3	3
Chad	2.4	2.00	2.7	3.0	1,821	2,200	54	10	-0.6	-0.6	3	6	52	44
Mali	2.4	2.58	2.3	3.0	2,114	2,300	35	10	-0.5	-0.5	2	4	49	42
Mauritania	2.6	2.59	0.7	3.0	2,465	2,400	25	10	-2.4	-0.6	0	1	74	63
Niger	3.5	2.92	—	3.0	2,321	2,450	28	5	-2.6	-0.7	3	6	53	45
Coastal West Africa														
Benin	3.2	1.60	3.6	4.0	2,115	2,400	18	0	-1.7	-0.3	17	20	15	13
Cape Verde	2.4	1.64	—	3.0	2,500	2,800	—	0	—	-0.3	10	12	0	0
Côte d'Ivoire	4.0	1.95	1.0	4.0	2,405	2,700	8	0	-5.2	-0.3	11	13	10	9
Gambia, The	3.3	2.22	7.1	4.5	2,339	2,700	19	0	-2.4	-0.3	17	20	0	0
Ghana	3.4	1.65	1.0	4.5	2,167	2,400	36	0	-0.8	-0.3	12	14	0	0
Guinea	2.4	2.25	—	4.5	2,007	2,400	—	0	-0.8	-0.3	6	7	6	0
Guinea-Bissau	1.9	1.61	5.7	4.5	2,437	2,400	—	0	-2.7	-0.3	12	14	0	0
Liberia	3.2	1.73	—	4.0	2,344	2,500	30	0	-2.3	-0.3	4	5	17	14
Nigeria	3.3	1.69	3.3	4.0	2,033	2,400	17	0	-2.7	-0.3	34	40	2	2
Senegal	3.0	2.21	3.1	4.0	2,162	2,500	21	0	-0.5	-0.3	27	32	11	9
Sierra Leone	2.4	2.24	2.6	4.0	1,813	2,400	23	0	-0.3	-0.3	25	30	0	0
Togo	3.5	1.90	5.7	4.0	2,110	2,400	29	0	-0.7	-0.3	26	30	0	0
Central Africa Forest Zone														
Angola	2.5	2.36	—	4.0	1,742	2,400	—	0	-0.2	-0.3	3	4	26	22
Cameroon	3.2	1.83	1.6	4.0	2,142	2,400	9	0	-0.4	-0.3	15	18	3	3

Central African Rep.	2.7	1.54	2.2	4.0	1,965	2,400	39	0	-0.2	-0.3	3	4	39	33
Congo	3.5	2.39	3.6	4.0	2,519	2,700	27	0	-0.1	-0.3	2	3	42	36
Equatorial Guinea	1.9	1.54	—	4.0	—	2,400	—	0	-0.2	-0.3	8	9	0	0
Gabon	3.9	2.19	—	4.0	2,398	2,600	0	0	-0.1	-0.3	2	3	35	30
Zaïre	3.1	1.83	2.5	4.0	2,079	2,400	42	0	-0.2	-0.3	3	4	6	5
Northern Sudanian Zone														
Djibouti	3.3	1.86	—	3.0	—	2,400	0	0	—	-0.6	—	—	0	0
Ethiopia	2.9	2.81	0.0	4.0	1,684	2,200	46	10	-0.3	-0.6	13	26	22	19
Somalia	3.0	2.31	3.3	3.0	1,781	2,400	50	10	-0.1	-0.6	1	2	24	20
Sudan	3.1	1.65	2.7	4.0	1,981	2,400	18	0	-1.1	-0.6	5	10	40	34
East Africa Mountain and Temperate Zones														
Burundi	2.8	2.27	3.1	4.0	2,320	2,400	26	5	-2.7	-0.2	52	52	0	0
Kenya	3.8	1.91	3.3	4.0	2,016	2,400	37	5	-1.7	-0.2	4	5	25	21
Lesotho	2.7	1.35	-0.7	3.0	2,275	2,500	—	0	—	-0.2	11	12	80	68
Madagascar	2.8	1.56	2.4	4.0	2,174	2,500	13	0	-1.2	-0.2	5	6	2	2
Malawi	3.4	2.61	2.0	4.0	2,057	2,400	24	5	-3.5	-0.2	25	28	10	9
Rwanda	3.3	2.84	-1.5	3.0	1,817	2,300	24	10	-2.3	-0.2	45	45	0	0
Swaziland	3.3	2.02	3.9	4.0	2,554	2,600	0	0	0.0	-0.2	10	11	0	0
Tanzania	3.5	2.24	4.1	4.0	2,186	2,400	35	0	-0.3	-0.2	6	7	10	9
Uganda	3.2	2.13	2.5	4.5	2,034	2,400	46	0	-0.8	-0.2	34	38	4	3
Zambia	3.9	1.93	3.1	4.5	2,028	2,400	48	0	-0.2	-0.2	7	8	24	20
Zimbabwe	3.7	1.20	2.4	4.5	2,193	2,400	—	0	-0.4	-0.2	7	8	0	0
Other South East Africa														
Botswana	3.4	1.33	-4.0	3.0	2,251	2,400	—	5	-0.1	-0.3	2	3	63	54
Comoros	3.5	2.12	—	3.0	2,059	2,300	—	5	-3.1	-0.3	44	44	—	—
Mauritius	1.0	0.50	2.6	4.0	2,690	2,900	9	0	-3.3	-0.3	58	58	—	—
Mozambique	2.7	2.38	1.3	4.0	1,604	2,200	49	5	-0.8	-0.3	4	5	9	8

— Not available.

Note: The methodology used to develop the targets appears on the following page.

a. Defined as percentage of population who do not have adequate food all the time.

b. Negative number means deforestation.

c. Average annual rate for 2020–2030 if the target of reducing the total fertility rates to 50 percent of their current levels is to be achieved by 2030; see Table A-4.

Methodology Used to Develop the Targets Shown in Table 6-2

(i) The target population growth rates were established as shown in Table A-4. They reflect the projected effect in each country of achieving a reduction in the total fertility rate by almost 50 percent by 2030.

(ii) The agricultural growth targets reflect what is necessary in the long term for each country to achieve an average annual economic growth rate of 4 percent.

(iii) The target for average daily calorie consumption was initially set for all countries to equal the present average in all the world's low-income countries; this target was then adjusted upwards for those countries that already have comparatively high average levels of per capita calorie consumption and downwards for those with currently very low levels.

(iv) While the objective should be to reduce to zero the percentage of each country's population that remains in conditions of food insecurity, the "targets" presented here are based on a qualitative assessment of the feasibility of reducing food insecurity in each country, given the extent of the problem at present and the target agricultural growth rate.

(v) The targets for reducing the rate of deforestation are based on estimates of the forest area required to satisfy, with improved management, projected wood needs of populations growing on average at 2.8 percent per year; they also take into account essential environmental objectives as well as some expansion of cropland. These targets were set by subregion rather than by country. The results, in millions of hectares of forest, are as follows:

	1990	2020
Sudano-Sahel	90.0	75.4
Humid West Africa	43.0	38.6
Central Africa	215.0	192.4
East Africa	46.0	42.8
Southern Africa	206.0	189.2
Total	600.0	538.4

(vi) The target percentage of land under crops was determined on the basis of available wilderness, forests, and other currently uncultivated land potentially available for future cultivation, given the constraint imposed by the need to reduce deforestation to the postulated target rates. For SSA as a whole, the target deforestation rate of 0.35 percent per year represents a reduction of the forested area by about 2.3 million ha per year. With only about 30 percent of the land taken out of forests cultivated each year, this implies an increase of about 650,000 ha annually in the area cultivated. By 2020, this would result in about 8.3 percent of SSA's land area being under crops. Since the rate of deforestation varies by subregion, a similar estimation was undertaken for each country to develop the specific targets shown.

(vii) The targets for the minimum of wilderness area to be retained were derived by deducting from the present wilderness area the postulated maximum increase in cultivated land (1.3 percent expansion by 2020) and the anticipated loss attributable to urban, industrial and infrastructure development at its present rate of 5.8 percent every 22 years (Table A-17). A similar calculation was undertaken for each country.

rizes the present situation and sets out some internally consistent targets for each SSA country with respect to population growth, agricultural growth, calorie supply, food insecurity, deforestation, percentage of land under cultivation, and percentage of land remaining as wilderness areas. There are some tradeoffs between growth of agriculture and environmental protection — but these are far outweighed by substantial and positive complementarity. Nevertheless, the tradeoffs require that choices be made — and these can be made only by the people in the countries themselves. The targets in the table are therefore also indicative of the tradeoffs.

There will be wide differences in the degree of difficulty various countries will experience in meeting the objectives. Some countries are already on course to meet some of the critical targets, but will need to do better in other respects. Others are faced with the necessity of drastic action in all areas concerned to attain a development path that would suggest any likelihood of success in reaching the targets postulated here. Still others are likely to face virtually insurmountable obstacles in certain respects, and solutions that go beyond national boundaries will need to be seriously considered.

Mauritius, for example, has already achieved the targets for population growth, calorie intake, and the percentage of its population facing food insecurity. It also has achieved modest agricultural growth, averaging about 2.6 percent a year during the 1980s. At present, the rate of deforestation is high (3.3 percent per year), and the objective should be to reduce it to about 0.3 percent per year. Cropland cannot be expanded on this island nation, underscoring the need for substantial effort at further agricultural intensification and/or economic diversification to meet rising needs for food and other agricultural products through international trade.

Ethiopia is at the other extreme. Adverse climatic conditions and prolonged civil strife have had a severe impact. Agricultural production has stagnated during the past decade, average daily food intake is a meager 1,684 calories per person, 46 percent of the population are food insecure, and forests are disappearing at a rate of 0.3 percent annually. At 2.9 percent per year, population growth is somewhat below the SSA average — not so much because of declining fertility, but because of the high child mortality and overall death rates. The targets set out here for Ethiopia are more modest than those for most other countries, simply because of its critical situation. The area under cultivation will need to increase from 13 percent to 26 percent of the total land area by 2020 to meet the target of 4.0 percent annual growth in agriculture. Deforestation cannot be halted with this expansion of cropped land, but is in fact likely to accelerate given the difficulty of intensifying agriculture in a dry environment.

Uganda provides yet another picture. Its agricultural performance has been poor, owing largely to civil strife, but with some impressive improvements in recent years. Agricultural growth averaged 2.5 percent annually during the 1980s. Population growth has been rapid (3.2 percent a year). Most of the arable land is already under cultivation (34 percent), and there is little wilderness area left (4.0 percent of total land). The rate of deforestation has averaged about 0.8 percent annually in recent years. Uganda has enormous agricultural potential: its agricultural sector could grow at a sustained rate of 4.5 percent annually. If population growth can be reduced to 2.7 percent a year by 2020, average daily calorie intake per person could rise from 2,034 to 2,400, and the number of people facing food insecurity could be brought down dramatically. This would have to occur mostly through intensification on currently cropped land, because there is little additional land left to cultivate. AIDS already is a more serious problem in Uganda than in many other African countries; this suggests that efforts to improve the reach and effectiveness of health care and family planning services are critical.

A number of countries are facing scenarios of extreme difficulties and constraints: Rwanda, Burundi, the Sahelian countries, Kenya, and Malawi. The case of *Rwanda* was particularly dramatic even before the recent social breakdown and civil war. Agricultural performance has been poor, with production declining at an average rate of 1.5 percent per year in the 1980s. Population growth averaged 3.3 percent per year during the 1980s. Per capita daily calorie consumption is only 1,817, and 24 percent of the people are food insecure. There is little wilderness left, although nearly 15 percent of the country has been set aside as protected areas. The rate of deforestation has been 2.3 percent per year, and 45 percent of the entire land area is cropped. The modest agricultural growth target of 3.0 percent per year can only be achieved through agricultural intensification. The very high population density may be creating demand for smaller family size; family planning interventions should seek to capitalize on this once stability is restored in the country. Reforestation must be intensified, on land unsuitable for crops. The difficulties are immense. Indeed, the targets spelled out here imply that 10 percent of the population will still be food insecure in the year 2020. Out-migration to other countries will clearly be inevitable.

Nigeria's example is important, if only because of the country's size. It's agricultural performance during the 1980s and early 1990s has been marked by widely fluctuating production, with a trend growth rate of 3.3 percent per year, somewhat ahead of the population growth rate. The country has such potential for growth that, with appropriate policy reforms in key areas, it can achieve 4.0 percent agricultural growth per year in the medium term. As much as four-fifths of this growth can be realized without expanding the area under cultivation, because of the availability of proven yield-increasing technology for a number of key crops and the scope for double-cropping through small-scale irrigation in many river valleys. The remainder will come from modest expansion of the area cropped. Realignment of public expenditure toward small-scale irrigation, provision and maintenance of rural roads, improvement in agricultural support services, elimination of the fertilizer subsidy, and liberalization of fertilizer imports and marketing are key areas requiring policy reform. Without such reforms, future agricultural growth would come primarily from area expansion which would not be sustainable. The country's family planning effort, still very weak, will have to improve considerably for the target population growth rate of 2.1 percent per year to be reached by 2020. As population pressure on cultivated land is rising, demand for family planning services appears to be increasing in parts of the country, and FP programs will need to foster such demand growth and meet this rising and largely unmet demand. Substantial policy reforms will be needed to stop the rapid destruction of existing forest resources and to induce sufficient private investment in agroforestry, fuelwood, and industrial plantations if the target of reducing deforestation to an annual rate of 0.3 percent is to be met.

7

Reducing Population Growth

Population Policy

Key Issues and Challenges

Chapter 3 suggested several avenues for reducing population growth. Fertility rates can be brought down by emphasizing direct actions such as improving knowledge and availability of family planning (FP) services. But to have maximum impact, these "supply-side" efforts need to be backed, if not preceded, by efforts to stimulate demand — such as improving education, especially of females, reducing infant mortality, reducing environmental degradation, and, possibly, improving food security. Family planning education can be provided through FP services, along with the means to control fertility. By providing nutrition advice, FP services can also help in reducing infant mortality and improving nutritional standards. Rising density of population on cultivable land may also stimulate demand for fewer children. Acceptance and adoption of family planning will spread most rapidly in countries where demand for FP services is increasing fastest. This is likely to be in countries with the highest levels of female education, the lowest infant mortality, the highest population densities on cultivated land, the least environmental degradation, and, possibly, the greatest food security.

Governments are increasingly aware of the consequences of rapid population growth. In 1974, only Botswana, Ghana, Kenya, and Mauritius had adopted policies to reduce population growth. By 1987, fourteen countries had adopted explicit national population policies (Cochrane, Sai and Nassim 1990:229), and a number of others have done so since then. In 1989, twenty-six governments in Sub-Saharan Africa considered their population growth rates, and twenty-nine their TFRs, to be too high (Stephens and others 1991:xxxv). But few have provided adequate technical, financial, and managerial resources to promote and deliver FP services broadly. Hence, progress has been slow.

Only a few countries on the continent — notably Botswana, Kenya, and Zimbabwe — have been implementing population programs that have shown some measurable success (Tables A-2 and A-8). The Contraceptive Prevalence Rate (CPR) in Botswana more than doubled, from 16 percent to 33 percent, between 1984 and 1990, as FP services were placed within easy reach of the majority of the population. Botswana's TFR declined from 6.9 in 1965 to 4.7 in 1988. Kenya succeeded in raising the CPR from 5 percent in the mid-1970s to 17 percent in 1984 and to 27 percent in 1989, and the TFR declined from 8.0 in 1965 to 6.5 in 1989. In Zimbabwe, the CPR is now estimated at 43 percent, and the TFR dropped from 8.0 to 5.3 between 1965 and 1988; the creation of a network of FP clinics and of a community-based outreach program which widely distributed contraceptives was instrumental in providing access to FP services. An indication of changing attitudes concerning fertility and of growing demand for FP services is evident in the number of children desired by women in these three countries. In 1988–1989, women wanted only 4.7, 4.4, and 4.9 children, respectively, in Botswana, Kenya, and Zimbabwe — far fewer than their counterparts in other SSA countries and also far fewer than women in the same three countries only ten years ago (Table A-8).

Government policies in these countries have played a major role in achieving fertility reduction through an expansion of FP services and education. However, in each of these countries the fundamental forces have also been working: relatively dense population on cultivated land, relatively high female school enrollments, good agricultural performance contributing to enhanced food security, and declining infant mortality. Yet even in these three relatively successful countries, the TFR must be brought down further.

To lower the population growth rate to 1.8 percent a year for Sub-Saharan Africa by 2030, the average TFR for Sub-Saharan Africa as a whole must drop steadily to 3.1 by that time (Table A-4). This is possible, as shown by evidence from countries outside Africa where per capita incomes are low and populations largely rural, and where infant mortality rates and life expectancy, when the effort was initiated, were comparable to those in Sub-Saharan Africa today. It requires determined effort and commitment from the political leadership to shape public attitudes and implement policies and programs to reduce population growth.

Significant reductions in fertility cannot be expected until the CPR reaches 25 to 30 percent. Slowing population growth to only 1.8 percent per year during the period 2020–2030 would require increasing the CPR substantially above even this level. This underscores the need for fostering greater awareness of the consequences of population growth as well as the need to stimulate demand for FP services. Increasing the availability of FP services raises the level of their use. There is evidence that, even at the present levels of demand for family planning, the CPR in Sub-Saharan Africa could be raised to 25 percent within the current decade by making services widely, regularly and reliably available. It requires a rapid expansion of access to FP services, and this, in turn, requires strengthening and expanding public health care systems and developing multiple channels (public sector, private commercial, NGO, community organizations) to deliver services as well as information, education, and communication (IEC). The progress achieved in Botswana, Kenya, and Zimbabwe shows what is possible when various other factors that bear upon demand for children are also moving in the right direction (Table A-8).

The ethical issues in family planning in Sub-Saharan Africa form a complex web of social, economic, cultural, and developmental concerns, and dialogue on ethical issues in family planning is crucial if the process of 'depoliticizing' family planning is to continue (Sai and Newman 1989). The promotion of family planning as a basic human right and as an important health measure has increased its acceptability, and family planning is now increasingly regarded a legitimate component of overall development efforts. But the "human right" to control one's own fertility, remains elusive without full and ready access to FP information, education, and services. This entails full and voluntary choice of method, right of access for young people, and financial affordability of fertility regulation services. Each of these has caused ethical controversy in some countries. The right of access to FP services is derived from the basic right to make decisions about reproductive behavior. This, too, has been controversial in some countries.

Family planning is also a major element of the rights of women. Many women prefer to have fewer children, but are discouraged from using family planning by sociocultural factors, including their husbands' wishes. This highlights the importance of reaching men, either at the workplace or through other means such as the agricultural extension services. It also suggests that women's groups would be an effective channel for delivering family planning services because they foster solidarity among women and may help them make fertility decisions on their own.

It is important to distinguish between population policies and family planning programs. Population policy includes family planning, but also includes a range of measures to influence decisions at the family and community levels as well as education and health programs effecting family size. It also comprises changing laws to encourage small families and providing effective incentives and disincentives (for example, cost sharing for health and education). A comprehensive population policy must also include policies to cope with the consequences of population growth. This means general development policies that encourage optimal use of resources in agriculture, urban development, and so on.

In about a dozen countries, fertility regulation programs are part of national population policies. In other countries with FP services, the rationale is not so much to reduce fertility but to improve maternal and child health (MCH). The health rationale for family planning, especially for preventing high-risk pregnancies, is proven and especially pertinent in Sub-Saharan Africa, where infant and maternal mortality and morbidity rates are high. One key element of primary health care is MCH care, and this includes family planning. By providing the means to postpone childbearing until after adolescence, space births at two-to-three-year intervals, and prevent pregnancies after the age of 35, family planning can greatly improve maternal and child health.

Where the rationale for FP programs is demographic, it is often a matter of controversy whether government has the right to influence the reproductive behavior of the people. Clearly, unless population policies command broad popular support, the prospects for reducing population growth are dim. And where poor governance causes people to question the legitimacy of governments, governmental population policies and FP programs tend to be viewed with particular skepticism. It is critical that anti-natalist policies be seen to apply to entire populations and be evenly implemented. Policies can justifiably become discredited when they appear designed to alter the balance of ethnic groups.

Needed is a deliberate fostering of pluralism in efforts to extend access to FP information and services by encouraging and supporting local government, community, and private initiatives. The successful involvement of nongovernmental groups in family planning in Sub-Saharan Africa strongly suggests the viability of such an approach. Fostering pluralism entails a broad agenda of activities to facilitate local and private initiatives and learn from them. It involves difficult choices about how and where to expend governments' limited technical and administrative resources. Governments must take the lead in promoting the dissemination of FP information and in developing a social consensus on its legitimacy. Especially in rural areas, where the government is the major provider of modern health care and specifically of MCH services, the public sector may have to be the principal provider of FP services for some time to come. Many factors still bear on the ethics of family planning in Sub-Saharan Africa, and these point to the need for a sensitive approach (Sai and Newman 1989).

Promoting Demand for Fewer Children

Even greatly improved supply of FP services will not succeed in bringing about the required declines in fertility, unless *demand* for fewer children rises considerably. Most past efforts in the FP field have been deficient in recognizing this. A recent evaluation of past World Bank operations in the population sector, for instance, found that FP services have been offered in many countries when there was little evidence of significant demand for them (World Bank 1991e). The evidence of attitudinal and behavioral changes regarding fertility in many parts of the continent suggests, however, that it is possible to create such demand. Between 20 and 40 percent of women in the countries of Sub-Saharan Africa wish to space their children at least two years apart (Table A-6). Rising pressure of rural populations on cultivated land is stimulating demand for smaller family size. Migration and urbanization are loosening extended family ties and raising the private costs of children. Education of women is increasing, there is a clear trend toward later marriage,[1] and there are indications of considerable unmet demand for modern contraception (Table A-6). These changes in attitudes can be encouraged, promoted, and accelerated by a variety of means, including effective information, education, and communication (IEC) programs, so as to lead to increased demand for FP services.

Improving the legal, economic, and social status of women is critical to overcoming the constraints imposed on them by their traditional roles that perpetuate high fertility. This entails, among other things, recognizing and emphasizing that women's status also derives from their *economic* contributions to family, community, and society. It requires, therefore, expanding the range of opportunities available to them and supporting developments that provide women with greater control over their own lives and the output and income generated by their work. Greater educational opportunities, removal of discriminatory laws, raising the age of marriage, ensuring women's rights to land, improving their access to credit and training, meeting their needs for technology and information, opening up employment and income-earning opportunities beyond those traditionally open to them, and strengthening women's organizations all help to raise women's status and give them greater control over their lives. At the same time, efforts must be made to relieve both the environmental degradation and the work burden on women, both of which fuel demand for additional family labor.

To promote demand for FP services, actions such as the following are essential:

- Political leaders and communities need to be sensitized to the environmental and economic consequences of rapid population growth. Demand for family planning and contraception, as well as for later female marriage, must be increased through widespread IEC programs. To ensure that people regard such programs as legitimate, governments must demonstrate continually their legitimacy and credibility, through good governance. Governments lacking credibility and popular acceptance are very likely to confront popular distrust of population programs.

- Effective measures are needed to expand education, especially for females, and to improve women's income-earning opportunities. This will tend to raise women's marriage age and reduce both their desired and actual number of children. To the extent that improved income-earning opportunities for women lead to increased control by women over such income, this will have strong positive effects on child health and welfare, on infant and child mortality, and, hence, on women's fertility preferences.

- Health services need to be expanded and improved to deal with major epidemic diseases and reduce infant and child mortality. This will greatly improve the probability of having descendants in one's old age and thereby weaken one of the major traditional motivations for desiring large families. It will also reduce the economic incentive for having larger families, since fewer, but surviving, children can ensure adequate availability of family labor.

- Expanding access to effective primary health care is also essential to address the problems of sexually transmitted diseases (STDs). STDs are major causes of infertility, which in some regions discourages any interest in fertility control. High incidences of STDs are also an important factor contributing to the rapid spread of AIDS.

- Incentives for smaller families and disincentives for large families (such as limitations on tax deductions for children) may help in the longer term. Community leaders, teachers, agricultural extension agents, and the mass media should be used to convince people of the economic, environmental, and health benefits of having fewer children.

- Land tenure reform as well as improved access of women to land, to agricultural extension, and to credit are likely to reduce the pressure on women to have many children. Greater food security may also lead to reductions in fertility rates.

Box 7-1   Increasing the Private Costs of Having Children

Some observers argue for deliberate policy actions designed to impose more of the social costs of children directly on their parents. In some countries and under certain conditions, this would create pressure for reducing family size. Where, for example, education is a highly valued commodity, shifting the cost of schooling increasingly to the parents is likely to have a dampening effect on fertility rates. This appears to have been an important factor contributing to the decline in the TFR in Kenya.

Such a policy thrust conflicts, of course, with the important development policy objective to meet basic needs. Moreover, such a policy potentially faces important pitfalls. There is a high likelihood that parents would, out of economic necessity, decide to ration access to education among their children, favoring boys at the expense of girls (even more so than is already the case). This would have profound longer-term implications — not least for fertility rates.

Moreover, in many SSA settings, the cost of children is not necessarily borne by those responsible for their having been born. Not only do fathers often have very limited responsibilities for child maintenance (or evade their responsibilities altogether through divorce or migration), but child fostering is a widespread custom in many societies.

Improving Access to Family Planning Services

Improving the supply and accessibility of FP services to respond to the demand created by measures such as those outlined above requires the combined efforts of governments, NGOs, and aid donors. The target must be to raise the CPR in each country sufficiently to achieve a 50 percent reduction in the TFR by 2030 (Tables A-4 and A-5). For Sub-Saharan Africa as a whole, this implies increasing the average CPR from less than 11 at present to over 45 by the year 2020 and to over 50 by 2025 (Table A-5).

The family planning effort of nearly every country in Sub-Saharan Africa ranks near the bottom of developing countries, with the notable exceptions of Botswana, Kenya, Mauritius, Zimbabwe, and, arguably, Ghana (Table A-7). Fertility can be reduced and population growth slowed if governments, schools, employers, and NGOs take measures to increase the demand for smaller families, while supplying the services needed for families to limit family size. The FP services provided must be of high quality and responsive to clients' needs, and there must be adequate provision for monitoring and evaluation.

In most SSA countries, FP services are integrated with and delivered through the public health system, usually as part of MCH care. But in many countries the public health system is unable to deliver widespread and effective FP services. Expanding the access to family planning requires strengthening and expanding public health care systems as well as developing alternative and supplementary channels to deliver FP services and IEC. Where AIDS is prevalent, this will be all the more critical, since health and sex education and the provision of condoms are the key instruments for combatting its spread.

The promotion of modern family planning can build on long-standing traditions of spacing births through prolonged breastfeeding and post-partum sexual abstinence. The significant potential health gains from family planning appeal to policymakers and to the people affected. And new methods of delivering FP services have been shown to be workable and to make a difference in parts of Sub-Saharan Africa. A focus on birth spacing, rather than on family size limitation, would appear to be most appropriate where demand for fewer children is not strong. This is most common in countries where population pressure on cultivated land is comparatively weak and where traditional incentives for wanting large families remain strong.

Supply and accessibility of FP services could be improved substantially by measures such as the following:

- Governments should establish and strengthen public institutions charged with population and FP programs. This will involve staff training, management improvements, and strengthened program content.

- The role of NGOs in family planning should be expanded. NGOs have demonstrated their effectiveness in dealing with family planning issues effectively all over the world.

- Private FP organizations, nongovernmental health care networks (churches, employers' schemes), private health care practitioners (including traditional health care providers), other nongovernmental development groups (women's groups and community associations), and nonhealth outreach networks (agricultural extension and community development workers) can all be effectively used as channels for FP services. So can commercial outlets such as pharmacies, traders, and rural stores, particularly for marketing contraceptives. With AIDS an increasingly severe problem in many countries, a massive effort to expand the range of providers of condoms will be critical.

- Community incentive schemes should be developed and funded to induce communities to take action to reduce population growth through community-managed family planning programs. These programs can be managed, with government funding, by schools, employers, and community groups.

Periodic demographic and health and contraceptive prevalence surveys are needed to establish baseline data and provide essential information on fertility, family planning, and maternal and child health to policymakers and planners. Such data would reveal unmet demand for family planning and would indicate where service expansion or improvement is warranted and most needed.

Primary Education

In most countries of Sub-Saharan Africa, two important development objectives are (a) to improve the quality of primary education and (b) to expand primary school enrollment, especially of girls. Indeed, one of the most critical issues in the education sector in much of Sub-Saharan Africa is the urgency to increase primary school enrollment of girls. In some countries, girls account for less than 20 percent of primary school enrollment and even less in secondary and tertiary education. The lower rates of female school enrollment and the higher rates of female dropout at earlier grades are due in large measure to the high demand for girls to help with domestic work, such as caring for younger siblings, fetching water and fuelwood, etc. (e.g., Ventura-Dias 1985:183). Caring for younger siblings is particularly prevalent among girls aged 6 to 9 — an age at which they should attend primary school. Once they have missed that, their chance to receive any schooling is almost inevitably lost forever. These girls are very likely to remain in the low-education, low-income, low-status, high-fertility trap.

The gender gap in education has a high cost. Primary schooling beyond the first three years lowers women's fertility. Female education also has a strong effect on family welfare: the mother's education may be the single most important determinant of child health and nutrition. Moreover, since the majority of agricultural subsistence producers are women, better education for women can be expected to improve agricultural productivity — as well as women's incomes, opportunities, and decisionmaking influence within the household.

A number of possibilities exist and have been successfully tried in various settings to increase primary and especially female school enrollment. One such possibility merits mention here, as it may be of particular relevance in the present context. It concerns changing school schedules

— daily hours as well as vacations — to fit better into rural production systems and agricultural seasons. Children need to help with farm work, especially at peak periods, and if school is scheduled accordingly, attendance could be improved. Current vacation schedules are often still those established on the model and patterns of the former colonial powers. School breaks in Europe were scheduled to allow child labor in farming activities (planting, weeding, harvesting). The farming seasons in Sub-Saharan Africa are different. Regional school administrations should be given authority to adjust schedules to local realities.

Conclusion

Rapid population growth is detrimental to achieving economic and social progress and to sustainable management of the natural resource base. But there remains a sizeable gap between the private and social interest in fertility reduction, and this gap needs to be narrowed. Policies and programs that influence health, education, the status of women, and the economic value of children in turn influence attitudes toward child-bearing, family planning, and people's ability to control family size. Efforts to reduce fertility through explicit population policies, therefore, should be integrated with policies to improve health, education, and the status of women.

The various components of human resource development programs are strongly synergistic. Family planning is more readily accepted when education levels are high and when mortality — and, in particular, child mortality — is low. Healthy children are more likely to attend school. Clean water and sanitation are more beneficial if combined with health education and nutrition education. Educated mothers are more likely to have fewer and healthier children. These human resource development efforts also have positive effects on agricultural productivity and, hence, on food security. This, in turn, stimulates demand for fewer children. Improvements in human resource development are therefore critical in multiple ways for long-term sustainable development.

Broad-based improvement in human resource development requires reorienting policies and financial resources to focus on delivery systems that respond to the critical needs of the majority of the population, including the poor. This calls for far greater emphasis on primary education and basic health care. It also requires financial resources and, hence, substantial and sustained economic growth to generate sufficient resources to invest in human resource development (the significant potential and need for improving cost effectiveness notwithstanding). Without substantially improved agricultural growth performance, this will not be attainable.

Note

1. Average age at marriage increases with education level — and this correlation is stronger in SSA than in other regions. This may be because education for women is more rare in SSA and differences in age at marriage therefore reflect the exceptional differences in the lives of the most educated. Since female education is a more recent phenomenon in SSA, the difference in age at marriage may also capture both education and cohort effects. Interestingly, these larger differences in age at marriage were not yet reflected in differences in fertility in the early 1980s (Cochrane and Farid 1989).

8

Promoting Sustainable Agricultural Development

Sustainable and Environmentally Benign Agriculture

As suggested by the analysis in Chapters 4, 5, and 6, agricultural development efforts must focus on innovations that improve the productivity of land and of farm labor. Incentives that encourage further expansion of the cultivated area are consistent with agricultural growth objectives, but *not* with environmental protection concerns. The objective, therefore, must be to increase the productivity of both land and labor, in order to permit output growth while minimizing the increase in the area farmed. The required increase in productivity must be achieved with the least possible destruction of the environment.

A critical issue is the extraordinarily high risk faced by most farmers and herders in Sub-Saharan Africa. Rainfall is unpredictable in all but the most humid zones, and much of the continent has a significant chance of drought each year. Even in years of adequate overall rainfall, rains may start late or end early, and dry spells can occur at crucial times in the growing season. Most African soils need skilled management to ensure sustainable production, and most are easily degraded when their vegetative cover is thinned or removed. The drier areas are dominated by sandy porous soils deficient in nutrients, while many of the humid lowlands have acidic soils where aluminum toxicity can damage plants. The most fertile soils are in the East African highlands, where slopes and intense downpours increase the risk of erosion. The dark clay and alluvial soils in valley bottoms are prone to waterlogging and difficult to cultivate without animal traction or mechanized equipment. And the potential for irrigation is limited.

Crop farming in Sub-Saharan Africa, as in other tropical regions, is also characterized by extreme seasonality of labor requirements and labor peaks. All farming systems research in SSA shows tight labor constraints at certain critical periods in the crop cycle. Labor shortages are very common at the stages of land preparation, weeding, and harvesting. With traditional tools, land can only be prepared once the rains have started — but then it must be done very quickly to allow sufficient time for crops to grow on the available moisture. With the onset of the rains, growth conditions also become ideal for weeds, and weeding becomes critical. Similar urgency prevails at harvest time to prevent crop losses. An obvious implication of this is the pressing need for technology that saves labor, particularly at times of peak labor demand.

The systemic labor constraints are compounded by the effects of climate, health, and nutrition. Work capacity declines very rapidly with rising temperatures as also with declining health. An important insight from data collected in northern Malawi is the relationship between labor demands and health: most illnesses were reported toward the end of the rainy season (February–April) and most deaths during March–June — explained largely by reduced food availability, heavy workloads, damp-ness, and water problems in the house (Due 1988:334). In humid tropical and subtropical climates, only light work is possible during the midday and early afternoon hours when there is no shade. Heavy work must be interrupted by frequent and prolonged rest periods. If people are poorly nourished and/or afflicted with disease, their capacity for hard and sustained work is further diminished.[1]

Generally poor and heavily dependent on local natural resources and family labor, farmers and herders in Sub-Saharan Africa cope with uncertainty and with sustainability problems by adopting a variety of flexible strategies that minimize risk and make optimal use of the resources available to them. Examples of such strategies include plant-ing multiple crops and multiple varieties of multiple crops, diversifying herds and maintaining a high degree of mobility, establishing social arrangements to gain access to additional resources at times of stress, and engaging in various off-farm income-generating activities, particu-larly during the off-season. These strategies aim to diversify income and food sources, stabilize aggregate production and income, minimize risk, and maximize returns to labor under low-technology conditions. In crop production strategies, the central objectives almost invariably are: (a) en-suring optimum stable aggregate output of multiple crops over time, rather than maximizing yields of individual crops, and (b) maximizing output per unit of labor, rather than per unit of land.

Farmers seek to maximize production per unit of land only when land becomes scarce relative to labor. This is now occurring in many parts of Sub-Saharan Africa. The weakness of the traditional coping strategies, as discussed in Chapter 4, is that they are not capable of adjusting quickly enough to prevent serious negative impact of rapid population growth and increasing population pressure on soil fertility, farm size, fuelwood availability, land tenure systems, and so forth. The challenge is to increase quickly and effectively farmers' and communities' ability to confront these problems, building on their traditional mechanisms of coping with their environment.

Another critical issue is that of ensuring the longer-term sustainability of agricultural production systems. Sustainability has several dimensions and must be considered in terms of environmental, technological, economic, social, and institutional aspects and constraints and of the interactions among them. It also must be considered in a dynamic sense, since there will be change, probably quite rapid in certain areas. If the rapidly rising demand for agricultural products is to be met without further depletion of the natural resource base, this requires modification of agricultural production systems in the direction of intensification (i.e., more output per unit of land).

Numerous environmentally benign agricultural technologies have been developed experimentally on a small scale throughout Sub-Saharan Africa. Examples include contour farming to reduce water runoff and soil erosion, mulching, minimum tillage, intensive fallowing, crop mixtures and rotations which ensure continuous soil cover, terracing and bunding, integration of livestock and cropping to maintain soil fertility, agroforestry, integrated pest management, and water harvesting. In some countries farmer-managed small-scale irrigation has considerable potential. Behind each of these terms lies a vast body of agricultural knowledge, which to date has found little application in Africa outside of a number of NGO projects. Accelerating the widespread adoption of such technology, carefully adapted to the widely varying local agroecological and socioeconomic conditions, is essential if the critical problems faced by African agriculture are to be overcome.

Such technologies need to be mastered by agricultural research and extension systems so that they can be widely adapted to local conditions. There is a key constraint, however, which is as much responsible for the lack of dissemination of these technologies as are poor research and extension. Farmers have not *demanded* these technologies — much as most people have not demanded family planning. There has been little incentive for farmers to adopt such technologies in place of traditional methods. As long as there is free land to open up for farming, investing labor and capital in more intensive agriculture makes little sense from a farmer's perspective. When poor macroeconomic and agricultural policies reduce the profitability of farming, the incentives to intensify are further weakened. But incentive policies that encourage converting more land to farming are not the answer, since the cost in environmental degradation can be substantial. This complicates the search for solutions.

Agricultural intensification on a wide scale requires more effective research and extension. It also requires policies that induce farmers to intensify production. Making intensive farming profitable requires the kind of price, tax, and exchange rate policy environment suggested in the World Bank's long-term perspective study for Sub-Saharan Africa (World Bank 1989d). Farm input and output prices must be determined not by decree or by monopolistic or monopsonistic parastatal marketing agencies, but by market forces and must be closely linked to world prices. Exchange rate policies must ensure efficient equilibration of international and internal prices. And marketing, trade, and investment policies must facilitate private response to market opportunities.

In the short to medium term, subsidies may be necessary for certain farm inputs (such as seeds of improved varieties) which are needed to introduce intensive sustainable farming techniques, while the conversion of forests, rangeland, and wetlands to cropland may need to be taxed for environmental reasons. Such measures improve the profitability of agricultural intensification and raise the cost of land. Another, complementary, approach would involve providing compensation to individuals and communities to narrow — or even eliminate — the gap between private and public costs and benefits of resource-conserving production methods. Such programs would need to be carefully designed and monitored. If, for example, constructing rock bunds on steep slopes or the afforestation of severely degraded land to prevent gully erosion provide high economic returns, but low financial returns to the farmers and communities who would be undertaking these works, it would make sense to provide appropriate compensation to cover the difference. This might take the form of partly or wholly subsidized provision of key inputs (such as seedlings) or of direct wage payments (under food-for-work schemes, for example). Or it might be done through the provision of village-level infrastructure facilities in exchange for community action on resource conservation.[2]

Environmentally benign and sustainable technologies of the type noted on page 125 and discussed further in the following sections are, by themselves, unlikely to be sufficient for most countries of Sub-Saharan Africa to achieve agricultural growth rates of 4 percent a year. Improved crop variety/fertilizer/farm mechanization technologies will also be necessary, and the most desirable scenario would involve the widespread adoption of location-specific appropriate combinations of both. A gradual shift to locally suitable higher-value crops and livestock products will also be necessary. Over time, this will be stimulated by the policy reforms summarized above, by increasing market orientation of agricultural production, and by rising urban incomes. Nevertheless, in certain agroecological settings, some tradeoffs between agricultural intensification and environmental resource protection will be inevitable. The following sections discuss environmentally benign low-input, low-risk technologies that deserve greater emphasis in research and extension.

Soil Conservation and Fertility Management

Soil erosion is influenced by a combination and interplay of many factors — including soil characteristics, climate, topography, land use, and farming practices. It is therefore site-specific, and individual control measures that are appropriate and successful in one set of circumstances cannot automatically be transferred without modification to another location.

Farmers adopt soil conservation measures when they clearly perceive them to be in their own interest. In low-resource and labor-constrained settings, and with risk-averse farmers, measures recommended for adoption must increase crop yields (probably by a fairly significant margin), require little or no cash outlays, and conflict as little as possible with existing peak labor demands. If tree planting is involved, local rules concerning tree tenure must be considered, as must the often considerable differences in the allocation of costs and benefits between genders. If men are to invest in tree planting and maintenance, trees must produce cash crops and/or timber (or fuelwood for sale). Women far more readily value trees that provide fuelwood for own use, livestock fodder, fruits, and other nonwood products.

Many soil conservation efforts require additional labor — which often has high opportunity costs or is simply not available. Even off-season labor availability cannot be taken for granted. Rural people pursue various nonfarm income-earning activities when farm labor needs are slack, and seasonal out-migration of men is common in many areas. The shortage of labor has been one major reason for the poor record of many soil conservation programs. The other has been the perceived low rate of financial return to most of the methods that would be technically effective. Where, however, the labor/land ratio is high, as in parts of the East African highlands, various labor-intensive soil conservation techniques are financially attractive and, indeed, widely used. This suggests that farmers' willingness to undertake soil conservation measures will increase as population densities rise, as soil degradation and erosion problems intensify, and as policy reforms make intensive farming more profitable.

African farmers already use a variety of techniques, highly adapted to local conditions, to manage soil fertility and conserve soil. Many of the "more innovative" practices now being evaluated and refined on research stations are in fact based on techniques developed by farmers themselves. These are founded on the recognition that the only effective way of minimizing, if not preventing, soil erosion is the maintenance of vegetative soil cover, especially during the rainy season. Many traditional farming practices contain features that are designed, in part, to meet this requirement: mixed cropping, intercropping, relay cropping, multistory farming, various forms of fallowing, crop rotations, no-tillage and minimum tillage, a variety of agroforestry techniques, and others. Farmers have also resorted to engineering techniques to combat soil erosion and improve water retention on farmland. In many parts of the Sahel, the construction of terraces, stone lines and stone bunds, and earthen ridges, often laid out in grids, have a long tradition; these methods are still used in Mali, Burkina Faso and Niger (Reij 1988:19–23).

The multistory garden found throughout much of Sub-Saharan Africa, and especially in the forest zones, is a particularly noteworthy example of farmers' ingenuity. These plots, almost always very near the homestead, contain a variety of plants that grow to different heights (trees, vines, bushes, low-growing plants, creepers, and root and tuber crops), attract or repel different animals and pests, and have widely different life cycles and, hence, labor requirements and yield peaks. In essence, multistory gardens represent farmers' efforts to utilize the synergies of the rainforest ecology for crop production. A recent survey of compound farms in eastern Nigeria identified 146 species being cultivated in compound farms, with as many as 57 grown in a single compound (Bass 1990:136).

All these techniques meet other important requirements as well. Particularly essential are these: spreading total labor requirements as evenly as possible over the year, making optimal use of cultivated land through spatial arrangement of crops in mixed cropping systems,[3] and minimizing risk and stabilizing aggregate output from multiple crop species in environments characterized by considerable climatic uncertainty. It has been repeatedly documented that African farmers "outperform" the weather: indices of crop yields over time fluctuate considerably less than indices of rainfall (Dommen 1988:27).

Basing improvements on this rich tradition of farmer ingenuity and adaptation to local circumstances and constraints holds the greatest promise for success in overcoming the problems now facing agriculture in Sub-Saharan Africa. By the same token, failure to recognize this potential and to tailor supportive efforts accordingly has been an important factor contributing to the nonadoption of many technical "solutions" proffered in the past to overcome the continent's agricultural crisis. A long-time student of the situation in northern Nigeria has written that the basic rationality of indigenous land use systems "emerges unfailingly from almost every field investigation" and "the rationale of indigenous land-use systems must become the basis for conservationary resource management for the simple reason that the land belongs to, and must continue to be occupied by, its present population" (Mortimore 1989a:207).

Numerous effective and low-cost or no-cost techniques can be made available to farmers that would permit intensification and greater sedentarization, improve yields, and maintain soil fertility. Which of these are appropriate — technically and economically — depends very much on local conditions. A few examples of techniques aimed at soil conservation and soil fertility management are the following:

- Vegetative soil and water conservation methods are highly effective and far less labor-intensive to establish and maintain than terraces and other soil-moving techniques. Except on very steep slopes, grassy strips (sometimes called infiltration bands) have been found to be as effective in combating erosion as bench terraces — these being the two most effective techniques. Permanent strips of suitable species (such as *Vetiveria spp.*, see Box 8-1), established on the contour at proper intervals down the slope, are highly effective in slowing runoff, reducing soil erosion, improving moisture retention, and creating natural terraces over time. If fodder grasses are used, periodic cuttings provide animal fodder. Variations of this method are already in use, for instance, in Ethiopia, Kenya, Madagascar, Nigeria, Rwanda, and Tanzania.

Box 8-1   Vetiver Grass: A Proven Remedy against Erosion

For best effect, the species used to establish vegetative antierosion strips on sloping land should be a grass or a shrub with deep roots and strong and dense leaves and stems. It should be drought, fire, livestock, and flood resistant, should not take up much cropland, and should not harbor pests or diseases. *Vetiveria zizanioides*, a clump grass, exhibits all these characteristics and more. It thrives in arid and humid conditions, seems to grow on any soil (including shallow rocky soils) and survives wide temperature ranges. It is virtually maintenance-free, produces a dense hedge, and is extremely effective in trapping silt, slowing runoff, and increasing water infiltration. It is used very successfully for soil conservation purposes in regions as diverse as China, Fiji, the Caribbean, and India, even on very steep slopes and in regions with extremely high and erosive rainfall. Following successful field trials, extension services in Nigeria are now promoting its use, as well as that of its close relative *V. nigritana*, which has long been used by farmers in parts of northern Nigeria to mark field boundaries, as a vegetative erosion barrier. For a comprehensive assessment of the experience with Vetiver and its potential as an effective low-cost means to control soil erosion, see National Research Council 1993.

- Where draft power is available, plowing along the contour on sloping land will considerably reduce soil erosion and increase water infiltration. The effectiveness of contour farming is further improved if permanent contour key lines are established at appropriate intervals down the slope by means of permanent strips of suitable plant species.

- "Intensive" or "managed" fallowing — sowing deep-rooted legumes when land is taken out of production, rather than simply waiting for natural revegetation—will greatly improve soil fertility even in a single year. Where new land remains available for clearing, however, or where livestock are allowed to graze fallow land, farmers may be slow to change their fallowing practices.

- Minimum tillage and no-tillage methods, which involve planting directly into a stubble mulch without plowing or hoeing, can virtually eliminate soil losses, increase water infiltration and retention, and reduce labor input per unit of output. Minimum tillage is, of course, a practice very familiar to farmers in forest fallow systems. Soils in forest fallow systems are, however, almost entirely free of weed seeds and very easy to work with a planting stick. Neither condition is likely to apply in minimum tillage or no-tillage systems practiced on permanently cultivated land.

- Mulching can considerably reduce soil erosion, improve in-situ water retention, raise soil fertility and increase yields. But mulching annual crops is difficult. It can only be done after the seedlings have emerged, so that the mulch will not prevent germination. Consequently, mulch will not be in place at the onset of the rains, when much soil erosion takes place. Moreover, many annuals are low to the ground and mulch, with its microenvironment that harbors insects and molds, is close to the leaves of the young plants. The techniques of mulching annual crops are proving to be extremely demanding. Most experimental work in this area has been conducted by the International Institute of Tropical Agriculture (IITA), which has generally had to resort to pesticides (Jones and Egli 1984).

Labor-intensive approaches and mechanical or engineering works (such as terracing and bunding) are suitable only in certain settings. Moreover, engineering works will not be satisfactory in isolation. The primary requirement is appropriate land use, and mechanical conservation works must be accompanied by good farming practices (Hudson 1987:158).

Terracing is common in some parts of Sub-Saharan Africa, mainly on steeply sloping land. (From 1976 to 1985, with support from several

---

Box 8-2   From Slash-and-Burn to Sustainable Farming

Results of ICRAF field tests of environmentally benign, low-input sustainable technologies for tropical forest areas suggest that farming on newly cleared land must begin with low-input cropping. The initial slashing and burning clears the land, adds nutrients to the soil, and reduces soil acidity for the first year of cultivation (tropical forest soils generally being very acidic). Acid-tolerant crops such as upland rice and cowpeas should then be planted. First-year yields are usually very high. All crop residues (cowpea tops and rice straw) should be returned to the soil to improve its organic content. The plot should then be sown to pasture legumes or grasses. This "managed fallow" is more effective than the traditional forest fallow in restoring soil fertility. In subsequent years, more intensive methods are needed to maintain soil fertility. This may involve agroforestry, tree crops, legume-based pasture, or, if the farmer can afford it, the use of chemical fertilizers (Sanchez 1991).

---

external aid agencies, Ethiopian farmers constructed 60,000 km of bunds and 470,000 km of terraces for reforestation; however, this covers just 6 percent of Ethiopia's threatened highlands.) When properly constructed and maintained, terraces are highly effective in preventing soil erosion and increasing the retention of water in the soil, but they have drawbacks. Most important, they require considerable labor to construct and maintain and are far more expensive per unit of soil retained than almost any other alternative for soil erosion control.

Earthen bunds also require frequent maintenance and repair. Unless properly maintained and stabilized with grasses, they last only two to five years. On slopes of more than 10 percent gradient, they silt up rapidly; their trap efficiency may be 30 to 50 percent in the first year but falls to zero in the second (Grimshaw 1989). They have been found useful only on well-drained soils. Elsewhere, they are susceptible to breaching or cause water logging.

In Rwanda and Burundi, contour ditches introduced by colonial governments to control soil loss were abandoned after independence because farmers, who have a good idea of the cost in labor of digging and maintaining ditches, felt the ditches were not worth the maintenance they required (Brown and Wolf 1985:42; Jones and Egli 1984). The practice is now slowly being reintroduced, along with tree planting, mulching, and other complementary conservation measures.

On the Yatenga Plateau in Burkina Faso, farmers have adopted a technique of placing lines of stones along the contour on land suffering from, or threatened by, erosion. The lines of stones slow water runoff, increase water infiltration, trap dislodged topsoil, and have helped revegetate heavily degraded land. Farming had become threatened, and because labor was available for this work, this comparatively heavy investment in soil conservation and land improvement works made economic sense to farmers. Some 6,000 ha have been treated in this manner, and yields have increased by 15 to 30 percent. Labor costs are high and rising, however, because rocks have to be brought from increasingly greater distances.

The success story of Yatenga could not be replicated in Mauritania's Affole mountains, where rainfall is much lower, slopes are steeper, and the population density far lower. This underscores the limitations to "technology transfer" and the critical importance of adapting "solutions" very carefully to local agroecological and socioeconomic conditions (Reij 1988: 27).

Another interesting dimension of the stone line technology has been observed on the Mossi Plateau in Burkina Faso. There, women do not own land and do not benefit directly from the profits of their husbands' fields. They do, however, benefit directly from working on their collective fields, which are "borrowed" from the men, because the yields are distributed to all participants. Most women were soon discouraged from building rock lines. They had labored hard to treat their fields, but then often found the men reclaiming these improved plots for their own crop production and forcing the women to move again to another untreated piece of land (Wardmann and Salas 1991:77).

Kenya offers an example of a promising combination of conservation and new farming practices that increases vegetative cover and reduces the likelihood of severe erosion. Farmers are free to choose which practices to adopt and which trees to plant. Hundreds of thousands of smallholdings have been terraced by now, with farmers doing the work themselves (see Box 8-3).

There are a number of other simple and effective ways in which farmers' production systems can be made significantly more productive and sustainable, without increasing farmers' risks or the requirements for additional labor and/or capital beyond what the productivity gains will cover. Table A-28 summarizes the results of a financial and economic analysis of many such techniques under current conditions in Nigeria (FAO/World Bank Cooperative Programme 1991). This analysis showed that many of these techniques are very effective in reducing the decline of crop yields on continuously cropped land by reducing, to varying degrees, soil fertility losses and erosion. Almost all of the techniques assessed showed high economic rates of return and financial rates of return of 10 percent and more.

However, the pitfalls of attempting to introduce such techniques on a wide scale are also evident in these data. A few, such as stone-faced

---

Box 8-3 Soil Conservation in Kenya

In Kenya, grass-roots interest in soil conservation began to emerge a few years after independence, encouraged by good leadership and a strong sense of national unity based on the *harambee* philosophy. An important step was the adoption of soil conservation by the *Mwethya* groups, voluntary self-help groups that form each year to carry out communal work during the dry season and disband with the onset of the rains to tend to their individual farming activities. Leadership comes from the women, but men are persuaded to join for some physically demanding tasks. Activities includes bush clearing, water carrying, management of grass and tree nurseries, and plowing arable land on group members' farms in turn.

Presidential support for a national conservation program and the creation of a Permanent Presidential Commission on Soil Conservation and Afforestation provided a strong boost to this movement. At the same time, the increasingly serious problem of soil erosion attracted the attention of national and international aid agencies, who supported development projects that included soil conservation elements. In 1974, the Ministry of Agriculture began a soil conservation extension program with assistance from SIDA. Farmers were encouraged to terrace sloping land by leaving unplowed strips along the contour, and the concept of a new type of terrace called *Fanya Juu* ("throwing upwards") emerged: a ditch is dug on the contour, with the excavated soil placed on the uphill side to form a bund. The steeply sloping riser and the bund are planted with grass, providing a self-terracing effect as the grass and the bund retain soil washed down the cultivated interterrace strip.

To compensate farmers for keeping some land out of crop production, fruit and fuelwood seedlings and cuttings of quality fodder grasses were provided for the unplowed strips. Tree crops diversified the produce farmers could sell. High-quality fodder enabled farmers to limit the free grazing of cattle. Terraces retained water and soil and raised yields on the upslope side. In Machakos District, maize production in some fields increased by half after introduction of the terraces.

By 1983, terraces had been built on 100,000 farms, and extension agents were reaching over 30,000 new farms each year (Brown and Wolf 1985:41–42; Hudson 1987:165–166).

---

terracing and improvements of grazing reserves, are either unprofitable or only marginally profitable. Moreover, even a financial rate of return of 10 or 15 percent may not be sufficient to induce investment by farmers whose private discount rates are likely to be as high as 25 percent and more because of the high risks and distorted markets they face. But as the costs of soil degradation and erosion rise, as labor availability increases, as economic policy renders agriculture more profitable, the financial returns to such investments will increase. Knowledge transfers through extension will find an increasingly favorable reception by farmers as these changes occur. This is evident in the Kenya and Burkina Faso cases reported above, in farmer investment in stone terracing and tree planting in Ethiopia, and in windbreak establishment to protect millet fields in Niger (FAO/ECA 1992:10–11).

Water Management

Highly variable rainfall makes water conservation vital, particularly in semiarid areas and where dry spells are frequent. In the Sahelo-Sudanian zone in particular, moisture deficiencies pose the primary constraint on cropping, and effective water management is critical to reduce erosive and wasteful runoff and to maximize water infiltration into the soil. In most settings, in-situ water management through improved infiltration and moisture conservation is likely to be far less costly, more effective, and less stressful for the environment than the construction of water harvesting and storage structures. Many techniques recommended to combat soil erosion (such as contour farming, establishing vegetative contour strips, intercropping, ridging) are also extremely useful for in-situ moisture conservation.

However, under certain conditions (notably in low-rainfall areas), water harvesting techniques may be both necessary and effective. Water harvesting involves the collection and utilization of runoff for farming or other uses. A common form of water harvesting involves collecting runoff from a large area by means of earthen or stone bunds and guiding it through ditches or channels to smaller areas where field crops or trees are grown. Another common traditional technique is water spreading: diverting runoff from seasonal streams or gullies to cultivated fields. By increasing the quantity of water available on cultivated land, these and other water harvesting techniques greatly improve land productivity; they usually require little capital and are labor-using. Water harvesting has proved effective and successful, for example, in Burkina Faso's Yatenga Region and in Kenya's Baringo District.[4]

Only about 5 million ha are irrigated in Sub-Saharan Africa today, about half by modern means and the rest by traditional small-scale methods. Sudan (1.75 million ha), Madagascar (0.96 million ha) and Nigeria (0.85 million ha) account for more than 70 percent of this total (Barghouti and Le Moigne 1990:7). The additional area potentially suitable for irrigation is estimated at about 15 million ha (Barghouti and Le Moigne 1990:9,13) — not much in terms of Sub-Saharan Africa's total potential arable land area. Topography, soil characteristics and high water losses due to evapotranspiration from reservoirs and ponds pose significant constraints to irrigation development. Moreover, irrigation development in many regions would entail very high environmental costs in terms of increased threats from water-related human diseases and of irreversible damage to ecologically valuable floodplain ecosystems (Barghouti and Le Moigne 1990:13). Nevertheless, in a number of countries — notably those of the Sahel, but also Ethiopia, Malawi, Nigeria, and Uganda — irrigation development holds considerable promise for improving the productivity of farmland in a manner consistent with resource conservation objectives.

The emphasis should lie on individually or communally managed systems with development costs of US$2,500 per ha or less, which can be developed and maintained by individual farmers themselves or by farmers' groups. Such low-cost schemes include irrigation from wells or pumps, controlled flooding, and small-scale development of inland valleys and flood plains. Such developments have often spread spontaneously. Good examples are the private small-scale schemes developed by Mauritanian farmers in the Senegal valley, the rapidly spreading development of small groundwater irrigation systems in northern Nigeria's *fadama* areas (alluvial valley bottoms), and shallow aquifer exploitation with low-cost tubewells and pumps in Chad and Niger. Common characteristics of a number of recently reviewed successful small-scale irrigation schemes in the Sahel are the following: simple and low-cost technology, institutional and management arrangements that rely on the private sector and on individual responsibility, adequate infrastructure to facilitate access to inputs and to output markets, active farmer participation in project design and implementation, and high financial (cash) returns to farmers (Brown and Nooter 1992).

Livestock Production and Utilization

Mixed farming, combining crop and livestock activities, holds considerable promise for meeting criteria of environmental sustainability and of improved productivity. Farm animals are an important link for recycling resources within the farming system, and draft animals represent a major step towards agricultural intensification and, through the provision of transport services, market orientation. Indeed, the largely unutilized potential for using animal traction in both farm operations and transport needs to be realized. Cattle acquisition and maintenance involve considerable capital expenditure, however, and are therefore likely to be feasible only for relatively better-endowed households. In fact, the switch from hoe to plow tillage is usually motivated by the desire to expand the area cultivated or to economize on the labor required for land preparation (Pingali and others 1987:104). In any case, switching to animal draft power becomes economical only when the cost of hoe cultivation exceeds the cost of the transition to animal power. This usually happens only with the emergence of continuous cultivation.

Moreover, animal traction is generally adopted first to provide transport services, and only later for purposes of land preparation (Pingali and others 1987). Maintaining draft animals will not be economically attractive to farmers if their sole use is in land preparation. This suggests that developing rural transport infrastructure — roads and tracks suitable for animal-powered traffic — is important to accelerate the incorporation of draft animals on a wide scale into rural economies and farming systems. Upgrading rural transport — the movement of farm inputs and output, fuelwood, construction materials, and water — from headloading to animal-powered means will also greatly ease the pressure on women's time.

Nevertheless, there is good potential for greater incorporation of livestock components into farming systems. In many mountainous areas, this process is already well under way. Approaches and solutions will vary. The full potential of sheep, goats, pigs, and poultry has not been exploited in much of Sub-Saharan Africa. Small ruminants, especially if herded together, are very efficient users of a wide variety of forage and browse resources. They are less restricted by seasonal variations in feed resources and maintain their body weight far better throughout the year than cattle. They also withstand the effects of drought, even a prolonged one, and recover far more quickly from its impact than do cattle (FAO 1991:28–36). Goats, pigs, and poultry are likely to be more easily integrated into farm operations managed by women, because they tend to stay near the compound. Sheep present a different management issue because they require herding (and this may have implications for boys' school attendance).

In humid and subhumid zones, the tsetse fly can be controlled (although not eradicated) through low-cost traps and spraying. Priorities for promoting the integration of cattle into farming systems should be to popularize breeds such as the N'Dama, which are tolerant to trypanosomiasis, and at the same time to develop transport and farm equipment that such animals can power. In the subhumid zone, where cattle are concentrated, it will also be important to develop fodder banks to provide feed reserves for the dry season; analysis in Nigeria suggests this to be potentially profitable (Table A-28).

In the drier cultivated zones, the integration of cattle into sedentary crop farmers' production systems will generate increasing pressure on the available pasture and forage resources, leading to stiffer competition and potential conflicts with transhumant pastoralists whose herds graze on crop stubble and bushy fallows during the dry season. The pastoralists' difficulties are further exacerbated by the increasing development of valley bottoms in many parts of the Sahel and Sudan for cropping, often year-round by means of small-scale irrigation facilities, because this closes off essential migration routes and feed resources for their herds during the dry season. Improved land allocation between pastoralists and farmers to permit both to survive would be desirable, but no effective means of achieving this has been found as yet. Better land use planning and appropriate land tenure arrangements would be needed.

Traditional pastoralists are very efficient users of the meager range-land resources in the arid and semiarid zones. They possess enormous knowledge and understanding of the steppe and savanna ecologies in which they live and upon which their economies depend. Their husbandry of land, water, plant, and animal resources and their migratory movements are highly skilled, complex, and organized, reflecting generations of careful observation, experimentation, and adaptation. Their livestock production systems are, as recent studies have demonstrated, extremely productive. They utilize the marginal resources to which they have access not only very efficiently, but also in a manner that is environmentally sustainable over time. Traditional pastoralists produce as much protein per hectare as do ranches in areas with similar rainfall in Australia and the United States — but with vastly lower capital inputs (Bass 1990; Odhiambo 1991:79–80; Independent Commission on International Humanitarian Issues 1985).

But the potential for increasing the output and productivity of pastoralist production systems is low. Moreover, the most critical aspect of their traditional resource management system — mobility — is under increasing pressure as sedentary farmers appropriate land resources for cropping, close off vital migration routes and seasonal feed sources, and lay claim to scarce water resources. Forcible (and often violent) prevention of herd movement across national borders, as well as armed raids on herds to procure food supplies for rival factions in civil wars, further threaten pastoralists' production systems and way of life. Overgrazing is acute around public waterholes and urban centers and a major cause of environmental degradation. In these regions, water resource development and utilization require a refocusing of efforts to develop a network of more widely dispersed wells tapping shallow aquifers. At the same time, water and range resources should be placed under the control and management of local communities to help prevent excessive concentration of livestock.[5] Integrated water/livestock/forestry management is required instead of investment and policy efforts that stress

---

Box 8-4   Kenya's Turkana District: Lessons Learned

In Kenya's Turkana District, costly lessons from previous failed projects appear to have been heeded. Young Turkana men have been trained as para-vets and are moving among the pastoralists as "livestock scouts" to promote improved husbandry methods and sell veterinary medicines. Mobile veterinary extension units have succeeded in sharply raising the percentage of vaccinated animals. Oxfam provided (on grant or loan basis) small herds of goats and sheep to families who had lost their animals to help them get started again in their traditional way of life. The Norwegian aid agency NORAD has funded a scheme to market livestock in Nairobi and other urban centers where demand for meat has been rising. Thousands of trees (especially *Acacia tortilis*, an important source of fodder, food, and fuelwood) have been planted by the Turkana with the help of NORAD in an effort to offset tree losses suffered because of drought and changes in the hydrology along the Turkwel River brought about by water abstraction for irrigation. And many Turkana have established small farms, utilizing water harvesting techniques taught to them by extension workers, to grow some crops for their own use (Harden 1990:205–208).

---

one objective to the detriment of overall efficiency or environmental sustainability.

To improve the incentives for livestock production, the linkages from rural producers to urban consumers of meat and milk need to be strengthened. Several countries, including Kenya and Tanzania, are now developing cooperative dairy collection and marketing systems, similar in some respects to the successful Indian model. Other countries, such as Ghana and Nigeria, are considering to do the same. Restrictions on cross-border trade in live cattle should be eliminated to improve producer incentives and consumer access to meat. Private abattoirs should be licensed (and regularly inspected) to provide market outlets for livestock producers and to serve urban concentrations of demand for meat.

The provision of veterinary services should be increasingly left to the private sector, with governmental efforts concentrating on regulating private veterinarians, organizing and subsidizing mass vaccinations, and responding to emergency situations. In more remote pastoral areas, improved livestock care should be provided through "para-vets," who could be compensated for their work through commissions on veterinary drug sales. In all areas, agricultural extension workers should be made competent in improved animal husbandry, forage production, and animal traction.

Inputs

For environmental as well as cost reasons, the use of organic fertilizers should be emphasized. The integration of livestock into farmers' production systems is especially important in this regard. Similarly, disease and pest control efforts should emphasize cultural and biological controls.[6] To support this, subsidies on inorganic fertilizers and pesticides should be drastically reduced, if not removed entirely. Needed are pest- and disease-resistant varieties, as well as cultivation methods and inter-cropping and crop rotation systems that reduce the spread of pests and diseases. Some positive results in this field have been achieved, for example, by IITA.

Integrated pest management (IPM) programs for rice and other tropical crops have been developed that minimize the need for chemical pesticides. Yet many governments continue to provide substantial subsidies on chemical pesticides that reduce farmers' incentives to adopt such techniques. Past efforts at biocontrol of pests have focused on predators and parasitoids of insects, but research is now also being directed at the development of biopesticides to replace chemical pesticides and of plant pathogens to replace herbicides. Research in all these areas deserves strong donor support. Much can be learned in such research from taking a close look at the many indigenous pest control techniques developed by farmers themselves. In The Gambia, for instance, harvested cowpeas are steamed or stored in oil, ash, or chilies to repel cowpea weevils. Broadcasting wood ash on plants, especially vegetables, is widely practiced to deter insect pests. Fresh cow dung, bran, or green baobab fruit are used to lure insects to a site away from the field, where they are killed by burning or burying. Burning of blister beetles is reported to produce an odor that repels other blister beetles. Dried *neem* tree berries are pounded and used as seed dressing to ward off pests (Norem and others 1988:311).

Chemical fertilizers and pesticides will be important, even essential, components of intensified cropping systems. But they are costly in terms of foreign exchange, and their subsidization discourages the use of available and less expensive alternatives. Policy and infrastructure constraints to the use of chemical farm inputs need to be removed, however. There are no gains to be obtained from shifting to a rigid antichemicals bias in agricultural policy.

More efficient tools and equipment are essential to raise the productivity of farm labor. Particularly useful are implements that can be manufactured locally (preferably from locally available materials), are cheap, require little maintenance, and are easy to use. There is a tremen-

---

**Box 8-5   Research in Integrated Pest Management (IPM):
Some Examples**

The International Centre of Insect Physiology and Ecology (ICIPE) in Kenya
is working on various techniques that would eliminate the threat of
periodic devastating invasions of desert locusts into Sahelian farming
regions. Work is ongoing, for example, to utilize the locust's natural
enemies (parasitoids and pathogens) and, more importantly, to use pher-
omones to control the locusts' gregarization and sexual maturation and
thereby prevent the emergence of marauding locust swarms while ensuring the locust's continuing existence as an important part of the African
savanna ecosystems (Odhiambo 1991:81).

The International Institute of Biological Control (IIBC), an affiliate of CAB
International conducting research and development work in IPM, is exploring the use of pathogens and the development of biopesticides to replace
chemical pesticides and of plant pathogens rather than herbicides to
combat weeds. Fungi sprays are being tested, in collaboration with IITA,
under Sahelian conditions to ascertain their utility in controlling locusts.
In collaboration with the Département de Formation en Protection des
Végétaux of Niger, IIBC is testing a fungal pathogen effective against desert
locusts, along with strains from Pakistan, for incorporation into formula-
tions for field trials. And, based on the confirmed key role of predatory
ants and beatles against the *Helicoverpas armigera* moth, IPM techniques are
being developed to combat moths that attack cotton, sunflower, and other
African crops (CAB International 1991).

---

dous need throughout much of rural Africa for more efficient tools for
land preparation, planting, weeding, harvesting, and crop processing,
as also for small carts, wheelbarrows, bicycles, and other locally suitable
transport aids. Efforts to develop, adapt, and disseminate such technology have been largely confined to NGOs. Research and extension programs need to place greater emphasis on these aspects of rural
technology development and dissemination, drawing on the experiences of NGOs and collaborating with them. The production and marketing of such technology are obvious areas for promoting the development
of a viable local artisanal and small-scale industrial sector.

Agroforestry

From an environmental and agricultural perspective, agroforestry holds
high promise. There are a variety of techniques and approaches for
different agroecological conditions and production systems which can
increase farm productivity and incomes and simultaneously improve

the prospects for environmental sustainability of rural production systems (Nair 1990). Indeed, a multitude of agroforestry systems and practices are already in use in different parts of Sub-Saharan Africa (Cook and Grut 1989). Utilizing indigenous trees and shrubs (such as *Acacia albida* in the Sahelian zone),[7] these are appropriate, low-cost, low-risk, and high-return means for maintaining soil fertility, improving soil structure, recycling water and nutrients from lower soil strata, combating soil erosion, and providing secure supplies of fuel, fruits, fodder, mulches, building and fencing materials, and the like. Increased supply of tree products from agroforestry will also help preserve the remaining forest resources. Agroforestry systems are likely to be particularly suitable in the context of buffer zone development around environmentally valuable forest stands that should remain under protection (see Box 10-1).

Whether agroforestry efforts should be based on individual planting or on some form of communal planting will need to be determined at each site and with each community. Farm forestry is likely to be more readily incorporated by farmers into their production system in densely populated areas where common forests are no longer available and wood needs must be met from the farm or where wood fetches a good market price. This is already happening in parts of East Africa: there may be more trees in Rwanda now than at independence, even though the natural forests have all but disappeared.

If trees are to play a greater role in soil conservation and agricultural production, it must be on farmed land — through farmers' agroforestry activities on their own land. This can take many forms: shade trees in and around living areas, live (wood-producing) fences replacing dead (wood-consuming) fences around fields and homesteads, and trees and shrubs planted very closely in lines along the contours of sloped fields to help prevent soil erosion. Cocoa, coffee, rubber, and tea are valuable not only as cash crops, but also as environmentally important components in agroforestry systems. More species should be added, especially trees that produce fruit, nuts, or fodder. Trees can diversify the basis of food production.

In semiarid areas where wind is a threat to farming through desiccation or eolian erosion, windbreaks can be very beneficial. Appropriately designed and managed multipurpose windbreaks of mixed species and heights are particularly attractive, since they will also yield sustainable flows of fuelwood and other tree products for the local people. Under the Majjia Valley Windbreak Project in Niger, initiated by CARE in 1975, farmers have established some 350 km of windbreaks to protect about 3,000 ha of rainfed millet and sorghum fields. Crop yields in protected fields have been 15 to 23 percent higher than in neighboring unprotected fields. Once fully established, the annual sustainable yield of firewood from the *Azadirachta indica* used in these windbreaks is about 5 kg per tree. Spaced 4 m apart, 400 m of double-row windbreaks provide 1 ton of fuelwood annually. The seed pods of *Acacia scorpioides*, also used in windbreaks in Niger, are sold for use in leather tanning (Nair 1990:45).

In humid areas, multistory farming may be desirable, in which various trees, shrubs, and crops of different heights are intercropped to provide complete and continuous ground cover and a variety of microclimates (see also p. 128). In humid and subhumid regions, alley-cropping — a variation of traditional agroforestry practices adapted to sedentary farming — might be effective and adopted by farmers, if the labor requirements involved can be made to fit actual on-farm labor availability. Crops are grown in 4–8 m alleys between rows of leguminous trees such as *Leucaena* or *Gliricidia*, with the prunings providing fuelwood, stakes and fodder, or nitrogen-rich mulch for fertilizer.

Farmers will not invest in agroforestry unless there are adequate incentives at the farm level to produce trees for own use or for the market. The emergence of such incentives depends on a combination of factors. Climate, stage of deforestation, institutional arrangements, tenurial conditions, effectiveness of forestry extension and other factors all are important (Barnes 1990a, 1990b) — along with pricing. If trees are to be grown for sale as fuelwood or construction material, the practice must be profitable. Such incentives are gradually emerging. As populations grow and trees are felled, fuelwood becomes scarcer. Although scarcity creates a market value for fuelwood, this market has been developing too slowly, for the reasons discussed earlier.

The development of fuelwood markets will be accelerated if: cutting in protected forest areas is restricted; farmers are not restricted or licensed/taxed in marketing fuelwood they produce on their farms; nurseries are established to produce appropriate species; research and extension services incorporate tree farming as a major theme; and land tenure reform provides ownership of forests to farmers and local communities so that they are more likely to invest in forests rather than merely mine them for fuelwood. If appropriate price signals are to be developed, fuelwood must not be obtainable as a free good. Provided the appropriate species are used, agroforestry techniques can be very profitable in many areas because of their potential to generate a combination of benefits (fuelwood, poles, fodder, fruits, and associated crop yield increases).

Even transhumant livestock herders will plant trees if they face the right incentives (notably clear economic benefits and uncontested resource ownership) and if the establishment and management techniques are suitable to their means and lifestyles. In Kenya's arid Turkana

District, the Turkana have long depended on the riverine forests along the Turkwel river for fodder, fuel, food, and other uses. These forests provide the Turkana with an important source of fodder for their herds in dry seasons and especially in drought years. Individual families own the user rights to each individual tree, *Acacia tortilis* with its long tap root and ample production of edible pods being the most important. Prolonged drought and irrigation and fishing schemes along the river had significantly reduced the number and productivity of trees by 1984 when NORAD began to assist the Kenya Forestry Department in seeking ways to conserve the woodlands in Turkana District. Well aware of the value of these trees for their herds' and their own survival, the Turkana dug thousands of planting pits with microcatchments around them, planted *A. tortilis* in the next few years, and made sure the trees were not destroyed by foraging herds (Harden 1990:206).

Economic pricing of woodfuels is critical to encourage conservation and interfuel substitution. Pricing policies based on taxing incoming supplies would encourage economies in the use of woodfuels in urban areas (UNDP/World Bank ESMAP 1988). Such policies can also provide a way to raise revenues that could be used to improve the forestry services (Falloux and Mukendi 1988). Higher taxes could be levied on fuelwood coming from open-access areas and lower taxes on fuelwood coming from wood plantations and private plots.

In many regions, there are significant sociocultural obstacles to widespread tree farming, at least in the short run. In Kenya's Kakamega District, for example, women are not allowed to plant trees because this would undermine their husbands' authority; they are subjected to superstitious threats of barrenness or widowhood (Aloo 1985:28). In many communities, trees have rarely been deliberately planted — even where their utility is recognized and they are protected and prized for their contribution to livelihood systems. Trees may in fact be regarded as an obstacle to crop cultivation, especially where tenurial considerations (such as separation of usufructual rights to land and to trees) or technology aspects (such as animal or mechanized plowing) are important. In some countries, because all forest land is owned by the state, people fear that if they plant trees their land will revert to the government. In parts of the Sahel, farmers are unwilling to plant certain trees because they are on the forest department's protected list; to crop or prune them would require going through tedious procedures to prove they own the land and planted the trees and to obtain a cutting permit (Timberlake 1986:56).

It is important to involve the local women in projects that concern fuelwood production, provision, and use. Men and women almost always have vastly different views concerning the utility of community or farm forestry activities (Molnar and Schreiber 1989). In Senegal, the men in the village councils planned to sell as poles the timber from community woodlots, which had in fact been established to provide fuelwood for local households and to reduce the workload of the women (Dankelman and Davidson 1988:54). Where women are actively involved, chances of success are high. In The Gambia, for example, the National Women's Bureau and the Forestry Department promoted the establishment of woodlots-cum-orchards managed by village women's groups; these are now producing locally significant quantities of fruits and vegetables as well as fuelwood (Marenha 1985:56; Dankelman and Davidson 1988:21). Where women face traditional restrictions concerning the planting of trees, careful investigation may reveal possibilities, acceptable under local norms, to plant certain species of brush that are suitable for fodder and fuel.

Several successful programs in Kenya are based on strong involvement of local women. One of the best known and most successful nongovernmental afforestation programs is the Green Belt Movement, started in 1977 by the National Council of Women of Kenya (Maathai 1988). Another successful program is that of the Kenya Energy Non-Governmental Organization (KENGO), an association of over 200 NGOs dealing with energy issues, which includes a number of women's groups and organizations. KENGO is active in the promotion of fuel-saving stoves as well as in reforestation with indigenous trees. Information on medical, cultural, ecological, and economic values of trees is collected from local women and passed on to women's groups through workshops, exhibitions, mass media, pamphlets, and posters. The Kenya Woodfuel Development Programme promotes a self-sustaining system of tree planting to supply fuelwood. Based on surveys of agroforestry practices and cultural background of local people, its approach accommodates indigenous expertise with traditional beliefs and taboos. Women are especially encouraged to develop solutions that will not conflict with traditional values (Chavangi, Engelhard and Jones 1985; Leach and Mearns 1988:142–145).

Stoves That Save Fuel and Women's Time

A second major effort to address the fuelwood and household energy problems has been aimed at improving the efficiency of energy use: slowing the rise in fuelwood consumption by introducing more fuel-efficient wood and charcoal stoves or stoves using nonwood energy sources (such as solar cookers). Most rural African women cook on some version of the three-stone stove or on other simple stoves with an energy efficiency of 10 percent or less. Various technical improvements have been advanced, tested, promoted — and in most cases not adopted by the women for whom they were meant. On the whole, little headway had been made by the mid-1980s: few programs had distributed more than 5,000–8,000 stoves (WRI/IIED 1987). But there have been exceptions — such as KENGO's projects (the ceramic *jiko* and the *kuni mbili* stoves) in Kenya, supported by USAID's Renewable Energy Development Project, and the program in Burkina Faso based on the stove design of the Burkina Energy Institute (see Box 8-6).

The reasons for failure have varied. The driving motive of those developing and promoting new stoves has usually been to save fuel, but women in the "target population" have often had a number of other, and frequently overriding, concerns which the designs proffered did not address to their satisfaction. Women in some villages in Mali responded poorly to cookstove programs because their perceptions of their time constraints differed from those of the program planners. These women considered the time required for food preparation and cooking to be more burdensome than the time needed to collect fuel; they preferred a stove that would reduce cooking time, rather than save fuel (Molnar 1989:41). Cultural and dietary reasons are important, as are cost, local availability of materials, convenience of use, cooking time, suitability for local cooking implements and utensils, suitability for different fuels, and a variety of other factors. Women may be averse to cooking outside. The stove's capacity may be too small to cook for large families or to prepare several dishes simultaneously. Where simmered stews are the mainstay of the diet, as in many parts of the Sahel, stove design must take this into account. Solar cookers are useless in the evening when meals are prepared. Stoves may be used not only for cooking, but also for heating (M. Carr 1985:133–134). Other important reasons for nonadoption include: unaffordable cost; nonportability; drastic changes required in cooking habits; cultural taboos; design inappropriate to multiple purposes, including water heating, space heating, and smoke generation to repel insects under the house roof. Complications also tend to arise because it is often men who buy the stoves while women operate them (Elnur 1985:36).

Stove promotion efforts must begin with careful studies of local dietary habits and cooking practices. It is particularly important to involve women from the start. Whatever replacement is recommended, it must address the common constraints to adoption listed above.

In addition to KENGO's projects in Kenya and the program in Burkina Faso, successful efforts which involved the targeted women from the inception of the program include: the *Ban-ak-Suuf* stoves program in Senegal; the ILO/World Bank Stoves Feasibility Project in Ethiopia, which focused on urban women in Addis Ababa; the portable metal *Mai*

Box 8-6   Two Successful Stove Programs in Sub-Saharan Africa

The Renewable Energy Development Project in **Kenya**, launched with support from USAID in 1982, sought to sell or give away 5,000 stoves by the end of 1986. By the end of 1985, promoted by the Kenya Energy NGO (KENGO), it had spawned a new industry whose main producers alone had sold 110,000 improved stoves at a profit. They had captured a large slice of the market previously dominated by the cheap one-unit-a-year *jikos*, scrap-metal charcoal stoves with a fuel efficiency of about 19 percent. The new stove was designed to compete directly with these traditional ones. Local participation in the design was extensive: scrap-metal artisans were consulted to ensure easy manufacture, and prototypes were tested in 600 households to ensure acceptability. The final design comprises a scrap-metal casing, waisted for stability, with an insulating ceramic liner, a grate in the top half, and an ash chamber at the bottom. The other main reason for success is the stove's very favorable cost-benefit ratio: it costs more, but lasts longer than the old stove, resulting in actual savings over two years. Its measured fuel efficiency is 29–30 percent, theoretically offering fuel savings of 34–37 percent, but many users reported savings of up to 50 percent (probably due to more careful fuel use). For the average user family in Nairobi, the stove paid for itself within eight weeks and provided an annual return of up to 1,000 percent on the investment (WRI/IIED 1987:232).

A promising approach for poor and scattered rural populations is indicated by the program in **Burkina Faso**. Based on a design developed at the Burkina Energy Institute, the stove is basically a shielded traditional three-stone stove, with a circular shield or shell built of clay, dung, millet chaff, and water around three stones that support the pot. A woman can build the stove in half a day to fit any desired pot size; the simple design and construction method require only half a day's training. There are no cash costs. Fuel savings range from 35 to 70 percent. Most women recoup the investment of a day's training and labor within one or two weeks through savings in fuelwood. By April 1986, some 85,000 improved three-stone stoves were in use (WRI/IIED 1987:232–233).

Sanki stove in Niger, under which more than 40,000 stoves were sold by 1987 and users recovered their investment cost through wood savings of 30 percent in two months; and the Women and Energy Project initiated in 1984 with GTZ support by Maendeleo Ya Wanawake in Kenya. Under the latter project, local women were trained to construct low-cost one- and two-pot woodburning stoves with clay liners, which use considerably less wood and allow the kitchen area to be kept much cleaner. This was backed up with training in agroforestry techniques and the establishment of nurseries and fuelwood plantations by village women's groups (Dankelman and Davidson 1988:85–86).

For urban users, reliable, economically accessible, and appropriately priced alternative energy sources, such as kerosene and LPG, must be developed. Low-income urban users may need assistance with appropriate credit schemes to purchase stoves and appliances that use these fuels.

Economizing on fuelwood is also important in many cottage industries — to improve profitability and to ease the pressure on forest resources. The successful introduction of more efficient, yet affordable fish smoking ovens in Ghana has considerably improved the profitability of women's fish smoking by lowering their wood requirements. A GTZ project in Zambia, where some 15,000 tons of wood are cut each year from the forests near Lake Kariba to smoke 4,300 tons of fish, is now drawing on this positive experience. Improved smoking ovens based on the Ghanaian model reduce wood consumption by two-thirds and are proving popular with the local fishermen and fish traders. The clay stoves can be easily built by the fishermen themselves, and the racks are made by local carpenters. The project is now testing the use of fast-growing trees such as *melia* and *neem* as fuel; since both contain insect-repellent essences which do not appear to be harmful to humans, their use would also eliminate the need for other methods to prevent insect infestation that might be costly and/or harmful to humans.

Policy and Institutional Aspects

Although environmentally benign technologies of the kind discussed here have been tested widely and successfully in Sub-Saharan Africa, they have generally not been adopted by large numbers of farmers. The "imported" technologies involving fertilizers, pesticides and herbicides, HYVs, and farm mechanization have not fared much better. The reasons for nonadoption vary, but the basic problem has almost always been a poor fit with the resources available to farmers, combined with farmers' risk aversion. Inappropriate price, tax and exchange rate policies, inadequate rural infrastructure, inefficient marketing systems, and poor agricultural support services have all contributed to keeping resources out of the reach of farmers and to increasing the risks inherent in innovation. In this situation, and as long as uncultivated land remained available for clearing and cropping, it made sense to farmers to cultivate new land rather than to use more labor-intensive and/or financially costly production methods. This continues to be the case in much of Sub-Saharan Africa.

These problems have been more apparent with respect to "imported" technologies — not only because these technologies have tended to be the ones promoted most actively by governments and aid agencies alike, but also because these technologies have tended to require significant departures from familiar resource management and production techniques and in relative factor utilization. Placing greater emphasis on improving and adapting the types of techniques discussed above should lower the adoption threshold considerably. But a number of measures will be necessary to create a policy and institutional environment that is conducive, rather than inimical, to agricultural intensification and resource conservation.

Farmers require incentives and assistance to adopt yield-enhancing and soil-conserving technologies. Sustainable farming methods must be made profitable — and environmentally unsustainable practices must be made unprofitable. To promote the switch to environmentally sustainable farming, the cost of resource degradation and destruction must be increasingly shifted to farmers instead of being borne entirely by society at large and, in effect, by future generations. Privatizing the social costs of resource-depleting farming practices will discourage their use. Government policy must permit farmers to profit from switching to sustainable agriculture but to incur obvious costs if they use environmentally destructive methods. The major tools for this are: (a) land tenure reform, (b) economic policy that increases the profitability of market-oriented farming, and (c) agricultural services that help farmers through the transition to sustainable agriculture.

Land Policy and Tenure Reform

It is essential to ensure the security of land tenure — to halt the erosion of security traditionally provided by customary tenure systems. Secure rights to land (individual or communal) are necessary to encourage management practices and investments that ensure sustainable use of a fragile natural resource base. Over time, population pressure and agricultural intensification will make formal land titling necessary. The administrative machinery for land titling needs to be established to permit those seeking titles to obtain them. The transition to full land titling will require more than a decade to achieve in most countries and should be undertaken only in response to demand from below, not imposed from above.

In the interim, respect for customary tenure systems needs to be codified. Judicial mechanisms for dealing with disputes between people claiming traditional versus modern land rights are needed. Land laws and regulations should respect customary tenure systems, permitting modern titles only when land is purchased fairly or acquired with the agreement of traditional owners. Women's tenurial/usufructual rights must be safeguarded, if not enhanced. Titles provided to groups for collective ownership should also be available. Kenya has begun this by providing land titles to group-owned ranches, with groups organized by clan. French aid projects and the World Bank are planning to experiment with community titles in several Sahelian countries.

Governments should divest themselves of most land, except parks, to individual or community owners. This would be a first step in inducing farmer landowners to conserve the land. Where such divestiture is impossible — because, for example, of the breakdown of traditional communities due to large-scale migration — governments might retain state ownership but provide legally protected use rights to local inhabitants.

Local people and communities must be given a direct and tangible interest in the sustainable management of ranges and woodlands and in the conservation of forests and wildlife. Communities cannot be effective at managing their natural resources unless their authority is clearly established and recognized. In particular, the appropriateness of statutes vesting residual control over all land in the state should be reexamined. In return for legal title, the populations of forests and rangelands must accept obligations for proper management of these areas. Economic incentives to conserve could be strengthened by allocating the benefits of forests and pastures to local populations in the form of logging, hunting, and gathering rights in forest areas and exclusive grazing rights in pasture areas. Opening up new land for cropping in certain areas might be made subject to heavy land taxes. Only by involving the local people as full partners in conservation, with appropriate incentives, will conservation occur.

Agricultural Support Services

Sub-Saharan Africa urgently needs farm technology development and dissemination mechanisms that are effective: agricultural research, extension, education, and farm input supply. Each of these activities will have to incorporate the soil conservation, fertility management, agroforestry, pest management, and environmentally sustainable farming techniques identified above. Not many of these services are working well today anywhere in Sub-Saharan Africa, and virtually none are competent as yet in environmentally sustainable agriculture.

Although there are success stories, agricultural research in Sub-Saharan Africa has, on the whole, not performed well. This has been largely because of weak government commitment and poor management, rather than inadequate funding. Externally financed projects have not provided the needed breakthrough as yet. To develop, test, and adapt technologies of the kind identified above, national agricultural

---

Box 8-7   Past Research Impact on Agricultural Productivity

The success of new crop varieties introduced into SSA in the past thirty years has been limited. Rice in a few parts of West Africa, hybrid maize in parts of Ghana, Kenya, Nigeria, Zambia, and Zimbabwe and, more recently, cassava varieties developed by IITA are among the few success stories of yield-increasing varietal improvements adopted by farmers. Productivity in tea production has risen impressively in Kenya, Burundi, and Rwanda. Maize yields have increased in Benin and Gabon, and cotton has done well in much of francophone West Africa, Swaziland, and Zimbabwe. Coconut in Côte d'Ivoire, oil palm in Zaïre, and control of coffee berry disease in Ethiopia and Kenya are other examples of positive research impact on production. Yield increases implied in aggregate data for sorghum and groundnuts, on the other hand, appear to be due to acreage reductions (abandonment of less suitable land and switching of unproductive farmers to other crops), rather than of technological improvements (Lipton and Longhurst 1985; World Bank 1987c, 1987d, 1989d).

---

research systems (NARSs) must be rehabilitated and given work programs relevant to the task. Most important will be strengthening national capacity to plan, manage, and carry out research focused on the issues identified above. Research as well as research management skills need to be developed. Faculties of agriculture, NGOs, and the private sector should be drawn into the effort. Aid donors should coordinate their activities so that external aid strengthens national agricultural research systems in this endeavor.

Agricultural research in and for Sub-Saharan Africa needs to focus on the conditions and constraints that prevail in Sub-Saharan Africa and that determine the production environment of farmers in Sub-Saharan Africa. Direct application of "off-the-shelf" technology imported from other regions has rarely proved successful. As already noted, African soils need careful management, rainfall is unpredictable, the likelihood of drought in any given year is high, and dry spells may occur at any time in the growing season. Since the many different combinations of soil, elevation, slope, aspect, rainfall, temperature, and solar radiation result in an enormous diversity of agroecological microenvironments, strong emphasis needs to be placed on location-specific adaptive research. For the same reasons, researchers need to pay more attention to the spontaneous experimentation and adaptation of farmers themselves —because that is where the real fine-tuning of technological innovations to farmers' complex agroecological and socioeconomic conditions occurs (Richards 1991; Chambers and Toulmin 1991). The similarly vast variety of farming systems — based not only on the local agroecological conditions, but just as firmly on the often poorly investigated and even more poorly understood socioeconomic arrangements, institutions, and traditions — lends further weight to this requirement. The highly pronounced gender-specificity of agricultural tasks and entire farming systems in many communities is one important manifestation of this aspect. The parallel existence of individual and communal fields in many communities' land use systems is another. The frequent distinction between rights to land and rights to trees under customary tenure systems is a third.

National research priorities must relate to the specific agroecological and socioeconomic characteristics, production patterns and development objectives of each country. Each country needs to test and adapt technology under its own specific conditions, but it will take time to rehabilitate and develop NARSs and for these systems to introduce the concerns of sustainable agriculture into their work programs. Moreover, most countries of Sub-Saharan Africa are too small to undertake the entire range of agricultural research needed. Much of the basic and applied research on sustainable agriculture will therefore need to be undertaken at the International Agricultural Research Centers (IARCs) and to some extent at universities and research centers in the industrial countries. Regional and international collaboration and African regional networks of researchers are needed to facilitate sharing of research results and experiments on the subjects relevant to sustainable agriculture.

The capability of national agricultural research systems to undertake multilocational verification of international and national research findings on farmers' fields and the analysis of farmers' constraints needs to be strengthened. There is an urgent need to identify more intensive farming systems that can sustain soil fertility and structure and conserve soil moisture. Better integration of livestock and of agroforestry into farming systems will be important in this regard. Low-cost, low-risk techniques found effective in similar environments elsewhere need to be tested and, if found suitable, appropriately adapted and promoted. Agricultural scientists must learn to fit their research to farmers' real situations. An intimate understanding of local constraints such as soil conditions, pests and diseases, moisture variation, seasonal labor shortages, and the gender aspects of farming systems is essential.

New crop varieties must be tested under zero- and low-input conditions and in mixed cropped and intercropped situations before being recommended to farmers through the extension services. Appropriate improved drought-resistant and short-duration varieties of millet and sorghum are urgently needed. Work on these and other important

---

**Box 8-8   Special Considerations Governing Agricultural
Research in Sub-Saharan Africa**

A 1987 review by the World Bank of agricultural research in East and
Southern Africa (World Bank 1987c) noted that the impact of agricultural
research on economic growth had been less than that experienced elsewhere because of a number of particular characteristics of Sub-Saharan
Africa:

- The relative insignificance of irrigation and the large agroecological
  diversity in rainfed farming in SSA.
- The hostile physical environment (droughts, fragile soils) and the
  more complex systems of farming that African farmers employ to
  diminish risks and conserve fertility.
- The relative shortage of labor at peak periods of demand for farm
  labor, which makes mechanization (not necessarily tractorization)
  important; at the same time, trypanosomiasis raises unique obstacles
  to the use of animal power in many areas.
- Inadequate macroeconomic policies, which have exacerbated deteriorating world market conditions and limited farmers' incentives to
  adopt new technology and expand production.
- The relatively low efficiency of agricultural support services (extension, input distribution, credit, marketing, and seed production).
- The fact that small countries find it difficult to sustain both adequate
  agricultural training facilities and a minimum research capacity to
  test and adapt imported technology to an often wide range of
  agroecological conditions.

---

indigenous food crops (roots, tubers, plantains) has long been neglected.
The enormous positive impact in recent years of IITA's new cassava
varieties and of the development and extension of the mini-sett planting
technique for yam on the food security and income of Nigerian smallholders shows what payoffs can be expected from effective and farmer-
oriented research on root crops.

Research on biological soil fertility maintenance, especially nitrogen
fixation and the ecology of microbes in the soil, should complement soil
conservation efforts (Brown and Wolf 1985:43). The enormous importance of insects — on plant and livestock health and performance and on
human health — in most of Sub-Saharan Africa is rarely reflected in
research programs; neither is the need for locally effective and appropriate nonchemical pest controls and integrated pest management. In both
these respects, NARSs would gain immensely by collaborating more

intensively with the International Centre of Insect Physiology and Ecology (ICIPE) in Nairobi.

Social science research, much neglected so far, should be an integral part of adaptive research. In particular, Farming Systems Research (FSR) must pay more attention to the importance of nonfarm and off-farm activities and incomes in rural households. These are critical elements of the resource- and risk-management strategies of such households. They also pose constraints and provide opportunities: off-farm work may preclude on-farm labor intensification, but off-farm income may allow cash expenditures not otherwise possible. Off-farm work is far more often recognized as important in the case of men — notably when and where it involves out-migration (be it daily, seasonal, or long-term) from the village. It is also very important for women — yet often totally ignored in rural/agricultural development planning and projects. Throughout Sub-Saharan Africa, women derive important income from such activities as beer brewing, produce marketing, and nonwood forest product gathering and processing. The cash income derived from such activities is often critical for family welfare.

Extension services that effectively transfer sustainable agriculture technologies to farmers are critical. Equally essential is the need for extension services to ascertain and transmit information to researchers regarding farmers' needs, problems, and constraints. Farming systems research is not likely ever to succeed in covering the vast diversity of microecologies of Sub-Saharan Africa or the countless permutations of crop and tree combinations that farmers use. Extension services therefore also need to facilitate farmers' own experimentation and the transmission of such indigenous adaptations from farmer to farmer. The International Center for Research on Women (ICRW) has reported excellent results with this approach in an extension program aimed at women farmers in Zaïre. If extension services are to offer farmers the best techniques to suit their specific circumstances, they must provide "menus" of options for farmers to choose from — rather than deliver prescriptive composite "technology packages." Farmers will then experiment to adapt research findings and extension recommendations to their own specific combination of needs and constraints. Extension services must collaborate with their respective NARSs in maintaining a continuous two-way flow of information between farmers and researchers and ensuring that research is geared to farmers' needs and meets the criteria of sustainability and profitability.

Given the high degree of gender-specificity in farming operations, the widespread prevalence of gender-segregated farming, and the increasing incidence of female-headed households and female-managed farms, it is imperative that extension services be more effectively oriented towards reaching women farmers. Steps to accomplish this have been initiated in a number of countries (see, for example, Murphy 1989; Saito and Weidemann 1990). They include: deployment of more female extension staff, properly trained and equipped; use of more female contact farmers and of women's groups to facilitate the delivery of extension messages and to obtain feedback; training of extension workers to be aware of, and responsive to, women's responsibilities, needs, and constraints; and adoption of special measures to reach women farmers. The latter include, for instance, timing of visits, selection of crops and impact points, and adaptation of technology messages to women's time and resource constraints and to their production objectives and risk perceptions.

Unified agricultural extension systems are more cost-effective and appropriate to farmers' needs than the multiple subsector-specific or single-commodity services currently operating in many countries, often supported by different aid donors. Such consolidation has been effected successfully in Kenya, Zimbabwe, Togo, Mali, and Burkina Faso and is now being implemented in Ghana and Nigeria.

The content of agricultural education will need to change. It must focus on training for low-input, labor-intensive environmentally sustainable smallholder agriculture under tropical and subtropical conditions, rather than for high-input, mechanized farming more suited to temperate climates. This will require teachers competent in these fields as well as appropriate texts and other teaching materials. Most important, it will require refocusing agricultural education in most SSA countries and widening it to include natural resource and environmental concerns.

Research and extension services, along with private voluntary organizations, should be active in developing and testing prototypes of inputs and investment goods consistent with sustainable agriculture: new hand tools, animal-drawn equipment, crossbred cattle, village- or farm-level grain storage facilities, more efficient stoves, hand pumps, small-scale agricultural processing technology, trees for agroforestry, organic fertilizers, etc. These can subsequently be produced and distributed by the private sector.

Exchange Rate, Trade, Fiscal, and Pricing Policies

Agricultural intensification requires that agricultural production be sufficiently profitable to induce and sustain this process. Profitability depends heavily on the policy environment which creates the incentives and disincentives to which farmers respond. Past government interventions have generally tended to turn the internal terms of trade against agriculture. Generally, the best policy has been found to be a relatively liberal market-based price system, with a fairly equilibrated exchange rate[8] and open entry to marketing and processing. Price stability might be pursued in the face of international price fluctuations through a system of variable export and import duties.

There also is a need to provide positive incentives for sustainable use of natural resources and negative incentives to reduce their inefficient use and prevent their destruction. Promoting environmentally benign and sustainable agriculture may therefore require taxing of environmentally unsustainable practices. It may also be advisable for society to assume some of the costs involved in moving farmers from unsustainable to sustainable production systems — in recognition of the socially desirable externalities involved. There may be a case for selective and temporary subsidizing of such activities as tree nurseries and seedling distribution, dissemination of more efficient prototype stoves, watershed stabilization and soil conservation, water harvesting and small-scale irrigation. Conversely, farm machinery powered by fossil fuels, logging, land clearing, and fuelwood extraction from public forests and woodlands should be taxed.

Subsidies influence decisions to employ commercially available inputs (such as chemical fertilizers, farm machinery, seedlings). The effects of subsidies on the environment can be beneficial or detrimental. Input subsidies compensate somewhat for low output prices received by farmers and, hence, may favor conservation — at least on farms producing for the market. But artificially lowering the price of inputs through subsidization may encourage the use of economically and environmentally inappropriate technologies. For instance, excessive or inappropriate use of chemical fertilizers and pesticides, stimulated by heavy subsidies, can do much environmental harm. Temporary subsidies may be justified and beneficial for environmentally benign inputs — to popularize a new technology. But in the long term, subsidization of any input is difficult to justify.

Subsidies for basic anti-erosion activities (especially engineering measures) are frequently advocated — but where such policies have been implemented, they have often had very undesirable effects. Lack of subsequent maintenance, lack of local identification with the effort, and disruption of local incentive systems (for instance, distortion in local wage labor markets, promotion of attitudes that favor new investments over maintenance) have been the most common and serious problems. Moreover, as noted above, engineering measures are rarely sufficient by themselves and must be combined with changes in on-farm soil and water management practices; these latter are often ignored when attention is focused on engineering works and subsidy administration. Finally, engineering is costly and rarely the most effective technique. Even if subsidies are to be considered for such initial investments (and this may be the case in particular for common investments that may be required, such as runoff evacuation channels and water harvesting/storage structures), the modalities and effects of subsidization must be carefully thought through in all their consequences.

Local Institutions: Involving the People

If farmers are to innovate and adopt sustainable agricultural production and resource management techniques, they must be given more responsibility for their own affairs. They should be allowed to associate freely in farmer-managed cooperatives and groups, to market their own produce, to own and manage their land. Tenurial security must be ensured. People will only cooperate in environmental resource conservation efforts if they have a stake in the resources to be conserved and incentives to manage their environment more prudently. Administrative regulations will not suffice — even if enforcement mechanisms were to be substantially strengthened. Responsibility and authority to manage rangeland should be vested with pastoral associations. Forest dwellers should be given responsibility to manage the forests where they live and they should be assured of priority, or even exclusive, rights to hunt, gather, and carry out artisanal logging. In return, they should be entrusted with the obligation and requisite authority to protect these forests against farmer encroachment, poaching, and illegal logging and fuelwood extraction. If the state is less intrusive and local people are given greater responsibility, people will tend to take more care in conserving their environment (especially if the other actions discussed here are also taken).

Resource management interventions must emphasize the social arrangements among people as they interact with each other and with their natural resource base, paying particular attention to incentives and sanctions for influencing individual behavior. "[Every] aspect of the interrelationship between society and nature plays a critical role and if one of them fails then the whole situation is likely to be severely affected" (Timberlake 1986:42). Natural resource management projects that do not actively involve the local users will fail. National, and even regional, governments cannot effectively manage local natural resources. The sheer scale of the soil and water conservation problems faced in many countries dictates the need to create the necessary conditions for local people and communities to take matters into their own hands again. Programs and projects must become more concerned with the people using natural resources and less preoccupied with the commodities around which projects have traditionally been organized. An essential ingredient in program and project formulation and implementation is the existence of incentives and sanctions for influencing the behavior of those who live in the area and who depend for their livelihood and survival on the natural resources in question (Bromley and Cernea 1989).

Traditional land and natural resource management systems may not have been ideal, but their subtleties need to be objectively and realistically assessed. There is the danger that an overly zealous, albeit well-meaning, effort will destroy an imperfect but functioning system, only to create a replacement that hardly functions at all. Promising pilot operations in land management are now under way in a number of countries. The existence of pastoral associations in Senegal and Niger, village land management and water conservation efforts in Burkina Faso, and the *comités du village* in Mali have demonstrated that careful attention to the needs and practices of local people can generate enthusiasm for positive action. These examples suggest that some governments are beginning to have enough political confidence to relinquish control over resources to local groups as well as the political determination to enact legislation that will support such initiatives. They also show that local communities can improve their situation when they believe their efforts will pay off (Falloux and Mukendi 1988).

Whether governments will be willing or able to recognize or create centers of authority and initiative in rural areas remains to be seen. Some governments are already making firm commitments in that direction. Smaller organizational units, such as village or pastoral associations, are better equipped to manage their own resources. Recognizing this is prerequisite for implementing strategies aimed at improving production systems and land use. These local associations might provide a more effective basis for rural development and rational resources management than previous efforts that imposed external institutions on rural societies. Group action is deeply rooted in most societies of Sub-Saharan Africa — for managing land, for cooperative marketing and input supply, for pooling savings and financing credit, for pooling labor for critical tasks at critical times. To succeed, cooperation has to be voluntary and managed from below. Grassroots management is one way to ensure this. Alternatively, cooperatives can be based on customary social structures and groups, as they often are. Governments can provide technical assistance, such as advice on accounting, legal rights, and technology, and should provide for legal arrangements that facilitate the creation, recognition, and dissolution of cooperatives.

The single most important lesson that has been learned is the need for popular participation and action at the village and community level — using and developing local skills and responding to the particular characteristics of each area (Shaxson and others 1989:12–14). Identifying concrete practical mechanisms to foster popular support is critical. Grassroots organizations and local NGOs have a particularly valuable role to play in this respect. Channeling financial resources, to the extent these are needed, to and through them is important, but more important will be meeting their urgent need for institutional strengthening and training in such critical areas as program planning, management and leadership skills, accounting, financial planning and management, and information sharing (Newman 1992). Governments, international aid agencies, and international NGOs alike will need to find ways to provide this critical support.

Conclusion

The experience of Machakos District in Kenya demonstrates that the right policy framework and investments of the kind recommended here will work to address agricultural growth, environmental conservation, and human resource development (English and others 1994; Tiffen and others 1994). Significant soil degradation and erosion was observed in Machakos as early as 1920. Substantial efforts have been undertaken over the past sixty years to combat these problems and to prevent further deterioration. By 1990, with nearly five times the population as in 1920, the district's agricultural production had increased more than fivefold — yet land degradation had not merely been arrested, it had been reversed. Real incomes and general welfare have increased.

The ingredients to this success have been those recommended in this chapter. The government has provided a generally good macroeconomic and agricultural policy environment, which has made intensive and market-oriented farming profitable. Relatively good transport infrastructure facilitated the movement of farm inputs and output at affordable costs. Land tenure security, achieved through a combination of respect for traditional land rights and slowly expanding individualized land titling, encouraged farmer investment in land. Rural education and health services have also been relatively good. Agricultural research and extension efforts in the district have been excellent since before independence and have included emphasis on soil conservation efforts, tree planting, and low-cost crop husbandry. In this setting, and particularly because the economic incentives were good, farmers were receptive to good extension advice regarding soil conservation, moisture retention, and the intensification of farming and tree planting, and they have applied these measures on a wide scale. Local farmers' groups are playing an increasingly important role in planning and implementing community activities. Efforts to slow population growth are only now beginning to show the desired impact, but the combined effect of these various measures has been so positive in Machakos District that photographs taken of the same sites in 1930 and again in 1989/90 show the improvement of the rural environment — including the increase in the number of trees.

Notes

1. According to medical studies, the "admissible workload" for a healthy person would be 300 kcal per hour in agricultural field work at 27°C (or about 80°F) with no insolation, but only 225 kcal working with full insolation. A sick worker working in full insolation can only expend about 180 kcal/hour. At 30°C, a healthy worker in the shade can put in about 150 kcal/hour, while sick people should be resting in the shade (Ruthenberg 1985:78, citing H. Brandt, "Work Capacity Constraints in Tropical Agriculture Development," in *Medizin in Entwicklungsländern*, 1980, Heft 8, Verlag P.D. Lang, Frankfurt, Germany).

2. This approach is discussed and analyzed in detail in FAO/World Bank Cooperative Programme (1991), and a pilot land resource conservation project recently initiated with World Bank support in Ghana will attempt to test it in practice (IBRD 1992c).

3. In mixed cropping systems in the humid tropical forest zone, twenty to thirty different species appear to be the "norm" on a single farm, but as many as sixty species have been found. In the semiarid regions, fifteen to twenty species appear to be the normal range for a single farm (Dommen 1988:36).

4. See Reij, Mulder and Begemann (1988) for an extensive review of technical, environmental, agronomic, economic, and sociological aspects of water harvesting.

5. This argument is well developed in Shanmugaratnam and others (1992).

6. Greathead and Waage (1983) discuss various possibilities for biological control of agricultural pests, and substantial research findings have been accumulated since then. See also Kiss and Meerman (1991), Singh (1990), and Odhiambo (1991).

7. The presence of *Acacia albida*, a leguminous tree often found in fields sown to millet, sorghum, or groundnut in much of the Sahelo-Sudanian Zone, consistently increases the yield of the associated field crops. The tree has many appealing features. A particularly important one is that it sheds its leaves during the rainy season and therefore does not compete with crops for light and moisture. The tree gives ample shade during the dry, hot season, and its leaf litter provides nitrogen and organic matter to farmers' fields. Yields have been found

to be about twice as high under the trees as they are beyond its crown. Each tree also supplies about 75–125 kg of nutritious pods per year for livestock feed (Gritzner 1988:99).

8. In the countries of the West African Sahelo-Sudanian Zone, exchange rate distortions have made the recommended agricultural intensification and anti-desertification activities simply not sufficiently productive, below the 800 mm isohyet, to make their widespread adoption financially worthwhile (Gorse and Steeds 1987:31–32). The recent exchange rate realignment for the countries of the CFA zone should considerably improve the financial viability of these techniques for farmers in these countries.

9

Infrastructure Development, Migration, and Urbanization

Infrastructure Development

The most basic elements of rural physical infrastructure comprise rural roads, markets in rural towns, and rural water supply facilities. In some areas, irrigation and drainage facilities would also be essential to facilitate agricultural production. At a somewhat higher level of development, infrastructure also includes rural electrification as well as telecommunications facilities and access to electronic mass media. Defined more broadly, rural infrastructure also includes educational, health, and sanitation facilities. Given the critical importance of such facilities — or, more importantly, of the services they provide — for the development and maintenance of "human capital" in rural areas, these are indeed crucial in the context of the nexus.

The importance of basic rural infrastructure for agricultural development is well established. Remunerative output prices accelerate the pace of agricultural intensification — provided they are effectively transmitted to the farm. Incentives to increase production and marketed output are blunted if the physical barriers and, hence, the costs of moving goods to and from local markets are too high. This is equally true of the national transport system linking local markets to cities and ports. Recent research in Asia found that in villages with better infrastructure, fertilizer costs were 14 percent lower, wages were 12 percent higher, and crop output was 32 percent higher (IFPRI 1991). Similar findings would be likely for Sub-Saharan Africa, though no comparable analysis is available yet. Research in a number of SSA countries has shown that adequate road links to product markets stimulate agricultural intensification — even where population densities are comparatively low (Pingali and others 1987). Farmers with access to roads and transport infrastructure use land more intensively, adopt efficient techniques and modern inputs, produce more for the market, and employ more labor.

Infrastructure development also has a major effect on the productivity of rural labor and on key determinants of human fertility, such as infant mortality and female education. Roads provide access to health facilities and schools, and water supply schemes and sanitation facilities have significant impact on health and on labor productivity. Education, health, water supply and sanitation facilities and services are particularly important in terms of their impact on female education and on infant mortality — both critical determinants of fertility preferences (see Chapters 3 and 7).

Transport

Rural transport infrastructure is highly deficient in most countries of Sub-Saharan Africa, and throughout most of the continent the distances from villages to major towns and to all-weather roads are substantial. Rural road density has been estimated at about 32 m/km^2 in West Africa and 36 m/km^2 in East Africa and southern Africa. Moreover, Nigeria, Cameroon, and Côte d'Ivoire account for more than half the rural roads in West Africa, and Tanzania, Zaïre, Zimbabwe, and Madagascar have more than two-thirds of the rural roads in East Africa and southern Africa (Riverson, Gaviria and Thriscutt 1991:4), so that these average data significantly overstate the true situation in most countries. In Nigeria, with its fairly dense network of rural roads by African standards, rural road density today is about 90 m/km^2, roughly equal that of India in 1951; a reasonable target density, based on Indian areas with comparable population densities would be 730 m/km^2 (Riverson, Gaviria and Thriscutt 1991:4). Rural road densities also vary considerably within countries, being generally higher in areas with higher population densities and productive natural resource endowments. In Kenya, for example, rural road density ranges from 400–500 m/km^2 to less than 30 m/km^2 (Riverson, Gaviria and Thriscutt 1991:4).

Where rural roads exist, they often are poorly maintained. Indeed, maintenance standards deteriorated considerably during the 1980s: 42 percent of unpaved roads in West Africa and 47 percent in East Africa were in poor condition in 1988, compared with 28 percent and 44 percent, respectively, in 1984 (Carapetis, Levy and Wolden 1991a:12).

The availability and reliability of transport services is frequently further compromised by restrictive transport sector policies and trucking regulations. Transport monopolies, for example, are often granted to parastatal companies or to well-connected individuals, and entry into the industry is often restricted even where there are no monopolies. Inefficient procurement and distribution of motor fuels by monopolistic parastatals is another impediment in a number of countries. Price con-

---

Box 9-1   Rural Transport in Ghana

A field study in Ghana's Ashanti, Volta, and Northern regions (Barwell and others 1987) found walking and headloading to be the predominant means of rural travel and transport. Transport activities for an average household, numbering 11.4 persons, involved an average of about 4,800 hours (with a range from 3,740 to 6,210 hours) per year and a load-carrying effort of 234 ton-km per year (ranging from 185 t-km to 315 t-km). It comprised 54 t-km for water fetching, 20 t-km for firewood gathering, 75 t-km for crop harvesting, 77 t-km for crop marketing, and 8 t-km for carrying produce to and from the food grinding mill. About three-quarters of the load-carrying effort and time spent involved transport in and around the village.

Women accounted for about three-fourths of the total loads carried. The average adult woman spent 977 hours per year, or 19 hours per week, on transport activities, mainly headloading. This involved water carrying (11.8 t-km per year per woman), crop harvesting (13.1 t-km), crop marketing (14.7 t-km), fuelwood collection (5.0 t-km), and food processing (2.0 t-km). Male involvement in transport was far less, about 346 hours per year per adult male, and was almost entirely crop-related (harvesting, 7.9 t-km; marketing, 2.9 t-km), with little involvement in transporting water (0.8 t-km) and fuelwood (0.5 t-km).

---

trols on motor fuels tend to reduce fuel availability in the countryside because they make it unprofitable to invest in transporting and selling motor fuels in locations distant from the port cities.

As a result, markets are poorly integrated, interregional and interseasonal price variations are far greater than they would be with efficient transport facilities, and incentives to switch from subsistence to market production are often weak. Where there is surplus farm produce, it often has to be carried over considerable distances to markets or to roadsides from where vehicles can move it to processing facilities or consuming centers. Women bear the brunt of the rural transport burden, because much of rural commodity transport (water, fuel, farm inputs, and farm produce) is done in the form of headloading by women. Studies throughout Sub-Saharan Africa show that women and older girls carry loads of 10–25 kg (sometimes as much as 40 kg) and can manage 3–5 km per hour, depending on terrain and load weight.

Rural roads and improved tracks navigable for animal-drawn vehicles are crucial for rural development. Planning, construction, and maintenance should involve the local communities as well as local contractors and technicians. This will help ensure that siting is in accordance with local needs, make maximum use of labor-intensive techniques to keep down costs, and provide local off-season employment.

Major efforts are also needed to promote the use of locally appropriate intermediate means of transport (IMT). Referring to transport technology intermediate between walking and headloading on the one hand and motor vehicles on the other, IMT cover a wide range: improved aids for human porterage (shoulder bars, yokes, backpacks), panniers and rigs for pack animals, animal-drawn sleds and wheeled vehicles, wheelbarrows and handcarts, bicycles, tricycles, trailers, and so on. Especially needed in rural SSA are animal-drawn implements and improved off-road transport. Governmental involvement here would have to be largely facilitative and promotional. Improvements in off-road transport are essential for the well-being and productivity of rural people. The extremely poor state of off-road transport in much of Sub-Saharan Africa severely reduces the timeliness and quantities of agricultural inputs and outputs moved to and from motorable roads, thus acting as a strong impediment to agricultural productivity and growth (Riverson, Gaviria and Thriscutt 1991; Riverson and Carapetis 1990). Rural women in particular will benefit considerably from such improvements — with significant follow-on benefits in terms of the various nexus linkages.

Farmers need information about technical options and market opportunities. Improved communications are required generally, including not only transportation but also telecommunications and access to electronic mass media. The latter also have significant potential for reaching rural populations with health and educational information, including information on family planning and the prevention of sexually transmitted diseases.

Water Supply

The rural water supply situation constitutes another key constraint — and an important link in the nexus. Less than 20 percent of Nigeria's rural population, for instance, have convenient access to safe water. There is a direct link between safe potable water and the reduction of infant mortality, and efforts to provide safe water and sanitation facilities have been motivated mainly by these and other direct health considerations. Throughout much of Sub-Saharan Africa water-borne and water-related pathogens are major causes of seasonally or permanently debilitating diseases, which severely effect, among other things, labor productivity — and often especially during periods of peak demand for farm labor. Women's stake in convenient access to safe water and sanitation facilities is particularly high. They have almost exclusive responsibility for collecting, transporting, boiling, and storing water for drinking and cooking and for washing household effects and laundry, for disposing of waste water, and for maintaining household sanitation standards and facilities. Women have to determine the water sources that can be used for various purposes (drinking, washing, cooking, watering domestic animals and home gardens, and so on); collect, transport, and store the water; and purify drinking water using simple techniques and locally available materials (Dankelman and Davidson 1988:32). In rural Kenya, 89 percent of the women over age 14, but only 5 percent of the men, reported fetching water as one of their normal tasks; the same percentages were reported for fetching fuelwood (Kenya 1980). Access to sufficient quantities of quality water is an increasingly more time-consuming problem for many rural women. A study in Kirinyaga, Kenya, found that 70 percent of trips that involve carrying a load are for fetching water (Kaira 1982).

Assuming a daily requirement of, say, only ten liters of water per person, a six-member household needs 60 liters of water daily — almost 22 *tons of water each year.* If a women carries 20 liters of water per trip (provided she has the appropriate vessels), she would have to make three trips daily to the water source — or have her daughter(s) help her with this chore. If the water source is twenty minutes away from the home, about two hours daily will be needed to meet the household's water needs. If young girls are responsible for fetching water, they carry smaller loads and, hence, will need to go more often. The workload increases substantially if water also has to be brought home for watering domestic animals and the home garden, brewing beer, processing cassava, making mud bricks, or other production tasks requiring water. Additional trips to the water source, each with considerable loads to be carried, are required for bathing small children and for washing laundry, pots, and kitchen utensils.

Drastic changes in the rural landscape brought about by deforestation, often exacerbated by prolonged drought, have made water more difficult to obtain. Springs and streams run dry for long periods, and wells go dry as the water table recedes. In some areas, water sources have become polluted or contaminated: in parts of Zimbabwe, for example, women used to get water from wells in the fields where they worked, but these have become contaminated by fertilizer (Nyoni 1985:55).

Convenient sources of safe water are of enormous importance for human health and, hence, labor productivity, and contribute substantially to reductions in infant mortality and child morbidity and mortality. A major benefit to women and girls of better access to safe water is that time formerly spent fetching water from distant sources and preparing it for human use can be used instead for other productive activities, attending school or training, tending to children's health and educational needs, or simply resting and recuperating. Water supply projects should be planned and implemented, if not operated, with and by local women. Good examples of successful water supply projects based on women's groups are those of the Kenya Water for Health Organisation (KWAHO), an NGO consortium supported by the government, UNDP, UNIFEM, and the World Bank. In Kwale district, KWAHO has organized cooperative handpump installation and maintenance using female extension workers, village decisionmaking, and local materials and labor, backed by training in health, water use, pump maintenance, bookkeeping, and group organization (Dankelman and Davidson 1988).

Infrastructure and Environmental Conservation

Infrastructure development is a major determinant of the way people use land and of the spatial allocation of people on land. Sound infrastructure policy is therefore a powerful instrument in the two-pronged strategy to intensify agricultural production and to limit further destruction of forest and pasture areas. The development of infrastructure tends to attract and retain people. The many instances of colonists invading forests via abandoned logging roads provide a powerful illustration. Conversely, the absence of infrastructure in areas that are environmentally delicate will tend to induce people to stay out of those areas. Careful locational targeting of infrastructure development can guide spontaneous population movement into environmentally robust or resilient areas with agricultural potential and into secondary towns and cities, and help keep migrants out of areas that should not be opened up to farming.

Infrastructure development, and especially road construction, should be focused where the potential for agricultural intensification is highest and settlement is to be encouraged. It should be avoided in forest areas that are to be conserved and in other environmentally fragile areas where an influx of people would lead to environmental degradation and destruction. Concentrating infrastructure development and thereby attracting/retaining people in areas of high production potential and keeping them out of environmentally fragile areas also allows considerable efficiencies in investments and service provision, since the per capita cost of infrastructure development and maintenance is inversely related to population density.

Migration and Settlement Policy

Given the considerable agroecological diversity in most countries of Sub-Saharan Africa, the development and adoption of suitable productivity-enhancing and environmentally appropriate agricultural technology will of necessity have to be highly region- and even location-specific. This will, over time, engender significant regional disparities in agricultural production and income growth. Governments will need to resist the urge to correct for this by targeting scarce public resources to the lagging regions. Allowing, facilitating, and encouraging migration from the lagging to the thriving regions is the appropriate policy response. This is particularly important when the lagging regions are likely to be those that have less agricultural potential and are environmentally more fragile.

In many areas, therefore, part of the solution to the problems of unsustainable agriculture and environmental destruction will have to involve some movement of people. This is the case, for example, in much of the Sahelo-Sudanian Zone, where movement should be encouraged to the Sudano-Guinean Zone farther south as well as to areas within the Sahelo-Sudanian Zone itself that can still absorb more people. Nigeria's "middle belt," for instance, remains relatively underpopulated, compared with the country's northern and southern regions, and holds considerable untapped potential for agricultural development. The same is true for much of Ghana's Brong-Ahafo and Northern regions. In both cases, as in other countries, ethnic diversity and land tenure issues help explain the uneven population distribution.

Migration is multisectoral in nature and, in the context of rural Sub-Saharan Africa, closely linked to the problems of rising population pressure, land tenure uncertainties, poor land use, and environmental resource degradation. Large-scale migration within and between African countries is inevitable in the future, given rapid population growth and the limited absorptive capacity in many rural areas. Without strengthening tenurial arrangements to provide greater security, it will be as difficult to channel migration and settle migrants as it will be to protect and improve their host environments. A sound migration policy must consider the land use rights of farmers, transhumant pastoralists, and forest dwellers.

Migration can be used as a positive development tool — if it is linked to a well-conceived settlement program. In many cases, migration can balance resource demand with resource availability. Regional surveys of migration, both quantitative (who, how many, from where, and to where) and qualitative (motivations and aspirations), should be carried out in the most sensitive areas of immigration. Without land rights that are confirmed by both custom and law, migrants have no incentive to protect or restore their land. Neither will the residents be able to protect themselves and their resource base from incoming migrants (Falloux and Mukendi 1988). This has happened in Côte d'Ivoire, for instance, where massive unplanned immigration of Sahelian farmers into open-access forests has contributed to rapid forest destruction, widespread land disputes, and a lack of incentives to conserve the land.

Redistributing population — to reduce pressures on the environment on the one hand and to accelerate the transition to intensive farming on the other — requires identifying areas of high agricultural and economic potential, improving infrastructure and services (roads, water supply, schools, health facilities, markets) in these areas, and encouraging people to move to the high potential areas and into rural towns and secondary cities. Governments should normally include population distribution as a part of their policy to accommodate population growth. Spontaneous movement of people, in search of a better livelihood, in pursuit of trade, and to find seasonal or permanent employment, has been occurring for a long time within countries and across borders. Cross-border movement has helped ease population pressure in the areas from which people emigrate — such as the Sahel or Rwanda. But such movements have sometimes been restricted or reversed because of political and ethnic conflicts. Benefits of population migration certainly accrue to the individual migrants and often to the communities from which they migrate. Often there also are significant economic benefits for the communities receiving the migrants. The Sahelian farmers settling in Côte d'Ivoire have been a dynamic force for agricultural growth (although, as noted above, there have also been significant costs associated with their absorption into the Ivorian environment). The benefits and costs need to be realistically assessed, and migration, though better anticipated and prepared for, must be allowed to continue. Such movement of people is also consistent with African aspirations to encourage and promote regional cooperation.

There are two main types of rural-rural migration: spontaneous and uncontrolled migration, and government-sponsored organized migration and resettlement. Spontaneous migration involves no direct costs to the public treasury. It is quick for the individuals who move, but in most cases takes place gradually enough to preclude social and economic upheavals in the receiving areas. Unfortunately, it also often tends to lead to poor land use practices, because migrants bring with them the farming and land use experiences and traditions from the area they left, and these are often inappropriate to their new environment. This is particularly the case where settlers invade forest areas opened up by loggers (see Chapter 8). Organized migration, on the other hand, usually entails high costs and is characterized by slow implementation. It, too, has often resulted in poor land use, as planning and implementing agencies have tended to promote settlement, resource use, and production patterns poorly matched to the settlers' own needs, perceptions, and capabilities.

The required strategy, therefore, lies somewhere between these two. It should channel, train, and support migrants, combining incentives for and controls over land use practices with the development of sustainable and viable production systems. It makes far more sense for governments to promote and support spontaneous migration and settlement than to undertake organized colonization schemes. It will be essential to devise and implement enforceable land use regulations to promote sustainable settlement.

An Appropriate Urbanization Policy

During the past three decades, Sub-Saharan Africa's urban population has grown about twice as fast as its total population. In a number of countries the rate of urbanization has been even faster. It has been especially high in West, Central, and East Africa, relatively more modest in southern Africa (Montgomery and Brown 1990:76). The rapid growth of cities is due not only to the persistent high fertility rates among urban women in SSA, but in large part to the very high rate of rural-urban migration. This "land flight" is caused in part by the strong urban bias inherent in the economic and investment policies of almost all SSA countries.

In much of Sub-Saharan Africa, rural out-migration involves predominantly young men (Russell, Jacobsen, and Stanley 1990a). Where policy has a heavy urban bias, this is particularly pronounced. As women, children, and the old stay behind, farm management is increasingly left to women, who already have multiple and very heavy workloads and who face far greater constraints in access to resources and services than men (see Chapter 5). Many rural areas are characterized today by severely imbalanced gender ratios in their adult population, with women substantially outnumbering men. In addition, if the migrants abandon resilient and productive areas in pursuit of urban jobs and in response to antiagricultural policy biases, this has a negative impact on agricultural production and rural development in the areas they leave.

Experience throughout the world suggests that urban populations have grown and will continue to grow much faster than rural populations — even if governments were to pursue policies that do not favor urban over rural dwellers. What is needed, therefore, is an urbanization and urban development policy that also promotes agricultural development and preserves the integrity of the environment.

Where government policy discourages agricultural production and encourages agricultural imports to supply urban needs, there will be no positive impact of urbanization on agriculture. This has tended to be the case in countries where urban development policy has focused heavily

**Figure 9-1   Urban Population as Percentage of Total Population
in Sub-Saharan Africa, 1960–1990**

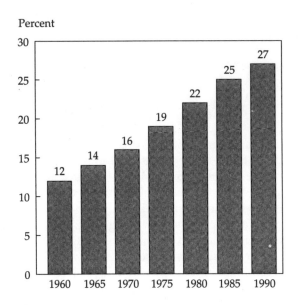

Percent

Note: Data for 41 countries of Sub-Saharan Africa.

on the capital or on a few dominant cities, inevitably more distant from rural hinterlands. Manifestations of such policy and expenditure bias are the subsidization of the consumption of urban populations (often based on imported food), preoccupation with large urban infrastructure projects, and focus of social expenditures in a few cities. The political influence of growing, massed, and vocal urban populations results in political pressure to keep food prices low and to target public investments and services disproportionately to the big cities. The result is the extraordinarily low level of public investment in rural roads, water, health, and education observed in much of Sub-Saharan Africa. Where governments have effectively resisted this pressure, the results have been positive for agricultural profitability and growth: Kenya, Togo, and Zimbabwe are cases in point.

Some countries have pursued policies that have led to the emergence of numerous and geographically dispersed secondary cities and rural towns closely linked with their surrounding rural areas (for example, Cameroon, Côte d'Ivoire, Kenya, Nigeria, Togo). They also have a few very large cities (notably Abidjan, Nairobi, Lagos, Ibadan), but urbanization in these countries has also been characterized by the development of many smaller cities and rural towns throughout much of the national territory. This has had important positive effects on agriculture. These towns and cities have created nonagricultural employment opportunities for some of the rural population, and this industrial and service sector development has been very closely linked to agriculture and to the needs of rural populations. Cash remittances to home villages are an important source of financing of both consumption and investment expenditures in rural areas. Urban growth creates expanding markets for farm products and tends to lead to increased supply and availability of farm inputs and services. This can make agriculture more profitable — provided there are adequate transport links and marketing arrangements. Where networks of rural towns and secondary cities exist, these links are more direct, immediate, and efficient. Dispersed rural towns and secondary cities tend to be associated with far greater penetration of rural areas with adequate transport links and marketing arrangements than are distant megacities. For areas that are approaching the limits of sustainable agricultural land use under existing tenurial, technological, and climatic conditions, migration to secondary towns and cities reduces the population pressure and provides an important safety valve.

Considered in the context of the nexus, urbanization is both a result and a cause of environmental resource degradation. People leave rural areas when they can no longer make a living there (or at least not year-round). Urban dwellers, especially the vast numbers of poor, require fuelwood and food. Urbanization concentrates demand at specific locations. The heavy concentration of urban populations in a single capital city (often on the coast, rather than at a central inland location) makes things worse. Huge concentrations of people in a single location, coupled with high transport costs for domestically produced supplies, tend to make it easier and cheaper to import food than to obtain it from domestic producers. Government policies in most of Sub-Saharan Africa tend to keep producer prices of food and fuelwood low, reducing incentives for intensification of local food and wood production. Food imports, often sold at subsidized prices, further undermine the incentives for domestic producers. Imports can also lead to major changes in consumer preferences that may diminish demand for local products and be nutritionally undesirable. Fuelwood suppliers, responding to the dual opportunities presented by large concentrations of demand and virtually free access to the raw material base, mine the forests and woodlands around the cities and along roads.

Ensuring that urbanization promotes agricultural development and environmental resource conservation requires economic policies that do not discriminate against rural areas (for instance through discriminatory pricing, tax, and investment promotion policies). It also requires a better balance between rural and urban areas in public investments in social and physical infrastructure. The more rapid agricultural growth that will occur in the absence of such discrimination is likely to have a positive impact on the economies of Africa's cities and their inhabitants.

Greater focus on secondary cities and rural towns, in infrastructure investment and urban development generally, and a reduced bias to invest in the megacities, will provide a beneficial rural-urban link. Powerful synergies can be tapped here. The examples of Cameroon, Kenya, and Togo show that rapid urbanization tends to occur in secondary cities and rural towns (rather than in megacities) if governments implement policies to promote agricultural development and rural growth (Becker and Morrison 1988). Agricultural growth is an essential lever to stimulate nonagricultural investment and growth as well as to influence population distribution.

A recent analysis of farm-nonfarm linkages in rural Sub-Saharan Africa found that each unit of increased agricultural income generated an additional increase of half a unit in nonagricultural rural incomes. The direction of causality was largely agricultural growth stimulating growth in services and manufacturing. Of the additional rural income generated, only about 20 percent was attributable to production linkages, but about 80 percent to consumption linkages (Haggblade and Hazell 1988; Haggblade, Hazell and Brown 1989). This stimulation of nonfarm activities and incomes in rural areas is less likely to occur when biased policies retard or prevent the development of secondary towns and cities and instead cut off rural areas and agriculture from the megacity and make the latter more dependent on imports. Sound urban policy, favoring rural towns and secondary cities over megacities, is an important element to ensure balanced urban and rural development.

The strong consumption linkages found between agricultural growth and nonagricultural production are likely to have significant positive effects on the real incomes of the rural poor — given the importance of female-dominated food processing and beverage production and of service and manufacturing activities with low investment requirements. They are also likely to stimulate production of fruits, vegetables, and meat and, thus, agricultural intensification and diversification into higher-value products, with positive effects for rural income equity where, if, and as long as these commodities are produced by smallholders and pastoralists. The production linkages of increased agricultural incomes on rural equity depend heavily on the respective rates of growth of demand for agricultural wage labor and for purchased inputs, both of which are currently at very low levels (Haggblade and Hazell 1988; Haggblade, Hazell and Brown 1989).

A sound urban development policy will involve relatively more public expenditure in secondary towns and cities and less in the few large cities than has generally been the case to date. It will require spatially well-distributed infrastructure investment throughout the country (not merely in the largest cities). Market-based petroleum pricing will be essential to promote the development of efficient transport fuel distribution systems throughout each country. Small and medium-scale industry will need to be promoted — through industrial extension as well as fiscal and credit policies. Sound policy will also require considerable decentralization of decisionmaking to local people and rural communities to avoid undue dominance of the major cities and their populations in national political decisionmaking. And there will have to be greater community control over urban resources: given adequate financial resources and the requisite technical and administrative assistance, local and community governments are more likely to create and maintain appropriately scaled and sited urban infrastructure facilities than are central governments. Investment in urban development should be responsive to demand for such investment, not driven by political considerations.

10
Managing the Natural Resource Base

Production versus Protection

The environmental issues that are linked to population and agriculture are primarily those involved with soil, water, and vegetation. There are, of course, many other environmental problems facing Sub-Saharan Africa — such as over-fishing in coastal waters, oil spills, dumping of hazardous wastes, pollution from urban sewage and industrial waste, land devastation from surface mining, and so forth. These problems are not, however, so closely related to rapid population growth and laggard agricultural growth and therefore are not dealt with here.

Governments must be more determined in developing and implementing environmental policies aimed at: (a) maintaining and restoring, in the face of increasing consumption demands, the soil, water, pasture, and forest resources on which agriculture will continue to be based, and (b) preserving ecosystems and plant and animal species — as repositories of genetic diversity that may underlie future production of many types of products, and as a national and global heritage. Solving the population and agricultural aspects of the problem are crucial to curtailing degradation of the natural environment. Agricultural intensification, farm forestry and fuelwood programs, and sensible land tenure reform are critical factors, as discussed in Chapter 8. However, moving from the present situation of rapid deforestation, wetland conversion, and land degradation to one of stabilizing the area under trees, raising the efficiency of fuelwood use, preserving much of the remaining wilderness areas, and reversing the degradation of soils will require an "affirmative action program" of considerable consequence. Such a program will need to comprise a number of elements beyond those discussed in Chapter 8.

An essential first step is to determine which areas should and can be maintained as protected areas, and which should be allowed to be

176

developed for production (cropping, forestry, livestock, fisheries). Criteria for selecting natural ecosystems for preservation and protection include:

- Biological importance, notably richness (diversity, numbers) and uniqueness of species and complexity of the ecosystem: the greater the importance, the more important the need for full protection.

- Provision of "environmental services," such as prevention of soil erosion or of destructive flooding, recharge of aquifers, maintenance of river flow, provision of breeding grounds for marine life: the greater the value of such services, the greater will be the importance of protection.

- Importance for the survival of indigenous peoples and their livelihood systems, especially of forest dwellers: where indigenous peoples depend for physical and/or cultural survival on an area remaining undisturbed, the need for protection becomes imperative.

- Productive potential if converted to other uses such as cropping or livestock production: the greater the productive potential under alternative uses, the less viable the decision to protect fully.

- Current status, i.e., whether or not the ecosystem is already degraded or spatially constricted to an extent where it is no longer stable and wildlife populations are no longer sustainable: the less viable a particular ecosystem, the less viable a decision to protect it fully.

- Likelihood of success of preservation — which depends on the type and degree of present threats (such as human population pressure) that reduce the likelihood of success versus the potential for supporting nonexploitative economic activities (such as eco-tourism), which increase the likelihood of success.

These criteria imply tradeoffs. In many cases they will involve the need to make difficult choices. If one basic objective is to limit the decline in Sub-Saharan Africa's total wilderness areas (from their present extent of 27 percent of the total land area to not less than 23 percent, as postulated in Chapter 6), these criteria will need to be applied with considerable stringency. Since natural resource systems, including forests, have multiple uses, there can be no substitute for some form of planning. Land use plans should identify conservation areas, parks, areas designated for sustainable logging, farming areas, pasture and rangeland, as well as areas needed and suitable for human settlements and physical infrastructure. Agricultural technology is location-specific in its applications, and land use plans therefore should identify, in broad terms, the appropriate technologies. Land tenure issues and fuelwood problems also are location-specific — as are many of the cultural factors that help determine human fertility. Regional plans should define these, with considerably more weight attached to resource conservation than in the past.

The widespread skepticism concerning the utility of such plans is based on the fact that most past attempts at land use planning and regional planning have not worked well in Sub-Saharan Africa. The reasons included often excessive complexity of such plans, lack of governmental capacity to prepare and implement realistic plans, and frequent lack of incentives to cooperate for the people living in the areas concerned. In most cases, and especially those concerning forest areas, very little, if any, attention was paid to land tenure issues, identification of appropriate agricultural technology in forest areas, participation of local people and of the private sector, and provision of adequate incentives to cooperate for loggers, farmers, hunter-gatherers, livestock owners, and forest dwellers. Instead, nearly universally applied were "engineering solutions," implemented by public sector agencies or donor-supported project management units which sought to manage forest areas independently of people and of companies operating in the forests.

A different approach is necessary — both for planning and for management. It must greatly increase the role of local people and the private sector in planning and implementation; it must be evolutionary and adaptive, rather than rigid; and it must be simple to execute. If the role of governments is confined primarily to providing the legislative backing and to planning and supervision, land use planning becomes more manageable. And if assistance for carrying out these more limited functions is provided through the collaborative mechanisms established for preparing National Environmental Action Plans (NEAPs) and Tropical Forestry Action Plans (TFAPs), adopting this approach is a realistic strategy.

It is increasingly recognized that maintenance of protected areas requires the direct involvement of the local and surrounding populations. It is unrealistic to expect local people to conserve forest and wildlife resources unless such conservation provides them with clear benefits. The exclusionary approach so often taken in protected areas in the past is neither workable nor sustainable nor equitable. Governments cannot financially afford and effectively provide the degree of enforcement needed. And the local people, frequently among the poorest, are left to bear the costs of restricted or prohibited access to resources, exposure to marauding wildlife, and other disadvantages associated with living on the edge of a closed off territory.

The local people therefore must be active participants in both planning and implementation of land and resource use. This requires: (a) appropriate incentives and (b) collaborative planning and implementation of resource management plans. Incentives are far more likely than governmental regulation, control, and enforcement to be effective tools for inducing people to conserve essential stocks of natural resources. The most important incentive to ensure resource conservation is clearly defined and uncontested resource ownership: it entails the certainty that the yield or benefits derived from resources conserved will continue to accrue to the current owners/users and their descendants, but also that resource degradation will be a cost directly borne by them. This is best accomplished by ensuring people's ownership of the land and of the natural resources on that land — or, where government ownership is to continue, by providing legally binding and protected long-term use rights. Under the right economic conditions, this provides strong and direct incentives to conserve and to invest in resource conservation or productivity enhancement. Conversely, loss of ownership or exclusive user rights, or ambiguities concerning these, create incentives to exploit without regard to sustainability.

Appropriate resource management plans should be prepared in a collaborative manner — involving the concerned communities, technically competent government agency staff, and, where they exist and enjoy the local people's confidence, grassroots organizations and NGOs. Participatory rural appraisal (PRA) techniques provide very effective tools to do this. These techniques have been developed and refined in the 1980s, evolving from Rapid Rural Appraisal (RRA) techniques and agroecosystem analyses, to ensure intensive involvement by the local populations in all aspects of local land use planning — such as resource inventory, problem diagnosis, resource use planning, action plan formulation, etc. (see, for instance, Chambers 1991).

Forests

About 30 percent of Sub-Saharan Africa's land area is classified as forests or woodlands. But only about 28 percent of this area is closed forest — compared with about two-thirds in Latin America and in Asia. About 34 percent is shrubland and 38 percent is savanna woodland; both are multiple-use resource systems, utilized for meeting local requirements for fuelwood and other tree and forest products as well as for farming and forage.

As discussed in Chapter 2, Sub-Saharan Africa's forest area is diminishing at a rate of about 2.9 million ha per year, and the rate of decline is accelerating. The most important causes of deforestation are conversion to farmland, infrastructure development in environmentally delicate

Box 10-1   Integrated Conservation and Development

Reflecting the recognition that effective resource conservation and management must involve strong local participation, the concept of "integrated conservation and development" is being developed. It involves the following key aspects:

- Local people retain the rights to continued traditional utilization of resources inside state-owned protected areas (to the extent that this is not detrimental to the ecosystem) and are, of course, allowed to continue such activities on all land returned outright to them.
- The local communities are allowed to generate income from protected areas through environmentally compatible activities such as tourism, hunting with traditional weapons, and gathering of non-timber forest products. All of these activities are directly dependent on the protected area. Local communities given exclusive rights to carry out these activities will have an incentive to conserve the forest or wilderness area.
- Commercial logging of protected areas is entirely excluded. Logging can be allowed and carefully managed only in those areas specifically identified for logging, but even then only with techniques and management practices that ensure long-term sustainability.
- Buffer zones are established around core protected areas, and ownership of the land and associated resources in them is returned to the local people. Buffer zones are meant to provide the local people with sufficient forest and agricultural products to prevent overexploitation of the protected areas. They also serve to keep potentially destructive wildlife away from villages, crops, and domestic livestock.
- Agriculture and social development activities can be provided outside protected areas to attract local people away from these areas and as an incentive to avoid encroachment.

Experience with implementing this concept is still limited in Sub-Saharan Africa. A number of pilot efforts have been initiated, but are at very early stages. A potential danger to watch for is the risk of the "magnet syndrome": priority provision of infrastructure and social services around areas to be protected may in fact *attract* people to the area if social and infrastructure development farther away is significantly lagging behind that around the area to be protected.

areas, timber extraction, and commercial fuelwood harvesting. Growing and migrating human populations as well as international demand for tropical timber drive these processes. Timber exports from Sub-Saharan Africa amount to about US$700 million per year at present. Cropland is expanding at a rate of 1 million ha annually — to a large extent at the expense of forest areas and woodlands. A number of agricultural development projects supported by external aid donors, including the World Bank, have facilitated the conversion of forest and rangelands into cropland.

The most important areas for action to stop the degradation of Sub-Saharan Africa's forest resources lie outside the immediate purview of forestry sector policy. They are: (a) reducing population growth, and (b) intensifying agricultural production at a rate which exceeds population growth, in order to encourage sedentary agriculture and livestock raising and to discourage further invasion of the remaining forests. Rapidly growing numbers of people, barely surviving in land-extensive agricultural systems, have no option than to continue to invade and destroy forests. This points again to the complex mutual dependency of agricultural and nonagricultural activities.

For the forests that remain, improved management for multiple uses will be vital. These uses range from the provision of critical environmental services to the supply of timber and nontimber products, and from tourism and recreational uses to mineral extraction. It is unrealistic to expect that all forests can be conserved in their present state. For almost all of Africa's forests the issue is not whether to use them or not to use them — but how to use them. If people (and governments) feel that there is little benefit from forests, they will continue to be mined for urgently needed export revenue or converted into agricultural land.

To address these problems effectively, there is no alternative to planning, orchestrated by governments. This can be done within Tropical Forestry Actions Plans (TFAPs), National Environmental Action Plans (NEAPs), or simply forestry master plans. Each will involve some form of land use and natural resource planning. Land use plans for forest areas should identify conservation areas, parks, areas designated for sustainable logging, mining areas, farming and grazing areas, and areas designated for infrastructure development.

Farmers have encroached into most forest areas in Sub-Saharan Africa, including into many government-managed "forest reserves." Removing and resettling these people would, in most cases, entail social and economic costs of a magnitude that render this option generally prohibitive. Even if farmers were to be expelled from areas they have invaded for farming, this would not restore the affected areas to their previous forested state. Consequently, areas that have already been largely converted to farmland should be formally relinquished for farming, and farmers already established there should be provided with secure use rights. Areas allocated to industrial wood production should be carefully managed in collaboration with logging companies (which should be compelled under their concession agreements to log in a sustainable manner) and with local populations. Areas designated for protection should be managed by government agencies in partnership with the local people. This will require giving these people specific user rights in protected areas and involving them in management decisions.

A key to improving forest management will be the direct involvement of the local people in both planning and execution of forest resource use plans. As already noted, the most effective manner to achieve this is to ensure their resource ownership or legally protected long-term use rights and to prepare forest resource management plans in a truly collaborative manner. Where local communities own the forest, governments should assist them, through forest and extension services, to manage their forests productively and sustainably. Indeed, since government agencies throughout most of Sub-Saharan Africa are stretched far too thin to manage even those forest resources that are legally under government ownership and control, and since in many cases local people and communities continue to consider these resources to be rightfully theirs, governments should consider divesting many (though not all) forest and range areas to local people. The traditional owner/user communities could obtain group title to these resources.

Sound forest management plans would allow some logging and artisanal wood harvesting on a sustainable basis (specifying concession fees, taxes, and so on), provide for essential infrastructure development, and identify areas suitable for crop and livestock production. Local people would utilize the forest and woodland resources for fuelwood and artisanal forestry, hunting and harvesting of nonwood forest products, the arable land for cropping, and the range and grazing land for livestock production. Royalties paid by "outside" users would accrue to the local communities; governments would share in such royalties through the tax system.

Where governments retain ownership of forests, the management will be more directly under government control. But even there, management plans will need to be responsive to local people's needs and should, therefore, be developed and implemented with their full participation. Local people will only be induced to cooperate if they are given secure and exclusive user rights: hunting, fishing, collection of nontimber forest products, some wood harvesting. They should also be given a significant share in the royalties received from other users, such as logging concessionaires; the certainty of such long-term sources of income will represent a significant benefit and an incentive to adhere to agreed use plans.

Governments will need to provide the essential policy and administrative framework: publishing standard concession agreements, establishing and collecting taxes and stumpage fees, and creating conservation areas, based on both land use plans and national forest policy parameters. Implementation would be the responsibility of the local communities, with the requisite technical assistance provided by government agencies, NGOs, or both. As these communities acquire experience and management acumen, the need for such outside assistance will decline and government support should be commensurately withdrawn. As emphasized above, strong and lasting incentives (embodied in resource ownership, user rights, revenue sharing, and the like) would need to be provided to ensure appropriate local interest in such an approach to resource management.

Whether any kind of commercial logging is compatible with sustainable management of primary humid forests is highly contentious. Although the evidence available at present may not be sufficient to make a definitive and categorical statement, there is increasing support among experts for entirely prohibiting logging in intact primary humid forests. Although considerable interest and optimism are often expressed with respect to sustainable exploitation of natural forests, ITTO has estimated that only one-fifth of one percent of the world's natural tropical forest areas are currently being harvested in an ecologically sustainable manner (Goodland 1991:14; Poore and others 1989). Even logging systems based on selective removal of certain species and age classes of trees may seriously disrupt the ecological balance of a tropical moist forest and destroy a significant portion of the remaining vegetation during the process of extraction. Recovery of the ecosystem can only be assured if the damaged area is very small and if it is surrounded by large areas of undamaged forest that can serve as a reservoir of recolonizing species. Thus, even though the area may remain forested, any type of commercial logging in a tropical moist forest may result in a fundamental and quite possibly irreversible degradation of the original ecosystem. This is in contrast to the less diverse and more resilient temperate forests, which can be logged productively on a sustainable basis.

Logging certainly should be stopped in ecologically delicate and in environmentally important areas in humid and savanna forests. There should be no logging where it is not possible to log on a sustainable basis. In secondary forests (those consisting of regrowth where primary forests have been logged or otherwise significantly disturbed before) and on forest plantations and tree farms, logging must be undertaken in accordance with sustainable management practices. These areas could, in many cases, be designated and managed as permanent sources of timber, pulpwood and woodfuels — provided the private owners (individuals or groups) agree. Logging companies unable to log in a sustainable manner should not be given concessions and permits, even in secondary forests. This will require governmental regulation of logging, even if it is undertaken on private land.

Loggers will have to improve their performance and show themselves to be responsible in their logging activities. To induce this behavior, concession agreements providing for logging company responsibilities as well as rights will be necessary. Payment of taxes — rather than tax evasion — should be the norm. Sustainable management of secondary growth forests and industrial plantations would then become a more important aspect of the business of logging companies than the mining of primary forests. Even where governments choose to continue to allow logging in primary forests, management of secondary growth should be strongly encouraged by levying much lower taxes on trees taken from replanted areas and industrial plantations than on trees harvested from primary forests. If international prices for tropical wood rise as currently projected, the profitability of forest plantations will increase, making such an approach even more feasible.

Where logging is still permitted in primary forests, it should be more heavily taxed — through area-based taxes levied on concessions. Part of the tax should be collected and retained by local communities owning the forests or having user rights in them. Concession agreements should be auctioned to the highest bidder. These measures would serve to return more of the benefit to the community and, in effect, impose a charge on the companies for the resource (the forest) exploited. Taxes should be high enough to reflect the economic and social value of the forest, including the environmental services it provides, and the cost of rehabilitation if the public sector or the local community undertakes that rehabilitation.

Governments will also need to develop the institutional and human capacity required to manage protected areas and to monitor logging as well as the use of farming, pasture, and fisheries resources made available for local people's use in forest areas. This is important to ensure that protected areas are in fact protected and that the areas made available for exploitation are used in a productive and sustainable manner. An example of management for sustainability is increasing the availability of wood products to keep pace with population growth — ensuring, for example, that replanting exceeds cutting. This could be done by inducing local communities and individual landowners to set aside sufficient land for wood production. The primary instrument to achieve this would be ensuring that price, tax, and other incentives make tree production and marketing profitable (and more profitable than other forms of land use on land most suitable for tree production). This requires planning and management capacity in government to help local populations manage natural resources. In parks and protected areas, governments will need the capacity to manage resources directly and effectively.

On privately and communally held forest land, government forest services can also help local landowners reforest degraded areas, by providing planning assistance, technical advice, training, and seedlings. But planting, maintenance, and harvesting must be done by the resource owners, the people themselves. NGOs can play an important role in assisting them. Forest services need to abandon their present almost exclusive focus on direct management of forests — which is all too often coupled with an adversarial relationship with the people living around the forests — and place far greater emphasis on extension functions targeted at private and community-owned land. And forestry research needs to pay more attention to the issues faced in private and community management of forestry resources.

Natural Resource Management in Farming Areas

Since much farming takes place within forest areas, there is not always a clear distinction between forest areas and farming areas. In large areas throughout Sub-Saharan Africa, forests have been almost totally replaced by farms. In these areas, the primary role of governments in natural resource management should be effective planning of land and water resource use. Even in areas predominately used for farming, land must still be allocated for various uses such as settlements, service and infrastructure facilities, parks and forests, grazing land and cropland, areas to be protected (watershed headlands, wetlands, water bodies), and so forth. Land use planning will need to take into account the important tradeoffs among these various uses. Land use and management plans for farming areas should be prepared in a collaborative manner, with the active participation of the local communities. They will need to cover such issues as watershed management, locally appropriate improved farming and livestock husbandry practices, farm tree planting, irrigation and drainage, domestic water supply and use, and the location of physical infrastructure.

Actual resource management and conservation in such areas will be almost entirely in the hands of the local farmers and livestock owners.

Box 10-2   A New Forest Policy in Côte d'Ivoire

In Côte d'Ivoire, about 12 million ha of tropical forest land have been lost during this century. To arrest this destruction, the government has begun to implement a number of the recommendations set out here. Wildlife and biodiversity would be conserved in parks covering 1.9 million ha, of which 600,000 ha are tropical forests. Sustainable wood production would be achieved through better management of production forests (all of which are secondary forests, previously logged), expansion of hardwood plantations, and assistance to farmers induced to resettle outside the forests.

This process began with detailed land use plans for existing "gazetted" forests, which belong to the government. These plans designate specific tracts for protection, logging, farming, and other uses. Park areas have already been delimited and are to be fully protected. In those areas that have been previously logged over and are to remain production forests, logging companies are receiving long-term concessions in accordance with detailed forest resource management plans and under governmental supervision. Loggers judged unable or unwilling to participate are not permitted to log. Taxes on logs have been increased, and concessions are auctioned to the highest qualified bidders. This is helping to eliminate the least efficient loggers. In effect, forests will no longer be treated as a virtually free good, but as a valuable resource, requiring high payment by loggers for exploitation. Intact primary forests are in parks and will not be logged at all.

Farmers are given incentives to leave those areas that are environmentally delicate or should be managed for logging. The key incentives are ownership titles for land outside these areas and access to agricultural inputs. Agricultural extension staff will provide technical advice to resettled farmers. No support services will be provided to farmers remaining in the forests. There will, however, be no coercion to move; the incentives are expected to be sufficiently persuasive to induce voluntary exit from the park and logging areas. Traditional forest dwellers will be allowed to remain in the forests; so would settlers in areas already so heavily encroached upon that forests have essentially disappeared. Government institutions in the forest sector will be strengthened to focus more on conservation and resource management, rather than on servicing the logging industry.

This new forestry policy fits into a broader national strategy for natural resource conservation, which includes accelerating agricultural intensification and improving land tenure security.

A major issue now is the need for an effective consultative process between farmers, forest dwellers, and the government. Such a process has been initiated in the form of local-level forest-farmer commissions for each forest, which will decide on resettlement questions as well as on other disputes between the government, traditional forest dwellers, and farmers who have settled in the forests. A second issue is land ownership. The government would continue to own the land in the gazetted forest areas, but would share the royalties with local populations to induce their support for the new policy.

The example of Machakos District in Kenya demonstrates that this works (see pp. 158–159). It will be essential to ensure tenurial security if there is to be significant private investment in land conservation and productivity enhancement. The agricultural research and extension systems will be the major governmental instruments for supporting farmers and private industry in managing the natural resources in farming areas.

Dryland and Range Areas

Many dryland and range areas will, like forest areas, require special protection. Actions in the agricultural, livestock, infrastructure, land tenure, and population spheres along the lines set out in previous chapters will be necessary, but not sufficient. Since agricultural technology adapted to dryland areas is so marginal, land tenure reform so exceedingly difficult to implement, and carrying capacity so low, sustainable management of dryland areas will be very problematic.

Land use planning will be important, since there are tradeoffs and potential conflicts here as well among the traditionally predominating pastoralists, new settlers who are moving into the better areas to farm, fuelwood collectors, and the preservation of biodiversity. Many pastoral areas contain forests and wildlands. Resolving land disputes is an important aspect of the solution to these problems, including that of ensuring adequate fuelwood supplies in drier areas. The management of rangeland by local people, grouped into voluntary and self-governing associations, is the most effective tool for managing these resource systems. But these associations must be provided undisputed ownership of, or assured long-term user rights to, the land and the associated water and vegetation if they are to manage them.

Two recent reviews of key issues in Sahelian dryland management highlighted a number of essential concerns that should be observed in attempts to ensure sustainable management and development (Nekby 1990; Shanmugaratnam and others 1992). These include the research and extension of appropriate crop and livestock technologies that are both soil conserving and more profitable for farmers and herdsmen, land tenure reform to eliminate open access, reduction of population growth through out-migration, and promotion of rural industries to reduce the pressure on land. One of these reviews (Nekby 1990) also suggested a return to holistic and integrated planning and execution — in effect, a return to the concept of integrated regional development based on land use plans that allocate land for pasture, cropping, reserves and parks, fuelwood production, forests, and other uses. Land ownership would be allocated, including to traditional community or clan owners. Agricultural and livestock technology would be developed to suit each particular agroclimatic situation. The technologies would include considerable soil conservation measures. It is, at present, not possible to envisage an alternative approach in dryland areas.

Box 10-3   Global Cost-Sharing of Tropical Forest Conservation

The benefits of conserving tropical forests will accrue to the entire world, while the costs will have to be borne almost entirely by the countries in which the forests are located. This has stimulated efforts to compensate the producing countries for income foregone as forests are taken out of production and placed under protection. The first such efforts were "debt-for-nature swaps." Although not many swaps have been organized in Sub-Saharan Africa, there is considerable potential for them in many parts of the continent. The principle is that governments set aside as a protected reserve large tracts of forest or wildland, usually managed with the help of an NGO, in return for the purchase of some amount of the country's discounted external debt by that NGO (or organized by it).

Another important recent initiative has been the Global Environment Facility (GEF), under which funds have been made available to countries as compensation for reducing activities that are remunerative but that significantly compromise biodiversity (such as logging), contribute to carbon dioxide emissions (such as forest burning), or produce CFCs. An evaluation of the first phase of the GEF has been published (UNDP, UNEP, and World Bank 1994). This has helped determine modalities for the second phase. A good candidate for funding under this facility would be the setting aside of intact tropical forests as reserves and parks.

Local initiative and management need to be mobilized to manage range, pasture, and dryland areas — in a manner similar to that outlined above for forest areas. Where traditional, community-based authority still exists, group land titles or secure long-term user rights should be provided. As in the case of forests and farmland, it is through the ownership of land and the associated natural resources, or at least the assurance of secure long-term exclusive use rights, that local participation in sustainable resource management can be mobilized and maintained. In better watered grazing areas, individual ownership of livestock farms will be possible (although crop farming may prove to be a more remunerative use of land and labor in many such situations), but this will be rarely feasible on drylands because of the patchy availability of water and the need for seasonal livestock movement. But exclusion of others — i.e., elimination of open-access conditions — is essential.

At the same time, local communities and individuals need to be supported in planning and managing resource use, particularly in view of the increasing limitations imposed on the geographic mobility of pastoralists' herds. The microproject funds which some donors have begun to establish are a suitable instrument to provide critically needed funding for this purpose. Technical assistance should come through extension agents, knowledgeable about conservation techniques.

Water

As noted in Chapter 2, water is a critical resource in limited supply in large parts of Sub-Saharan Africa. Conflicts over competing uses are already evident in many cases. In some areas, groundwater reserves are being drawn down for irrigation much faster than they can be replenished. Damming and diversion of rivers for irrigation or hydropower development have often created serious problems downstream. These include the spread of water-borne and water-related diseases, intrusion of saltwater into groundwater aquifers in coastal areas, destruction of riverine woodlands and of wetlands of importance as wildlife habitat, destruction of downstream fisheries and of coastal wetlands critical for marine life and migratory birds, and coastal erosion. Water pollution from domestic sources has become a major concern in many areas, particularly around major cities, but also in countless rural areas where lack of safe potable water is the most serious public health problem. In some regions, pollution from agrochemicals is emerging as a problem, as it already is in other parts of the world.

With the primary exceptions of parts of coastal West Africa and the Congo/Zaïre River basin and adjoining parts of humid Central Africa, most of Sub-Saharan Africa is not endowed with abundant water. Moreover, only a portion of total potentially available water is actually accessible and usable. Geographical distribution of supplies, seasonal and annual variations in flows, topographic conditions, and evaporation losses drive a large wedge between potentially available and realistically accessible water. Conflicting demands on water use and environmental considerations pose further constraints on the utilization of water (Falkenmark and Suprapto 1992:33–34). In Europe, water management problems began to be encountered when water demand exceeded 20 percent of potential water availability (Falkenmark 1991:88–89). Water quality is an important consideration as well. Not all sources of water are suitable for all uses, and water impurities and pollution can severely limit the range of uses to which a particular source of water can be put.

Demand for water is rising rapidly, driven by population growth and economic development. Except for the humid regions of Central and coastal West Africa, almost all of Sub-Saharan Africa will be facing water shortages or water scarcity early in the next century. In many of the arid regions, this is already the case — particularly during the dry season. WHO has suggested an average of 30 liters per capita daily (or about 11 m^3 per person annually) as the minimum needed to ensure adequate hygiene for urban populations in developing countries. Industrial water requirements depend very much on the size and type of industries; in industrialized countries, these requirements considerably exceed household consumption, even though the latter surpass the WHO standard cited above five to ten times.

Agriculture is, and will continue to be, the largest consumer of water. In dry climates, the photosynthesis process consumes about 1,000 m^3 of water to produce one ton of biomass (Falkenmark and Suprapto 1992:31). Depending on agroecological factors (crops grown, soil characteristics, evapotranspiration rates, etc.) and on technical efficiency, feeding people by means of irrigated agriculture requires anywhere from 500 m^3 to 2,500 m^3 of water per capita per year.

For many SSA countries, the water that can be utilized at reasonable cost with available technological means will not be more than about 250 m^3 per capita annually by the year 2025, and for some (such as Kenya, Burundi, Rwanda, Malawi) it may be as little as half that amount. This has important implications for the agricultural and overall economic development strategies these countries will need to pursue. It certainly underscores the urgency of initiating effective water resource monitoring and planning and of maximizing efficiency in water use.[1]

The many different uses of water can be variably grouped, depending on the objective of the analysis. One categorization distinguishes between consumptive, nonconsumptive, and polluting uses (Frederiksen 1993:24–25). Another differentiates between withdrawal uses and instream uses. Water used by households and industries and for watering livestock and irrigated crops represents withdrawal uses. Instream uses include water flow for fisheries and wetlands, for maintaining downstream water quality, for water transport, and for recreational uses. Power generation may involve instream uses (for hydropower generation) or withdrawal uses (for cooling thermal and nuclear power plants). While some instream uses are compatible with others, most demands for different water uses compete with each other and, in situations of increasing water scarcity, imply important tradeoffs and potential conflicts.

This points to the urgent need for effective hydrological planning and for prudent demand management which involves planning, regulation, technology, and pricing. Demand management means allocating among alternative uses, encouraging conservation, and protecting instream flow and water quality. Market mechanisms alone will not be adequate: "...the nature of the resource makes it difficult and in many cases impossible to establish efficient markets" (Frederick 1993:23). Well-defined and transferable property rights are usually missing and very difficult, if at all, to establish. The full benefits and costs of a water transfer are not likely to be borne by the buyer and seller, because there are multiple and important externalities. And rarely will there be multiple and competitive suppliers of water, since the nature of the resource makes water supply a natural monopoly (Frederick 1993:24–25).

Water must be recognized as the critical and limiting resource it is. It must be carefully allocated, beginning with the development of local and regional water use plans, and it must be protected against pollution. Project-by-project and sector-by-sector planning for water uses (water and sewage services, irrigation, flood control, hydropower, navigation, fisheries, industrial uses, and so forth) is prone to lead to conflicting and inefficient investment decisions. In the absence of prices for water that reflect its scarcity, planning must be based on natural hydrological units such as river basins to ensure that the opportunity costs associated with different water uses are properly considered. Such planning should be integrated with planning for land use and other activities that affect, and are affected by, water development. Water management plans will need to assess water availability against likely demand (taking into account anticipated population growth and urban/industrial development) and develop options for water supply (including costs) as well as options for demand management and conservation.

Given the frequent occurrence of drought, many water sources in semiarid and arid parts of Sub-Saharan Africa are very vulnerable to wide annual variations in flow volume and, hence, in supply. In these regions, water use plans must allow adequate margins for safety and establish clear priorities among competing uses. In many arid and semiarid regions, water supply constraints will imply that large-scale irrigation cannot be the first priority in allocating water among different uses. Where this is not recognized, capital investments designed to abstract surface or groundwater for irrigation and to develop land for irrigated farming may later need to be abandoned as the requirements for human and livestock use increase.[2]

Water resources frequently are shared among countries. This underscores the importance of close cooperation in planning for long-term water sharing if riparian disputes are to be avoided.

The economics of water supply are important. Many irrigation and water supply schemes are excessively costly — and uneconomic. Conservation efforts on currently used supplies or demand management through more rational water charges can obviate expensive new investments in water supply, especially for irrigation. Water user associations should be given much greater management responsibility in operation and maintenance of rural potable water supply schemes as well as in irrigation systems.

Common Elements

There are a number of common elements to the recommended strategies and approaches for conserving and sustainably managing Africa's natural resources, and a number of basic lessons from the, admittedly limited, experience to date:

- The overall policy and legal framework must be consistent with the conservation objective. For example, local communities need to be authorized to participate in the management and benefits of protected areas and the wildlife and other resources they contain. Resistance to this concept remains strong in most of Sub-Saharan Africa, as governments generally believe that benefits reaped from conservation areas should accrue to all citizens. Compromises will have to be made. For example, taxes can be levied on local community receipts from tourism, so that benefits may be shared more widely.

- Social and institutional factors constrain implementation of community-based conservation strategies. The major problems are the general weakness of community organizations and the vastly unequal distribution of authority between the national and local levels. Most local communities in forest, range, and wilderness areas are poorly organized and difficult to organize. Outside assistance is nearly always necessary.

- Only in a few cases can protected areas be expected to generate sufficient revenues from nonexploitative uses (such as eco-tourism) to provide significant local income or to support significant rural development. In most cases, external financing will be needed on a long-term basis. The national and international communities must contribute to the cost of maintaining the national and global heritage represented by the areas being protected.

- Creation of an institutional and management capacity in government is a difficult process. This is rarely, if ever, the highest priority of governments; as a result, government agencies charged with managing natural resources are usually neglected and financially strained. Again, international assistance is essential.

- In the absence of agricultural intensification outside the areas to be protected, conservation efforts are bound to fail. Only rapid gains in output per unit of land will induce fast growing populations to stay out of the remaining intact forests and other ecosystems that should remain undisturbed.

Conservation of biodiversity depends directly upon preservation of natural habitats, particularly tropical primary moist forests which contain the greatest diversity of species outside of certain marine environments. Habitat destruction is the greatest cause of extinction of species overall. For species that are acutely endangered by commercial exploitation, additional protection is needed in the form of controls on harvesting and on international trade. Such controls can only be effective if the governments of both producing and consuming countries are committed to enforcing them.

The single most important factor to ensure the preservation of land-based natural ecosystems will be meeting the demand for food, wood, and other agricultural and forest products on a sustainable basis. Soil and water resources must be protected by protecting important watersheds — by maintaining natural forests and, where these are already degraded, by replanting or allowing natural regeneration to take place. The critical issue of meeting the needs for woodfuels and timber must be addressed from both the production and the demand side. While commercial logging of remaining primary moist forests should be greatly reduced (if not banned entirely), because the available evidence indicates that it cannot be sustainable, there must be a major increase in resources for the sustainable production of fuelwood, lumber, and pulpwood. This must come from farm forestry, as well as from plantations and well-managed production forests located in areas where the original forest system has already been substantially altered by logging. At the same time, energy conservation must be promoted, both through economic policy measures such as appropriate pricing and through the development and extension of technical innovations.

The most important element is agricultural intensification outside of forests and wilderness areas. Without it, Africa's forests and wilderness areas stand little, if any, chance of survival in the longer run. The ultimate environmental collapse can be postponed by reducing the rate of population growth. The preferred option combines maximum agricultural intensification with sharply curtailing population growth and far more determined and effective management of environmental resources.

The Role of Governments

There are important functions to be fulfilled by government agencies, and there is an urgent need to develop the requisite institutional and human capacity to undertake these. They include carrying out resource inventories and mapping, preparing land use plans, managing protected areas, and monitoring logging and the use of agricultural, pasture, wetland, and fisheries resources. Governments also need to develop the capacity to undertake environmental assessments of development projects in order to avoid unacceptably negative environmental impact.

Governments should focus their direct management efforts on a much smaller portion of the total national land and forest resources — i.e., those areas that provide public (and global) benefits and goods. This will consist mainly of parks and other protected conservation areas where there are important externalities that local populations cannot be expected to finance or otherwise support. Even there, local participation will be necessary. The local people should be given incentives to conserve the resource endowment of the protected area through the confirmation of exclusive hunting and gathering rights, the provision of employment opportunities in the various support services required to manage protected areas, and a share of any user fees that are collected from outsiders.

NGOs can play important roles in assisting local people in managing natural resources. Where they are ready and willing to assume this role, they should be given wide room to do so.

Governments should also intensify their efforts to provide effective and locally relevant environmental education through the school system and through mass media. Agricultural extension staff should similarly be utilized to spread awareness of environmental issues, and especially of soil, water, and tree conservation techniques, among rural populations.

A problem common to all natural resources is that financial returns to conservation are often lower than economic returns. Individuals and private enterprises will therefore tend to undertake less conservation and more exploitation than is economically optimal. In circumstances where the economic returns to conservation are high, but the financial returns too low to induce adequate conservation by private resource users, taxes on natural resource use (logging fees, mining royalties, water charges) and subsidies for conservation (free extension advice to farmers, cost-sharing for soil conservation activities) are likely to be justified to close the gap between economic and financial returns. Making this determination, and imposing the necessary taxes or providing the required subsidies, are functions of government.

National Environmental Action Plans

The development of national environmental resource management strategies must be a national affair. The main instrument for this process is the National Environmental Action Plan (NEAP). NEAPs are currently being prepared or implemented with World Bank support by most African countries. They should contain strategies for addressing all of the issues of the nexus. The NEAP concept is multisectoral in approach, and oriented to bottom-up participatory planning and implementation. It provides a framework for integrating environmental concerns with social and economic planning within a country. The objective is to identify priority areas and actions, develop institutional awareness and processes, and mobilize popular participation through an intensive consultation process with NGOs and community representatives. Donor collaboration can also be effectively mobilized in this manner.

A successful national approach to environmental concerns involves several important steps:

- Establishing policies and legislation for resource conservation and environmental protection that are integrated into the macroeconomic framework and, if possible, assessing the costs of degradation. These were, for example, estimated to be between 5 and 15 percent of GNP in Madagascar and more than 5 percent of GDP in Ghana.

- Setting up the institutional framework, usually involving a ministerial or higher-level environmental policy body, developing mechanisms for coordination between agencies, building concern in these agencies, balancing private and public sector concerns, decentralizing environmental management, and assuring continuous contact with local people. The preparation of regional land use plans could be an important component. The basic framework needed to guide the implementation of land tenure reform, forest policy reform, and other elements discussed above can also be included in NEAPs.

- Strengthening national capacity to carry out environmental assessments and establishing environmental information systems. This can be done to some extent by restructuring existing data and making them available to users. Pilot demand-driven information systems should also be initiated to strengthen national capacity to monitor and manage environmental resources. Local and regional research capacity will be crucial to the development of plant varieties and technologies which are truly adapted to local conditions.

- Developing human resources through formal and on-the-job training; introducing environmental concerns into educational curricula and agricultural extension messages; and increasing public awareness through media coverage, general awareness campaigns, and extension services.

- Establishing Geographical Information Systems (GISs) that incorporate adequate environmental information. Lack of operationally meaningful and reliable environmental data is a major problem. It tends to result in misconceptions about natural resource problems and the consequent risk that policy measures will be misdirected. Urgent needs include assessments of forest cover, soil erosion and soil capability, desertification risks, and the distribution of human and livestock populations. This is clearly an area in which donors can provide support and expertise and governments need to act. It is important to develop national capacity to gather and analyze information in-country: properly designed and operated Geographical Information Systems can be extremely helpful in this regard. GISs make use of aerial photography, remote sensing, and actual ground inspections and data collection. GISs will be particularly useful not only to monitor the progress of natural resource degradation and destruction, but — more importantly — to assess land capability for various uses and, thus, to provide the basis for sound land use planning.

NEAPs are intended to be evolutionary — developing policies through field experience as well as national-level analysis. They should lead to the empowerment of the nongovernmental sector, not just by providing funds for small-scale community activities through national environmental funds, but also by drawing large numbers of village and district representatives into consultative forums. A nongovernmental advisory body was part of the institutional arrangements set up, for example, under the Lesotho NEAP.

Considerable external support has been provided for the NEAP process, from bilateral and multilateral agencies and NGOs (such as the World Wildlife Fund, the World Resources Institute, and the International Institute for Environment and Development). External expertise is made available to the countries undertaking NEAP preparation, and aid agency policies are coordinated in the process, with the NEAP forming the basis for coordination. Where NEAPs have led to the preparation of national environmental investment plans (as in Madagascar and Mauritius), donors have substantially oversubscribed the programs. A National Environmental Action Plan can therefore become the major preparatory instrument for addressing the issues discussed in this chapter.

Notes

1. An effort has been under way since 1986 to establish the information base for sound water resource planning in Sub-Saharan Africa. A number of multilateral and bilateral agencies and donors (including the ADB, UNDP, UNDTCD, WMO, the World Bank, the EEC and France) are collaborating in a multiyear program,

Sub-Saharan Africa Hydrological Assessment, to assist all SSA countries in creating or improving a sound hydrometric base for the purpose of planning and evaluating water resource development programs and projects. This effort covers surface water resources, hydrometeorology, and groundwater. Initial reports for a number of countries are available from the World Bank's Agriculture and Rural Development Department.

2. Climate change is likely to have significant impact on water supplies and regional hydrological systems, particularly in regions already facing water shortages. This makes prudent planning so much more important. Even relatively small changes in precipitation and temperature can have significant effects on the volume and timing of runoff, especially in arid and semiarid regions (Frederick 1993:63).

11
Conclusion

The Problem

The countries of Sub-Saharan Africa face three important challenges: (1) reducing the rate of population growth, (2) safeguarding their natural resource base, and (3) making agriculture, as quickly as possible, sufficiently productive to ensure rising standards of living for the rapidly increasing population without further endangering the resource base available for this purpose. Because these three challenges are closely interlocking, the ambitious indicative targets set out in Chapter 6 are more likely to be achieved if the actions suggested in each specific area are successful.

Rapid population growth, environmental degradation, and slow agricultural growth in Sub-Saharan Africa are closely linked. The principal problem is that the technologies applied in shifting cultivation and transhumant pastoralist systems, appropriate under conditions of low population density on Africa's fragile natural resource base, are environmentally damaging when practiced by rapidly increasing populations. When population densities increase and shifting around on the land becomes impossible, but farming practices do not change, soils degrade and forests are destroyed. Soil degradation and deforestation constrain agricultural growth. Lagging agricultural growth perpetuates rural poverty and food insecurity, which in turn impede the onset of the demographic transition to lower human fertility rates.

Past efforts have, on the whole, failed to reverse the downward direction of the spiral that is driven by the synergetic forces of this nexus. The explanation, at least in part, appears to be that past efforts have been pursued too narrowly along conventional sectoral lines — matching established institutional arrangements and traditional academic disciplines — while crucial cross-sectoral linkages and synergies have been ignored. Environmental integrity and resource conservation are critical for sustainable long-term growth of agriculture, and of the economy. But this will be very difficult to achieve if present rates of population growth

---

Box 11-1   Kenya: The Nexus Synergies at Work

In Kenya, population density on cultivated land is high. Education is relatively good, and females participate. Infant mortality has declined due to relatively good health care, food security, and women's education. Agricultural policy has been quite good, smallholder commercial farming is profitable, and private sector participation in all aspects of agricultural production, marketing, and processing is high. Land tenure security is assured (although there have been problems with land grabbing by influential elites as well as with the land rights of livestock herders and of women). Women are receiving attention from the agricultural extension service. Family planning programs are in place. Popular sensitivity to the costs of environmental degradation is high, and there has been successful environmental conservation action in the form of a national soil conservation program, the maintenance of sizeable national parks, and the widespread tree planting under the Greenbelt Movement promoted by a national NGO working almost entirely with women. Urban bias in economic policy is less pronounced than elsewhere in Sub-Saharan Africa, and the development of secondary towns and cities characterizes Kenya's urbanization policy. Relatively good infrastructure, including a countrywide network of roads, has been developed.

The combination of these (and other) factors has had a number of desirable results. Agricultural growth has been averaging between 3 and 5 percent per year. Tree farming and other agroforestry activities have increased, and the area under trees may now in fact be expanding. There is at least marginally effective protection of national parks and of wildlife. Farmers participate in marketing decisions, with farmer-managed cooperatives playing a significant role. Kenya's urban markets are stocked with Kenyan farm products, assembled in rural markets and secondary towns and brought to market largely by private traders. And the TFR has begun to decline measurably in recent years.

---

persist. Population growth is unlikely to decelerate unless there is more vigorous growth of agriculture, and of the economies dependent on agriculture. At the same time, agricultural growth based on traditional patterns of resource use and production technologies will be increasingly constrained by rapid population growth and the degradation of the environmental resource base.

A key conclusion of this study is that far more emphasis needs to be placed on efforts designed to promote effective *demand* for sustainable and environmentally benign farming technologies, for family planning services, and for resource conservation. In most past sectoral development efforts, emphasis has been placed largely on the supply side (efforts to develop and deliver technology and services), while the need to generate demand has remained largely unrecognized — or at least poorly served. The synergies inherent in the nexus provide considerable potential for addressing the demand side of these important problems.

There is low demand for small families, and there is inadequate supply of family planning services. Both are keeping total fertility rates (TFRs) high. Low demand for small families is due to cultural factors, high infant mortality, low education for girls, and limited family planning services. More contentious is the impact of economic incentives. High demand for child labor may be created by systems of shifting cultivation, severely constrained access by rural women to production inputs other than child labor, the need for child labor as part of a survival strategy in the face of poor food security, and increasing degradation and depletion of soil and water resources. Demand for smaller families is manifesting itself, however, where the density of population on cultivated land is high, infant mortality is low, food security is high, and female school enrollment rates are high. Countries with these characteristics are entering the demographic transition, and family planning programs are likely to be extremely effective there in responding to the strongly emerging demand for family planning services.

Forest degradation is stimulated by rapid population growth combined with shifting cultivation (people moving into forests to farm), poorly regulated logging, and "open access" land tenure. Open access occurs when there is no effective regulation of land use, either traditional or modern. This allows farmers and others to exploit the land, and the resources on it, in an unsustainable manner. Fuelwood prices, which are too low to cover replanting costs, are constraining fuelwood planting. Fuelwood prices are low because fuelwood can be mined, nearly freely, from open-access areas. Where there is open access, trees can be cleared for farmland by migrant farmers.

Women's time is increasingly constrained in rural areas, as fuelwood and water become scarce, and women have to walk farther for water and fuelwood. With less time available, women have difficulty maintaining food output, and this contributes to food security problems.

Technological innovation, which could permit traditional farming and livestock practices to evolve in an environmentally sustainable manner, is not keeping up with the present rapid rate of population growth. The gap between population growth and the rate of agrotechnological innovation is enormous.

Lack of demand by farmers for new agricultural technology is as important as lack of supply of appropriate technology in explaining slow agricultural growth. Lack of demand is related to several factors:

- Open-access land tenure conditions are replacing customary land tenure systems. With open access, land occupation and use is temporary and there is no incentive for the farmer to invest in farm intensification. Open access also reduces the incentive for farmers to conserve the land (since it is not theirs).

• There is often a lack of financial resources with which farmers (especially women) can invest. This low-income trap is operable in much of subsistence agriculture.

• Labor constraints on women often prevent them from adopting those technologies that are labor intensive.

• In much of Sub-Saharan Africa poor agricultural and economic policies, combined with currently low world prices for many agricultural products, have reduced the profitability of farming and hence the incentive to intensify farming. They have often restricted farmers' ability to participate fully in land management, marketing, or price setting.

• Appropriate improved agricultural technology for farmers is often locally unavailable or unknown; there can be no effective demand for what does not exist or is not known to exist.

Recommendations for Action

To correct the current disastrous trends, a set of mutually reinforcing actions need to be undertaken by governments and external aid agencies. One of the most important will be to promote demand for smaller families and for family planning (FP) services. This needs to be effected through determined action in several areas — notably expanding primary and secondary education for females, reducing infant mortality, and providing culturally sensitive FP advice and services. Field surveys to identify the determinants of fertility and attitudes to family planning will be essential. Population programs are being prepared in about half of the countries of Sub-Saharan Africa. Political commitment will be necessary to implement them. In establishing FP programs that emphasize increased supply, priority should be given to countries where demand for fewer children is emerging — as a consequence of increasing population density on cultivated land, improving female education, declining infant mortality rates, improved food security, and better conservation of environmental resources. Where these factors are not present, demand for children will remain strong and will blunt the effectiveness of programs oriented towards increasing the supply and accessibility of FP services.

Where AIDS is a serious concern, even in the absence of the elements that appear to spur the onset of the demographic transition, high priority must be placed on providing appropriate information and education regarding the prevention of sexually transmitted diseases as well as on supplying condoms through all available channels, such as schools, health facilities, traditional health providers, FP programs, pharmacies, and NGOs.

Strong efforts are also needed to create farmer demand for environmentally sustainable agricultural technology. Means to accomplish this include expansion of appropriate research and extension to farmers, the elimination of open access to land resources, and agricultural policy that makes agricultural intensification profitable (and reduces the relative profitability of shifting cultivation). The priority development of rural roads and markets in areas designated for agricultural development will be important in this regard. Agricultural research systems must be developed to supply the appropriate technology. The elaboration of Frameworks for Action under the auspices of the Special Program for African Agricultural Research (SPAAR) merits strong support, as do related efforts to improve other agricultural support services such as extension. The problem is not so much funding, but organization and management.

Agricultural services and education must serve women as much as men — to improve women's farming practices, raise their productivity and incomes, and stimulate reduced demand for children. Successful introduction of agroforestry and fuelwood production on farms would significantly reduce women's work burden in fuelwood gathering. Introduction of appropriate transport improvements and stoves that save both fuel and time would also help. Improving rural water supply will save women's time. It will also reduce infant mortality, thus reducing the demand for more children. Success in these areas will free more of women's time for family management, agricultural production, and other economic activities.

Measures necessary to create a market for fuelwood should be pursued. Fuelwood prices should reflect the scarcity value and replanting costs of trees. Higher prices would stimulate farmers and entrepreneurs to plant trees. This will require land tenure reform to eliminate open access to free fuelwood by farmers and entrepreneurs. It will also require extension advice to farmers on agroforestry and fuelwood plantations. Eliminating price and taxation disincentives to the marketing of kerosene and other replacement fuels would stimulate the substitution of such fuels for woodfuels over time, particularly in urban areas.

The rate of degradation and destruction of forests and wildlands can be reduced by determined pursuit of agricultural intensification. This needs to be promoted through the measures indicated above, the elimination of open-access land tenure situations, keeping infrastructure out of environmentally sensitive areas, and more effective regulation and taxation of logging.

In each country, Environmental Action Plans should be prepared, and they should focus heavily on agricultural and demographic causes of environmental degradation in rural areas. A key instrument to be used in preparing solutions will be land use plans. These define the use, given various demands, to which various types of land are to be put (forest, protected areas, agriculture, settlements, infrastructure, and so forth). A meaningful National Environmental Action Plan should be based on careful analyses of the issues discussed here and should incorporate an action plan for governments, affected communities, and external aid agencies to address these issues and the linkages and synergies among them. In most cases, the action plan will consist of: changes to agricultural research, extension, and investment policy; increased focus on creating demand for family planning services and increased resources for population policy; greater emphasis on fuelwood and industrial forestry plantations and private tree farming; greater sensitivity to the environmental impact of all investments; more investment in natural resource conservation and protection; and land tenure reform. The needs of women must be addressed far more effectively, notably in the areas of agricultural development, natural resource management, and education.

Infrastructure development in rural areas, particularly roads and water supply, is important for agricultural development and for focusing population settlement outside of environmentally sensitive areas. Keeping infrastructure out of environmentally fragile areas is an important tool for safeguarding their integrity. Developing infrastructure in rural areas and in secondary towns merits considerably higher priority than it has received in most countries in the past. Infrastructure development should be in response to demand. This is likely to result in smaller-scale investments — rather than in major engineering efforts, which have characterized much government and aid agency spending to date. Responsiveness to demand will be stimulated by more community and local control over design and siting, by the use of local contractors, and by funding of facilities built and maintained by the user communities themselves.

Urban areas represent outlets for population increases, markets for agricultural products and fuelwood, sources of manufactured inputs and consumer goods for farmers, and centers for the provision of education, health, and other services. Urban development needs to be one component of land use plans. Further, urban policy should be developed in part as a function of likely growth of the urban population, linkages between urban and rural product and labor markets, communications needs in rural areas, and environmental constraints. Generally, policies that promote development of secondary cities and rural towns, rather than of a few megacities, will be far more conducive to efficient, equitable, and sustainable rural development. This requires spatially well-distributed public investment that is not biased in favor of a few major cities — i.e., sound and substantial investment in infrastructure throughout each country (rather than concentration in megacities). It further requires functioning markets and market-based pricing for petroleum and other energy sources, avoidance of transport monopolies to increase the likelihood that the entire country is adequately served by private transport providers, promotion (through industrial extension, investment codes, credit facilities) of small and medium enterprises located in secondary cities and rural towns, and decentralization of political decisionmaking outside capital areas to facilitate greater responsiveness to demand. These are not only crucial elements of sound urbanization policy, but are important for rural development because well-functioning secondary towns and cities are more likely to provide services and markets for rural areas than are distant megacities, which tend to be heavily oriented to overseas suppliers.

Local communities need to be empowered to participate in all of the above. Without participation, people will not demand smaller families, sustainable agricultural technologies, road maintenance, or forest conservation. Participation is more likely to result in development initiatives that respond to felt needs rather than to short-term political imperatives and expediencies. People should become managers of actions conceived in partnership with governments.

Multisectoral and cross-sectoral analysis is needed to resolve agricultural, population, settlement, and environmental problems — because of the important linkages and synergies between them. Environmental protection will be very difficult to achieve if present rates of population growth continue. Population growth is unlikely to decelerate unless agriculture, and the economies dependent on agriculture, grow more rapidly. Agriculture will be increasingly constrained by rapid population growth. Settlement and urban development policies are important factors influencing population growth and movement, agriculture, and environmental resource use. In this regard, the analysis suggests that spatial planning is desirable and that action plans covering the various sectors should be integrated at the regional level.

In particular, land use plans should be developed with a spatial and regional focus. These should identify conservation areas, logging areas, farming areas, and locations for settlements and infrastructure development. Appropriate farming technologies vary from one micro-agroclimatic zone to the next. Infrastructure development is location-specific. Land tenure systems, fuelwood problems, gender responsibilities in farming, and cultural factors affecting attitudes towards human fertility vary among regions, and often from place to place, within the same country. There is therefore merit to developing integrated action plans for regions within countries. Such plans would address the wide range of issues and concerns applicable within that region — including appropriate land uses; demographic trends; likely migration patterns; natural resource management; the development of transport and other infrastructure; agricultural technology; land tenure reform and land ownership; fuelwood demand and supply; forestry development and utilization; and likely development of markets, towns, and cities.

Far greater community involvement in the preparation and the execution of these location-specific plans will be essential. Communities and individuals must be given ownership of natural resources as an incentive for them to manage and conserve these resources. Better planning, particularly spatial planning, community and individual ownership of assets, and community management of implementation are the main directions in which donors and governments must move.

Because such multisectoral action plans will be complex and difficult to implement, they should in most cases not be implemented through integrated multicomponent projects. Conservation and land use plans specified by location would be one cluster of projects. Appropriate agricultural technology for each microregion could be developed and extended through national research and extension programs, with regional implementing divisions. Regionally specific land tenure reform could be implemented under national tenure reform programs. Family planning programs adapted to particular communities would be implemented through national population and family planning programs. Urban and infrastructure development will constitute separate projects. But there needs to be a sensible fit between these separate projects and investments, given the synergies and complementarities between them.

Several other important recommendations emerge from this study concerning analytical work that should precede the formulation of action plans and, particularly, of developmental interventions — be they investment projects or institutional and policy reforms:

- Far greater attention needs to be paid to the social organization of production and consumption, of decisionmaking and resource allocation, of access to resources and services. These systems and structures can be very complex and often differ substantially among communities (and certainly among countries) throughout Sub-Saharan Africa.

- This implies the need to use relevant units of analysis. The casual and often indiscriminate use, for example, of the "household," the "family," and the "family farm" may not be appropriate if these terms are simply assumed to convey concepts of social and economic arrangements familiar to 20th-century industrialized economies. Most African societies are characterized by complex systems of resource-allocation and -pooling arrangements for both production and consumption purposes, based on lineage, kinship, gender, and age-groups — often with multiple overlaps. It is imperative to be cognizant of, and sensitive to, these arrangements and to analyze the impact of development interventions on individuals in this context.

- Gender issues are critical, especially in terms of gender-specific divisions of responsibilities, tasks, and budgets, as well as in terms of access to resources, information, and markets. Interventions and incentives do not necessarily work in the same direction or with the same intensity for men and women.

- More input is needed from sociologists and anthropologists to understand socioeconomic systems and relationships. Social scientists should collaborate closely with agricultural scientists and economists in researching farming systems, cultures, and socioeconomic institutions into which new varieties and technologies are to be introduced. Agriculturalists and economists in turn should receive special training to raise their awareness of these issues. Local expertise needs to be much more drawn upon to improve our understanding of how things operate, why they operate this way, and what may work under these conditions.

- It is extremely important to take into account the risk perception of the local people — their absolute requirement for ensuring survival in the short term even under worst case scenarios.

Status of Implementation

The above recommendations are broad and need to be adapted to the special circumstances of each country. In some countries, these ideas are already being pursued, with varying degrees of success.

- Many countries in Sub-Saharan Africa are pursuing macroeconomic and agricultural policy reform programs designed in part to improve the profitability of agriculture; this will stimulate the needed agricultural intensification. Other countries do not yet pursue policies that would make agriculture profitable. Also, many donor countries maintain a combination of import barriers and agricultural subsidies to assist their own farmers, and this harms African producers of these commodities. These policies need to be changed.

- An increasing number of countries in Sub-Saharan Africa are developing Environmental Action Plans. For these countries, implementation is the watchword. In the others, the process should be launched. Donor support should be intensified.

- Agricultural research and extension systems in a number of countries are slowly shifting to a greater focus on "sustainable" agricultural technology and responsiveness to varying farmer demand. Collaborating within SPAAR, countries in the Sahel and SADC regions are planning the improvement of their agricultural research systems. Others should follow suit, and donors should collaborate in implementing SPAAR's "Frameworks for Action."

- At least four Sub-Saharan African countries (Botswana, Kenya, Mauritius, and Zimbabwe) have, with considerable effort, succeeded in bringing down fertility rates. Much more needs to be done here as in all SSA countries, but these four provide relatively successful models. Several other countries are developing promising population and family planning programs. Genuine and sustained political commitment will be essential. Donor support should be channelled through the ongoing African Population Action Plans.

- Improved health programs to address the AIDS problem, including health education and the distribution of condoms, are starting up in several countries.

- The empowerment of local communities to manage development in each of the above areas is now beginning to be accepted in some countries; it requires much more effort.

- Weak and eroding land tenure security, inappropriate fuelwood pricing, and feeble rural infrastructure programs are major weak points almost everywhere.

- In many countries, major deficiencies remain to be addressed in rural health care and education (and particularly female education), rural infrastructure, participation of local communities in development efforts, forest and conservation policy, sound urbanization policy, and effective family planning programs.

Several countries are already pursuing many of the policies and approaches suggested here. They are capitalizing on the positive synergies between agricultural growth and productivity gains, environmental resource protection and reduction in human fertility rates and achieving measurable improvements in the welfare of rural people. Kenya, Zimbabwe, Botswana, and Mauritius are examples. They strongly suggest that the type of measures recommended here are likely to be effective. Others, such as Benin, Burkina Faso, Ghana, Tanzania, and Uganda, are moving in the right direction.

Issues and Follow-Up

Many of the issues touched upon here require more focused and detailed research and analysis. Among them are the following:

- There is a need for further research to ascertain the relative importance of the various factors that influence human fertility decisions and trends. Gender-specific analysis is particularly essential in this area.

- The expected impact of AIDS on population growth has been incorporated in the most recent population projections used here. However, given the difficulty of predicting its impact, the possible margin of error is considerable. More research is needed. Should AIDS turn out to have even more devastating impact on demographics than currently anticipated, improved health care, FP services, and education focused on preventing sexually transmitted diseases and increasing the use of condoms could become the single most important intervention to be undertaken in Sub-Saharan Africa.

- More analysis is needed concerning the productivity potential of the environmentally benign and "sustainable" agricultural technologies identified. The environmental effects of "green revolution" technologies also need careful study.

- Work is needed to determine and test the degree to which communities and community groups will be conservation-minded if and when natural resource management is turned over to them by governments.

- Urbanization and the urban-rural link are important determinants of key aspects of the agriculture-population-environment nexus. More research is required in this direction.

- There is some argument with the contention of this study that, although multisector planning is necessary, multisectoral projects to implement such plans will generally be undesirable. Some writers suggest that regional development plans could in many cases be implemented in an integrated fashion. Although this makes conceptual sense, the disappointing past experience with integrated rural development projects suggests that such programs are too complex to be managed as integrated wholes. How best to implement integrated location-specific plans through manageable components remains an issue to be explored.

- The equity impact of these recommendations needs further scrutiny. Reducing open access to land, expanding the areas under protection, and raising the price of woodfuels will have negative effects on some of the poor. However, improved agricultural technology, successful family planning, better access to rural health and education facilities and services, improved rural infrastructure, and sound urban development will have positive impact on the poor.

The follow-up to this study includes the preparation of country-specific population, agriculture, and environment nexus studies in Côte d'Ivoire, Ethiopia, Malawi, Kenya's Machakos District, Nigeria, and the Sahelian countries as a group. These studies will help firm up the analytical framework and will be instrumental in adapting the analysis to the situation of specific countries. *Reversing the Spiral* was the most important input for a revised agricultural development strategy for Sub-Saharan Africa recently prepared by the World Bank's Africa Region (Cleaver 1993). Follow-up also includes widespread incorporation of nexus issues in Environmental Action Plans and in investment projects. Concurrent monitoring is under way regarding the progress of preparation and implementation of National Environmental Action Plans and of national population programs. The institutional locus for the former is the "Club of Dublin," comprising representatives of African governments and donor agencies. The institutional arrangement for deepening the population agenda for SSA and for monitoring its progress is the African Population Advisory Committee, with similar membership. It is hoped that a similar African Agricultural Advisory Committee, managed by prominent Africans, will also be established.

Statistical Appendix

Table A-1. Basic Indicators

Country	Population ('000) Mid-1990	Area ('000 km²) 1990	GNP per capita (US$) 1990	Life expectancy (years) Mid-1960s	Life expectancy (years) 1990	Primary school enrollment (percentage of age group) Mid-1960s	Primary school enrollment (percentage of age group) 1990	Adult illiteracy (age 15+) 1990
Sub-Saharan Africa	**473,634**	**22,240**	**350**	**43**	**51**	**44**	**70**	**51**
Angola	10,012	1,247	—	35	46	39	95	58
Benin	4,740	113	360	42	51	34	61	77
Botswana	1,254	582	2,190	48	68	65	110	26
Burkina Faso	9,016	274	270	38	48	12	36	82
Burundi	5,427	28	210	43	48	26	72	50
Cameroon	11,739	475	950	42	55	94	101	46
Cape Verde	371	4	680	54	67	—	116	—
Central African Rep.	3,035	623	400	41	47	56	67	62
Chad	5,680	1,284	180	36	47	34	59	70
Comoros	475	2	480	44	56	24	75	—
Congo	2,276	342	1,000	44	52	114	—	43
Côte d'Ivoire	11,902	322	760	42	52	60	75	46
Djibouti	427	23	—	38	49	—	47	—
Equatorial Guinea	417	28	340	38	47	65	—	50
Ethiopia	51,180	1,222	120	43	48	11	38	—
Gabon	1,136	268	3,550	42	53	134	—	39
Gambia, The	875	11	340	34	44	21	64	73
Ghana	14,870	239	390	47	55	69	75	40
Guinea	5,717	246	440	35	43	31	37	76
Guinea-Bissau	980	36	180	35	39	59	26	64
Kenya	24,160	580	370	47	59	54	94	31
Lesotho	1,768	30	550	48	56	94	107	26
Liberia	2,561	111	—	44	55	41	35	61
Madagascar	11,673	587	230	43	51	65	92	20
Malawi	8,507	118	200	39	45	44	71	59

Mali	8,460	1,240	280	38	48	24	24	68
Mauritania	1,969	1,026	500	37	47	13	51	66
Mauritius	1,074	2	2,310	61	70	101	106	17
Mozambique	15,707	802	80	38	47	37	58	67
Niger	7,666	1,267	310	37	46	11	29	72
Nigeria[a]	96,203	924	340	39	51	32	70	49
Rwanda	7,118	26	320	44	46	53	69	50
São Tomé and Principe	17	1	410	—	67	—	138	33
Senegal	7,404	197	720	41	48	40	59	62
Seychelles	68	..	5,100	—	71	—	—	—
Sierra Leone	4,136	72	250	33	42	29	53	79
Somalia	7,805	638	120	38	48	10	15	76
Sudan	25,188	2,506	—	40	51	29	49	73
Swaziland	797	17	1,030	43	57	74	104	32
Tanzania	24,517	945	100	43	51	32	63	—
Togo	3,638	57	410	42	54	55	103	57
Uganda	16,330	236	180	47	46	67	71	52
Zaïre	37,320	2,345	220	43	52	70	79	28
Zambia	8,111	753	460	44	49	53	95	27
Zimbabwe	9,805	391	680	48	60	110	125	33
India	**849,515**	**3,288**	**360**	**47**	**60**	**74**	**97**	**52**
China	**1,133,698**	**9,561**	**370**	**55**	**70**	**89**	**135**	**27**

— Not available.
.. Less than 0.5.
Note: Excludes Namibia (pop. 1,780,000) and South Africa (pop. 35,919,000), as well as Mayotte (pop. 73,000), Réunion (pop. 593,000), Ascension (pop. 1,000), St. Helena (pop. 6,000), and Tristan da Cunha (pop. 300).
a. Following the 1992 Census, Nigeria's population estimates have been revised downward.
Source: World Bank 1992b, 1993a, 1993b, 1993c; UNDP/World Bank 1992; Bos and others 1992.

Table A-2. Population Growth and Fertility Rates

Country	Average Annual Growth of Population (percent)		Projected[a]		Total fertility rate[b]	
	1965–80	1980–90	1990–95	1995–2000	1965	1990
Sub-Saharan Africa	**2.7**	**3.1**	**2.9**	**2.8**	**6.6**	**6.4**
Angola	2.8	2.6	2.8	3.1	6.4	6.5
Benin	2.7	3.2	3.0	2.7	6.8	6.4
Botswana	3.6	3.3	2.8	2.2	6.9	4.7
Burkina Faso	2.1	2.6	2.8	2.9	6.4	6.5
Burundi	1.9	2.8	3.1	3.1	6.4	6.8
Cameroon	2.7	3.0	2.9	2.9	5.2	5.9
Cape Verde	1.6	2.4	3.2	2.8	—	—
Central African Rep.	1.8	2.7	2.5	2.4	4.5	5.8
Chad	2.0	2.4	2.6	2.8	6.0	6.0
Comoros	2.2	3.5	3.5	3.3	—	—
Congo	2.8	3.4	3.2	3.2	5.7	6.6
Côte d'Ivoire	4.1	3.8	3.5	3.3	7.4	6.7
Djibouti	—	3.3	3.1	3.1	—	—
Equatorial Guinea	1.7	1.9	2.2	2.3	—	—
Ethiopia	2.7	3.1	3.3	3.4	5.8	7.5
Gabon	3.6	3.6	2.7	2.8	4.1	5.7
Gambia, The	3.0	3.3	2.9	2.8	—	—
Ghana	2.2	3.4	3.1	2.9	6.8	6.3
Guinea	1.5	2.5	2.7	2.9	5.9	6.5
Guinea-Buissau	2.9	1.9	1.9	2.0	—	—
Kenya	3.6	3.8	3.5	3.3	8.0	6.6
Lesotho	2.3	2.7	2.7	2.5	5.8	5.6
Liberia	3.0	3.1	3.0	2.9	6.4	6.3
Madagascar	2.5	3.0	2.9	2.7	6.6	6.3
Malawi	2.9	3.4	3.3	3.3	7.8	7.6

Mali	2.1	2.5	2.9	3.1	6.5	7.0
Mauritania	2.4	2.4	2.7	2.9	6.5	6.8
Mauritius	1.6	1.0	0.9	0.9	4.8	1.9
Mozambique	2.5	2.6	2.9	3.1	6.8	6.4
Niger	2.6	3.3	3.1	3.3	7.1	7.1
Nigeria	2.5	3.2	2.9	2.8	6.9	6.0
Rwanda	3.3	3.3	3.9	3.7	7.5	8.3
São Tomé and Principe	2.1	2.7	2.6	2.4	—	—
Senegal	2.9	2.9	3.0	3.1	6.4	6.5
Seychelles	1.9	0.7	1.0	1.0	—	—
Sierra Leone	2.0	2.4	2.5	2.6	6.4	6.5
Somalia	2.9	3.1	3.0	3.1	6.7	6.8
Sudan	3.0	2.7	2.8	2.7	6.7	6.3
Swaziland	2.8	3.3	3.4	3.3	—	—
Tanzania	2.9	3.1	3.0	3.1	6.6	6.6
Togo	3.0	3.5	3.3	3.1	6.5	6.7
Uganda	3.0	2.5	3.3	3.2	7.0	7.3
Zaïre	3.1	3.2	3.0	2.9	6.0	6.3
Zambia	3.0	3.7	3.2	2.9	6.6	6.7
Zimbabwe	3.1	3.4	2.7	2.1	8.0	5.0
India	**2.3**	**2.1**	**1.8**	**1.6**	**6.2**	**4.0**
China	**2.2**	**1.4**	**1.4**	**1.2**	**6.4**	**2.5**

— Not available.

a. Projections are based on present trends; hence the slight decline in growth rates results only from the slightly declining trend in a few countries. The projections include the probable impact of AIDS. They do not include the impact of more successful population programs.

b. The Total Fertility Rate (TFR) is the average number of children who would be born alive to a woman during her lifetime if she were to pass through her childbearing years conforming to the age-specific fertility rates of a given year.

Source: World Bank 1992b, 1993c; Bos and others 1992.

Table A-3. Crude Birth and Death Rates, Infant and Child Mortality Rates, 1965 and 1990

| Country | Crude birth rate per 1,000 population | | Crude death rate per 1,000 population | | Infant mortality per 1,000 live births | | Child mortality (under age 5) per 1,000 live births |
	1965	1990	mid-1960s	1990	mid-1960s	MRY	MRY
Sub-Saharan Africa	**48**	**46**	**23**	**16**	**157**	**107**	**177**
Angola	49	47	29	19	192	127	214
Benin	49	46	24	15	166	111	166
Botswana	53	35	19	6	112	36	40
Burkina Faso	48	47	26	18	190	133	199
Burundi	47	49	24	18	144	107	179
Cameroon	40	41	20	12	143	64	121
Cape Verde	—	—	—	—	97	43	50
Central African Rep.	34	42	24	16	157	106	129
Chad	45	44	28	18	183	124	208
Comoros	—	—	—	—	152	90	128
Congo	42	48	18	15	129	115	168
Côte d'Ivoire	52	45	22	12	149	95	154
Djibouti	—	—	—	—	171	113	189
Equatorial Guinea	—	—	—	—	177	118	198
Ethiopia	43	51	20	18	165	130	195
Gabon	31	42	22	15	153	95	154
Gambia, The	—	—	—	—	199	134	227
Ghana	47	44	18	13	120	83	131
Guinea	46	48	29	21	191	136	227
Guinea-Bissau	—	—	—	—	192	148	249
Kenya	52	45	20	10	112	67	105
Lesotho	42	40	18	12	142	81	157
Liberia	46	44	20	14	176	134	218
Madagascar	47	45	22	15	201	114	165
Malawi	56	54	26	20	200	143	195

Mali	50	50	27	19	207	161	193
Mauritania	47	48	26	19	178	119	199
Mauritius	36	17	8	6	65	19	25
Mozambique	49	46	27	18	179	149	280
Niger	48	51	29	20	180	126	320
Nigeria	51	43	23	14	162	85	186
Rwanda	52	54	17	18	145	111	222
São Tomé and Principe	—	—	—	—	—	67	88
Senegal	47	45	23	17	160	81	150
Seychelles	—	—	—	7	—	17	21
Sierra Leone	48	47	31	22	208	145	359
Somalia	50	48	26	18	165	128	210
Sudan	47	44	24	15	160	101	166
Swaziland	—	—	—	—	148	110	144
Tanzania	49	48	23	18	138	115	162
Togo	50	48	22	14	153	87	140
Uganda	49	51	19	19	119	118	185
Zaire	47	45	21	14	140	95	150
Zambia	49	49	20	15	121	106	176
Zimbabwe	55	37	17	8	103	48	57
India	**45**	**30**	**20**	**11**	**150**	**90**	**124**
China	**38**	**22**	**10**	**7**	**90**	**38**	**43**

—Not available.

MRY Most recent year (usually 1990).

Source: World Bank 1992b, 1993a.

Table A-4. Population Estimates and Projections Based on Targeted Decline of 50 Percent in Total Fertility Rate by 2030

Country	Population (thousands)				Hypothetical stationary population[a] (millions)	Average annual population growth (percent)			Total fertility rate (TFR)			Assumed year of reaching NRR=1[b]
	1980	1990	2020	2030		1990–95	2020–25	2025–30	1990–95	2020–25	2025–30	
Sub-Saharan Africa[c]	**351,114**	**476,086**	**1,071,870**	**1,305,581**	**2,604**	**2.99**	**2.05**	**1.84**	**6.24**	**3.53**	**3.12**	**2055**
Angola	6,993	10,012	23,662	29,604	61	2.84	2.36	2.12	6.56	4.19	3.59	2045
Benin	3,464	4,740	9,647	11,223	19	2.97	1.60	1.43	6.20	2.88	2.59	2035
Botswana	902	1,277	2,303	2,613	4	2.75	1.33	1.20	4.33	2.09	2.08	2015
Burkina Faso	6,962	9,016	20,110	24,511	48	2.79	2.12	1.84	6.50	3.80	3.20	2045
Burundi	4,130	5,492	12,544	15,522	32	3.14	2.27	1.99	6.80	4.10	3.50	2045
Cameroon	8,701	11,524	25,793	30,622	53	2.87	1.83	1.63	5.85	2.93	2.57	2035
Cape Verde	289	371	768	898	1	3.16	1.64	1.47	5.28	2.23	2.10	2025
Central African Rep.	2,320	3,008	5,706	6,607	11	2.53	1.54	1.39	5.75	2.98	2.65	2035
Chad	4,477	5,680	12,229	14,786	28	2.56	2.00	1.79	6.03	3.60	3.10	2040
Comoros	333	475	1,163	1,416	3	3.45	2.12	1.81	6.70	3.13	2.65	2035
Congo	1,630	2,276	5,638	7,050	14	3.23	2.39	2.08	6.61	3.84	3.24	2045
Côte d'Ivoire	8,194	11,902	28,499	34,343	63	3.54	1.95	1.78	6.61	3.23	2.86	2040
Djibouti	304	427	967	1,153	2	3.13	1.86	1.67	6.60	3.30	2.91	2040
Equatorial Guinea	341	417	773	894	2	2.22	1.54	1.37	5.50	3.00	2.65	2035
Ethiopia	37,717	51,180	135,523	177,229	417	3.29	2.81	2.56	7.50	4.80	4.20	2050
Gabon	797	1,136	2,524	3,097	6	2.74	2.19	1.91	5.92	3.75	3.15	2045
Gambia, The	634	875	1,953	2,413	5	2.88	2.22	2.01	6.50	4.40	3.80	2045
Ghana	10,740	14,870	31,765	36,944	62	3.09	1.65	1.37	6.10	2.72	2.34	2030
Guinea	4,461	5,717	13,005	16,112	33	2.70	2.25	2.04	6.50	4.40	3.80	2045
Guinea-Bissau	809	980	1,760	2,054	4	1.90	1.61	1.48	6.00	3.90	3.39	2040
Kenya	16,632	24,160	58,239	70,146	124	3.48	1.99	1.73	6.43	3.02	2.61	2035
Lesotho	1,339	1,768	3,398	3,867	6	2.69	1.35	1.24	5.50	2.34	2.20	2025
Liberia	1,879	2,561	5,463	6,427	11	3.01	1.73	1.52	6.20	2.85	2.54	2035
Madagascar	8,714	11,673	23,781	27,437	45	2.89	1.56	1.30	6.16	2.79	2.40	2030
Malawi	6,138	8,507	21,263	27,323	62	3.34	2.61	2.40	7.60	4.90	4.30	2050

Mali	6,590	8,460	20,643	26,399	57	2.87	2.58	2.34	7.06	4.47	3.87	2050
Mauritania	1,551	1,969	4,700	6,027	14	2.69	2.59	2.38	6.80	4.70	4.10	2050
Mauritius	966	1,075	1,362	1,427	2	0.86	0.50	0.42	1.75	2.01	2.06	2030
Mozambique	12,103	15,707	36,906	46,257	96	2.88	2.38	2.14	6.52	4.26	3.66	2045
Namibia[d]	1,066	1,439	3,759	4,374	7	3.01	1.64	1.39	5.79	2.59	2.27	2030
Niger	5,515	7,666	20,434	27,115	72	3.12	2.92	2.74	7.18	5.25	4.65	2055
Nigeria	71,148	96,203	197,719	231,711	398	2.87	1.69	1.48	5.86	2.89	2.57	2035
Réunion	506	593	849	919	1	1.51	0.83	0.75	2.16	2.05	2.05	1995
Rwanda[d]	5,163	6,921	19,567	25,700	65	3.93	2.84	2.61	8.29	4.99	4.39	2055
São Tomé and Principe	94	115	220	249	..	2.60	1.31	1.19	4.95	2.16	2.06	2025
Senegal	5,538	7,404	17,347	21,332	43	3.04	2.21	1.92	6.50	3.80	3.20	2045
Seychelles	63	68	92	102	..	0.95	1.01	0.90	2.70	2.07	2.07	2005
Sierra Leone	3,263	4,136	8,986	11,127	23	2.46	2.24	2.04	6.50	4.40	3.80	2045
Somalia	5,746	7,805	18,571	23,092	47	2.98	2.31	2.04	6.77	4.07	3.47	2045
South Africa[d]	29,529	37,959	61,183	68,300	96	2.32	1.14	1.06	4.08	2.12	2.11	2020
Sudan	19,152	25,118	51,095	59,662	101	2.84	1.65	1.45	6.22	3.00	2.65	2035
Swaziland	565	797	1,938	2,338	4	3.44	2.02	1.73	6.57	3.07	2.64	2035
Tanzania	18,098	24,470	56,990	70,466	144	3.02	2.24	2.00	6.61	4.13	3.53	2045
Togo	2,615	3,638	8,289	9,896	17	3.32	1.90	1.64	6.50	3.04	2.65	2035
Uganda	12,807	16,330	37,416	45,670	91	3.29	2.13	1.86	7.30	4.00	3.40	2045
Zaïre	27,009	37,391	81,408	96,557	171	3.04	1.83	1.58	6.22	3.15	2.72	2035
Zambia	5,647	8,050	17,949	21,553	41	3.18	1.93	1.73	6.67	3.51	3.06	2040
Zimbabwe	7,009	9,805	16,964	19,046	28	2.65	1.20	1.11	4.55	2.22	2.19	2015
India	**687,332**	**849,515**	**1,284,486**	**1,407,236**	**1,855**	**1.81**	**0.96**	**0.87**	**3.74**	**2.15**	**2.12**	**2015**
China	**981,234**	**1,133,698**	**1,540,268**	**1,647,707**	**1,886**	**1.44**	**0.73**	**0.62**	**2.37**	**2.08**	**2.08**	**2000**

.. Less than 500,000.

a. Assumes that a fertility transition will start in any country in the 5-year period when the combined male and female life expectancy reaches 50 years, but in any case no later than in 2005. This implies that for SSA as a whole the TFR will be 50 percent lower during 2025–2030 than it is today.

(Table continues on the following page.)

Table A-4 (*continued*)

  b. Even when the net reproduction rate (NRR) reaches one, the age structure is such that the number of women in, or yet to enter, their childbearing years causes total births to exceed total deaths. Populations will therefore continue to increase for considerable periods before reaching their hypothetical stationary levels.

  c. Sub-Saharan Africa here excludes Namibia and South Africa.

  d. Population estimates for Namibia (1980 and 1990), Rwanda (1990) and South Africa (1980 and 1990) as shown here and reported in World Bank 1993b have been significantly revised since the publication of demographic projections in Bos and others 1992.

  Source: Bos and others 1992; World Bank 1993b.

Table A-5. Contraceptive Prevalence Rates Required to Achieve Target Population Projections in Table A-4

Country	Estimated contraceptive prevalence rates (percent)[a]			
	1990	2020	2025	2030
Sub-Saharan Africa	**10.8**	**45.3**	**50.5**	**55.5**
Angola	4.0	30.9	34.9	38.8
Botswana	35.8	63.5	68.1	72.8
Burkina Faso	7.0	36.2	41.0	45.7
Burundi	12.5	46.9	52.1	57.2
Cameroon	7.9	42.4	47.6	52.6
Chad	6.1	35.2	39.9	44.4
Côte d'Ivoire	7.8	41.7	46.8	51.7
Ethiopia	4.6	27.6	31.9	36.4
Ghana	16.8	53.8	59.7	65.7
Guinea	7.4	48.7	55.2	61.6
Kenya	28.1	63.6	72.1	78.8
Liberia	11.3	49.8	56.5	63.4
Madagascar	6.7	49.2	56.3	63.4
Malawi	4.9	30.7	34.6	38.5
Mali	7.0	29.6	33.4	37.2
Mozambique	4.6	36.4	41.2	45.8
Niger	5.0	24.1	27.2	30.1
Nigeria	9.2	49.5	56.0	62.4
Rwanda	13.5	39.7	44.4	49.1
Senegal	14.2	42.0	46.5	50.9
Somalia	5.7	33.4	38.3	43.2
Sudan	10.6	47.8	54.2	60.7
Tanzania	11.9	47.6	53.1	58.5
Togo	36.9	63.3	67.2	71.0
Uganda	7.2	40.1	45.7	51.4
Zaïre	5.3	41.4	47.8	54.5
Zambia	8.2	41.7	47.6	53.5
Zimbabwe	45.8	72.8	77.3	81.9
India	**37.7**	**64.2**	**61.4**	**64.8**
China	**81.2**	**85.0**	**82.6**	**82.8**

a. The estimated contraceptive prevalence rates (CPR) were derived by applying Bongaarts' model to available country-specific information, including data on CPR, contraceptive mix and proportion married, with assumptions on likely changes. (For countries without such information, proxy data from countries with a similar socio-cultural background were utilized.) The CPR estimates refer to the percentage of women aged 14–49 using contraception (both modern and traditional). For India and China, they refer to married women aged 15–44. Countries in this table are selected on the basis of the size of their population (over 5 million) and/or availability of information from Phase 1 of the Demographic and Health Surveys (Oct. 1984–Sept. 1989).

Source: World Bank; Demographic and Health Surveys, Institute of Resource Development/Macro System, Inc., Columbia, Md.

Table A-6. Demand for Contraception and its Components Among Currently Married Women

Country	Demand for Contraception			Unmet Needs			Current Use			Percent of Demand Satisfied		
	Total	For spacing	For limiting	Total	For spacing	For limiting	Total	For spacing	For limiting	Total	For spacing	For limiting
Sub-Saharan Africa												
Botswana	61.6	38.6	23.0	26.9	19.4	7.4	33.0	17.9	15.1	53.6	46.4	65.7
Burundi	33.8	23.5	10.3	25.1	17.7	7.4	8.7	5.8	2.9	25.8	24.7	28.2
Ghana	48.1	34.2	13.9	35.2	26.2	9.0	12.9	8.0	4.9	26.8	23.4	35.3
Kenya	64.9	31.0	33.9	38.0	22.4	15.5	26.9	8.6	18.3	41.5	27.7	54.0
Liberia	39.3	23.4	15.8	32.8	19.8	13.0	6.4	3.6	2.9	16.4	15.4	18.4
Mali	27.6	21.2	6.4	22.9	17.2	5.7	4.7	4.0	0.7	17.0	18.9	10.9
Togo	52.2	36.4	15.8	40.1	28.5	11.7	12.1	8.0	4.1	23.2	22.0	25.9
Uganda	32.1	22.0	10.1	27.2	19.9	7.3	4.9	2.1	2.8	15.2	9.5	27.7
Zimbabwe	64.8	37.6	27.2	21.7	10.1	11.6	43.1	27.5	15.6	66.5	73.1	57.4
North Africa												
Egypt	64.8	16.5	48.3	25.2	10.1	15.0	37.8	5.9	31.9	58.4	35.8	66.0
Morocco	60.8	26.4	34.4	22.1	12.5	9.6	35.9	12.7	23.2	59.1	48.1	67.4
Tunisia	71.1	24.9	46.2	19.7	10.6	9.1	49.8	13.5	36.3	70.0	54.2	78.6

Asia

Indonesia	64.7	28.5	36.1	16.0	10.1	6.0	47.8	17.8	29.9	73.8	62.5	82.8
Sri Lanka	73.9	21.5	54.4	12.3	7.2	5.1	61.7	13.1	48.6	81.3	60.9	89.3
Thailand	77.1	21.8	55.3	11.1	5.6	5.5	65.5	15.9	49.6	85.0	72.9	89.7

Latin America and the Caribbean

Bolivia	69.8	17.5	52.3	35.7	9.5	26.2	30.3	6.5	23.8	43.4	37.1	45.5
Brazil	81.1	24.2	56.9	12.8	4.8	8.0	66.2	17.9	48.3	81.6	74.0	84.9
Colombia	80.9	22.1	58.9	13.5	5.1	8.3	64.8	15.4	49.4	80.1	69.7	83.9
Dominican Rep.	71.2	20.8	50.4	19.4	10.0	9.4	49.8	9.6	40.1	69.9	46.2	79.6
Ecuador	70.8	23.8	47.0	24.2	10.8	13.4	44.3	11.6	32.7	62.5	48.7	69.6
Guatemala	53.4	22.1	31.4	29.4	16.4	13.0	23.2	5.1	18.1	43.3	23.1	57.6
Mexico	79.0	25.9	53.1	24.1	11.0	13.1	52.7	13.5	39.2	66.7	52.1	73.8
Peru	77.8	21.7	56.1	27.7	8.1	19.6	45.8	11.2	34.6	58.8	51.6	61.7
El Salvador	73.8	22.3	51.5	26.0	13.9	12.1	47.3	8.1	39.2	64.1	36.3	76.1
Trinidad and Tobago	71.1	28.6	42.5	16.1	8.3	7.9	52.7	18.9	33.8	74.2	66.1	79.5

Note: Data are for the late 1980s. Except for several countries in the last column, all data shown represent the percentage of currently married women. Total demand includes current use, method failures, and unmet needs. Unmet needs include nonuse among women who would like to regulate their fertility. Percent of demand satisfied is the proportion of current use to total demand.

Source: Westoff and Ochoa 1991.

Table A-7. Developing Countries by Strength of Family Planning Programs, 1989

Strong	Moderate	Weak	Very weak or none
Bangladesh	Algeria	Afghanistan	Argentina
Botswana	Chile	**Angola**	Bhutan
China	Colombia	**Benin**	Cambodia
El Salvador	Costa Rica	Bolivia	**Chad**
India	Cuba	Brazil	**Gabon**
Indonesia	Dominican Rep.	**Burkina Faso**	Iraq
Korea, Rep. of	Ecuador	**Burundi**	**Côte d'Ivoire**
Mexico	Egypt	**Cameroon**	Kuwait
Sri Lanka	**Ghana**	**Central Afr. Rep.**	Lao, P.D.R.
Taiwan	Guatemala	**Congo**	**Liberia**
Thailand	Guyana	**Ethiopia**	Libya
Tunisia	Honduras	**Guinea**	**Malawi**
Vietnam	Iran	**Guinea-Bissau**	Myanmar
	Jamaica	Haiti	**Namibia**
	Kenya	Jordan	Oman
	Korea, P.D.R.	**Lesotho**	Saudi Arabia
	Lebanon	**Madagascar**	**Somalia**
	Malaysia	**Mali**	**Sudan**
	Mauritius	**Mauritania**	United Arab Emirates
	Morocco	**Mozambique**	
	Nepal	**Niger**	
	Pakistan	**Nigeria**	
	Panama	Papua New Guinea	
	Peru	Paraguay	
	Philippines	**Rwanda**	
	South Africa	**Senegal**	
	Singapore	**Sierra Leone**	
	Trinidad and Tobago	Syria	
	Venezuela	**Tanzania**	
	Zambia	**Togo**	
	Zimbabwe	Turkey	
		Uganda	
		Uruguay	
		Yemen	
		Zaïre	

Bold type denotes countries in Sub-Saharan Africa.

Note: The maximum possible score for program effort was 120. Country program effort scores were divided into four groups: strong = 80+; moderate = 55–79; weak = 25–54; very weak or none = 0–24. The average score was 53.

Source: Mauldin and Ross 1991.

Table A-8. Total Fertility Rates, Desired Number of Children, Infant and Child Mortality Rates, and Contraceptive Prevalence Rates

Country	DHS survey year	Total fertility rates[b]	Desired number of children		Infant mortality rate[c]	Child mortality rate[c,d]	Contraceptive prevalence rates (% of currently married women)[a]	
			Mean, all women	Mean, women in union			Currently using any method[e]	Currently using any modern method[f]
Botswana	1988	4.7	4.7	5.4	37	53	33	32
Burundi	1987	6.5	5.3	5.5	75	152	7	1
Ghana	1988	6.1	5.3	5.5	77	155	13	5
Kenya	1989	6.5	4.4	4.8	60	89	27	18
Liberia	1986	6.4	6.0	6.5	144	220	6	6
Mali	1987	6.9	6.9	6.9	108	250	3	1
Nigeria	1990	5.7	—	—	87	192	6	4
Nigeria-Ondo State	1986/87	5.7	5.7	6.1	56	108	6	4
Senegal	1986	6.2	6.8	7.2	86	191	5	2
Sudan	1989/90	4.6	—	—	70	123	9	6
Togo	1988	6.1	5.3	5.6	81	158	12	3
Uganda	1988/89	7.2	6.5	6.8	101	180	5	3
Zimbabwe	1988/89	5.3	4.9	5.4	53	75	43	36

— Not available.
a. Women aged 15–49.
b. Based on 3 years preceding the survey; women aged 15–44.
c. Based on 5 years preceding the survey; per thousand.
d. Children under 5 years of age.
e. Excluding prolonged sexual abstinence.
f. Excluding periodic abstinence, withdrawal, and "other" methods.
Source: Demographic and Health Surveys, Institute of Resource Development/Macro International, Columbia, Md.

Table A-9. Performance of the Agriculture Sector

Country	Agricultural GDP, average annual growth (percent)		Agricultural share of GDP (percent)	
	1970–80	1980–91[a]	1965	1991[b]
Sub-Saharan Africa	**1.5**	**1.8**	**40**	**31**
Angola	—	-0.5	—	13
Benin	1.8	4.9	59	37
Botswana	8.3	3.0	34	5
Burkina Faso	1.0	3.2	37	44
Burundi	3.2	3.1	—	55
Cameroon	4.0	1.1	33	27
Cape Verde	—	—	—	—
Central African Rep.	1.9	2.4	46	41
Chad	-0.4	3.4	42	43
Comoros	—	—	—	—
Congo	2.5	3.3	19	12
Côte d'Ivoire	2.7	-1.2	47	38
Djibouti	—	—	—	—
Equatorial Guinea	—	—	—	—
Ethiopia	0.7	0.3	58	47
Gabon	—	0.9	26	9
Gambia, The	—	7.1	—	—
Ghana	-0.3	1.2	44	53
Guinea	—	—	—	29
Guinea-Bissau	-1.2	5.0	—	46
Kenya	4.8	3.2	35	27
Lesotho	0.2	1.8	65	14
Liberia	—	—	27	—
Madagascar	0.4	2.4	25	33
Malawi	4.4	2.4	50	35

Mali	4.2	2.4	65	44
Mauritania	-1.0	0.7	32	22
Mauritius	-3.3	3.2	16	11
Mozambique	—	16	—	64
Niger	-3.7	—	68	38
Nigeria	-0.1	3.5	55	37
Rwanda	7.1	-1.5	75	38
São Tomé and Principe	—	-1.3	—	—
Senegal	1.3	2.7	25	20
Seychelles	—	-2.9	—	—
Sierra Leone	6.0	2.7	34	43
Somalia	—	3.3	71	65
Sudan	3.3	—	54	—
Swaziland	—	3.9	—	—
Tanzania	0.7	4.4	46	61
Togo	1.9	5.3	45	33
Uganda	—	2.5	52	51
Zaïre	—	2.5	20	30
Zambia	2.1	3.3	14	16
Zimbabwe	0.6	2.2	18	20
India	1.8	3.2	44	31
China	2.6	5.7	38	27

— Not available.

a. 1980–1988 for The Gambia, São Tomé and Principe, Seychelles, Swaziland; 1980–90 for Angola, Somalia, Uganda, Zaïre.

b. 1990 for Angola, Somalia, Zaïre.

Source: World Bank 1992b, 1993c.

Table A-10. Food Security

Country	Population facing food insecurity 1980/82 (millions)	(percent of total)	Average daily supply of calories per capita 1965	Average 1986–89	Average supply as percentage of minimum requirement[a]	Average annual cereal imports ('000 tons) 1974	1990	Index of per capita food production (1979–81 = 100) 1964–66	1989–90
Sub-Saharan Africa	98	28	2,074	2,027	87	4,209	7,838	—	94
Angola	—	—	1,907	1,742	74	149	272	127	81
Benin	1	18	2,019	2,115	92	8	126	94	112
Botswana	—	—	2,025	2,251	97	21	87	134	113
Burkina Faso	2	32	1,882	2,002	84	99	145	113	114
Burundi	1	26	2,131	2,320	100	7	17	100	92
Cameroon	1	9	2,011	2,142	92	81	398	89	89
Cape Verde	—	—	—	2,500	107	—	—	163	—
Central African Rep.	1	29	2,055	1,965	87	7	37	94	91
Chad	2	54	2,395	1,821	76	37	36	124	85
Comoros	—	—	—	2,059	88	—	—	114	—
Congo	0	27	2,260	2,519	114	34	94	110	94
Côte d'Ivoire	1	8	2,352	2,405	104	172	502	73	101
Djibouti	—	—	—	—	—	—	—	—	—
Equatorial Guinea	—	—	—	—	—	—	—	—	—
Ethiopia	15	46	1,853	1,684	72	118	687	111	84
Gabon	0	7	1,955	2,398	103	24	57	110	84
Gambia, The	0	19	—	2,339	98	—	—	152	—
Ghana	4	36	1,937	2,167	94	177	337	120	97
Guinea	—	—	2,187	2,007	87	63	210	106	87
Guinea-Bissau	—	—	—	2,437	106	—	—	140	—

228

Country									
Kenya	6	37	2,208	2,016	87	15	188	119	106
Lesotho	—	—	2,049	2,275	100	48	97	120	86
Liberia	1	30	2,158	2,344	101	42	70	95	84
Madagascar	1	13	2,447	2,174	95	114	183	105	88
Malawi	1	24	2,259	2,057	89	17	115	87	83
Mali	3	35	1,938	2,114	90	281	61	100	97
Mauritania	0	25	1,903	2,465	107	116	85	143	86
Mauritius	0	9	2,269	2,690	118	160	210	111	100
Mozambique	6	49	1,712	1,604	68	62	416	132	81
Niger	2	28	1,996	2,321	98	155	86	105	71
Nigeria	14	17	2,185	2,083	88	389	502	125	106
Rwanda	1	24	1,856	1,817	78	3	21	78	77
São Tomé and Principe	—	—	—	2,529	108	—	—	—	—
Senegal	1	21	2,372	2,162	91	341	534	156	102
Seychelles	—	—	—	2,117	91	—	—	—	—
Sierra Leone	1	23	2,014	1,813	79	72	146	99	89
Somalia	2	50	1,718	1,781	77	42	194	144	94
Sudan	3	18	1,938	1,981	84	125	186	89	71
Swaziland	—	—	—	2,554	110	—	—	68	—
Tanzania	7	35	1,831	2,186	94	431	73	87	88
Togo	1	29	2,454	2,110	92	6	111	118	88
Uganda	6	46	2,361	2,034	88	36	7	110	95
Zaïre	12	42	2,187	2,079	93	343	336	110	97
Zambia	3	48	2,072	2,028	87	93	100	98	103
Zimbabwe	—	—	2,075	2,193	92	56	83	96	94

— Not available.

a. Average per capita daily calorie supply data for 1986–89 divided by requirement established by WHO for each country.

Note: Food security is defined as access to enough food for an active and healthy life. The minimum daily calorie requirement to meet the energy needs of an average healthy person, as calculated by the World Health Organization for each country, is taken into account.

Source: Index of food production, cereal imports, per capita calorie supply 1965 from World Bank 1992b; except for Cape Verde, Comoros, The Gambia, Guinea-Bissau, São Tomé and Principe, Seychelles, Swaziland for which the source is World Bank 1989d. Per capita calorie supply 1986–89 is taken from UNDP/World Bank 1992 (Table 13-8).

Table A-11. Crop Yields

Country	Cereals		Roots and tubers	
	Tons/ha 1989	Average annual percentage change over 1964–66	Tons/ha 1989	Average annual percentage change over 1964–66
Angola	0.3	-4.2	4.1	1.1
Benin	0.9	1.8	9.3	1.2
Botswana	0.3	-2.1	5.4	1.7
Burkina Faso	0.7	1.6	6.0	4.3
Burundi	1.2	0.8	8.1	0.0
Cameroon	1.3	2.0	2.6	0.8
Cape Verde	—	—	—	—
Central African Rep.	1.0	0.9	3.5	0.7
Chad	0.5	-0.5	5.5	1.3
Comoros	—	—	—	—
Congo	0.7	-2.0	6.4	2.1
Côte d'Ivoire	0.9	0.3	6.1	2.3
Djibouti	—	—	—	—
Equatorial Guinea	—	—	—	—
Ethiopia	1.2	2.0	3.3	-0.2
Gabon	1.4	0.4	6.2	1.1
Gambia, The	—	—	—	—
Ghana	1.0	-0.3	6.2	-0.7
Guinea	0.9	-0.4	5.5	-0.6
Guinea-Bissau	—	—	—	—
Kenya	1.7	1.0	8.6	0.3
Lesotho	0.8	0.3	14.0	0.4
Liberia	1.2	1.3	7.2	1.0
Madagascar	2.0	0.2	6.4	-0.1
Malawi	1.2	0.6	3.1	-1.8

Mali	0.9	1.0	8.5	0.4
Mauritania	1.0	4.2	1.8	0.0
Mauritius	3.8	2.4	20.2	2.1
Mozambique	0.5	-3.0	6.3	0.7
Niger	0.4	-0.8	7.1	0.2
Nigeria	1.2	3.2	12.4	1.2
Rwanda	1.1	0.4	7.8	0.7
São Tomé and Principe	—	—	—	—
Senegal	0.8	1.7	4.3	0.5
Seychelles	—	—	—	—
Sierra Leone	1.4	0.2	3.3	-1.0
Somalia	0.8	2.1	10.4	0.2
Sudan	0.4	-2.4	2.2	-1.4
Swaziland	—	—	—	—
Tanzania	1.5	3.6	7.3	2.7
Togo	0.9	1.6	8.3	-2.7
Uganda	1.5	1.6	6.3	2.0
Zaïre	0.8	0.6	7.5	0.4
Zambia	1.7	4.6	3.7	0.5
Zimbabwe	1.5	0.7	4.8	0.9
India	**2.0**	**2.8**	**15.7**	**2.2**
China	**4.0**	**3.9**	**15.0**	**1.9**

— Not available.

Source: World Bank 1992b (pp. 202–203).

Table A-12. Growth Rates of Average Yields of Major Cereal and Export Crops

	Average annual growth rate (percent)					
	Major cereal crop			Major export crop		
Country/crops	1975–80	1980–85	1986–MRY	1975–80	1980–85	1986–MRY
Angola (maize, coffee)	-6.1	-4.5	-6.9	-21.4	-19.7	-14.3
Benin (maize, cotton)	1.2	3.8	7.0	-2.0	13.6	-0.8
Botswana (maize, n.a.)	-28.7	-11.9	-16.2	—	—	—
Burkina Faso (maize, cotton)	7.4	-1.9	7.7	5.5	7.3	-5.3
Burundi (maize, coffee)	-1.3	0.6	-0.8	4.2	9.6	-1.3
Cameroon (maize, coffee)	-7.3	0.3	4.0	2.8	0.6	-10.3
Central African Rep. (maize, coffee)	-2.4	16.9	-4.6	-1.0	1.6	4.4
Chad (sorghum, cotton)	-0.8	-1.8	0.0	2.0	6.9	-4.8
Congo (maize, coffee)	3.7	-4.5	7.4	18.7	1.0	16.2
Côte d'Ivoire (maize, coffee)	6.3	1.8	-1.2	-6.5	-10.8	-8.4
Equatorial Guinea (n.a., coffee)	—	—	—	0.8	1.4	0.0
Ethiopia (maize, coffee)	-2.5	-5.1	1.2	3.7	1.0	3.2
Gabon (maize, coffee)	4.1	-3.0	7.6	1.6	9.9	2.9
Gambia, The (rice, groundnuts)	7.3	5.9	-0.5	-9.3	3.4	0.9
Ghana (maize, cocoa)	-2.9	-0.5	5.9	-3.6	-1.0	11.2
Guinea (maize, coffee)	-3.3	2.4	-0.1	-0.1	-3.7	-2.2
Guinea-Bissau (rice, groundnuts)	-6.6	6.2	4.5	-3.5	5.1	2.5
Kenya (maize, coffee)	-7.2	4.0	-1.3	3.9	-5.9	-0.6
Lesotho (maize, wheat)	11.4	-4.6	6.3	3.8	-12.3	3.5
Liberia (rice, coffee)	0.5	0.0	-1.0	7.5	3.9	-23.2

Madagascar (rice, coffee)	-1.4	1.5	3.3	-1.7	-1.1	0.6
Malawi (maize, tea)	3.5	-0.1	4.3	1.6	1.1	1.8
Mali (sorghum, cotton)	0.6	8.6	3.0	1.2	2.6	-3.1
Mauritania (sorghum, n.a.)	-12.8	-4.1	-5.8	—	—	—
Mauritius[a] (potatoes, sugarcane)	1.7	8.7	0.3	1.1	2.1	-3.7
Mozambique (maize, cotton)	4.7	-2.7	0.0	1.3	-7.4	-11.8
Namibia (maize, wheat)	-0.9	0.6	2.9	0.0	4.3	-5.3
Niger (sorghum, groundnuts)	6.3	-10.2	-0.2	28.7	-11.5	9.2
Nigeria (maize, cocoa)	-1.3	-5.2	1.5	-4.5	-6.7	15.9
Rwanda (maize, coffee)	1.4	0.5	0.4	3.3	2.2	7.9
Senegal (maize, cotton)	-6.5	9.7	6.4	-3.7	-1.4	7.6
Sierra Leone (rice, coffee)	-3.8	2.5	-4.3	13.7	-11.2	-17.8
Somalia (maize, bananas)	-1.4	8.5	-6.7	1.0	-0.1	-0.8
Sudan (sorghum, cotton)	-2.7	-9.1	-4.8	-4.5	20.0	5.3
Swaziland (maize, cotton)	-3.6	-0.8	7.7	6.4	-1.5	0.0
Tanzania (maize, coffee)	1.0	1.1	9.7	-1.8	-0.4	-8.3
Togo (maize, coffee)	-0.8	-1.5	20.9	-5.7	-13.1	4.6
Uganda (maize, coffee)	1.1	-3.1	2.7	-8.3	4.9	10.2
Zaïre (maize, coffee)	2.1	1.0	2.4	-4.3	-0.2	0.4
Zambia (maize, cotton)	3.3	0.9	3.9	-5.4	11.5	-2.5
Zimbabwe (maize, cotton)	-6.0	-1.5	1.1	0.8	3.3	-15.0

— Not available.

MRY Most recent year.

a. Data shown for major cereal crop refer to potatoes.

Source: UNDP/World Bank 1992 (Table 8-15).

233

Table A-13. Growth of Agricultural Exports (Value and Volume)

| Country | Average annual growth rate (percent) | | | | | |
| | Value | | | Volume | | |
	1975–80	1980–85	1986–MRY	1975–80	1980–85	1986–MRY
Sub-Saharan Africa	**9.6**	**-2.4**	**-3.1**	**-0.8**	**-2.9**	**-2.5**
Angola	-2.4	-13.0	-36.5	-19.1	-14.2	-12.3
Benin	12.9	17.6	5.4	1.6	5.9	2.8
Botswana	3.2	0.8	3.5	-10.0	10.4	-28.0
Burkina Faso	10.9	-5.1	17.5	-0.8	-8.1	0.9
Burundi	13.2	9.5	-15.9	-14.4	10.0	10.2
Cameroon	17.7	-5.2	-1.2	-1.2	0.0	1.5
Central African Rep.	13.2	-0.9	-5.0	-5.6	-0.3	1.8
Chad	14.2	6.1	9.0	3.2	-6.6	-4.2
Comoros	9.7	0.9	-5.9	-1.6	8.5	-32.3
Congo	6.6	4.1	-3.5	-24.8	34.2	1.6
Côte d'Ivoire	19.9	1.5	-8.6	2.3	3.6	-4.0
Djibouti	—	10.3	9.3	—	28.8	19.9
Equatorial Guinea	2.5	8.7	-16.4	-7.2	7.7	4.4
Ethiopia	13.7	-2.9	-11.2	-14.5	8.1	11.2
Gabon	48.9	-10.0	-19.3	13.5	-3.0	-11.5
Gambia, The	-9.1	-1.6	3.1	-11.6	-3.6	23.2
Ghana	7.2	-10.6	-7.4	-13.4	-5.1	8.6
Guinea	13.3	-10.4	0.2	3.4	-8.2	-1.3
Guinea-Bissau	7.8	81	11.5	0.6	0.2	-3.8
Kenya	15.2	1.7	-4.6	1.8	0.5	-1.7
Lesotho	12.2	4.2	16.2	-3.8	-5.6	-56.9
Liberia	21.4	-2.5	-5.0	0.9	2.3	-2.5
Madagascar	9.8	-6.1	-10.4	-5.5	-3.4	1.6
Malawi	13.5	0.7	10.0	11.3	5.0	-11.7
Mali	20.7	-2.1	9.6	13.0	-0.5	-6.0

234

Mauritania	15.9	-3.9	1.5	0.1	-6.7	-6.0
Mauritius	4.5	-4.8	4.9	4.4	-0.7	1.7
Mozambique	7.0	-26.7	-1.1	-6.8	-23.9	17.0
Namibia	7.9	-3.8	9.5	—	-2.1	10.0
Niger	18.6	-6.6	-7.2	5.5	-3.3	-14.0
Nigeria	3.2	-6.1	-7.4	-3.5	-17.2	1.8
Rwanda	10.3	1.6	-11.4	-19.7	6.0	-0.3
São Tomé and Principe	24.7	-14.8	-10.4	6.2	-12.5	-3.1
Senegal	-12.4	6.7	22.0	-18.1	-3.0	33.2
Seychelles	13.4	-14.9	-19.4	-4.7	-7.9	-37.2
Sierra Leone	18.7	-1.7	-24.2	-7.3	-2.4	-0.4
Somalia	11.2	-14.3	-7.8	6.4	-10.6	-21.7
Sudan	4.2	-4.1	13.4	6.6	-6.9	24.2
Swaziland	14.0	-12.7	6.2	7.0	2.3	-8.0
Tanzania	4.2	-10.0	-3.1	-4.6	-10.4	7.0
Togo	18.3	1.3	-4.8	0.9	0.6	-8.9
Uganda	4.8	5.1	-18.8	-15.3	8.2	2.1
Zaïre	0.3	2.8	-19.3	-6.5	-2.7	-12.6
Zambia	-2.6	4.9	2.7	-18.7	31.0	-31.6
Zimbabwe	2.4	-1.2	8.3	-11.8	3.6	-10.7

— Not available.

MRY Most recent year.

Note: Based on values in U.S. dollars (at current prices and exchange rates).

Source: UNDP/World Bank 1992 (Tables 8-8 and 8-9).

Table A-14. Incentive Strength of Official Agricultural Producer Prices

		Ratio of official producers' price to international reference price		
Country	Crop	Average 1975–79	Average 1980–85	Average 1986–MRY
Angola	Coffee	0.22	0.45	0.96
Benin	Cotton (lint)	0.45	0.41	0.54
Botswana	Groundnuts	—	0.61	—
Burkina Faso	Cotton (lint)	0.42	0.34	0.56
Burundi	Coffee	0.51	0.60	0.60
Cameroon	Cotton (lint)	0.42	0.37	0.40
Central African Rep.	Coffee	0.29	0.18	0.34
Chad	Cotton (lint)	0.75	0.51	0.54
Comoros	Vanilla (dried)	0.43	0.32	0.42
Congo	Coffee	0.21	0.26	1.09
Côte d'Ivoire	Cocoa	0.40	0.51	0.79
Equatorial Guinea	Cocoa	—	0.74	0.90
Ethiopia	Coffee	0.45	0.39	0.42
Gabon	Cocoa	0.57	0.49	0.63
Gambia, The	Groundnuts	0.54	0.62	0.71
Ghana	Cocoa	0.30	0.87	0.25
Guinea	Palm kernels	1.08	0.86	0.62
Guinea-Bissau	Groundnuts	0.63	0.51	0.34
Kenya	Coffee	0.82	0.88	0.95
Lesotho	Wheat	—	1.40	1.26

Country	Crop			
Liberia	Coffee	0.42	0.64	0.79
Madagascar	Coffee	0.40	0.29	0.38
Malawi	Groundnuts	0.47	0.65	1.01
Mali	Cotton (lint)	0.34	0.39	0.50
Mauritius	Sugar	0.90	0.61	0.52
Mozambique	Tea	0.64	0.56	0.33
Niger	Cotton (lint)	0.35	0.45	1.13
Nigeria	Cocoa	0.53	1.12	0.49
Rwanda	Coffee	0.58	0.89	0.81
São Tomé and Príncipe	Cocoa	0.36	0.99	—
Senegal	Groundnuts	0.42	0.42	0.81
Sierra Leone	Cocoa	0.47	0.66	0.42
Somalia	Bananas	—	0.43	0.33
Sudan	Groundnuts	0.55	0.40	0.96
Swaziland	Cotton (lint)	0.46	0.29	0.27
Tanzania	Coffee	0.39	0.55	0.36
Togo	Coffee	0.24	0.31	0.54
Uganda	Coffee	0.13	0.22	0.14
Zaïre	Coffee	0.18	0.45	—
Zambia	Tobacco	0.75	0.87	0.36
Zimbabwe	Tobacco	0.66	0.62	0.58

— Not available/not applicable.

MRY Most recent year.

Note: Prices reflect official producers' prices, *not* actual farmgate prices.

Source: UNDP/World Bank 1992 (Table 8-2).

Table A-15. Irrigation and Fertilizer Use

	Percentage of agricultural land irrigated[a]		Fertilizer consumption[b] (100 g/ha)		
Country	1989	Average annual change in percent 1965–89	1970/71	1979/80	1990/91
Sub-Saharan Africa	—	—	**33**	**59**	**90**
Angola	—	—	33	—	—
Benin	0.3	5.8	36	77	38
Botswana	..	3.5	15	8	7
Burkina Faso	0.1	8.0	3	26	39
Burundi	3.2	6.9	5	7	16
Cameroon	0.2	8.5	34	47	31
Cape Verde	—	—	—	—	—
Central African Rep.	—	—	12	1	4
Chad	..	3.6	7	—	18
Comoros	—	—	—	—	—
Congo	..	8.7	525	6	119
Côte d'Ivoire	0.4	8.4	74	165	97
Djibouti	—	—	—	—	—
Equatorial Guinea	—	—	—	—	—
Ethiopia	0.3	0.3	4	27	80
Gabon	—	—	—	3	25
Gambia, The	0.1	4.5	11	65	48
Ghana	0.4	7.3	44	31	7
Guinea	—	—	—	5	17
Guinea-Bissau	—	—	—	—	—
Kenya	0.1	3.9	238	169	477
Lesotho	—	—	10	144	144
Liberia	..	—	63	—	—
Madagascar	2.4	5.3	61	25	26
Malawi	0.5	10.9	52	110	198

	a		b		
Mali	0.6	5.6	31	69	73
Mauritania	..	2.2	11	108	93
Mauritius	15.0	1.0	2,095	2,564	2,616
Mozambique	0.2	8.8	22	78	8
Niger	0.3	3.5	1	5	3
Nigeria	1.2	0.3	2	36	124
Rwanda	0.3	..	3	3	26
São Tomé and Principe	—	—	—	—	—
Senegal	1.7	3.1	17	123	50
Seychelles	—	—	—	—	—
Sierra Leone	0.9	11.7	17	46	20
Somalia	0.3	0.9	27	—	—
Sudan	1.7	0.9	28	27	63
Swaziland	—	—	—	—	—
Tanzania	0.4	8.4	31	90	144
Togo	0.2	4.2	3	49	172
Uganda	0.1	4.8	14	—	—
Zaïre	..	10.9	6	—	—
Zambia	0.1	9.8	73	114	113
Zimbabwe	2.9	9.2	446	443	606
India	**23.8**	**2.3**	**137**	**313**	**743**
China	**10.8**	**1.2**	**410**	**1,273**	**2,777**

— Not available.
.. Less than 0.05 percent.
a. Irrigated land as percentage of arable land and permanent cropland (World Bank 1992b, Table A.7).
b. Fertilizer consumption in terms of plant nutrients per hectare of arable land.
Source: World Bank 1992b, 1993c.

239

Table A-16. Climatic Classes and Soil Constraints

Country	Total land area ('000 ha)	Percent of total land area						Land with no inherent soil constraints (percent)				
		Tropical	Subtropical	Arid	Semiarid	Humid	Cold	'000 ha	Arid	Semiarid	Humid	Cold
Sub-Saharan Africa	**2,437,491**	**87**	**13**	**38**	**10**	**53**	—	**361,996**	**68**	**9**	**24**	—
Angola	124,670	99	1	4	8	87	—	15,726	17	15	68	—
Benin	11,062	100	—	—	1	99	—	360	—	6	94	—
Botswana	56,673	87	13	62	38	—	—	4,792	72	27	1	—
Burkina Faso	27,380	100	—	1	15	84	—	6,899	1	19	80	—
Burundi	2,565	100	—	—	—	100	—	66	—	—	100	—
Cameroon	46,540	100	—	—	1	99	—	1,949	—	2	98	—
Cape Verde	403	100	—	100	—	—	—	84	100	—	—	—
Central African Rep.	62,298	100	—	—	—	100	—	800	—	—	100	—
Chad	125,920	84	16	67	7	27	—	34,160	81	1	17	—
Comoros	223	100	—	—	—	100	—	43	—	—	100	—
Congo	34,150	100	—	—	—	100	—	—	—	—	100	—
Côte d'Ivoire	31,800	100	—	—	—	100	—	730	—	—	100	—
Djibouti	2,318	100	—	100	—	—	—	757	100	—	—	—
Equatorial Guinea	2,805	100	—	—	—	100	—	21	—	—	100	—
Ethiopia	110,100	100	—	38	16	44	—	30,079	38	21	38	3
Gabon	25,767	100	—	—	—	100	—	—	—	—	100	—
Gambia, The	1,000	100	—	—	—	100	—	355	—	—	100	—
Ghana	23,002	100	—	—	—	100	—	878	—	—	100	—
Guinea	24,586	100	—	—	—	100	—	479	—	—	100	—
Guinea-Bissau	2,812	100	—	—	—	100	—	—	—	—	100	—
Kenya	56,697	100	—	71	14	15	—	7,342	79	11	10	—
Lesotho	3,035	100	—	15	13	66	6	1	100	—	—	—
Liberia	9,632	100	—	—	—	100	—	348	—	—	100	—
Madagascar	58,154	100	—	5	8	87	—	2,273	7	30	62	—
Malawi	9,408	100	—	—	—	100	—	1,097	—	—	100	—

Mali	122,019	77	23	64	15	21	—	40,865	81	8	10	—
Mauritania	102,522	60	40	94	5	1	—	58,867	99	1	—	—
Mauritius	185	100	—	—	—	100	—	7	—	—	100	—
Mozambique	78,409	100	—	8	9	82	—	4,952	7	7	86	—
Namibia	82,329	59	41	78	21	1	—	9,308	81	18	1	—
Niger	126,670	77	23	86	13	1	—	41,388	94	5	—	—
Nigeria	91,077	100	—	—	8	92	—	7,797	—	6	94	—
Rwanda	2,495	100	—	—	—	100	—	91	—	—	100	—
Senegal	19,253	100	—	7	14	80	—	2,957	10	20	71	—
Sierra Leone	7,162	100	—	—	—	100	—	187	—	—	100	—
Somalia	62,734	100	—	93	7	—	—	4,519	98	2	—	—
South Africa	122,104	5	95	55	13	32	—	7,482	47	18	34	2
Sudan	237,600	99	1	55	11	34	—	50,390	77	8	15	—
Swaziland	1,720	14	86	—	26	74	—	178	—	7	93	—
Tanzania	88,604	100	—	7	15	78	—	5,052	6	21	74	—
Togo	5,439	100	—	—	—	100	—	319	—	—	100	—
Uganda	19,955	100	—	—	5	95	—	1,210	—	8	92	—
Zaïre	226,760	100	—	—	—	100	—	5,079	—	—	100	—
Zambia	74,072	100	—	—	2	98	—	2,426	—	—	100	—
Zimbabwe	38,667	100	—	8	41	15	—	958	12	65	23	—

— Not available.

Source: WRI 1992 (p. 281).

Table A-17. Land Use

Country	Total land area ('000 ha)	Cropland 1965	Cropland 1980	Cropland 1987	Pasture 1965	Pasture 1980	Pasture 1987	Forest 1965	Forest 1980	Forest 1987	Other 1965	Other 1980	Other 1987	Wilderness 1985	Wilderness 1988
					Land use as a percentage of total land									Wilderness area as percent of total land area[a]	
Sub-Saharan Africa	**2,158,466**	**6**	**7**	**7**	**27**	**27**	**27**	**33**	**31**	**30**	**34**	**35**	**36**	**28**	**25**
Angola	124,670	3	3	3	23	23	23	44	43	43	30	31	31	26	22
Benin	11,062	13	16	17	4	4	4	44	36	33	39	44	47	15	11
Botswana	56,673	2	2	2	74	78	78	2	2	2	23	18	18	63	54
Burkina Faso	27,380	8	10	11	37	37	37	30	26	25	26	27	27	3	3
Burundi	2,565	39	51	52	24	35	36	2	2	3	35	11	10	0	0
Cameroon	46,540	12	15	15	19	18	18	59	55	53	10	12	14	3	3
Cape Verde	403	10	10	10	6	6	6	0	0	0	84	84	84	0	0
Central African Rep.	62,298	3	3	3	5	5	5	58	58	58	34	34	34	39	34
Chad	125,920	2	3	3	36	36	36	12	11	10	50	51	51	52	48
Comoros	223	38	41	44	7	7	7	16	16	16	39	37	34	—	0
Congo	34,150	2	2	2	29	29	29	64	63	62	5	6	7	42	35
Côte d'Ivoire	31,800	8	10	11	9	9	9	60	31	20	22	50	59	16	13
Djibouti	2,318	—	—	—	9	9	9	0	0	0	91	91	91	0	0
Equatorial Guinea	2,805	8	8	8	4	4	4	46	46	46	42	42	42	0	0
Ethiopia	110,100	11	13	13	42	41	41	27	26	25	20	21	22	22	16
Gabon	25,767	1	2	2	20	18	18	78	78	78	2	2	2	35	27
Gambia, The	1,000	13	16	17	9	9	9	30	22	17	48	54	57	0	0
Ghana	23,002	12	12	12	16	15	15	43	38	36	31	35	37	0	0
Guinea	24,586	6	6	6	12	12	12	49	43	41	33	38	41	0	0
Guinea-Bissau	2,812	9	10	12	38	38	38	39	38	38	13	13	12	0	0

	Area														
Kenya	56,969	3	4	4	7	7	7	8	7	6	82	83	83	25	19
Lesotho	3,035	13	10	11	73	66	66	—	—	—	15	24	24	80	70
Liberia	9,632	4	4	4	2	2	2	22	22	22	72	72	72	17	13
Madagascar	58,154	4	5	5	58	58	58	31	27	25	7	9	11	2	1
Malawi	9,408	21	25	25	20	20	20	54	54	46	5	2	9	10	7
Mali	122,019	1	2	2	25	25	25	8	7	7	66	67	67	49	47
Mauritania	102,522	0	0	0	38	38	38	15	15	15	47	47	47	74	70
Mauritius	185	51	58	58	4	4	4	34	31	31	12	7	7	—	0
Mozambique	78,409	3	4	4	56	56	56	22	20	19	18	20	21	9	8
Niger	126,670	2	3	3	8	8	7	3	2	2	87	87	88	53	52
Nigeria	91,077	32	33	34	21	23	23	23	18	16	24	26	27	2	2
Rwanda	2,467	26	41	45	34	19	16	23	21	20	17	20	19	0	0
São Tomé and Principe	96	35	38	39	1	1	1	—	—	—	64	61	60	—	—
Senegal	19,253	23	27	27	30	30	30	35	31	31	12	12	12	11	8
Seychelles	27	19	19	22	—	—	—	19	19	19	63	63	59	—	—
Sierra Leone	7,162	20	25	25	31	31	31	30	30	29	19	15	15	0	0
Somalia	62,734	1	1	1	46	46	46	16	15	14	37	38	38	24	16
Sudan	237,600	5	5	5	24	24	24	24	21	20	47	51	51	40	32
Swaziland	1,720	8	11	10	78	64	68	8	6	6	6	19	16	0	0
Tanzania	88,604	4	6	6	40	40	40	51	49	48	5	6	7	10	7
Togo	5,439	20	26	26	4	4	4	45	31	25	31	39	45	0	0
Uganda	19,955	24	28	34	25	25	25	32	30	29	19	16	13	4	2
Zaïre	226,760	3	3	3	4	4	4	80	78	77	13	15	16	6	5
Zambia	74,339	7	7	7	47	47	47	42	40	39	4	6	6	24	20
Zimbabwe	38,667	5	7	7	13	13	13	52	52	52	30	29	29	0	0
India	**297,319**	**55**	—	**57**	**5**	—	**4**	**20**	—	**22**	**20**	—	**17**	**1**	**0**
China	**932,641**	**11**	—	**11**	**31**	—	**31**	**12**	—	**14**	**46**	—	**44**	**20**	**22**

— Not available.

a. Refers only to areas larger than 4,000 square kilometers. Wilderness area is defined as land left in its natural state without any transformation by human action. These areas may partly include forests, pasture, and other lands as classified by FAO.

Source: FAO; WRI/IIED 1988 (pp. 264–265); WRI 1992 (p. 262).

Table A-18. Arable Land Per Capita, 1965–90

Country	Per capita arable land area (hectares)			
	1965	1980	1987	1990
Sub-Saharan Africa	**0.5**	**0.4**	**0.3**	**0.29**
Angola	0.6	0.5	0.4	0.36
Benin	0.6	0.5	0.4	0.40
Botswana	1.9	1.5	1.2	1.06
Burkina Faso	0.5	0.4	0.4	0.40
Burundi	0.3	0.3	0.3	0.24
Cameroon	1.0	0.8	0.6	0.59
Cape Verde	0.2	0.1	0.1	0.10
Central African Rep.	1.0	0.9	0.7	0.66
Chad	0.9	0.7	0.6	0.56
Comoros	0.4	0.3	0.2	0.18
Congo	0.6	0.4	0.3	0.27
Côte d'Ivoire	0.6	0.4	0.3	0.30
Djibouti	—	—	—	—
Equatorial Guinea	0.8	0.7	0.6	0.60
Ethiopia	0.5	0.4	0.3	0.28
Gabon	0.4	0.6	0.4	0.39
Gambia, The	0.3	0.2	0.2	0.20
Ghana	0.3	0.3	0.2	0.18
Guinea	0.4	0.3	0.2	0.13
Guinea-Bissau	0.5	0.4	0.4	0.35
Kenya	0.2	0.1	0.1	0.10
Lesotho	0.4	0.2	0.2	0.18
Liberia	0.3	0.2	0.2	0.14
Madagascar	0.4	0.3	0.3	0.26
Malawi	0.5	0.4	0.3	0.28
Mali	0.4	0.3	0.3	0.23
Mauritania	0.2	0.1	0.1	0.10
Mauritius	0.1	0.1	0.1	0.10
Mozambique	0.3	0.3	0.2	0.20
Niger	0.6	0.6	0.5	0.47
Nigeria	0.5	0.4	0.3	0.29
Rwanda	0.2	0.2	0.2	0.16
São Tomé and Principe	0.5	0.4	0.3	0.30
Senegal	1.1	0.9	0.8	0.71
Seychelles	0.1	0.1	0.1	0.10
Sierra Leone	0.6	0.5	0.5	0.43
Somalia	0.3	0.2	0.2	0.14
Sudan	0.9	0.7	0.5	0.50
Swaziland	0.4	0.3	0.2	0.20
Tanzania	0.3	0.3	0.2	0.19
Togo	0.7	0.6	0.4	0.40
Uganda	0.6	0.4	0.4	0.36
Zaïre	0.3	0.2	0.2	0.20
Zambia	1.3	0.9	0.7	0.62
Zimbabwe	0.5	0.4	0.3	0.29
For Comparison:				
India	**0.3**	—	**0.2**	—
China	**0.6**	—	**0.4**	—

— Not available.

Source: FAO; World Bank 1991c; 1990: World Resources Institute.

Table A-19. Forest Area, Deforestation, and Reforestation

Country	Forests and woodland ('000 ha)		Deforestation, annual average 1980s		Reforestation, annual average 1980s
	1980	1988	Percent per year	('000 ha per year)	('000 ha per year)
Sub-Saharan Africa	645,869	622,544	0.5	2,916	133
Angola	53,760	53,040	0.2	94	3
Benin	3,970	3,570	1.7	67	..
Botswana	962	962	0.1	20	—
Burkina Faso	7,200	6,720	1.7	80	2
Burundi	62	65	2.7	1	3
Cameroon	25,640	24,760	0.8	190	1
Cape Verde	1	1	—	—	1
Central African Rep.	35,895	35,820	0.2	55	..
Chad	13,532	12,890	0.6	160	—
Comoros	35	35	3.1	1	..
Congo	21,360	21,200	0.1	22	—
Côte d'Ivoire	9,880	5,880	5.2	510	6
Djibouti	6	6	—	—	—
Equatorial Guinea	1,295	1,295	0.2	3	—
Ethiopia	28,132	23,700	0.3	88	1
Gabon	20,000	20,000	0.1	15	1
Gambia, The	216	168	2.4	5	..
Ghana	8,770	8,210	0.8	72	2
Guinea	10,650	9,652	0.8	86	..
Guinea-Bissau	1,070	1,070	2.7	57	..
Kenya	3,860	3,620	1.7	39	10
Lesotho	—	—	—	—	1
Liberia	2,103	2,103	2.3	46	2
Madagascar	15,860	14,580	1.2	156	12
Malawi	5,074	4,190	3.5	150	1
Mali	8,800	8,480	0.5	36	1
Mauritania	15,000	15,000	2.4	14	..
Mauritius	58	57	3.3	..	..
Mozambique	15,689	14,730	0.8	120	4
Namibia	18,420	18,420	0.0	0	—
Niger	2,900	2,420	2.6	68	—
Nigeria	16,383	14,000	2.7	400	32
Rwanda	520	497	2.3	5	3
São Tomé and Principe	—	—	—	—	—
Senegal	6,000	5,930	0.5	50	3
Seychelles	5	5	—	—	..
Sierra Leone	2,113	2,070	0.3	6	..
Somalia	9,160	8,750	0.1	14	1
Sudan	48,940	46,460	1.1	504	13
Swaziland	103	108	—	1	5
Tanzania	43,260	42,305	0.3	130	9
Togo	1,700	1,300	0.7	12	..
Uganda	6,060	5,660	0.8	50	2
Zaïre	177,610	174,970	0.2	370	..
Zambia	29,890	29,090	0.2	70	2
Zimbabwe	19,930	19,930	0.4	80	4

— Not available.
.. Less than 500 ha.
Source: UNDP/World Bank 1992 (Tables 14-2 and 14-3).

Table A-20. Wood Production, 1977-89

	Roundwood production						Processed wood production					
	Total		Fuel and charcoal		Industrial roundwood		Sawnwood		Panels		Paper	
Country	'000 m³ 1987-89	% change since 1977-79	'000 m³ 1987-89	% change since 1977-79	'000 m³ 1987-89	% change since 1977-79	'000 m³ 1987-89	% change since 1977-79	'000 m³ 1987-89	% change since 1977-79	'000 m³ 1987-89	% change since 1977-79
Sub-Saharan Africa	**475,475**	**34**	**421,079**	**36**	**54,394**	**19**	**8,577**	**38**	**1,532**	**42**	**1,961**	**63**
Angola	5,262	26	4,217	31	1,045	8	5	-88	2	-74	15	15
Benin	4,845	35	4,591	35	254	35	11	22	0	—	0	—
Botswana	1,276	43	1,197	42	79	44	0	—	0	—	0	—
Burkina Faso	8,300	29	7,925	29	375	28	1	0	0	—	0	—
Burundi	3,969	31	3,921	31	48	43	3	200	0	—	0	—
Cameroon	12,615	31	9,886	31	2,730	31	652	58	80	10	5	0
Cape Verde	—	—	—	—	—	—	—	—	—	—	—	—
Central African Rep.	3,449	19	3,055	29	394	-24	52	-40	4	-20	0	—
Chad	3,837	26	3,294	26	542	26	1	0	0	—	0	—
Comoros	—	—	—	—	—	—	—	—	—	—	—	—
Congo	3,119	59	1,729	31	1,390	118	54	12	56	-26	0	—
Côte d'Ivoire	12,799	10	9,437	52	3,362	-38	775	15	260	133	0	—
Djibouti	0	—	0	—	0	—	0	—	0	—	0	—
Equatorial Guinea	607	46	447	10	160	1,614	51	993	10	2,900	0	—
Ethiopia	38,859	21	37,100	21	1,759	26	39	-46	15	10	10	25
Gabon	3,618	24	2,396	49	1,222	-6	126	17	228	75	0	—
Gambia, The	912	7	891	6	21	110	1	0	0	—	0	—
Ghana	17,006	56	15,905	71	1,101	-31	482	10	60	-11	0	—
Guinea	4,560	25	3,924	26	636	18	90	0	0	-100	0	—
Guinea-Bissau	565	6	422	2	143	19	16	0	0	—	0	—

Country												
Kenya	34,206	46	32,495	47	1,711	23	189	25	45	172	99	71
Lesotho	579	32	579	32	0	—	0	—	0	—	0	—
Liberia	5,825	31	4,736	30	1,089	33	411	129	5	-44	0	—
Madagascar	7,637	31	6,830	36	807	0	234	0	6	467	7	67
Malawi	7,366	36	7,016	37	351	19	31	-27	6	13	0	—
Mali	5,359	32	5,016	32	342	32	12	106	0	—	0	—
Mauritania	12	33	7	40	5	25	0	—	0	—	0	—
Mauritius	32	-27	20	-14	13	-38	4	-19	0	—	0	—
Mozambique	16,001	31	15,022	33	979	9	38	-59	6	113	2	0
Namibia	—	—	—	—	—	—	—	—	0	—	—	—
Niger	4,287	33	4,023	33	264	33	0	—	0	—	0	—
Nigeria	104,926	41	97,058	40	7,868	48	2,712	70	233	102	81	419
Rwanda	5,842	14	5,602	12	240	87	13	550	2	500	0	—
Senegal	4,286	25	3,697	24	589	32	11	32	0	—	0	—
Sierra Leone	2,941	23	2,801	26	140	-18	12	-37	0	—	0	—
Somalia	6,757	47	6,669	47	88	28	14	0	1	-33	0	—
South Africa	19,246	14	7,078	0	12,168	23	1,827	18	398	10	1,614	55
Sudan	21,584	36	19,554	36	2,030	35	13	-7	2	-40	10	43
Swaziland	2,223	-6	560	10	1,663	-10	136	27	8	118	0	—
Tanzania	31,966	46	30,019	44	1,947	87	156	78	13	39	28	—
Togo	840	33	662	34	178	30	5	0	0	—	0	—
Uganda	13,880	40	12,080	40	1,800	36	26	10	3	233	2	500
Zaïre	34,255	36	31,540	37	2,715	34	121	4	53	109	2	0
Zambia	12,030	43	11,424	44	606	38	68	61	8	92	3	—
Zimbabwe	7,755	32	6,226	31	1,530	36	185	22	28	-11	82	74

— Not available.
Source: WRI 1992 (p. 288).

247

Table A-21. Fuelwood Supply and Demand

Country	Fuelwood supply-demand balance (million cubic meters) 1980	Fuelwood supply-demand balance (million cubic meters) 2000
Angola	—	—
Benin	17.6	8.9
Botswana	25.6	23.9
Burkina Faso	−2.6	−11.2
Burundi	−3.2	−7.0
Cameroon	72.6	59.6
Cape Verde	—	—
Central African Rep.	111.5	105.6
Chad	−1.2	9.8
Comoros	—	—
Congo	46.4	43.2
Côte d'Ivoire	43.9	14.4
Djibouti	—	—
Equatorial Guinea	4.6	4.0
Ethiopia	4.4	−30.8
Gabon	42.8	40.9
Gambia, The	−0.6	−1.5
Ghana	29.3	13.8
Guinea	38.6	29.6
Guinea-Bissau	4.8	1.1
Kenya	−4.5	−58.4
Lesotho	—	—
Liberia	11.1	−4.4
Madagascar	5.2	4.4
Malawi	−3.1	−13.1
Mali	0.4	−5.0
Mauritania	3.8	3.8
Mauritius	—	—
Mozambique	16.8	0.3
Niger	−0.9	−5.5
Nigeria	57.5	−89.6
Rwanda	−5.5	−16.0
São Tomé and Principe	—	—
Senegal	0.3	−4.4
Seychelles	—	—
Sierra Leone	5.0	−1.5
Somalia	11.1	6.5
Sudan	6.1	−39.5
Swaziland	−0.5	−1.3
Tanzania	−5.1	−74.0
Togo	10.3	13.1
Uganda	−18.7	−57.3
Zaïre	388.2	327.9
Zambia	15.2	5.4
Zimbabwe	2.8	−12.2

— Not available.

Note: The fuelwood supply-demand balance is defined as the increase in the stock of fuelwood minus the total utilization of fuelwood in the same year.

Source: FAO.

Table A-22. Wildlife Habitat Loss in Afrotropical Nations, 1986

Country	Original wildlife habitat ('000 km^2)	Area remaining ('000 km^2)	Loss (percent)
Angola	1,246.7	760.8	39
Benin	115.8	46.3	60
Botswana	585.4	257.6	56
Burkina Faso	273.8	54.8	80
Burundi	25.7	3.6	86
Cameroon	469.4	192.5	59
Central African Rep.	623.0	274.1	56
Chad	720.8	173.0	76
Congo	342.0	174.4	49
Côte d'Ivoire	318.0	66.8	79
Djibouti	21.8	11.1	49
Equatorial Guinea	26.0	12.7	51
Ethiopia	1,101.0	30.3	70
Gabon	267.0	173.6	35
Gambia, The	11.3	1.2	89
Ghana	230.0	46.0	80
Guinea	245.9	73.8	70
Guinea-Bissau	36.1	7.9	78
Kenya	569.5	296.1	48
Lesotho	30.4	9.7	68
Liberia	111.4	14.5	87
Madagascar	595.2	148.8	75
Malawi	94.1	40.5	57
Mali	754.1	158.4	79
Mauritania	388.6	73.8	81
Mozambique	783.2	36.8	57
Niger	566.0	127.9	77
Nigeria	919.8	230.0	75
Rwanda	25.1	3.3	87
Senegal	196.2	35.3	82
Sierra Leone	71.7	10.8	85
Somalia	637.7	376.2	41
Sudan	1,703.0	510.9	70
Swaziland	17.4	7.7	56
Tanzania	886.2	505.1	43
Togo	56.0	19.0	66
Uganda	193.7	42.6	78
Zaïre	2,335.9	1,051.2	55
Zambia	752.6	534.3	29
Zimbabwe	390.2	171.7	56
Total	18,737.7	7,364.7	64
Namibia	823.2	444.5	46
South Africa	1,236.5	531.7	57

Note: Habitat is a place or type of site where a plant or animal naturally or normally lives and grows. The afrotropical realm is defined as all of the continent south of the Sahara Desert, including the island of Madagascar. Therefore, data for Chad, Mali, Mauritania, Niger and Sudan cover only parts of these countries. The Comoros, Seychelles, São Tomé and Principe, Mauritius, Réunion, Rodrigues, and the extreme southeastern corner of Egypt are not included.

Source: WRI/IIED 1988 (p. 94).

Table A-23. Known and Threatened Animal Species, 1990

Country	Mammals (number)		Birds (number)		Reptiles (number)		Amphibians (number)		Freshwater fish (number)	
	Known species	Threatened species	Known species	Threatened species	Known species	Threatened species	Known species	Threatened species	Known species	Threatened species
Angola	275	14	872	12	—	2	—	0	268	0
Benin	187	11	630	1	—	2	—	0	150	0
Botswana	154	9	549	6	158	1	38	0	81	0
Burkina Faso	147	10	497	1	—	2	—	0	120	0
Burundi	103	4	633	5	—	1	—	0	—	0
Cameroon	297	27	848	17	—	2	—	1	—	11
Cape Verde	9	0	103	3	—	1	—	0	—	0
Central African Rep.	208	12	668	2	—	2	—	0	400	0
Chad	131	18	496	4	—	2	—	0	130	0
Comoros	17	3	99	5	26	0	2	0	16	0
Congo	198	12	500	3	—	2	—	0	500	0
Côte d'Ivoire	226	18	683	9	—	1	—	1	200	0
Djibouti	22	6	311	3	—	0	—	0	—	0
Equatorial Guinea	141	15	392	3	—	2	—	1	—	0
Ethiopia	265	25	836	14	6	1	—	0	100	0
Gabon	190	14	617	4	—	2	—	0	200	0
Gambia, The	108	7	489	1	—	2	—	0	80	0
Ghana	222	13	721	8	—	2	—	0	180	0
Guinea	188	17	529	6	—	1	—	1	250	0
Guinea-Bissau	109	5	376	2	—	2	—	0	90	0
Kenya	314	15	1,067	18	191	2	88	0	180	0
Lesotho	54	2	288	7	—	0	—	0	8	0
Liberia	193	18	590	10	—	2	—	0	130	0
Madagascar	105	53	250	28	259	10	144	0	—	0
Malawi	187	10	630	7	124	1	69	0	600	0

Mali	136	16	647	4	16	2	—	0	160	0
Mauritania	61	14	550	5	—	1	—	0	15	0
Mauritius	4	3	102	10	19	6	2	0	—	0
Mozambique	205	10	666	11	170	1	—	0	—	1
Namibia	190	11	640	7	—	2	—	0	97	4
Niger	131	15	473	1	—	1	—	0	140	0
Nigeria	274	25	831	10	114	2	19	0	200	0
Reunion	2	0	33	1	6	0	—	0	—	0
Rwanda	147	11	669	7	—	2	—	0	—	0
São Tomé and Principe	7	1	124	7	—	0	—	0	—	0
Senegal	166	11	625	5	—	2	—	3	140	0
Seychelles	2	1	126	9	—	2	12	0	—	0
Sierra Leone	178	13	614	7	—	2	—	0	130	0
Somalia	173	16	639	7	—	1	—	1	—	0
South Africa	283	26	774	13	301	3	95	0	220	28
Sudan	266	17	938	8	—	1	—	0	120	0
Swaziland	46	0	477	5	—	1	—	0	45	0
Tanzania	310	30	1,016	26	273	3	—	0	—	0
Togo	196	9	630	1	—	2	—	0	160	0
Uganda	311	16	989	12	—	1	—	0	300	0
Zaïre	409	22	1,086	27	—	2	—	0	700	1
Zambia	228	10	732	10	152	2	83	0	156	0
Zimbabwe	194	9	635	6	155	1	120	0	132	0

— Not available.
Source: WRI 1992 (p. 304).

Table A-24. Rare and Threatened Plants, 1991

Country	Number of plant taxa	Endemic flora as percentage of total	Number of rare and threatened plant taxa	Rare and threatened plant taxa per 1,000 existing taxa
Angola	5,000	25	19	4
Benin	2,000	1	3	2
Botswana	2,600–2,800	17	4	1–2
Burkina Faso	1,096	—	0	0
Burundi	2,500	—	0	0
Cameroon	8,000	2	74	9
Cape Verde	659	14	1	2
Central African Rep.	3,600	4	0	0
Chad	1,600	—	14	9
Comoros	416	33	3	7
Congo	4,000	22	4	1
Côte d'Ivoire	3,660	2	70	19
Djibouti	534	—	3	6
Equatorial Guinea	—	—	—	—
Bioko	1,150	4	8	7
Pagula	208	8	2	10
Ethiopia	6,283	8	44	7
Gabon	8,000	22	80	10
Gambia, The	530	1	0	0
Ghana	3,600	1	34	9
Guinea	—	88[a]	36	—
Guinea-Bissau	1,000	—	0	0
Kenya	6,500	4	144	22
Lesotho	1,591	—	7	4
Liberia	—	59[a]	1	—
Madagascar	10,000–12,000	80	193	16–19

Malawi	3,600	2	61	17
Mali	1,600	1	15	9
Mauritania	1,100	—	3	3
Mauritius	800–900	33	240	267–300
Mozambique	5,500	4	84	15
Namibia	3,159	11[a]	18	6
Niger	1,178	—	1	1
Nigeria	4,614	5	9	2
Reunion	720	30	99	138
Rwanda	2,150	—	0	0
São Tomé and Principe	—		—	—
São Tomé	601	18	0	0
Principe	314	11	1	3
Senegal	2,100	1	32	15
Seychelles	274	15	73	266
Sierra Leone	2,480	3	12	5
Somalia	3,000	17	51	17
South Africa	23,000	80	1,145	50
Sudan	3,200	2	9	3
Swaziland	2,715	—	25	9
Tanzania	10,000	11	158	16
Togo	2,302[b]	1	0	0
Uganda	5,000	1	11	2
Zaïre	11,000	29	3	..
Zambia	4,600	5	1	..
Zimbabwe	5,428[c]	2	96	18

— Not available.
.. Less than 0.5.
a. Number of endemic taxa (includes species, subspecies and varieties).
b. Number of vascular taxa (includes species, subspecies and varieties).
c. Number of seed plants.
Source: WRI 1992 (p. 306).

253

Table A-25. Incidence of Drought, 1980–90

Country	1980	1981	1982	1983	1984	1985	1986	1987	1988	1989	1990
Angola	—	—	—	—	—	—	—	—	—	—	—
Benin	—	—	—	—	—	—	—	—	—	—	—
Botswana	—	—	D	D	D	D	D	D	—	—	—
Burkina Faso	—	—	D	D	D	—	—	—	—	—	—
Burundi	—	—	—	—	—	—	—	—	—	—	—
Cameroon	—	—	—	D	D	D	—	—	—	—	—
Cape Verde	—	D	D	D	D	—	—	—	—	—	—
Central African Rep.	—	—	—	D	D	—	—	—	—	—	—
Chad	—	—	—	D	D	—	—	—	—	—	—
Congo	—	—	—	—	—	—	—	—	—	—	—
Côte d'Ivoire	D	—	—	D	—	—	—	—	—	—	—
Equatorial Guinea	—	D	—	—	—	—	—	—	—	—	—
Ethiopia	—	—	—	—	D	D	—	D	D	—	—
Gabon	—	—	—	—	—	—	—	—	—	—	—
Gambia, The	—	—	—	—	—	—	—	—	—	—	—
Ghana	—	—	D	D	D	—	—	—	—	—	—
Guinea	—	—	—	—	—	—	—	—	—	—	—
Guinea-Bissau	—	—	—	—	—	—	—	—	—	—	—
Kenya	—	—	—	—	D	—	—	—	—	—	—
Lesotho	—	—	D	D	—	—	—	—	—	—	—

Country									
Liberia	—	—	—	—	—	—	—	—	—
Madagascar	D	—	—	—	—	—	—	—	—
Malawi	—	D	D	D	—	—	—	—	—
Mali	—	—	D	D	—	—	—	—	—
Mauritania	—	—	—	—	—	—	—	—	—
Mauritius	—	D	—	—	—	—	—	—	—
Mozambique	—	—	D	—	—	—	—	—	—
Namibia	—	—	—	—	—	—	—	—	—
Niger	—	—	D	D	—	D	—	—	D
Nigeria	—	—	—	—	—	—	—	—	—
Rwanda	—	—	D	D	—	—	—	—	—
São Tomé and Príncipe	D	—	D	—	—	—	—	—	—
Senegal	—	—	D	D	—	—	—	—	—
Sierra Leone	—	—	—	—	—	—	—	—	—
Somalia	—	—	—	—	—	—	—	—	—
Sudan	—	—	D	D	—	—	—	D	D
Swaziland	—	—	—	D	D	D	—	—	—
Tanzania	—	—	—	—	—	D	—	—	—
Togo	—	—	—	—	—	—	—	—	—
Uganda	—	—	—	—	—	—	—	—	—
Zaïre	—	—	—	—	—	—	—	—	—
Zambia	—	—	D	D	—	—	—	—	—
Zimbabwe	—	—	D	D	—	—	—	—	—

— Not available.

D Significant rainfall shortfall from long-term average.

Source: UNDP/World Bank 1992 (p. 242).

Table A-26. Soil Erosion in Selected Countries of Sub-Saharan Africa, 1970–86

Country	Location (and extent)	Affected area as percentage of national area	Amount of erosion (metric tons per year)	Amount of erosion (tons per hectare per year)	Year of estimate
Burkina Faso	Central Plateau	—	—	5–35	1970s
Ethiopia	Total cropland (12 million ha)	10	500 million	42	1986
	Central highland plateau (47 million ha)	43	1,600 million	—	1970s
Kenya	Njemps Flats	—	—	138	mid-1980s
	Tugen Plateau	—	—	72	mid-1980s
Lesotho	Grazing and croplands (2.7 million ha)	88	18.5 million	7	—
Madagascar	Mostly cropland (45.9 million ha)	79	—	25–250	1970s
	High central plateau	—	12–40 million	25–250	1980s
Niger	Small watershed (11,700 ha)	0.01	468,000	40	—
Nigeria	Imo State (900,000 ha)	1	13 million	14.4	1974
	Jos Plateau	—	6 million	—	1975
	Anambra	—	10–15 million	—	1975
Zimbabwe	Area with moderate to severe erosion (304,000 ha)	0.8	15 million	50	1979

— Not available.
Source: WRI/IIED 1988 (p. 282).

Table A-27. Extent of Soil Degradation in Major Regions of the World, Early 1980s

| | Total productive drylands | | Productive dryland types | | | | | |
| | | | Rangelands | | Rainfed croplands | | Irrigated lands | |
	Area (million hectares)	Percent degraded	Area (million hectares)	Percent degraded	Area (million hectares)	Percent degraded	Area (million hectares)	Percent degraded
Total	**3,257**	**61**	**2,556**	**62**	**570**	**60**	**131**	**30**
Sudano-Sahelian Africa	473	88	380	90	90	80	3	30
Southern Africa	304	80	250	80	52	80	2	30
Mediterranean Africa	101	83	80	85	20	75	1	40
Western Asia	142	82	116	85	18	85	8	40
Southern Asia	359	70	150	85	150	70	59	35
Former U.S.S.R. in Asia	298	55	250	60	40	30	8	25
China and Mongolia	315	69	300	70	5	60	10	30
Australia	491	23	450	22	39	30	2	19
Mediterranean Europe	76	39	30	30	40	32	6	25
South America and Mexico	293	71	250	72	31	77	12	33
North America	405	40	300	42	85	39	20	20

Note: The term "desertification" used in the original source has been replaced here by the more appropriate term "degradation."
Source: WRI/IIED 1988 (p. 291).

Table A-28. Results of Financial and Economic Analysis of Various Land Resource Management Technologies in Nigeria

Zone/technology		Yield increment benefit (percent)	Annual average yield decline		Financial analysis results				Economic analysis results				Conservation benefits as % of total benefits[c]
			Without project (percent)	With project (percent)	Base case[a]		Degraded case[b]		Base case[a]		Degraded case[b]		
					IRR (percent)	B:C ratio	IRR (percent)	B:C ratio	IRR (percent)	B:C ratio	IRR (percent)	B:C ratio	
Very humid zone:													
Vetiver grass contour strips	Sheet erosion; incipient gullying	5	3	1	20.5	.20	50.0	2.53	15.7	1.27	40.4	2.91	70
Fanya Juu contour bunds	Sheet erosion; incipient gullying	5	3	1	8.5	0.77	30.6	1.68	23.1	1.91	48.2	4.08	59
Stone-faced terracing	Sheet erosion; incipient gullying	5	3	1	-11.1	0.37	7.5	0.76	11.5	1.16	34.4	2.42	94
Wave bedding	Gullying	—	—	—	11.4	0.73	12.8	0.83	13.2	1.82	13.6	1.87	90
Improved acioa system	Declining fertility	0	—	—	—	1.45	—	1.12	—	1.81	—	1.40	92
Alley cropping	Declining fertility	20	5	2	17.7	1.06	14.7	1.00	9.5	1.05	4.2	0.94	45
Sub-humid zone:													
Animal traction	Declining fertility	5	2	1	16.6	1.06	24.2	1.39	14.2	1.34	22.0	1.79	17
Fodder banks	Declining fertility	40	2	—	25.3	1.33	23.7	1.27	10.6	1.07	5.8	0.97	11
Grazing reserve improvement	Overgrazing	33	2	—	7.9	0.80	23.5	1.25	-0.2	0.68	8.3	1.04	100

Plateau zone:													
Community woodlot	Woodland degradation	—	—	—	14.5	0.95	—	—	8.0	1.06	8.5	1.11	76
Dry sub-humid zone:													
Tree shelterbelts	Wind erosion	20	2	1	11.5	0.75	18.7	1.31	7.6	1.01	11.6	1.39	75
Vetiver grass contour strips	Wind erosion	10	2	1	29.8	1.32	71.6	2.14	11.0	1.10	38.0	1.92	77
Farm forestry	Wind erosion; declining fertility; woodland-degradation	10	2	1	15.0	1.00	16.6	0.12	12.5	1.67	14.2	1.96	5
Private woodlots	Woodland degradation	—	—	—	10.5	0.65	—	—	4.5	0.76	4.9	0.79	76
Rock bunds	Sheet erosion; incipient gullying	25	2	1	24.2	1.17	66.6	1.84	64.8	2.09	165.2	3.04	57

— Not available.

IRR Internal rate of return

B:C ratio Benefit/cost ratio

a. Assumes average yields, cropping intensity, and yield decline as indicated.

b. Assumes yields at 75 percent of average, cropping intensity doubled, and yield decline at 50 percent of the value indicated above (except for wave bedding where no yield loss is assumed, and alley cropping where the cropping intensity already is 100 percent).

c. Measured as the value of the potential food imports displaced by yield benefits plus fuelwood benefits divided by total benefits.

Source: FAO/World Bank Cooperative Program 1991, Vol. III, Annex 7.

Bibliography

Abeillé, Bernard, and Jean-Marie Lantran. 1993. *Social Infrastructure Construction in the Sahel: Options for Improving Current Practices.* World Bank Discussion Paper No. 200. World Bank, Washington, D.C.

Acsadi, George T. F., and Gwendolyn Johnson-Acsadi. 1990a. "Effects of Timing of Marriage on Reproductive Health." In Acsadi, Johnson-Acsadi, Bulatao 1990, pp. 105–114.

————. 1990b. "Demand for Children and for Childspacing." In Acsadi, Johnson-Acsadi, Bulatao 1990, pp. 155–185.

————, and Rodolfo Bulatao (eds.). 1990. *Population Growth and Reproduction in Sub-Saharan Africa: Technical Analyses of Fertility and its Consequences.* A World Bank Symposium. World Bank, Washington, D.C.

Adarkwa, Kazi. 1989. "Final Report on a Pilot Project to Improve Rural Mobility and Access Using Low Cost Roads and Non-Motorized Transport." Republic of Ghana, Ministry of Roads and Highways, Accra, Ghana.

Adekanya, Tomilayo O. 1985. "Innovation and Rural Women in Nigeria: Cassava Processing and Food Production." In Ahmed 1985, pp. 252–283.

Advocates for African Food Security/Lessening the Burden for Women. 1987. *Case Studies from Africa: Towards Food Security.* UN Non-Governmental Liaison Service, New York.

African Development Bank and Economic Commission for Africa. 1988. *Economic Report on Africa 1988.* Abidjan and Addis Ababa.

Agarwal, Bina. 1986. *Cold Hearths and Barren Slopes: The Woodfuel Crisis in the Third World.* Studies in Economic Development and Planning No. 40, Institute of Economic Growth. Allied Publishers, New Delhi, India.

Agyepong, G. T., J. E. Fleisher, R. D. Asiamah, H. K. Quartey-Papafio, Nana Addo Dankwa, and J. A. Allotey. 1988. *Report of Land Management Group on Preparation of Environmental Action Plan.* Prepared for the Environmental Protection Council, Accra, Ghana.

Ahlberg, Beth Maina. 1991. *Women, Sexuality and the Changing Social Order: The Impact of Government Policies on Reproductive Behavior in Kenya.* Gordon and Breach, Philadelphia.

Ahmad, Yusuf J., Salah El Serafy, Ernst Lutz (eds.). 1989. *Environmental Accounting for Sustainable Development: Selected Papers From Joint UNEP/World Bank Workshops.* World Bank, Washington, D.C..

Ahmed, Iftikhar (ed.). 1985. *Technology and Rural Women: Conceptual and Empirical Issues* (Study prepared for the International Labour Office within the Framework of the World Employment Programme). George Allen and Unwin, London.

Ainsworth, Martha. 1989. *Socioeconomic Determinants of Fertility in Côte d'Ivoire.* Living Standards Measurement Study, Working Paper No. 53. World Bank, Washington, D.C.

————, and Mead Over. 1992. *The Economic Impact of AIDS: Shocks, Responses and Outcomes.* Technical Working Paper No. 1, Population, Health and Nutrition Division, Africa Technical Department. World Bank, Washington, D.C.

Akuffo, Felix Odei. 1987. "Teenage Pregnancies and School Drop-outs: The Relevance of Family Life Education and Vocational Training to Girls' Employment Opportunities." In Oppong 1987, pp. 154–164.

Alebikiya, Malex. 1993. "The Association of Church Development Projects (ACDEP) in Northern Ghana." In Wellard and Copestake 1993, pp. 195–201.

Aloo, Theresa. 1985. "Forestry and the Untrained Kenyan Women." In *Women and the Environmental Crisis*. Report of the Proceedings of the Workshops on Women, Environment and Development, Nairobi, 10–20 July 1985. Environmental Liaison Center, Nairobi; pp. 26–28.

Amankwah, H. A. 1989. *The Legal Regime of Land Use in West Africa: Ghana and Nigeria*. Pacific Law Press, Hobart, Tasmania, Australia.

Ames, David W. 1959. "Wolof Co-operative Work Groups." In Bascom and Herskovits 1959, pp. 224–237.

Anderson, Dennis. 1987. *The Economics of Afforestation: A Case Study in Africa*. World Bank Occasional Papers, New Series, No. 1. Johns Hopkins University Press, Baltimore, Md.
———, and Robert Fishwick. 1984. *Fuelwood Consumption and Deforestation in Developing Countries*. World Bank Staff Working Paper No. 704. World Bank, Washington, D.C.

Anderson, Jock R., and Jesuthason Thampapillai. 1990. *Soil Conservation in Developing Countries: Project and Policy Intervention*. Policy and Research Series No. 8. World Bank, Washington, D.C.

Andreae, Meinrat O. 1991. "Biomass Burning in the Tropics: Impact on Environmental Quality and Global Climate." In Davis and Bernstam 1991, pp. 268–291.
———, and Johann Georg Goldammer. 1992. "Tropical Wildland Fires and Other Biomass Burning: Environmental Impacts and Implications for Land-Use and Fire Management." In Cleaver et al. 1992, pp. 79–109.

Anker, Richard, Mayra Buvinic and Nadia H. Youssef (eds.). 1982. *Women's Roles and Population Trends in the Third World*. International Labour Office. Croon Helm, London and Sidney.

Appleton, Simon, Paul Collier, and Paul Horsnell. 1990. *Gender, Education, and Employment in Côte d'Ivoire*. Social Dimensions of Adjustment in Sub-Saharan Africa, Working Paper No. 8. World Bank, Washington, D.C.

Ardayfio, Elizabeth. 1986. *The Rural Energy Crisis in Ghana: Its Implications for Women's Work and Household Survival*. World Employment Programme Research Working Paper (WEP 10/WP. 39). International Labour Office, Geneva, Switzerland.

Armitage, Jane, and Gunter Schramm. 1989. "Managing the Supply of and Demand for Fuelwood in Africa." In Schramm and Warford 1989, pp. 139–171.

Arnold, Fred. 1989. *Revised Estimates and Projections of International Migration 1980–2000*. PPR Working Paper WPS 275. World Bank, Washington, D.C.

Arrhenius, Erik A., and Thomas W. Waltz. 1990. "The Greenhouse Effect: Implications for Economic Development." World Bank Discussion Paper No. 78. World Bank, Washington, D.C.

Arum, Gilbert. 1993. "Kenya Energy and Environment Organization (1981–90)." In Wellard and Copestake 1993, pp. 145–158.

Ascher, William, and Robert Healy. 1990. *Natural Resource Policymaking in Developing Countries: Environment, Economic Growth and Income Distribution*. Duke University Press, Durham and London.

Babalola, S. O., and Carolyne Dennis. 1988. "Returns to Women's Labour in Cash Crop Production: Tobacco in Igboho, Oyo State, Nigeria." In Davison 1988c, pp. 79–89.

Bailey, Robert C., Serge Bahuchet, and Barry Hewlett. 1992. "Development in Central African Rainforest: Concern for Forest Peoples." In Cleaver et al. 1992, pp. 202–211.

Balassa, Bela. 1988. *Incentive Policies and Agricultural Performance in Sub-Saharan Africa*. PPR Working Paper WPS 77. World Bank, Washington, D.C.

Balcet, Jean-Claude, and Wilfred Candler. 1982. *Farm Technology Adoption in Northern Nigeria*. 2 vols. Final Report of the World Bank Research Project RPO 671–88. World Bank, Washington, D.C.

Bamba, Nonny. 1985. "Ivory Coast: Living with Diminishing Forests." In *Women and the Environmental Crisis*, Report of the Proceedings of the Workshops on Women, Environment and Development, Nairobi, 10–20 July 1985. Environmental Liaison Center, Nairobi; pp. 23–25.

Barbier, Edward B. 1988. *New Approaches in Environmental and Resource Economics: Towards an Economics of Sustainable Development*. International Institute for Environment and Development, London/Washington/Buenos Aires, and New Economics Foundation, London.

———. 1989. *Economics, Natural-Resource Scarcity and Development: Conventional and Alternative Views*. Earthscan, London.

——— and Joanne C. Burgess. 1992. *Agricultural Pricing and Environmental Degradation*. Policy Research Working Paper WPS 960 (Background Paper for World Development Report 1992). World Bank, Washington, D.C.

Barghouti, Shawki, and Guy LeMoigne. 1990. *Irrigation in Sub-Saharan Africa: The Development of Public and Private Systems*. World Bank Technical Paper No. 123. World Bank, Washington, D.C.

Barghouti, Shawki, Lisa Garbus, and Dina Umali (eds.). 1992. *Trends in Agricultural Diversification: Regional Perspectives*. World Bank Technical Paper No. 180. World Bank, Washington, D.C.

Barnes, Douglas F. 1990a. *Population Growth, Wood Fuels, and Resource Problems in Sub-Saharan Africa*. Industry and Energy Department Working Paper, Energy Series Paper No. 26. World Bank, Washington, D.C.

———. 1990b. "Population Growth, Wood Fuels, and Resource Problems." In Acsadi, Johnson-Acsadi, Bulatao 1990, pp. 44–59.

———, and José Olivares. 1988. *Sustainable Resource Management in Agriculture and Rural Development Projects: A Review of World Bank Policies, Procedures, and Results*. Environment Department Working Paper No. 5. World Bank, Washington, D.C.

Barrier, Christian. 1990. "Développement Rural en Afrique de l'Ouest Soudano-Sahélienne: Premier Bilan sur l'Approche Gestion de Terroir Villageois." (mimeo.). Caisse Centrale de Cooperation Economique, Paris.

Barth, Ursula. 1986. "Transportbedarf und Arbeitsaufwand von Frauen in der Subsistenzlandwirtschaft afrikanischer Länder südlich der Sahara." Berliner Sommerseminar: Verkehrsplanung in Entwicklungsländern, Institut für Verkehrsplanung und Verkehrswegebau. Technische Universität Berlin, Berlin, Germany.

———. 1989. "Rural Transport in Sub-Saharan Africa: Problems of Perceiving Women's Transport Tasks." *GATE - German Appropriate Technology Exchange*, No. 1/89, May 1989, Deutsches Zentrum für Entwicklungstechnologien, Eschborn, Germany; pp. 23–27.

Barwell, Ian J., Geoff A. Edmonds, John D. G. F. Howe and Jan de Veen. 1985. *Rural Transport in Developing Countries*. A Study Prepared for the International Labour Office within the Framework of the World Employment Programme. Intermediate Technology Publications, London.

Barwell, Ian J., John D. G. F. Howe and Paul Zille. 1987. "Household Time Use and Agricultural Productivity in Sub-Saharan Africa: A Synthesis of I.T. Transport Research" (Draft). I.T. Transport Ltd., Ardington, Oxon, U.K.

Bascom, William R., and Melville J. Herskovits (eds.). 1959. *Continuity and Change in African Cultures*. University of Chicago Press, Chicago.

Bass, Thomas A. 1990. *Camping with the Prince and Other Tales of Science in Africa*. Houghton Mifflin, Boston.

Bates, Robin W. 1991. *Energy Conservation Policy, Energy Markets and the Environment in Developing Countries*. Environment Working Paper No. 45, Environment Department. World Bank, Washington, D.C.

Bauer, Dan. 1987. "The Dynamics of Communal and Hereditary Land Tenure Among the Tigray of Ethiopia." In McCay and Acheson 1987, pp. 217–230.

Bay, Edna G. (ed.). 1982. *Women and Work in Africa*. Westview Press, Boulder, Colorado.

Becker, Charles M., and Andrew R. Morrison. 1988. "The Determinants of Urban Population Growth in Sub-Saharan Africa." *Economic Development and Cultural Change* 36(2):259–278.

Beenhakker, Henri L., with S. Carapetis, L. Crowther and S. Hertel. 1987. *Rural Transport Services: A Guide to Their Planning and Implementation*. Intermediate Technology Publications, London, and Westview Press, Boulder, Colorado.

Behnke, Roy H., and Ian Scoones. 1992. *Rethinking Range Ecology: Implications for Rangeland Management in Africa.* Environment Working Paper No. 53, Environment Department. World Bank, Washington, D.C.

Bell, Clive. 1990. "Reforming Property Rights in Land and Tenancy." *The World Bank Research Observer* 5(2):143–166.

Bellew, Rosemary T., and Elizabeth M. King. 1991. *Promoting Girls' and Women's Education: Lessons from the Past.* PRE Working Paper WPS 715. World Bank, Washington, D.C.

———. 1993. "Educating Women: Lessons from Experience." In King and Hill 1993, pp. 285–326.

Berg, Alan, and Susan Brems. 1989. *A Case for Promoting Breastfeeding in Projects to Limit Fertility.* World Bank Technical Paper No. 102. World Bank, Washington, D.C.

Bernal, Victoria. 1988. "Losing Ground — Women and Agriculture on Sudan's Irrigated Schemes: Lessons from a Blue Nile Village." In Davison 1988c, pp. 131–156.

Bernard, F. E. 1993. "Increasing Variability in Agricultural Production: Meru District, Kenya, in the Twentieth Century." In Turner, Hyden, and Kates 1993, pp. 80–113.

Bernhard, Michael H. 1992. *Strategic Management of Population Programs.* Policy Research Working Paper WPS 996, Population and Human Resources Department. World Bank, Washington, D.C.

Berry, Sara. 1986. "Social Science Perspective on Food in Africa." In Hansen and McMillan 1986, pp. 64–81.

Bertrand, Alain, Gerard Madon and Michel Matly. 1990. "République du Niger: Proposi-tions de Reforme du Dispositif de Controle Forestier et de Taxation du Bois-Energie." Rapport Technique No. 2. Groupement SEED-CTFT, Paris.

Bertrand, Jane T., and Judith E. Brown. 1992. *Family Planning Success in Two Cities in Zaïre.* Policy Research Working Paper WPS 1042, Population and Human Resources Depart-ment. World Bank, Washington, D.C.

Besley, Timothy, and Ravi Kanbur. 1990. *The Principles of Targeting.* PRE Working Paper WPS 385. World Bank, Washington, D.C.

Besong, Joseph Bawak, and François L. Wencélius. 1992. "Realistic Strategies for Conser-vation of Biodiversity in the Tropical Moist Forests of Africa: Regional Overview." In Cleaver *et al.* 1992, pp. 21–31.

Bhandari, Anil, C. Harral, E. Holland and A. Faiz. 1987. "Technical Options for Road Maintenance in Developing Countries and the Economic Consequences." In National Research Council, Transportation Research Board, *Road Deterioration in Developing Coun-tries and Low-Volume Road Engineering.* Transportation Research Record 1128. National Research Council, Washington, D.C.; pp. 18–27.

Bidol, Patricia, and James E. Crowfoot. 1991. "Toward an Interactive Process for Siting National Parks in Developing Nations." In West and Brechin 1991, pp. 283–300.

Bie, Stein W. 1990. *Dryland Degradation Measurement Techniques.* Environment Working Paper No. 26, Environment Department. World Bank, Washington, D.C.

Bilsborrow, Richard E., and Pamela F. DeLargy. 1991. "Land Use, Migration, and Natural Resource Deterioration: The Experience of Guatemala and the Sudan." In Davis and Bernstam 1991, pp. 125–147.

Binswanger, Hans P., and Prabhu L. Pingali. 1984. "The Evolution of Farming Systems and Agricultural Technology in Sub-Saharan Africa." Discussion Paper ARU 23, Agriculture and Rural Development Department. World Bank, Washington, D.C.

———. 1987. "Resource Endowments, Farming Systems and Technology Priorities for Sub-Saharan Africa." Discussion Paper ARU 60, Agriculture and Rural Development Department. World Bank, Washington, D.C.

———. 1988. "Technological Priorities for Farming in Sub-Saharan Africa." *The World Bank Research Observer* 3(1):81–98.

Binswanger, Hans P., Klaus Deininger and Gershon Feder. 1993. *Power, Distortions, Revolt, and Reform in Agricultural Land Relations.* Policy Research Working Paper WPS 1164. LAC Technical Department and Agriculture and Rural Development Department. World Bank, Washington, D.C.

Birdsall, Nancy. 1992. *Another Look at Population and Global Warming.* Policy Research Working Paper WPS 1020. Country Economics Department. World Bank, Washington, D.C.

Bishop, Joshua, and Jennifer Allen. 1989. *The On-Site Costs of Soil Erosion in Mali.* Environment Department Working Paper No. 21. World Bank, Washington, D.C.

Blackwell, Jonathan M., Roger N. Goodwillie, Richard Webb. 1991. *Environment and Development in Africa: Selected Case Studies.* EDI Development Policy Case Series, Analytical Case Studies, Number 6. Economic Development Institute. World Bank, Washington, D.C.

Blaikie, Piers, and Harold Brookfield. 1987. *Land Degradation and Society.* Methuen, London and New York.

Blarcom, Bonni van, Odin Knudsen, John Nash. 1993. *The Reform of Public Expenditures for Agriculture.* World Bank Discussion Paper 216. World Bank, Washington, D.C.

Bleek, Wolf. 1987. "Family and Family Planning in Southern Ghana." In Oppong 1987, pp. 138–153.

Blumberg, Rae Lesser. 1989. *Making the Case for the Gender Variable: Women and the Wealth and Well-Being of Nations.* Technical Reports in Gender and Development No. 1/1989. Office of Women in Development. USAID, Washington, D.C.

Bojö, Jan. 1991. *The Economics of Land Degradation: Theory and Applications to Lesotho.* (A Dissertation for the Doctor's Degree in Economics). Economic Research Institute/EFI, Stockholm School of Economics, Stockholm, Sweden.

Bonfiglioli, Angelo Maliki. 1993. *Agro-Pastoralism in Chad as a Strategy for Survival: An Essay on the Relationship between Anthropology and Statistics.* World Bank Technical Paper No. 214, Africa Technical Department Series. World Bank, Washington, D.C.

Bongaarts, John, Odile Frank, and Ron Lesthaege. 1990. "The Proximate Determinants of Fertility." In Acsadi, Johnson-Acsadi, Bulatao 1990, pp. 133–143.

Borlaugh, Norman E. 1991. "Reaching Sub-Saharan Africa's Small-Scale Farmers with Improved Technology: The Sasakawa-Global 2000 Experience." In Garbus, Pritchard, and Knudsen 1991, pp. 7–21.

Bos, Eduard, My T. Vu, Ann Levin, and Rodolfo Bulatao. 1992. *World Population Projections 1992–93 Edition: Estimates and Projections with Related Demographic Statistics.* Published for the World Bank. The Johns Hopkins University Press, Baltimore and London.

Bosc, Pierre-Marie, Peter Calkins and Jean-Michel Yung. 1991. "Technology Adoption in the Sahelian and Sudanese Regions: Approach and Major Findings." In Gnaegy and Anderson 1991, pp. 45–59.

Boserup, Ester. 1965. *The Conditions of Agricultural Growth: The Economics of Agrarian Change Under Population Pressure.* George Allen and Unwin, London.

———. 1970. *Woman's Role in Economic Development.* St. Martin's Press, George Allen and Unwin, New York.

———. 1981. *Population and Technological Change: A Study of Long-Term Trends.* University of Chicago Press, Chicago.

Bradley, P. N., and K. McNamara (eds.). 1993. *Living with Trees: Policies for Forestry Management in Zimbabwe.* World Bank Technical Paper No. 210. World Bank, Washington, D.C.

Bratton, Michael. 1987. "Drought, Food and the Social Organization of Small Farmers in Zimbabwe." In Glantz 1987, pp. 213–244.

Braun, Joachim von, Hartwig de Haen, and Juergen Blanken. 1991. *Commercialization of Agriculture under Population Pressure: Effects on Production, Consumption, and Nutrition in Rwanda.* Research Report 85. International Food Policy Research Institute, Washington, D.C.

Briscoe, John, and David de Ferranti. 1988. *Water for Rural Communities: Helping People Help Themselves.* World Bank, Washington, D.C.

Bromley, Daniel W., and Michael M. Cernea. 1989. *The Management of Common Property Natural Resources: Some Conceptual and Operational Fallacies.* World Bank Discussion Paper No. 57. World Bank, Washington, D.C.

Brown, Ellen, and Robert Nooter. 1992. *Successful Small-Scale Irrigation in the Sahel.* World Bank Technical Paper No. 171. World Bank, Washington, D.C.

Brown, Lester, and Edward C. Wolf. 1984. *Soil Erosion: Quiet Crisis in the World Economy.* Worldwatch Paper 60. Worldwatch Institute, Washington, D.C.

———. 1985. *Reversing Africa's Decline.* Worldwatch Paper 65. Worldwatch Institute, Washington, D.C.

———, and Jodi L. Jacobson. 1986. *Our Demographically Divided World*. Worldwatch Paper 74. Worldwatch Institute, Washington, D.C.

Brown, Lester R., William U. Chandler, Christopher Flavin, Cynthia Pollock, Sandra Postel, Linda Starke, and Edward C. Wolf. 1985. *State of the World 1985: A Worldwatch Institute Report on Progress Toward a Sustainable Society*. Worldwatch Institute. W. W. Norton, New York and London.

Brown, Lester R., Alan Durning, Christopher Flavin, Hilary French, Jodi Jacobson, Marcia Lowe, Sandra Postel, Michael Renner, Linda Starke, and John Young. 1990. *State of the World 1990: A Worldwatch Institute Report on Progress Toward a Sustainable Society*. Worldwatch Institute. W.W. Norton, New York and London.

Bryson, Judy C. 1981. "Women and Agriculture in Sub-Saharan Africa: Implications for Development (An Exploratory Study)." *The Journal of Development Studies* 17(3), Special Issue on African Women in the Development Process; pp. 29–46.

Buck, Louise E. 1993. "Development of Participatory Approaches for Promoting Agroforestry: Collaboration between the Mazingira Institute, ICRAF, CARE-Kenya, KEFRI and the Forestry Department (1980–91)." In Wellard and Copestake 1993, pp. 118–135.

Bulatao, Rodolfo A. 1984. *Reducing Fertility in Developing Countries: A Review of Determinants and Policy Levers*. World Bank Staff Working Paper No. 680, Population and Development Series No. 5. World Bank, Washington, D.C.

———, and Ann Elwan. 1985. *Fertility and Mortality Transition: Patterns, Projections, and Interdependence*. World Bank Staff Working Paper No. 681, Population and Development Series No. 6. World Bank, Washington, D.C.

Bulatao, Rodolfo A., Eduard Bos, Patience W. Stephens, and My T. Vu. 1989. *Africa Region Population Projections, 1989–90 Edition*. PPR Working Paper WPS 330. World Bank, Washington, D.C.

Bulatao, Rodolfo A., and Eduard Bos. 1992. *Projecting the Demographic Impact of AIDS*. Policy Research Working Paper WPS 941. World Bank, Washington, D.C.

Bunting, A. H. (ed.). 1970. *Change in Agriculture*. Gerald Duckworth, London.

Burfisher, Mary E., and Nadine R. Horenstein. 1985. *Sex Roles in the Nigerian Tiv Farm Household*. The Population Council, New York. Kumarian Press, West Hartford, Conn., USA.

CAB International. 1991. *CAB International: 1990 in Review*. Wallingford, Oxon, U.K.

Cain, Mead. 1984. *Women's Status and Fertility in Developing Countries: Son Preference and Economic Security*. World Bank Staff Working Paper No. 682, Population and Development Series No. 7. World Bank, Washington, D.C.

Caldwell, John C. 1991. "The Soft Underbelly of Development: Demographic Transition in Conditions of Limited Economic Change." In Stanley Fisher, Dennis de Tray and Shekar Shah, eds., *Proceedings of the World Bank Annual Conference on Development Economics 1990*, Supplement to *The World Bank Economic Review* and *The World Bank Research Observer*, Washington, D.C.; pp. 207–253.

———, and Pat Caldwell. 1990a. "Cultural Forces Tending to Sustain High Fertility." In Acsadi, Johnson-Acsadi, Bulatao 1990, pp. 199–214.

———. 1990b. "High Fertility in Sub-Saharan Africa." *Scientific American*, May 1990; pp. 118–125.

Calhoun, John B. 1991. "The Plight of the Ik." In West and Brechin 1991, pp. 55–60.

Canadian International Development Agency (CIDA). 1990. *The Water Utilization Project: A Case Study on a Water and Health Education Project in Northern Ghana*. Social Dimension Division, Canadian International Development Agency, Hull, Quebec, Canada.

Carapetis, Steve, Hernán Levy, Terje Wolden. 1991. *Sub-Saharan Africa Transport Program. The Road Maintenance Initiative: Building Capacity for Policy Reform. Volume 1: Report on the Policy Seminars*. EDI Seminar Series, Economic Development Institute. World Bank, Washington, D.C.

Carney, Judith A. 1988. "Struggles over Land and Crops in an Irrigated Rice Scheme: The Gambia." In Davison 1988c, pp. 59–78.

Carr, Marilyn. 1985. "Technologies for Rural Women: Impact and Dissemination." In Ahmed 1985, pp. 115–153.

————, Michael Ayre and Gordon Hathway. 1984. *Reducing the Woman's Burden: A Proposal for Initiatives to Improve the Efficiency of Load Movement.* Intermediate Technology Development Group, London.

Carr, Marilyn, and Ruby Sandhu. 1988. *Women, Technology and Rural Productivity: An Analysis of the Impact of Time and Energy-Saving Technologies on Women.* UNIFEM Occasional Paper No. 6. United Nations Development Fund for Women, New York.

Carr, Stephen J. 1989. *Technology for Small-Scale Farmers in Sub-Saharan Africa: Experience with Food Crop Production in Five Major Ecological Zones.* World Bank Technical Paper No. 109. World Bank, Washington, D.C.

————. 1993. *Improving Cash Crops in Africa: Factors Influencing the Productivity of Cotton, Coffee, and Tea Grown by Smallholders.* World Bank Technical Paper No. 216. World Bank, Washington, D.C.

Centre for Development Cooperation Services. 1986. "Soil and Water Conservation in Sub-Saharan Africa: Issues and Options." Prepared for the International Fund for Agricultural Development (IFAD). Centre for Development Cooperation Services, Free University, Amsterdam.

————. 1992. *Soil and Water Conservation in Sub-Saharan Africa: Towards Sustainable Production by the Rural Poor.* A Report prepared for the International Fund for Agricultural Development by the Centre for Development Cooperation Services. Free University, Amsterdam.

Cernea, Michael M. 1981. *Land Tenure Systems and Social Implications of Forestry Development Programs.* World Bank Staff Working Paper No. 452. World Bank, Washington, D.C.

————. 1989. *User Groups as Producers in Participatory Afforestation Strategies.* World Bank Discussion Paper No. 70. World Bank, Washington, D.C.

———— (ed.). 1991. *Putting People First: Sociological Variables in Rural Development.* (Second Edition, revised and expanded.) Oxford University Press, New York and London.

Chaguma, Arthur, and Davison Gumbo. 1993. "ENDA-Zimbabwe and Community Research." In Wellard and Copestake 1993, pp. 67–76.

Chambers, Robert. 1991. "In Search of Professionalism, Bureaucracy and Sustainable Livelihoods for the 21st Century." *IDS Bulletin* 22(4):5–11.

————, Arnold Pacey, and Lori Ann Thrupp (eds.). 1989. *Farmer First: Farmer Innovation and Agricultural Research.* Intermediate Technology Publications, London.

Chambers, Robert, and Camilla Toulmin. 1991. "Farmer-First: Achieving Sustainable Dryland Development in Africa." In Haswell and Hunt 1991, pp. 23–48.

Chapman, Duane (ed.). 1990. *Arresting Renewable Resource Degradation in the Third World.* Environment Department Working Paper No. 44. World Bank, Washington, D.C.

Charles, Rosemary Achieng, and Kate Wellard. 1993. "Agricultural Activities and NGOs in Siaya District." In Wellard and Copestake 1993, pp. 100–110.

Chavangi, Noel A. 1992. "Household Based Tree Planting Activities for Fuelwood Supply in Rural Kenya: The Role of the Kenya Woodfuel Development Programme." In Taylor and Mackenzie 1992, pp. 148–169.

————, Rutger J. Engelhard and Valerie Jones. 1985. *Culture as the Basis for Implementing Self-Sustaining Woodfuel Development Programs.* Beijer Institute, Nairobi.

Chernichowsky, Dov, Robert E. B. Lucas and Eva Mueller. 1985. *The Household Economy of Rural Botswana: An African Case.* World Bank Staff Working Paper No. 715. World Bank, Washington, D.C.

Chomitz, Kenneth M., and Nancy Birdsall. 1991. "Incentives for Small Families: Concepts and Issues." In Stanley Fisher, Dennis de Tray and Shekar Shah, eds., *Proceedings of the World Bank Annual Conference on Development Economics 1990*, Supplement to *The World Bank Economic Review* and *The World Bank Research Observer*, Washington, D.C.; pp. 309–339.

Christiansson, Carl, and Eva Tobisson. 1989. "Environmental Degradation as a Consequence of Socio-Political Conflict in Eastern Mara Region, Tanzania." In Hjort af Ornäs and Salih 1989, pp. 51–66.

Clark, Garcia. 1985. *Fighting the African Food Crisis: Women Food Farmers and Food Workers.* UNIFEM Occasional Paper No. 1. United Nations Development Fund for Women, New York.

Clarke, John I., and Leszek A. Kosinski (eds.). 1982. *Redistribution of Population in Africa.* Heinemann, London.

Cleaver, Kevin M. 1993. *A Strategy to Develop Agriculture in Sub-Saharan Africa and a Focus for the World Bank.* World Bank Technical Paper No. 203, Africa Technical Department Series. World Bank, Washington, D.C.

———, Mohan Munasinghe, Mary Dyson, Nicolas Egli, Axel Peuker, François Wencélius (eds.). 1992. *Conservation of West and Central African Rainforests.* Selected Papers from the Conference on Conservation of West and Central African Rainforests, held in Abidjan, November 5–9, 1990. World Bank Environment Paper No. 1. Published in cooperation with IUCN—The World Conservation Union. World Bank, Washington, D.C.

Cleland, John. 1985. "Marital Fertility Decline in Developing Countries: Theories and the Evidence." In Cleland and Hobcraft 1985, pp. 223–252.

———, and John Hobcraft (eds.). 1985. *Reproductive Change in Developing Countries: Insights from the World Fertility Survey.* Oxford University Press, London.

Cochrane, Susan H. 1985. *Development Consequences of Rapid Population Growth: A Review from the Perspective of Sub-Saharan Africa.* PHN Technical Note 85–8, Population, Health and Nutrition Department. World Bank, Washington, D.C.

———, and Samir M. Farid. 1989. *Fertility in Sub-Saharan Africa: Analysis and Explanation.* World Bank Discussion Paper No. 43. World Bank, Washington, D.C.

———, and Samir M. Farid. 1990. "Socioeconomic Differentials in Fertility and Their Explanation." In Acsadi, Johnson-Acsadi, Bulatao 1990, pp. 144–154.

———, Fred T. Sai, and Janet Nassim. 1990. "The Development of Population and Family Planning Policies." In Acsadi, Johnson-Acsadi, Bulatao 1990, pp. 217–233.

Colby, Michael E. 1989. *The Evolution of Paradigms of Environmental Management in Development.* Discussion Paper No. 1, Strategic Planning and Review Department. World Bank, Washington, D.C.

Connell, John, and Michael Lipton. 1977. *Assessing Village Labour Situations in Developing Countries.* Oxford University Press, London.

Cook, Cynthia C., and Mikael Grut. 1989. *Agroforestry in Sub-Saharan Africa: A Farmer's Perspective.* World Bank Technical Paper No. 112. World Bank, Washington, D.C.

Cook, Cynthia C., and Aleki Mukendi. 1992. *Involuntary Resettlement in Bank-Financed Projects: Lessons from Sub-Saharan Africa.* AFTEN Working Paper No. 3. Africa Technical Department, Environment Division. World Bank, Washington, D.C.

Copestake, James G. 1993. "The Contribution to Agricultural Technology Development of the Gwembe Valley Agricultural Mission (1985–90)." In Wellard and Copestake 1993, pp. 174–179.

Creevey, Lucy E. (ed.). 1986. *Women Farmers in Africa: Rural Development in Mali and the Sahel.* Syracuse University Press, Syracuse, N.Y.

Creightney, Cavelle D. 1993. *Transport and Economic Performance: A Survey of Developing Countries.* World Bank Technical Paper No. 232, Africa Technical Department Series. World Bank, Washington, D.C.

Critchley, William, Chris Reij, and Alain Seznec. 1992. *Water Harvesting for Plant Production; Volume II: Case Studies and Conclusions for Sub-Saharan Africa.* World Bank Technical Paper No. 157, Africa Technical Department Series. World Bank, Washington, D.C.

Croft, Trevor A. 1991. "Lake Malawi National Park: A Case Study in Conservation Planning." In West and Brechin 1991, pp. 138–149.

Csapo, Marg. 1983. "Universal Primary Education in Nigeria: Its Problems and Implications." *The African Studies Review* 26(1):91–106.

Curtis, Val. 1986. *Women and the Transport of Water.* Intermediate Technology Publications, London.

Daly, Herman E., and John B. Cobb, Jr. 1989. *For the Common Good: Redirecting the Economy Toward Community, the Environment and a Sustainable Future.* Beacon Press, Boston.

Dankelman, Irene, and Joan Davidson. 1988. *Women and Environment in the Third World: Alliance for the Future.* Earthscan Publications/International Union for Conservation of Nature, London.

Dasgupta, Partha. 1992. "Population, Resources, and Poverty." *Ambio* 21(1):95–101. Royal Swedish Academy of Sciences, Stockholm.

————. 1993. "Poverty, Resources, and Fertility: The Household as a Reproductive Partnership." In Munasinghe 1993, pp. 73–102.

————, and Karl-Gøran Maler. 1991. "The Environment and Emerging Development Issues." In Stanley Fisher, Dennis de Tray and Shekar Shah, eds., *Proceedings of the World Bank Annual Conference on Development Economics 1990*, Supplement to *The World Bank Economic Review* and *The World Bank Research Observer*, Washington, D.C.; pp. 101–131.

Date-Bah, Eugenia. 1985. "Technologies for Rural Women of Ghana: Role of Socio-Cultural Factors." In Ahmed 1985, pp. 211–251.

Dauber, Roslyn, and Melinda L. Cain (eds.). 1981. *Women and Technological Change in Developing Countries*. Westview Press, Boulder, Colorado.

Davis, Kingsley, and Mikhail S. Bernstam (eds.). 1991. *Resources, Environment, and Population: Present Knowledge, Future Options*. (Supplement to *Population and Development Review*, Vol. 16, 1990). The Population Council, New York. Oxford University Press, New York and Oxford.

Davis, Sheldon H. (ed.). 1993. *Indigenous Views of Land and the Environment*. World Bank Discussion Paper No. 188. World Bank, Washington, D.C.

Davis, Ted J. (ed.) 1985. *Proceedings of the Fifth Agriculture Sector Symposium*. World Bank, Washington, D.C.

————, and Isabelle A. Schirmer (eds.). 1987. *Sustainability Issues in Agricultural Development: Proceedings of the Seventh Agriculture Sector Symposium*. World Bank, Washington, D.C.

Davison, Jean. 1988a. "Who Owns What? Land Registration and Tensions in Gender Relations of Production in Kenya." In Davison 1988c, pp. 157–176.

————. 1988b. "Land Distribution in Mozambique and its Effects on Women's Collective Production: Case Studies from Sofala Province." In Davison 1988c, pp. 228–249.

———— (ed.). 1988c. *Agriculture, Women, and Land: The African Experience*. Westview Special Studies on Africa. Westview Press, Boulder, Colorado.

Dei, George J. S. 1992. "A Ghanaian Rural Community: Indigenous Responses to Seasonal Food Supply Cycles and the Socio-Environmental Stresses of the 1980s." In Taylor and Mackenzie 1992, pp. 58–81.

Dejene, Alemneh, and José Olivares. 1991. *Integrating Environmental Issues into a Strategy for Sustainable Agricultural Development: The Case of Mozambique*. World Bank Technical Paper No. 146. World Bank, Washington, D.C.

DeJong, Jocelyn. 1991. *Traditional Medicine in Sub-Saharan Africa: Its Importance and Potential Policy Options*. PRE Working Paper WPS 735, Population and Human Resources Department. World Bank, Washington, D.C.

DeLancey, Virginia. 1990. "Socioeconomic Consequences of High Fertility for the Family." In Acsadi, Johnson-Acsadi, Bulatao 1990, pp. 115–130.

Devres Inc. 1980. *Socio-Economic and Environmental Impacts of Low-Volume Rural Roads — A Review of the Literature*. AID Program Evaluation Discussion Paper No. 7. USAID, Washington, D.C.

Dey, Jennie. 1984a. *Women in Food Production and Food Security in Africa*. Women in Agriculture No. 3. Food and Agriculture Organization of the United Nations, Rome.

————. 1984b. *Women in Rice Farming Systems (Focus: Sub-Saharan Africa)*. Women in Agriculture No. 2. Food and Agriculture Organization of the United Nations, Rome.

Dia, Mamadou. 1993. *A Governance Approach to Civil Service Reform in Sub-Saharan Africa*. World Bank Technical Paper No. 225, Africa Technical Department Series. World Bank, Washington, D.C.

Dianzinga, Scolastique, and Paulette Yambo. 1992. "Les Femmes et la Forêt: Utilisation et Conservation des Ressources Forestières Autres que le Bois." In Cleaver *et al.* 1992, pp. 233–238.

Diop, Amadou Moctar. 1993. "Rodale Institute/Rodale International/CRAR Senegal." In Wellard and Copestake 1993, pp. 264–269.

Dixon, John A., David E. James and Paul B. Sherman. 1989. *The Economics of Dryland Management*. Earthscan Publications, London.

Dixon, John A., and Paul B. Sherman. 1990. *Economics of Protected Areas: A New Look at Benefits and Costs*. Island Press, Washington, D.C.

Dixon, John A., David E. James, and Paul B. Sherman (eds.). 1990. *Dryland Management: Economic Case Studies*. Earthscan Publications, London.

Dixon-Mueller, Ruth. 1985. *Women's Work in Third World Agriculture: Concepts and Indicators*. International Labour Office, Geneva.

Dommen, Arthur John. 1988. *Innovation in African Agriculture*. Westview Press, Boulder, Colorado.

Doorenbos, J., B. Haverkort and J. Jiggins. 1988. "Women and the Rationalisation of Smallholder Agriculture." *Agricultural Administration and Extension* 28:101–112.

Dorjahn, Vernon R. 1959. "The Factor of Polygyny in African Demography." In Bascom and Herskovits 1959, pp. 87–112.

Due, Jean M. 1988. "Intra-Household Gender Issues in Farming Systems in Tanzania, Zambia, and Malawi." In Poats, Schmink and Spring 1988, pp. 331–344.

Dugue, Patrick. 1993. "The Senegalese Institute for Agricultural Research (ISRA) and the Fatick Region Farmers' Association (ARAF)." In Wellard and Copestake 1993, pp. 270–282.

Dwyer, Daisy, and Judith Bruce (eds.) 1988. *A Home Divided: Women and Income in the Third World*. Stanford University Press, Stanford, California.

Dyson, Mary. 1992. "Concern for African Forest Peoples: A Touchstone of a Sustainable Development Policy." In Cleaver *et al.* 1992, pp. 212–221.

Easter, K. William, and Robert R. Hearne. 1993. *Decentralizing Water Resource Management: Economic Incentives, Accountability, and Assurance*. Policy Research Working Paper 1219, Agriculture and Natural Resources Department. World Bank, Washington, D.C.

Edungbola, Luke D., Eka I. Braide, A. C. Nwosu, B. Aripo. E. I. I. Gemade, K. S. Adeyemi, and C. de Rooy. 1987. *Guinea Worm Control as a Major Contributor to Self-Sufficiency in Rice Production in Nigeria*. Water and Sanitation Section, UNICEF Nigeria, Lagos.

Ehrlich, Paul R. 1986. "Extinction: What Is Happening Now and What Needs to Be Done." In Elliott 1986, pp. 157–164.

————, and Anne H. Ehrlich. 1981. *Extinction: The Causes and Consequences of the Disappearance of Species*. Random House, New York.

Eicher, Carl K. 1984a. "Facing up to Africa's Food Crisis." In Carl K. Eicher and John M. Staatz, eds., *Agricultural Development in the Third World*. Johns Hopkins University Press, Baltimore and London; pp. 453–479.

————. 1984b. "International Technology Transfer and the African Farmer: Theory and Practice." Working Paper 3/84. Department of Land Management, University of Zimbabwe, Harare.

————. 1985. "Agricultural Research for African Development: Problems and Priorities for 1985–2000." Paper prepared for a World Bank Conference on Research Priorities for Sub-Saharan Africa, Bellagio, February 25 - March 1, 1985. Department of Agricultural Economics, Michigan State University, East Lansing, Michigan.

————. 1986. *Transforming African Agriculture*. The Hunger Project Papers, No. 4, San Francisco.

————. 1989. *Sustainable Institutions for African Agricultural Development*. Working Paper No. 19. International Service for National Agricultural Research, The Hague, The Netherlands.

————, and Doyle C. Baker. 1982. *Research on Agricultural Development in Sub-Saharan Africa: A Critical Survey*. MSU International Development Paper No. 1. Department of Agricultural Economics, Michigan State University, East Lansing, Mich.

Elliot, David (ed.). 1986. *Dynamics of Extinction*. John Wiley and Sons, New York.

Elnur, Awatif Mahmoud. 1985. "Renewable Options for the Sudanese Women." In Environmental Liaison Center, *Women and the Environmental Crisis*. Report of the Proceedings of the Workshops on Women, Environment and Development, Nairobi, 10–20 July 1985. Environmental Liaison Center, Nairobi; pp. 35–36.

Engberg, Lila E., Jean H. Sabry, and Susan A. Beckerson. 1988. "A Comparison of Rural Women's Time Use and Nutritional Consequences in Two Villages in Malawi." In Poats, Schmink and Spring 1988, pp. 99–110.

Engel, J. Ronald, and Joan Gibb Engel (eds.). 1990. *Ethics of Environment and Development: Global Challenge, International Response*. University of Arizona Press, Tucson, Arizona.

English, John, Mary Tiffen and Michael Mortimore. 1994. *Land Resource Management in Machakos District, Kenya, 1930–1990.* World Bank Environment Paper No. 5. World Bank, Washington, D.C.

Ewing, Andrew J., and Raymond Chalk. 1988. *The Forest Industries Sector: An Operational Strategy for Developing Countries.* World Bank Technical Paper No. 83, Industry and Energy Series. World Bank, Washington, D.C.

Faiz, Asif, Clell Harral and Frida Johansen. 1987. "State of the Road Networks in Developing Countries and a Country Typology of Response Measures." In National Research Council, Transportation Research Board, *Road Deterioration in Developing Countries and Low-Volume Road Engineering.* Transportation Research Record 1128. National Research Council, Washington, D.C.; pp. 1–17.

Falconer, Julia. 1992. "Non-Timber Forest Products in Ghana's Forest Zone: Issues for Forest Conservation." In Cleaver *et al.* 1992, pp. 177–181.

Falkenmark, Malin. 1991. "Rapid Population Growth and Water Scarcity: The Predicament of Tomorrow's Africa." In Davis and Bernstam 1991, pp. 81–94.

———, and Riga Adiwoso Suprapto. 1992. "Population-Landscape Interactions in Development: A Water Perspective to Environmental Sustainability." *Ambio* 21(1):31–36. Royal Swedish Academy of Sciences, Stockholm.

Falloux, François. 1989. *Land Information and Remote Sensing for Renewable Resource Management in Sub-Saharan Africa: A Demand-Driven Approach.* World Bank Technical Paper No. 108. World Bank, Washington, D.C.

———, and Aleki Mukendi (eds.). 1988. *Desertification Control and Renewable Resource Management in the Sahelian and Sudanian Zones of West Africa.* World Bank Technical Paper No. 70. World Bank, Washington, D.C.

Falloux, François, Lee Talbot, Jeri Larson. 1991. *Progress and Next Steps for National Environmental Action Plans in Africa.* Environment Division, Africa Technical Department. World Bank, Washington, D.C.

Falloux, François, and Lee M. Talbot. 1992. *Crise et Opportunité: Environnement et Développement en Afrique.* Masonneuve and Larose, Paris.

———. 1993. *Crisis and Opportunity: Environment and Development in Africa.* Earthscan, London.

Famoriyo, Segun. 1979. *Land Tenure and Agricultural Development in Nigeria.* Nigerian Institute of Social and Economic Research, Ibadan. Ibadan University Press, Ibadan, Nigeria.

Food and Agriculture Organization of the United Nations (FAO). 1983. *Food Aid in Figures.* Food and Agriculture Organization of the United Nations, Rome.

———. 1984a. *Changes in Shifting Cultivation in Africa.* FAO Forestry Paper No. 50. Food and Agriculture Organization of the United Nations, Rome.

———. 1984b. *Land, Food and People.* Food and Agriculture Organization of the United Nations, Rome.

———. 1984c. *Women in Agricultural Production.* Women in Agriculture No. 1. Food and Agriculture Organization of the United Nations, Rome.

———. 1984d. *Women in Food Production (Report of the Expert Consultation Held in Rome, 7–14 December 1983).* Food and Agriculture Organization of the United Nations, Rome.

———. 1985. *Women in Developing Agriculture.* Women in Agriculture No. 4. Food and Agriculture Organization of the United Nations, Rome.

———. 1986. *Atlas of African Agriculture.* Food and Agriculture Organization of the United Nations, Rome.

———. 1989. *Forestry and Nutrition: A Reference Manual.* Food and Agriculture Organization of the United Nations, Rome.

———. 1990a. *The Major Significance of 'Minor' Forest Products: The Local Use and Value of Forests in the West African Humid Forest Zone.* Prepared by Julia Falconer. Community Forestry Note 6. Food and Agriculture Organization of the United Nations, Rome.

———. 1990b. *The Conservation and Rehabilitation of African Lands: An International Scheme.* ARC/90/4. Food and Agriculture Organization of the United Nations, Rome.

———. 1991. *Small Ruminant Production and the Small Ruminant Genetic Resource in Tropical Africa.* FAO Animal Production and Health Paper 88. By R. Trevor Wilson. Food and Agriculture Organization of the United Nations, Rome.

————and United Nations Economic Commission for Africa (ECA). 1992. *Land Degradation and Food Supply: Issues and Options for Food Self-Sufficiency in Africa.* Food and Agriculture Organization of the United Nations, Rome, and United Nations Economic Commission for Africa, Addis Ababa.

———— and United Nations Environment Programme (UNEP). 1981. *Forest Resources of Tropical Africa, Part I: Regional Synthesis.* Food and Agriculture Organization of the United Nations, Rome.

FAO/World Bank Cooperative Programme. 1991. *Nigeria: Land Resources Management Study.* Report No. 32/91 CP-NIR 42 SPN (3 vols.). Food and Agriculture Organization of the United Nations, Investment Centre, FAO/World Bank Cooperative Programme, Rome.

Fapohunda, Eleanor R. 1988. "The Nonpooling Household: A Challenge to Theory." In Dwyer and Bruce 1988, pp. 143–154.

Farooq, Ghazi M., Ita I. Ekanem and Sina Ojelade. 1987. "Family Size Preferences and Fertility in South-Western Nigeria." In Oppong 1987, pp. 75–85.

Farah, Jumanah. 1994. *Pesticide Policies in Developing Countries: Do They Encourage Excessive Use?* World Bank Discussion Paper No. 238, World Bank, Washington, D.C.

Feder, Gershon, and David Feeny. 1991. "Land Tenure and Property Rights: Theory and Implications for Development Policy." *The World Bank Economic Review* 5(1):135–153.

Feierman, Steven. 1993. "Defending the Promise of Subsistence: Population Growth and Agriculture in the West Usambara Mountains, 1920–1980." In Turner, Hyden, and Kates 1993, pp. 114–144.

Ferguson-Bisson, Darlène. 1992. "Rational Land Management in the Face of Demographic Pressure: Obstacles and Opportunities for Rural Men and Women." *Ambio* 21(1):90–94. Royal Swedish Academy of Sciences, Stockholm.

Ford, Robert E. 1993. "Marginal Coping in Extreme Land Pressures: Ruhengeri, Rwanda." In Turner, Hyden, and Kates 1993, pp. 145–186.

Foreit, Karen G. 1992. *Private Sector Approaches to Effective Family Planning.* Policy Research Working Paper WPS 940, Population and Human Resources Department. World Bank, Washington, D.C.

Fortmann, Louise. 1981. "The Plight of the Invisible Farmer: The Effect of National Agricultural Policy on Women in Africa." In Dauber and Cain 1981, pp. 205–214.

————, and John W. Bruce (eds.). 1988. *Whose Trees? Proprietary Dimensions of Forestry.* Westview Press, Boulder and London.

Frank, Odile. 1990. "The Demand for Fertility Control." In Acsadi, Johnson-Acsadi, Bulatao 1990, pp. 186–198.

Frederick, Kenneth D. 1993. *Balancing Water Demands with Supplies: The Role of Management in a World of Increasing Scarcity.* World Bank Technical Paper No. 189. World Bank, Washington, D.C.

Frederiksen, Harald D. 1993. *Drought Planning and Water Efficiency Implications in Water Resources Management.* World Bank Technical Paper No. 185. World Bank, Washington, D.C.

Freeman, Peter H., with J. K. Rennie. 1985. "Desertification in the Sahel: Diagnosis and Proposals for IUCN's Response." International Union for Conservation of Nature and Natural Resources (IUCN), Gland, Switzerland.

Funk, Ursula. 1988. "Land Tenure, Agriculture, and Gender in Guinea-Bissau." In Jean Davison, ed., 1988c, pp. 33–58.

The Futures Group. 1976. *Effects of Population on Development Objectives: A Demonstration.* (RAPID - Resources for the Awareness of Population Impacts on Development). The Futures Group, Washington, D.C.

————. 1981. *Rwanda: The Effects of Population Factors on Social and Economic Development.* (RAPID - Resources for the Awareness of Population Impacts on Development). The Futures Group, Washington, D.C.

————. 1983. *Mali: The Effects of Population Factors on Social and Economic Development.* (RAPID - Resources for the Awareness of Population Impacts on Development). The Futures Group, Washington, D.C.

―――. 1985. *Nigeria: The Effects of Population Factors on Social and Economic Development.* (RAPID - Resources for the Awareness of Population Impacts on Development). The Futures Group, Washington, D.C.

―――. 1991. *Population et Environnement au Rwanda.* Deuxième édition. The Futures Group, Washington, D.C.

Garbus, Lisa, Anthony Pritchard, and Odin Knudsen (eds.). 1991. *Agricultural Issues in the 1990s: Proceedings of the Eleventh Agriculture Sector Symposium.* World Bank, Washington, D.C.

Gaviria, Juan, Vishva Bindlish and Uma Lele. 1989. *The Rural Road Question and Nigeria's Agricultural Development.* MADIA Discussion Paper 10. World Bank, Washington, D.C.

Gerhart, John D. 1986. "Farming Systems Research, Productivity, and Equity." In Moock 1986, pp. 58–70.

Ghana, Government of; Land Use Planning Committee. 1979. *Report of the Land Use Planning Committee.* Accra, Ghana.

Ghana, Republic of, and United Nations Children Fund. 1990. *Children and Women of Ghana: A Situation Analysis 1989–90.* Accra, Ghana.

Gibbon, Peter, Kjell J. Havnevik, and Kenneth Hermele. 1993. *A Blighted Harvest: The World Bank and African Agriculture in the 1980s.* Africa World Press, Trenton, N.J., USA.

Gille, Halvor. 1985. "Policy Implications." In Cleland and Hobcraft 1985, pp. 273–295.

Glantz, Michael H. (ed.). 1987. *Drought and Hunger in Africa: Denying Famine a Future.* Cambridge University Press, Cambridge, England.

Glewwe, Paul, and Kwaku A. Twum-Baah. 1991. *The Distribution of Welfare in Ghana, 1987–88.* Living Standards Measurement Study, Working Paper No. 75. World Bank, Washington, D.C.

Gnaegy, Suzanne, and Jock R. Anderson (eds.). 1991. *Agricultural Technology in Sub-Saharan Africa: A Workshop on Research Issues.* World Bank Discussion Paper No. 126. World Bank, Washington, D.C.

Goheen, Miriam. 1988. "Land and the Household Economy: Women Farmers of the Grassfields Today." In Davison 1988c, pp. 90–105.

Goldman, Abe. 1993. "Population Growth and Agricultural Change in Imo State, Southeastern Nigeria." In Turner, Hyden, and Kates 1993, pp. 250–301.

Goodland, Robert. 1991. *Tropical Deforestation: Solutions, Ethics and Religions.* Environment Working Paper No. 43, Environment Department. World Bank, Washington, D.C.

Goody, Jack, and Joan Buckley. 1973. "Inheritance and Women's Labour in Africa." *Africa* 43(2):108–121.

Gorse, Jean Eugene, and David R. Steeds. 1987. *Desertification in the Sahelian and Sudanian Zones of West Africa.* World Bank Technical Paper No. 61. World Bank, Washington, D.C.

Gray, John W. 1983. *Forest Revenue Systems in Developing Countries: Their Role in Income Generation and Forest Management Strategies.* FAO Forestry Paper No. 43. Food and Agriculture Organization of the United Nations, Rome.

Greathead, David John, and J. K. Waage. 1983. *Opportunities for Biological Control of Agricultural Pests in Developing Countries.* World Bank Technical Paper No. 11. World Bank, Washington, D.C.

Gregersen, Hans, Sydney Draper and Dieter Elz (eds.). 1989. *People and Trees: The Role of Social Forestry in Sustainable Development.* EDI Seminar Series. World Bank, Washington, D.C.

Grimshaw, Richard G. 1989. "A Review of Existing Soil Conservation Technologies and a Proposed Method of Soil Conservation Using Contour Farming Practices Backed by Vetiver Grass Hedge Barriers." In Meyers 1989, pp. 81–97.

Gritzner, Jeffrey Allman. 1988. *The West African Sahel: Human Agency and Environmental Change.* Geography Research Paper No. 226. University of Chicago, Chicago.

Grut, Mikael, John A. Gray, and Nicolas Egli. 1991. *Forest Pricing and Concession Policies: Managing the High Forests of West and Central Africa.* World Bank Technical Paper No. 143, Africa Technical Department Series. World Bank, Washington, D.C.

Guyer, Jane I. 1986. "Intra-Household Processes and Farming Systems Research: Perspectives from Anthropology." In Moock 1986, pp. 92–104.

————. 1988. "Dynamic Approaches to Domestic Budgeting: Cases and Methods from Africa." In Dwyer and Bruce 1988, pp. 155–172.

Gumbo, Davison J. 1992. "Technology Generation and its Niche in Integrated Natural Resources Management." In World Bank 1992a, pp. 191–195.

Haan, Cees de. 1991. "Developments in Animal Technology." In Garbus, Pritchard, and Knudsen 1991, pp. 57–69.

Haan, Cornelis de, and Nico J. Nissen. 1985. *Animal Health Services in Sub-Saharan Africa: Alternative Approaches.* World Bank Technical Paper No. 44. World Bank, Washington, D.C.

Haddad, Lawrence, and Ravi Kanbur. 1990. *Are Better-off Households More Unequal or Less Unequal?* PRE Working Paper WPS 373. World Bank, Washington, D.C.

Haggblade, Steven, and Peter B. Hazell. 1988. "Prospects for Equitable Growth in Rural Sub-Saharan Africa." AGRAP Economic Discussion Paper No. 3, Agriculture and Rural Development Department. World Bank, Washington, D.C.

————, and James Brown. 1989. "Farm-Nonfarm Linkages in Rural Sub-Saharan Africa." *World Development* 17(8):1173–1201.

Hammond, Peter B. 1959. "Economic Change and Mossi Acculturation." In Bascom and Herskovits 1959, pp. 238–256.

Hansen, Art. 1988. "Correcting the Underestimated Frequency of the Head-of-Household Experience for Women Farmers." In Poats, Schmink and Spring 1988, pp. 111–126.

————, and Della E. McMillan (eds.). 1986. *Food in Sub-Saharan Africa.* Lynne Rienner, Boulder, Colorado.

Hansen, Stein. 1990. "Absorbing a Rapidly Growing Labor Force." In Acsadi, Johnson-Acsadi, Bulatao 1990, pp. 60–73.

Harden, Blaine. 1990. *Africa: Dispatches from a Fragile Continent.* W.W. Norton and Co., New York and London.

Harral, Clell. 1987. "Organization and Management of Road Maintenance in Developing Countries." In National Research Council, Transportation Research Board, *Road Deterioration in Developing Countries and Low-Volume Road Engineering.* Transportation Research Record 1128. National Research Council, Washington, D.C.; pp. 36–41.

Harrison, Paul. 1987. *The Greening of Africa: Breaking Through in the Battle for Land and Food.* An International Institute for Environment and Development - Earthscan Study. Penguin, London/New York.

Harrison, Peter, and John Howe. 1989. "Measuring Transport Demands of the Rural Poor: Experience from Africa." *GATE -German Appropriate Technology Exchange,* No. 1/89. Deutsches Zentrum für Entwicklungstechnologien, Eschborn, Germany; pp. 3–6.

Hart, Keith. 1982. *The Political Economy of West African Agriculture.* Cambridge University Press, Cambridge, U.K.

Haswell, Margaret, and Diana Hunt (eds.). 1991. *Rural Households in Emerging Societies: Technology and Change in Sub-Saharan Africa.* Berg Publishers, Oxford/New York.

Hathway, Gordon. 1985. *Low-Cost Vehicles: Options for Moving People and Goods.* Intermediate Technology Publications, London.

Heggie, Ian G. 1987. "Transport and Environment: A Review of Current Policies and Procedures." Discussion Paper, Transportation Issues Series, Report No. TRP6, Transportation Department. World Bank, Washington, D.C.

Heidemann, Claus, and Charles K. Kaira. 1984. "Transport Planning in Rural Regions in Developing Countries." *Economics* 30:142-157.

Hemmings-Gapihan, Grace S. 1982. "International Development and the Evolution of Women's Economic Roles: A Case Study from Northern Gulma, Upper Volta." In Bay 1982, pp. 171–189.

Henderson, Helen. 1986. "The Grassroots Women's Committee as a Development Strategy in an Upper Volta Village." In Creevey 1986, pp. 133–152.

Henn, Jeanne Koopman. 1988. "Intra-Household Dynamics and State Policies as Constraints on Food Production: Results of a 1985 Agroeconomic Survey in Cameroon." In Poats, Schmink and Spring 1988, pp. 315–330.

Heyer, Judith, Pepe Roberts and Gavin Williams (eds.). 1981. *Rural Development in Tropical Africa.* St. Martin's Press, New York.

Higgins, G. M., A. H. Kassam, L. Naiken, G. Fischer, and M. M. Shah. 1982. *Potential Population Supporting Capacities of Land in the Developing World.* Technical Report of

Project INT/75/P13, "Land Resources for Populations of the Future." FAO, UNDP and IIASA, Rome.

Hill, Althea. 1990. "Population Conditions in Mainland Sub-Saharan Africa." In Acsadi, Johnson-Acsadi, Bulatao 1990, pp. 3–27.

Hill, Ian D. 1982. "Natural Resource Surveys in Agricultural Development Planning: A Quick and Clean Method." *Agricultural Administration* 10:181–188. Applied Science Publishers, Barking, Essex, England.

Hill, M. Anne, and Elizabeth M. King. 1993. "Women's Education in Developing Countries: An Overview." In King and Hill 1993, pp. 1–50.

Hill, Polly. 1963. *The Migrant Cocoa Farmers of Southern Ghana.* Cambridge University Press, Cambridge.

———. 1982. *Dry Grain Farming Families: Hausaland (Nigeria) and Karnataka (India) Compared.* Cambridge University Press, Cambridge.

Hirschmann, David, and Megan Vaughan. 1983. "Food Production and Income Generation in a Matrilineal Society: Rural Women in Zomba, Malawi." *Journal of Southern African Studies* 10(1):86–99.

Hjort af Ornäs, Anders, and M. A. Mohamed Salih (eds.). 1989. *Ecology and Politics: Environmental Stress and Security in Africa.* Scandinavian Institute of African Studies, Uppsala, Sweden.

Ho, Teresa J. 1985. "Population Growth and Agricultural Productivity in Sub-Saharan Africa." In Davis 1985, pp. 92–128.

———. 1990. "Population Growth and Agricultural Productivity." In Acsadi, Johnson-Acsadi, Bulatao 1990, pp. 31–43.

Hoff, Karla. 1991. "Introduction: Agricultural Taxation and Land Rights Systems." *The World Bank Economic Review* 5(1):85–91.

Holcombe, Susan. 1988. *Profiles of Women Agricultural Producers: A Tool for Development Planners — A Sudan Example.* UNIFEM Occasional Paper No. 7. United Nations Development Fund for Women, New York.

Holden, Dennis, Peter Hazell, and Anthony Pritchard (eds.). 1991. *Risk in Agriculture: Proceedings of the Tenth Agriculture Sector Symposium.* World Bank, Washington, D.C.

Horenstein, Nadine. 1987. *Supporting Women's Involvement in African Agriculture: An Assessment of Selected Agencies' Approaches.* Report prepared for the World Bank, Women in Development Division. International Center for Research on Women, Washington, D.C.

———. 1989. *Women and Food Security in Kenya.* PPR Working Paper WPS 232. World Bank, Washington, D.C.

Horowitz, Michael M., and Peter D. Little. 1987. "African Pastoralism and Poverty: Some Implications for Drought and Famine." In Glantz 1987, pp. 59–82.

Horowitz, Michael M., and Muneera Salem-Murdock. 1993. "River Basin Development Policy, Women and Children: A Case Study from the Senegal River Valley." In Steady 1993, pp. 317–338.

Hoskins, Marilyn. 1979. "Women in Forestry for Local Community Development: A Programming Guide." Office of Women in Development, USAID, Washington, D.C.

Hough, John. 1991a. "Michiru Mountain Conservation Area: Integrating Conservation with Human Needs." In West and Brechin 1991, pp. 130–137.

———. 1991b. "Social Impact Assessment: Its Role in Protected Area Planning and Management." In West and Brechin 1991, pp. 274–283.

Howarth, Richard B., and Richard B. Norgaard. 1990. "Intergenerational Resource Rights, Efficiency, and Social Optimality." *Land Economics* 66(1):1–11.

Hoyle, B. S. (ed.). 1974. *Spatial Aspects of Development.* John Wiley and Sons, London and New York.

Hudgens, Robert. 1988. "A Diagnostic Survey of Female Headed Households in the Central Province of Zambia." In Poats, Schmink and Spring 1988, pp. 373–387.

Hudson, N. W. 1987. "Limiting Degradation Caused by Soil Erosion." In Wolman and Fournier 1987, pp. 153–169.

Hurlich, Susan. 1986. *Women in Zambia.* Rural Science and Technology Institute, Canadian International Development Agency, Hull, Quebec, Canada.

Hyde, Karin A. L. 1993. "Sub-Saharan Africa." In King and Hill 1993, pp. 100–135.

Hyde, William F., and David H. Newman, with a contribution by Roger A. Sedjo. 1991. *Forest Economics and Policy Analysis: An Overview*. World Bank Discussion Paper No. 134. World Bank, Washington, D.C.

Hyden, Goran. 1986. "The Invisible Economy of Smallholder Agriculture in Africa." In Moock 1986, pp. 11–35.

———, Robert W. Kates, and B. L. Turner II. 1993. "Beyond Intensification." In Turner, Hyden, and Kates 1993, pp. 401–439.

Ibrahim, Fouad N. 1987. "Ecology and Land Use Changes in the Semiarid Zone of the Sudan." In Little and Horowitz 1987, pp. 213–229.

Immers, Ben H., Ernst J. Malipaard and Michel J. H. Oldenhof. 1989. "Rural Transport in Developing Countries: A Case Study of Western Province, Zambia." *GATE — German Appropriate Technology Exchange*, No. 1/89, pp. 7–11. Deutsches Zentrum für Entwicklungstechnologien, Eschborn, Germany.

Independent Commission on International Humanitarian Issues (ICIHI). 1985. *Famine: A Man-Made Disaster?* A Report for the Independent Commission on International Humanitarian Issues. Pan Books, London and Sidney.

Inter-African Committee on Medicinal Plants and African Tropical Medicine and Scientific, Technical and Research Commission of the Organization of African Unity. 1985. *African Pharmacopeia* (Vol. I). OAU-STRC Scientific Publication No. 2. Lagos, Nigeria.

International Center for Research on Women (ICRW). 1989. *Strengthening Women: Health Research Priorities for Women in Developing Countries*. ICRW, Washington, D.C.

International Food Policy Research Institute (IFPRI). 1991. *IFPRI Report 1990*. Washington, D.C.

International Labour Office (ILO). 1989. *Women and Land*. Report on the Regional African Workshop on Women's Access to Land as a Strategy for Employment Promotion, Poverty Alleviation and Household Food Security, organized by the International Labour Office in Collaboration with the University of Zimbabwe, in Harare, Zimbabwe, from 17 to 21 October 1988. Programme on Rural Women, Rural Employment Policies Branch. International Labour Office, Geneva.

International Service for National Agricultural Research (ISNAR) and Special Program for African Agricultural Research (SPAAR). 1987. *Guidelines for Strengthening National Agricultural Research Systems in Sub-Saharan Africa*. World Bank, Washington, D.C.

Jackai, L. E. N., A. R. Panizzi, G. G. Kundu and K. P. Srivastava. 1990. "Insect Pests of Soybeans in the Tropics." In S. R. Singh 1990, pp. 91–156.

Jackson, Cecile. 1985. *The Kano River Irrigation Project*. The Population Council. Kumarian Press, West Hartford, Conn., USA.

Jaeger, William K. 1992. *The Effects of Economic Policies on African Agriculture*. World Bank Discussion Paper No. 147, Africa Technical Department Series. World Bank, Washington, D.C.

Jaffee, Steven, and Jitendra Srivastava. 1992. *Seed System Development: The Appropriate Roles of the Private and Public Sectors*. World Bank Discussion Paper No. 167. World Bank, Washington, D.C.

Jagannathan, Vijay. 1989. *Poverty, Public Policies and the Environment*. Environment Department Working Paper No. 24. World Bank, Washington, D.C.

Jahnke, Hans, Dieter Kirschke and Johannes Lagemann. 1987. *The Impact of Agricultural Research in Tropical Africa: A Study of the Collaboration between the International and National Research Systems*. Consultative Group on International Agricultural Research, CGIAR Study Paper No. 21. World Bank, Washington, D.C.

Jansen, Doris. 1988. *Trade, Exchange Rate, and Agricultural Pricing Policies in Zambia*. World Bank Comparative Studies: The Political Economy of Agricultural Pricing Policy. World Bank, Washington, D.C.

Jayne, Thomas S., John C. Day, and Harold E. Dregne. 1989. *Technology and Agricultural Productivity in the Sahel*. USDA, Economic Research Service, Agricultural Economic Report No. 612. U.S. Department of Agriculture, Washington, D.C.

Jiggins, Janice. 1986. *Gender-Related Impacts and the Work of the International Agricultural Research Centers*. Consultative Group on International Agricultural Research, CGIAR Study Paper No. 17. World Bank, Washington, D.C.

Jodha, N. S. 1992. *Common Property Resources: A Missing Dimension of Development Strategies.* World Bank Discussion Paper No. 169. World Bank, Washington, D.C.

Joekes, Susan. 1989. "Women's Programmes and the Environment." *Populi,* Journal of the United Nations Population Fund, 16(3):4–12.

Jones, Christine W. 1986. "Intra-Household Bargaining in Response to the Introduction of New Crops: A Case Study from North Cameroon." In Moock 1986, pp. 105–123.

Jones, William I., and Roberto Egli. 1984. *Farming Systems in Africa: The Great Lakes Highlands of Zaïre, Rwanda, and Burundi.* World Bank Technical Paper No. 27. World Bank, Washington, D.C.

Kaira, Charles K. 1982. "A Field Survey of Transportation Requirements for Subsistence Farmers of Mwea Division in Kirinyaga." Institute for Development Studies, Nairobi.

Kaluli, James. 1993. "NGO Involvement in Agricultural Activities in Machakos District." In Wellard and Copestake 1993, pp. 111–117.

Kamarck, Andrew M. 1976. *The Tropics and Economic Development: A Provocative Inquiry into the Poverty of Nations.* Johns Hopkins University Press, Baltimore and London.

Kandiyoti, Deniz. 1985. *Women in Rural Production Systems: Problems and Policies.* UNESCO, Paris.

Kasfir, Nelson. 1993. "Agricultural Transformation in the Robusta Coffee/Banana Zone of Bushenyi, Uganda." In Turner, Hyden, and Kates 1993, pp. 41–79.

Kassogué, Armand, with Jean Dolo and Tom Ponsioen. 1990. *Traditional Soil and Water Conservation on the Dogon Plateau, Mali.* International Institute for Environment and Development (IIED), Dryland Networks Programme, Issues Paper No. 23. IIED, London.

Kelley, Allen C., and Charles E. Nobbe. 1990. *Kenya at the Demographic Turning Point? Hypotheses and a Proposed Research Agenda.* World Bank Discussion Paper No. 107. World Bank, Washington, D.C.

Kennedy, Eileen T., and Bruce Cogill. 1987. *Income and Nutritional Effects of the Commercialization of Agriculture in Southwestern Kenya.* Research Report 63. International Food Policy Research Institute, Washington, D.C.

Kenya, Republic of. 1980. *The Integrated Rural Surveys 1976–79.* Central Bureau of Statistics, Nairobi, Kenya.

King, Elizabeth M., and M. Anne Hill (eds.). 1991. *Women's Education in Developing Countries: Barriers, Benefits and Policy.* PHREE Background Paper PHREE/91/40, Population and Human Resources Department. World Bank, Washington, D.C.

———, and M. Anne Hill (eds.). 1993. *Women's Education in Developing Countries: Barriers, Benefits, and Policies.* Published for the World Bank. The Johns Hopkins University Press, Baltimore and London.

Kiss, Agnes, and Frans Meerman. 1991. *Integrated Pest Management and African Agriculture.* World Bank Technical Paper No. 142, Africa Technical Department Series. World Bank, Washington, D.C.

Knudsen, Odin, John Nash with contributions by James Brovard, Bruce Gardner, and L. Alan Winters. 1990. *Redefining the Role of Government in Agriculture for the 1990s.* World Bank Discussion Paper No. 105. World Bank, Washington, D.C.

Kocher, James E. 1973. *Rural Development, Income Distribution, and Fertility.* The Population Council, New York.

Kolbilla, Dan, and Kate Wellard. 1993. "Langbesi Agricultural Station: Experiences in Agricultural Research." In Wellard and Copestake 1993, pp. 202–209.

Kreimer, Alcira, and Mohan Munasinghe (eds.). 1991. *Managing Natural Disasters and the Environment: Selected Materials from the Colloquium on the Environment and Natural Disaster Management Sponsored by The World Bank, June 27–28, 1990, Washington, D.C.* Environment Department. World Bank, Washington, D.C.

Lal, Rattan, and Bede Okigbo. 1990. *Assessment of Soil Degradation in the Southern States of Nigeria.* Environment Department Working Paper No. 39. World Bank, Washington, D.C.

Lanly, Jean Paul. 1982. *Tropical Forest Resources.* FAO Forestry Paper No. 30. Food and Agriculture Organization of the United Nations, Rome.

Ladipo, Patricia. 1987. "Women in a Maize Storage Co-operative in Nigeria: Family Planning, Credit and Technological Change." In Oppong 1987, pp. 101–117.

Leach, Gerald, and Robin Mearns. 1988. *Beyond the Woodfuel Crisis: People, Land and Trees in Africa.* Earthscan Publications, London.

Leach, Melissa. 1991. "Engendered Environments: Understanding Natural Resource Management in the West African Forest Zone." *IDS Bulletin* 22(4):17–24.

Ledec, George, and Robert Goodland. 1988. *Wildlands: Their Protection and Economic Management in Economic Development.* World Bank, Washington, D.C.

Lee, Ronald D. and Timothy Miller. 1990. "Population Growth, Externalities to Childbearing, and Fertility Policy in the Third World." In Stanley Fisher, Dennis de Tray and Shekar Shah, eds., *Proceedings of the World Bank Annual Conference on Development Economics 1990.* Supplement to *The World Bank Economic Review* and *The World Bank Research Observer.* World Bank, Washington, D.C.; pp. 275–304.

Lele, Uma. 1986. "Women and Structural Transformation." *Economic Development and Cultural Change* 34(2):195–221.

————. 1989a. *Agricultural Growth, Domestic Policies, the External Environment, and Assistance to Africa: Lessons of a Quarter Century.* MADIA Discussion Paper 1. World Bank, Washington, D.C.

————. 1989b. *Structural Adjustment, Agricultural Development and the Poor: Lessons from the Malawian Experience.* MADIA Discussion Paper 9. World Bank, Washington, D.C.

———— (ed.). 1989c. *Managing Agricultural Development in Africa: Three Articles on Lessons from Experience.* MADIA Discussion Paper 2. World Bank, Washington, D.C.

————, and Manmohan Agarwal. 1989. *Smallholder and Large-Scale Agriculture in Africa: Are There Tradeoffs Between Growth and Equity?* MADIA Discussion Paper 6. World Bank, Washington, D.C.

Lele, Uma, and Robert E. Christiansen. 1989. *Markets, Marketing Boards, and Cooperatives in Africa: Issues in Adjustment Policy.* MADIA Discussion Paper 11. World Bank, Washington, D.C.

Lele, Uma, and L. Richard Meyers. 1989. *Growth and Structural Change in East Africa: Domestic Policies, Agricultural Performance and World Bank Assistance, 1963–86, Parts I and II.* MADIA Discussion Paper 3. World Bank, Washington, D.C.

Lele, Uma, and Steven W. Stone. 1989. *Population Pressure, the Environment and Agricultural Intensification: Variations on the Boserup Hypothesis.* MADIA Discussion Paper 4. World Bank, Washington, D.C.

Lele, Uma, Robert E. Christiansen, Kundhavi Kadiresan. 1989. *Fertilizer Policy in Africa: Lessons from Development Programs and Adjustment Lending, 1970–87.* MADIA Discussion Paper 5. World Bank, Washington, D.C.

Lemma, Aklilu, and Pentti Malaska (eds.). 1989. *Africa Beyond Famine: A Report to the Club of Rome.* Tycooly, London and New York.

LeMoigne, Guy, Shawki Barghouti, Gershon Feder, Lisa Garbus and Mei Xie (eds.). 1992. *Country Experiences with Water Resource Management: Economic, Institutional, Technological and Environmental Issues.* World Bank Technical Paper No. 175. World Bank, Washington, D.C.

Leonard, Jeffrey H., and contributors. 1989. *Environment and the Poor: Development Strategies for a Common Agenda.* U.S.-Third World Policy Perspectives, No. 11. Overseas Development Council. Transaction Books, New Brunswick, New Jersey.

Leridon, Henri, and Benoît Ferry. 1985. "Biological and Traditional Restraints on Fertility." In Cleland and Hobcraft 1985, pp. 139–164.

Leslie, Joanne, and Michael Paolisso (eds.). 1989. *Women, Work, and Child Welfare in the Third World.* AAAS Selected Symposium 110. Westview Press, Boulder, Colorado.

Lewis, Barbara. 1982. "Fertility and Employment: An Assessment of Role Incompatibility among African Urban Women." In Bay 1982, pp. 249–276.

Levinson, F. James. 1991. *Addressing Malnutrition in Africa: Low-Cost Program Possibilities for Government Agencies and Donors.* Social Dimensions of Adjustment in Sub-Saharan Africa, SDA Working Paper No. 13, Africa Technical Department. World Bank, Washington, D.C.

Liebenow, J. Gus. 1987. "Food Self-Sufficiency in Malawi: Are Successes Transferable?" In Glantz 1987, pp. 369–392.

Lifton, Carey. 1991. "Social Soundness and WID Analyses for USAID Legal Reform Project Paper." Paper prepared for USAID/Bissau, Guinea-Bissau.

Lightbourne, R. E. 1985. "Individual Preferences and Fertility Behaviour." In Cleland and Hobcraft 1985, pp. 165–198.

Lipton, Michael, and Carol Heald. 1984. "African Food Strategies and the EEC's Role: An Interim Review." IDS Commission Study No. 6. Centre for European Policy Studies, Brussels, Belgium, and Institute of Development Studies, Sussex, U.K.

Lipton, Michael, and Richard Longhurst. 1985. *Modern Varieties, International Agricultural Research, and the Poor*. Consultative Group on International Agricultural Research, CGIAR Study Paper No. 2. World Bank, Washington, D.C.

Lisk, Franklyn, and Yvette Stevens. 1987. "Government Policy and Rural Women's Work in Sierra Leone." In Oppong 1987, pp. 182–202.

Little, Peter D. 1987. "Land Use Conflicts in the Agricultural/Pastoral Borderlands: The Case of Kenya." In Little and Horowitz 1987, pp. 195–212.

———, and Michael M. Horowitz (eds.). 1987. *Lands at Risk in the Third World: Local-Level Perspectives*. Westview Press, Boulder and London.

Lofchie, Michael F. 1987. "The Decline of African Agriculture: An Internalist Perspective." In Glantz 1987, pp. 85–109.

Loose, E. 1979. "Women in Rural Senegal: Some Economic and Social Observations." Paper presented at the Workshop on Sahelian Agriculture, Department of Agricultural Economics; Purdue University, West Lafayette, Indiana, USA, February 1979.

Low, Allan. 1986. "On-Farm Research and Household Economics." In Moock 1986, pp. 71–91.

Ludwig, Heinz-Dieter. 1968. "Permanent Farming on Ukara: The Impact of Land Shortage on Husbandry Practices." In Hans Ruthenberg, ed., *Smallholder Farming and Smallholder Development in Tanzania*. Afrika-Studien, No. 24. Weltforum, Munich, pp. 87–135.

Lundgren, Lill. 1992. "The Kenyan National Soil Conservation Project: An Example of an Integrated Natural Resources Management Project." In World Bank 1992a, pp. 69–92.

Lusigi, Walter (ed.). 1992. *Managing Protected Areas in Africa*. Report from a Workshop on Protected Area Management in Africa, Mweka, Tanzania. UNESCO - World Heritage Fund, Paris.

Lutz, Ernst, and Michael Young. 1990. *Agricultural Policies in Industrial Countries and Their Environmental Impacts: Applicability to and Comparisons with Developing Nations*. Environment Department Working Paper No. 25. World Bank, Washington, D.C.

Maathai, Wangari. 1988. *The Green Belt Movement: Sharing the Approach and the Experience*. Environment Liaison Centre International, Nairobi.

Mabbut, J. A., and C. Floret (eds.). 1980. *Case Studies on Desertification*. Unesco, Paris.

Mabogunje, Akin L. 1992. *Perspective on Urban Land and Urban Management Policies in Sub-Saharan Africa*. World Bank Technical Paper No. 196. Africa Technical Department Series. World Bank, Washington, D.C.

MacGarry, Brian. 1993. "Silveira House: Promoting the Use of Hybrid Seed (1968–83)." In Wellard and Copestake 1993, pp. 50–66.

Mackenzie, Fiona. 1992. "Development from Within? The Struggle to Survive." In Taylor and Mackenzie 1992, pp. 1–32.

MacNeill, Jim, Pieter Winsemius, Taizo Yakushiji. 1991. *Beyond Interdependence: The Meshing of the World's Economy and the Earth's Ecology*. A Trilateral Commission Book. Oxford University Press, New York.

Magrath, William. 1989. *The Challenge of the Commons: The Allocation of Nonexclusive Resources*. Environment Department Working Paper No. 14. World Bank, Washington, D.C.

———, and Peter Arens. 1989. *The Costs of Soil Erosion on Java: A Natural Resource Accounting Approach*. Environment Department Working Paper No. 18. World Bank, Washington, D.C.

Mahar, Dennis J. (ed.). 1985. *Rapid Population Growth and Human Carrying Capacity: Two Perspectives*. World Bank Staff Working Paper No. 690, Population and Development Series No. 15. World Bank, Washington, D.C.

Maine, Deborah, Regina McNamara, Joe Wray, Abdul-Aziz Farah, and Marylin Wallace. 1990. "Effects of Fertility Change on Maternal and Child Survival." In Acsadi, Johnson-Acsadi, Bulatao 1990, pp. 91–104.

Makinwa, Paulina Kofoworola. 1981. *Internal Migration and Rural Development in Nigeria: Lessons From Bendel State*. Heinemann Educational Books (Nig.) Ltd., Ibadan, Nigeria.

Mannathoko, Bob. 1992. "People's Participation in Natural Resources Management: Some Examples from Botswana." In World Bank 1992a, pp. 135–142.

Manuh, Takyiwaa. 1992. "Survival in Rural Africa: The Salt Co-operatives in Ada District, Ghana." In Taylor and Mackenzie 1992, pp. 102–124.

Marek, Tonia. 1992. *Ending Malnutrition: Why Increasing Income Is Not Enough*. Technical Working Paper No. 5, Population and Health Division, Africa Technical Department. World Bank, Washington, D.C.

Marenha, Comba. 1985. "Producing Food: The Gambian Women's Burden." In Environmental Liaison Center, *Women and the Environmental Crisis*. Report of the Proceedings of the Workshops on Women, Environment and Development, Nairobi, 10–20 July 1985. Environmental Liaison Center, Nairobi; pp. 55–57.

Marks, Stuart A. 1991. "Some Reflections on Participation and Co-management from Zambia's Central Luangwa Valley." In West and Brechin 1991, pp. 346–358.

Martin, Susan. 1993. "From Agricultural Growth to Stagnation: The Case of the Ngwa, Nigeria, 1900–1980." In Turner, Hyden, and Kates 1993, pp. 302–323.

Mathews, Jessica T. 1988. "Africa: Continent in Crisis" (mimeo.). World Resources Institute, Washington, D.C.

Matlon, Peter J. 1990. "Improving Productivity in Sorghum and Pearl Millet in Semi-Arid Africa." *Food Research Institute Studies* XXII(1):1–43. Food Research Institute, Stanford University, Stanford, California.

———. 1991. "Farmer Risk Management Strategies: The Case of the West African Semi-Arid Tropics." In Holden, Hazell, and Pritchard 1991, pp. 51–79.

Mauldin, W. Parker, and Sheldon J. Segal. 1988. "Prevalence of Contraceptive Use: Trends and Issues." *Studies in Family Planning* 19(6):335–353.

Mauldin, W. Parker, and John A. Ross. 1991. "Family Planning Programs: Efforts and Results, 1982–1989." *Studies in Family Planning* 22(6):350–367.

Mbilinyi, Marjorie J. 1971. "The Participation of Women in African Economies." ERB Paper 71.12. Economic Research Bureau, University of Dar es Salaam, Tanzania.

McCann, James. 1987. "The Social Impact of Drought in Ethiopia: Oxen, Households, and Some Implications for Rehabilitation." In Glantz 1987, pp. 245–267.

McCay, Bonnie J., and James M. Acheson (eds.). 1987. *The Question of the Commons: The Culture and Ecology of Communal Resources*. University of Arizona Press, Tucson, Arizona.

McDonald, Peter. 1985. "Social Organization and Nuptiality in Developing Societies." In Cleland and Hobcraft 1985, pp. 87–114.

McGuire, Judith S., and Barry M. Popkin. 1990. *Helping Women Improve Nutrition in the Developing World: Beating the Zero Sum Game*. World Bank Technical Paper No. 114. World Bank, Washington, D.C.

McIntyre, John. 1991. "Managing Risk in African Pastoralism." In Holden, Hazell, and Pritchard 1991, pp. 129–142.

McLoughlin, Peter F. M. (ed.). 1970. *African Food Production Systems: Cases and Theory*. Johns Hopkins University Press, Baltimore and London.

McMillan, Della E. 1987. "The Social Impact of Planned Settlement in Burkina Faso." In Glantz 1987, pp. 297–322.

———, Thomas Painter, and Thayer Scudder. 1992. *Settlement and Development in the River Blindness Control Zone*. World Bank Technical Paper No. 192, Series on River Blindness Control in West Africa. World Bank, Washington, D.C.

McNamara, Regina, Therese McGinn, Donald Lauro and John Ross. 1992. *Family Planning Programs in Sub-Saharan Africa: Case Studies from Ghana, Rwanda, and the Sudan*. Policy Research Working Paper WPS 1004, Population and Human Resources Department. World Bank, Washington, D.C.

McNicoll, Geoffrey. 1984. *Consequences of Rapid Population Growth: An Overview*. World Bank Staff Working Paper No. 691, Population and Development Series No. 16. World Bank, Washington, D.C.

Mellor, John W., and Bruce F. Johnston. 1984. "The World Food Equation." *Journal of Economic Literature* XXII(2):531–774.

Mellor, John W., Christopher L. Delgado and Malcolm J. Blackie (eds.). 1987. *Accelerating Food Production in Sub-Saharan Africa*. Johns Hopkins University Press, Baltimore and London.

Meyers, Richard L. (ed.). 1989. *Innovation in Resource Management: Proceedings of the Ninth Agriculture Sector Symposium.* World Bank, Washington, D.C.

Migot-Adholla, Shem, Peter Hazell, Benoît Blarel and Frank Place. 1989. "Land Tenure Security and Agricultural Production in Sub-Saharan Africa." In Meyers 1989, pp. 105–119.

Migot-Adholla, Shem, Frank Place, George Benneh and Steven Atsu. 1990. "Land Use Rights and Agricultural Productivity of Ghanaian Farmers" (Draft). Agriculture Department. World Bank, Washington, D.C.

Migot-Adholla, Shem, Peter Hazell, Benoît Blarel, and Frank Place. 1991. "Indigenous Land Rights Systems in Sub-Saharan Africa: A Constraint on Productivity?" *The World Bank Economic Review* 5(1):155–175.

Mitchell, Donald O., and Merlinda D. Ingco. 1993. *The World Food Outlook.* International Economics Department. World Bank, Washington, D.C.

Molnar, Augusta. 1989. *Community Forestry: Rapid Appraisal.* Food and Agriculture Organization of the United Nations, Rome.

———, and Götz Schreiber. 1989. *Women and Forestry: Operational Issues.* PPR Working Paper WPS 184. World Bank, Washington, D.C.

Montalembert, M. R. de, and J. Clement. 1983. *Fuelwood Supplies in the Developing Countries.* FAO Forestry Paper No. 42. Food and Agriculture Organization of the United Nations, Rome.

Montgomery, Mark R., and Edward K. Brown. 1990. "Accommodating Urban Growth in Sub-Saharan Africa." In Acsadi, Johnson-Acsadi, Bulatao 1990, pp. 74–88.

Moock, Joyce Lewinger (ed.). 1986. *Understanding Africa's Rural Households and Farming Systems.* Westview Special Studies on Africa. Westview Press, Boulder, Colorado.

Moris, Jon. 1991. *Extension Alternatives in Tropical Africa.* Agricultural Administration Unit, Occasional Paper 7. Overseas Development Institute, London.

Mortimore, Michael. 1989a. *Adapting to Drought: Farmers, Famines and Desertification in West Africa.* Cambridge University Press, Cambridge, England.

———. 1989b. *The Causes, Nature and Rate of Soil Degradation in the Northernmost States of Nigeria and an Assessment of the Role of Fertilizer in Counteracting the Processes of Degradation.* Environment Department Working Paper No. 17. World Bank, Washington, D.C.

———. 1993. "The Intensification of Peri-Urban Agriculture: The Kano Close-Settled Zone, 1964–1986." In Turner, Hyden, and Kates 1993, pp. 358–400.

———, Emmanuel A. Olofin, Riginand A. Cline-Cole, Ahmadu Abdulkadir (eds.). 1987. *Perspectives on Land Administration and Development in Northern Nigeria.* Proceedings of the Workshop on Land Resources, Kano, September 25–28, 1986. Department of Geography, Bayero University, Kano, Nigeria.

———, and others. 1990. "The Nature, Rate and Effective Limits of Intensification in the Small Holder Farming System of the Kano Close-Settled Zone." Study for the Federal Agricultural Coordinating Unit, Government of Nigeria. Department of Geography, Bayero University, Kano, Nigeria.

Moser, Caroline. 1986. "Women's Needs in the Urban System: Training Strategies in Gender Aware Planning." In Judith Bruce and Marilyn Kohn, eds., *Learning about Women and Urban Services in Latin America and the Caribbean (A Report on the Women, Low-Income Households and Urban Services Project of the Population Council).* The Population Council, New York; pp. 40–61.

Mtoi, Manasse Timmy. 1988. "Institutional and Policy Parameters Affecting Gender Issues in Farming Systems Research in Tanzania." In Poats, Schmink and Spring 1988, pp. 345–359.

Mueller, Eva. 1982. "The Allocation of Women's Time and Its Relation to Fertility." In Anker, Buvinic and Youssef 1982, pp. 55–86.

Munasinghe, Mohan, and Michael Wells. 1992. "Protection of Natural Habitats and Sustainable Development of Local Communities." In Cleaver *et al.* 1992, pp. 161–168.

Munasinghe, Mohan, and Ernst Lutz. 1993. "Environmental Economics and Valuation in Development Decisionmaking." In Munasinghe 1993, pp. 17–72.

Munasinghe, Mohan (ed.). 1993. *Environmental Economics and Natural Resource Management in Developing Countries.* (Compiled by Adelaida Schwab.) Committee of International Development Institutions on the Environment (CIDIE). Distributed for CIDIE by the World Bank, Washington, D.C.

Mung'ala, Patrick M. 1993. "Government Experiences of Collaboration with NGOs in Rural Afforestation." In Wellard and Copestake 1993, pp. 136–144.

Mungate, David. 1993. "Government Experience of Collaboration with NGOs in Agricultural Research and Extension." In Wellard and Copestake 1993, pp. 26–37.

Muntemba, Shimwaayi (ed.). 1985. *Rural Development and Women: Lessons from the Field.* 2 vols. International Labour Office, Geneva.

Murdoch, William W. 1980. *The Poverty of Nations: The Political Economy of Hunger and Population.* Johns Hopkins University Press, Baltimore, Md.

Murdock, George P., and Caterina Provost. 1973. "Factors in the Division of Labor by Sex: A Cross-Cultural Analysis." *Ethnology* 12:203–225. University of Pittsburgh Press, Pittsburgh, Pennsylvania.

Murphy, Josette. 1989. *Women and Agriculture in Africa: A Guide to Bank Policy and Programs for Operations Staff.* Africa Technical Department, Agriculture Division. World Bank, Washington, D.C.

Mvududu, Sara. 1993. "Forestry Commission Links with NGOs in Rural Afforestation." In Wellard and Copestake 1993, pp. 38–49.

Myers, Norman. 1987. "The Environmental Basis of Sustainable Development." *The Annals of Regional Science, Special Edition: Environmental Management and Economic Development* XXI(3):33–43. Western Washington University, Bellingham, Wash., USA.

———. 1988. *Natural Resource Systems and Human Exploitation Systems: Physiobiotic and Ecological Linkages.* Environment Department Working Paper No. 12. World Bank, Washington, D.C.

———. 1989. "Population Growth, Environmental Decline and Security Issues in Sub-Saharan Africa." In Hjort af Ornäs and Salih 1989, pp. 211–231.

———. 1992. "Population/Environment Linkages: Discontinuities Ahead." *Ambio* 21(1):116–118. Royal Swedish Academy of Sciences, Stockholm.

Nair, P. K. R. 1990. *The Prospects for Agroforestry in the Tropics.* World Bank Technical Paper No. 131. World Bank, Washington, D.C.

National Research Council. 1993. *Vetiver Grass: A Thin Green Line Against Erosion.* National Academy Press, Washington, D.C.

Ndaro, Japheth M. M. 1992. "Local Coping Strategies in Dodoma District, Tanzania." In Taylor and Mackenzie 1992, pp. 170–196.

Ndiweni, Mpuliso. 1993. "The Organization of Rural Associations for Progress and Grassroots Development." In Wellard and Copestake 1993, pp. 77–84.

Nelson, Ridley. 1988. *Dryland Management: The 'Desertification' Problem.* Environment Department Working Paper No. 8. World Bank, Washington, D.C.

Nekby, Bengt A. 1990. "Sub-Saharan Africa — Dryland Management: The Search for Sustainable Development Options" (mimeo.). Africa Technical Department, Environment Division. World Bank, Washington, D.C.

———. 1992. "Technology Generation." In World Bank 1992a, pp. 185–189.

Netting, Robert McC. 1993. *Smallholders, Householders: Farm Families and the Ecology of Intensive, Sustainable Agriculture.* Stanford University Press, Stanford, California.

———, Glenn Davis Stone, and M. Priscilla Stone. 1993. "Agricultural Expansion among the Kofyar, Jos Plateau, Nigeria." In Turner, Hyden, and Kates 1993, pp. 206–249.

Newcombe, Kenneth J. 1989. "An Economic Justification for Rural Afforestation: The Case of Ethiopia." In Schramm and Warford 1989, pp. 117–138.

Newman, Kate. 1992. "Forest People and People in the Forest: Investing in Local Community Development." In Cleaver *et al.* 1992, pp. 229–232.

Nicholson, Sharon E. 1989. "Long-Term Changes in African Rainfall." *Weather* 44:46–56.

Nigerian Environmental Study Action Team (NEST). 1991. *Nigeria's Threatened Environment: A National Profile.* Ibadan, Nigeria.

Nijkamp, Peter, Jeroen C.J.M. van den Bergh and Frits J. Soeteman. 1991. "Regional Sustainable Development and Natural Resource Use." In Stanley Fisher, Dennis de Tray and Shekar Shah, eds., *Proceedings of the World Bank Annual Conference on Development Economics 1990*, Supplement to *The World Bank Economic Review* and *The World Bank Research Observer*, Washington, D.C.; pp. 153–188.

Nkhoma-Wamunza, Alice. 1992. "The Informal Sector: A Strategy for Survival in Tanzania." In Taylor and Mackenzie 1992, pp. 197–213.

Norem, Margaret, Sandra Russo, Marie Sambou and Melanie Marlett. 1988. "The Women's Program of the Gambian Mixed Farming Project." In Poats, Schmink and Spring 1988, pp. 303–313.

Noronha, Raymond. 1985. "A Review of the Literature on Land Tenure Systems in Sub-Saharan Africa." Discussion Paper ARU 43, Agriculture and Rural Development Department. World Bank, Washington, D.C.

Norse, David, and Reshma Saigal. 1993. "National Economic Cost of Soil Erosion in Zimbabwe." In Munasinghe 1993, pp. 229–240.

Ntshalinsthali, Concelia, and Carmelita McGurk. 1991. "Resident Peoples and Swaziland's Malolotja National Park: A Success Story." In West and Brechin 1991, pp. 61–67.

Nyerges, A. Endre. 1987. "The Development Potential of the Guinea Savanna: Social and Ecological Constraints in the West African 'Middle Belt.'" In Little and Horowitz 1987, pp. 316–336.

Nyoni, Sithembiso. 1985. "Africa's Food Crisis: Price of Ignoring Village Women?" In Environmental Liaison Center, *Women and the Environmental Crisis*. Report of the Proceedings of the Workshops on Women, Environment and Development, Nairobi, 10–20 July 1985. Environmental Liaison Center, Nairobi; pp. 53–55.

Odhiambo, Thomas R. 1989. "Visions for IPM in Africa." In Ole Zethner, ed., *Pest Management and the African Farmer*. Proceedings of an ICIPE/World Bank Conference on Integrated Pest Management in Africa, Nairobi, Kenya, May 22–26, 1989. International Centre of Insect Physiology and Ecology, ICIPE Science Press, Nairobi; pp. 137–142.

———. 1991. "Managing Drought and Locust Invasions in Africa." In Kreimer and Munasinghe 1991, pp. 77–81.

Ofomata, Godfrey Ezediaso Kingsley. 1987. *Soil Erosion in Nigeria: The Views of a Geomorphologist*. University of Nigeria, Inaugural Lecture Series No. 7. University of Nigeria Press, Nsukka, Nigeria.

Okafor, Francis C. 1993. "Agricultural Stagnation and Economic Diversification: Awka-Nnewi Region, Nigeria, 1930–1980." In Turner, Hyden, and Kates 1993, pp. 324–357.

Okali, C., and J. E. Sumberg. 1986. "Sheep and Goats, Men and Women: Household Relations and Small Ruminant Production in Southwest Nigeria." In Moock 1986, pp. 166–181.

Okoth-Ogendo, H. W. O., and John O. Oucho. 1993. "Population Growth and Agricultural Change in Kisii District, Kenya: A Sustained Symbiosis?" In Turner, Hyden, and Kates 1993, pp. 187–205.

Oldeman, L. R., V. W. P. van Engelen, and J. H. M. Pulles. 1990. "The Extent of Human-Induced Soil Degradation." In L. R. Oldeman, R. T. A. Hakkeling, and W. G. Sombroek, *World Map of the Status of Human-Induced Soil Degradation: An Explanatory Note*. 2nd revised edition. International Soil Reference and Information Centre, Wageningen, The Netherlands.

Olson, Jennifer Maria. 1990. "The Impact of Changing Socioeconomic Factors on Migration Patterns in Rwanda" (M.A. thesis). Department of Geography, Michigan State University, Ann Arbor, Michigan.

Omari, C. K. 1990. "Traditional African Land Ethics." In J. Ronald Engel and Joan Gibb Engel, eds., *Ethics of Environment and Development: Global Challenge, International Response*. University of Arizona Press, Tucson, Arizona; pp. 167–175.

Omo-Fadaka, Jimoh. 1990. "Communalism: The Moral Factor in African Development." In Engel and Engel 1990, pp. 176–182.

Ondiege, Peter O. 1992. "Local Coping Strategies in Machakos District, Kenya." In Taylor and Mackenzie 1992, pp. 125–147.

Openshaw, Keith, and Charles Feinstein. 1989a. *Fuelwood Stumpage: Considerations for Developing Country Energy Planning*. Industry and Energy Department Working Paper, Energy Series Paper No. 16. World Bank, Washington, D.C.

———. 1989b. *Fuelwood Stumpage: Financing Renewable Energy for the World's Other Half*. PPR Working Paper WPS 270, Industry and Energy Department. World Bank, Washington, D.C.

Opole, Monica. 1985. "With Culture in Mind: Improved Cookstoves and Kenyan Women." In Environmental Liaison Center, *Women and the Environmental Crisis*. Report of the Proceedings of the Workshops on Women, Environment and Development, Nairobi, 10–20 July 1985. Environmental Liaison Center, Nairobi; pp. 33–34.

Oppong, Christine. 1982. "Family Structure and Women's Reproductive and Productive Roles: Some Conceptual and Methodological Issues." In Anker, Buvinic and Youssef 1982, pp. 133–150.

———— (ed.). 1987. *Sex Roles, Population and Development in West Africa: Policy-Related Studies on Work and Demographic Issues.* International Labour Office. Heinemann, Portsmouth, New Hampshire and James Currey, London.

Orubuloye, Oyetunji. 1987. "Values and Costs of Daughters and Sons to Yoruba Mothers and Fathers." In Oppong 1987, pp. 86–90.

Ottenberg, Phoebe V. 1959. "The Changing Economic Position of Women Among the Afikpo Ibo." In Bascom and Herskovits 1959, pp. 205–223.

Ottenberg, Simon. 1959. "Ibo Receptivity to Change." In Bascom and Herskovits 1959, pp. 130–143.

Over, Mead. 1992. *The Macroeconomic Impact of AIDS in Sub-Saharan Africa.* Technical Working Paper No. 3, Population, Health and Nutrition Division, Africa Technical Department. World Bank, Washington, D.C.

Owens, Solomon. 1993. "Catholic Relief Services in The Gambia: Evolution from Agricultural Research to Community-Based Experimentation." In Wellard and Copestake 1993, pp. 239–250.

Painter, Thomas M. 1987. "Bringing Land Back in: Changing Strategies to Improve Agricultural Production in the West African Sahel." In Little and Horowitz 1987, pp. 144–163.

————. 1991. "Approaches to Improving Natural Resource Use for Agriculture in Sahelian West Africa: A Sociological Analysis of the 'Aménagement/Gestion des Terroirs Villageois' Approach and its Implications for Non-Government Organizations." CARE Agriculture and Natural Resources Technical Report Series No. 3. CARE, New York.

Palmer, Ingrid. 1985a. *The Impact of Agrarian Reform on Women.* The Population Council. Kumarian Press, West Hartford, Conn., USA.

————. 1985b. *The Impact of Out-Migration on Women in Farming.* The Population Council. Kumarian Press, West Hartford, Conn., USA.

Palo, Maati, and Jyrki Salmi (eds.). 1987. *Deforestation or Development in the Third World?* Volume I. Finnish Forest Research Institute, Helsinki.

Panayotou, Theodore, and Peter S. Ashton. 1992. *Not By Timber Alone: Economics and Ecology for Sustaining Tropical Forests.* Island Press, Washington, D.C.

Panin, Anthony. 1988. *Hoe and Bullock Farming Systems in Northern Ghana: A Comparative Analysis.* Nyankpala Agricultural Research Report 1/1988. TRIOPS Tropical Scientific Books, Langen, Germany.

Pankhurst, Donna, and Susie Jacobs. 1988. "Land Tenure, Gender Relations, and Agricultural Production: The Case of Zimbabwe's Peasantry." In Davison 1988c, pp. 202–227.

Paolisso, Michael, Michael Baksh and J. Conley Thomas. 1989. "Women's Agricultural Work, Child Care, and Infant Diarrhea in Rural Kenya." In Leslie and Paolisso 1989, pp. 217–236.

Pearce, David W., and Anil Markandya. 1987. "Marginal Opportunity Cost as a Planning Concept in Natural Resource Management." *The Annals of Regional Science, Special Edition: Environmental Management and Economic Development* XXI(3):18–32. Western Washington University, Bellingham, Wash., USA.

Pearch, David W., Edward B. Barbier, Anil Markandya. 1988. *Environmental Economics and Decision-Making in Sub-Saharan Africa.* IIED/UCL London Environmental Economics Centre, LEEC Paper 88–01. International Institute for Environment and Development/University College London, London.

Peters, Pauline E. 1986. "Household Management in Botswana: Cattle, Crops, and Wage Labor." In Moock 1986, pp. 133–154.

————. 1987. "Embedded Systems and Rooted Models: The Grazing Lands of Botswana and the Commons Debate." In McCay and Acheson 1987, pp. 171–194.

Peterson, Richard B. 1992. "Kutafuta Maisha: Searching for Life on Zaïre's Ituri Forest Frontier." In Cleaver et al. 1992, pp. 193–201.

Pezzey, John. 1989. *Economic Analysis of Sustainable Growth and Sustainable Development.* Environment Department Working Paper No. 15. World Bank, Washington, D.C.

Pingali, Prabhu, Yves Bigot and Hans Binswanger. 1987. *Agricultural Mechanization and the Evolution of Farming Systems in Sub-Saharan Africa*. World Bank, Johns Hopkins University Press, Baltimore and London.

Pittin, Renée. 1987. "Documentation of Women's Work in Nigeria: Problems and Solutions." In Oppong 1987, pp. 25–44.

Platteau, J.-Ph. 1992. *Formalization and Privatization of Land Rights in Sub-Saharan Africa: A Critique of Current Orthodoxies and Structural Adjustment Programmes*. Development Economics Research Programme Discussion Paper DEP/34. London School of Economics, London.

Poats, Susan V. 1990. "Gender Issues in the CGIAR System: Lessons and Strategies from Within." Paper prepared for the 1990 CGIAR Mid-Term Meeting, The Hague, 21–25 May, 1990. Consultative Group on International Agricultural Research. World Bank, Washington, D.C.

———, Marianne Schmink and Anita Spring (eds.). 1988. *Gender Issues in Farming Systems Research and Extension*. Westview Press, Boulder, Colorado.

Poore, Duncan, Peter Burgess, John Palmer, Simon Rietbergen and Timothy Synnott. 1989. *No Timber Without Trees: Sustainability in the Tropical Forest*. A Study for ITTO. Earthscan Publications, London.

Pottier, Johan P. 1986. "The Politics of Famine Prevention: Ecology, Regional Production and Food Complementarity in Western Rwanda." *African Affairs*, Journal of the Royal African Society, 85(339):207–237.

Prah, Kwesi K. 1989. "Land Degradation and Class Struggle in Rural Lesotho." In Hjort af Ornäs and Salih 1989, pp. 117–129.

Preston, Samuel H. 1985. "Mortality in Childhood: Lessons from WFS." In Cleland and Hobcraft 1985, pp. 253–272.

Raintree, John B. (ed.). 1987. *Land, Trees, and Tenure*. Proceedings of an International Workshop on Tenure Issues in Agroforestry, Nairobi, May 27–31, 1985, Sponsored by the Ford Foundation. International Council for Research on Agroforestry, Nairobi, and Land Tenure Center, University of Wisconsin, Madison, Wisconsin.

Rasmusson, Eugene M. 1987. "Global Climate Change and Variability: Effects on Drought and Desertification in Africa." In Glantz 1987, pp. 3–22.

Reardon, Thomas, Peter Matlon and Christopher Delgado. 1988. "Coping with Household-Level Food Insecurity in Drought-Affected Areas of Burkina Faso." *World Development* 16(9):1065–1074.

Redclift, Michael. 1987. *Sustainable Development: Exploring the Contradictions*. Methuen, London and New York.

Reij, Chris. 1988. *The Present State of Soil and Water Conservation in the Sahel*. Organisation for Economic Co-operation and Development/Permanent Interstate Committee for Drought Control in the Sahel/Club du Sahel, SAHEL D(89)329. OECD, Paris.

———. 1990. "Indigenous Soil and Water Conservation in Africa: An Assessment of Current Knowledge." Paper Presented to the Workshop on 'Conservation in Africa: Indigenous Knowledge and Conservation Strategies,' Harare, Zimbabwe, 2–7 December 1990. Social Science Research Council/American Council of Learned Societies: The Joint Committee on African Studies. Center for Development Cooperation Services, Free University, Amsterdam.

———, Stephen Turner and Tom Kuhlman. 1986. *Soil and Water Conservation in Sub-Saharan Africa: Issues and Options*. Centre for Development Cooperation Services, Free University, Amsterdam, and International Fund for Agricultural Development, Rome.

———, Paul Mulder, and Louis Begemann. 1988. *Water Harvesting for Plant Production*. World Bank Technical Paper No. 91. World Bank, Washington, D.C.

Repetto, Robert. 1986. *World Enough and Time: Successful Strategies for Resource Management*. Yale University Press, New Haven, Conn., USA.

———. 1987. "Economic Incentives for Sustainable Production." *The Annals of Regional Science, Special Edition: Environmental Management and Economic Development* XXI(3):44–59. Western Washington University, Bellingham, Wash., USA.

———. 1988a. *The Forest for the Trees? Government Policies and the Misuse of Forest Resources*. World Resources Institute, Washington, D.C.

————. 1988b. *Economic Policy Reform for Natural Resource Conservation.* Environment Department Working Paper No. 4. World Bank, Washington, D.C.

————. 1989. *Population, Resources, Environment: An Uncertain Future.* Population Bulletin 42(2), April 1989 Reprint. Population Reference Bureau, Inc., Washington, D.C.

———— (ed.). 1985. *The Global Possible: Resources, Development and the New Century.* Yale University Press, New Haven, Conn.

————, and Thomas Holmes. 1983. "The Role of Population in Resource Depletion in Developing Countries." *Population and Development Review* 9(4):609–632.

————, and John Pezzey. 1990. "The Economics of Sustainable Development." Overview Paper Prepared for the UNECE/USEPA Workshop on the Economics of Sustainable Development, Washington, D.C., January 23–26, 1990. World Resources Institute, Washington, D.C.

Richards, Paul. 1983. "Ecological Change and the Politics of African Land Use." *The African Studies Review* 26(2):1–72.

————. 1985. *Indigenous Agricultural Revolution: Ecology and Food Production in West Africa.* Hutchinson, London and Westview Press, Boulder, Colorado.

————. 1991. "Experimenting Farmers and Agricultural Research." In Haswell and Hunt 1991, pp. 11–21.

Riverson, John D. N., and Steve Carapetis. 1991. *Intermediate Means of Transport in Sub-Saharan Africa: Its Potential for Improving Rural Travel and Transport.* World Bank Technical Paper No. 161, Africa Technical Department Series. World Bank, Washington, D.C.

Riverson, John D. N., Juan Gaviria, and Sydney Thriscutt. 1991. *Rural Roads in Sub-Saharan Africa: Lessons from World Bank Experience.* World Bank Technical Paper No. 141, Africa Technical Department Series. World Bank, Washington, D.C.

Rodda, Annabel (ed.). 1991. *Women and the Environment.* Joint UN NGO Group on Women and Development, United Nations Non-Governmental Liaison Service. Zed Books, London and Atlantic Highlands, New Jersey.

Rose, Laurel. 1988. "'A Woman is Like a Field': Women's Strategies for Land Access in Swaziland." In Davison 1988c, pp. 177–201.

Ross, John A., Marjorie Rich, Janet P. Molzan and Michael Pensak. 1988. *Family Planning and Child Survival: 100 Developing Countries.* Center for Population and Family Health, Columbia University, New York.

Runge-Metzger, Artur. 1988. *Variability in Agronomic Practices and Allocative Efficiency Among Farm Households in Northern Ghana: A Case Study in On-Farm Research.* Nyankpala Agricultural Research Report 2/1988. Josef Margraf Scientific Books, Weikersheim, Germany.

Russell, Sharon Stanton, Karen Jacobsen, and William Deane Stanley. 1990. *International Migration and Development in Sub-Saharan Africa.* Vol. I: Overview; Vol. II: Country Analyses. World Bank Discussion Papers No. 101 and No. 102. World Bank, Washington, D.C.

Ruthenberg, Hans. 1980. *Farming Systems in the Tropics.* Third Edition. Oxford University Press, Oxford, England.

———— (Hans E. Jahnke, ed.). 1985. *Innovation Policy for Small Farmers in the Tropics: The Economics of Technical Innovations for Agricultural Development.* Clarendon Press, Oxford, England.

Ruttan, Vernon W. 1991. "Constraints on Sustainable Growth in Agricultural Production: Into the 21st Century." In Garbus, Pritchard, and Knudsen 1991, pp. 23–35.

Safilios-Rothschild, Constantina. 1982. "Female Power, Autonomy and Demographic Change in the Third World." In Anker, Buvinic and Youssef 1982, pp. 117–132.

Sahn, David E. 1990. *Malnutrition in Côte d'Ivoire: Prevalence and Determinants.* Social Dimensions of Adjustment in Sub-Saharan Africa, Working Paper No. 4. World Bank, Washington, D.C.

Sai, Fred T. 1986. "Africa's Parliamentarians and Population." Keynote Speech at the All-Africa Conference of Parliamentarians and Development, Harare, May 12–16, 1986 (mimeo.). Population and Human Resources Department. World Bank, Washington, D.C.

————, and K. Newman. 1989. *Ethical Approaches to Family Planning in Africa.* PPR Working Paper WPS 324. World Bank, Washington, D.C.

Salem-Murdock, Muneera. 1987. "Rehabilitation Efforts and Household Production Strategies: The New Halfa Agricultural Scheme in Eastern Sudan." In Little and Horowitz 1987, pp. 337–351.

Sanchez, Pedro A. 1991. "Alternatives to Slash and Burn: A Pragmatic Approach to Mitigate Tropical Deforestation" (mimeo.). Paper presented at the World Bank Conference on "Agricultural Technology for Sustainable Economic Development in the New Century: Policy Issues for the International Community," Washington, D.C., 23 October 1991. Africa Technical Department. World Bank, Washington, D.C.

Sarch, Marie-Therese. 1993. "Case Study of the Farmer Innovation and Technology Testing Programme in The Gambia." In Wellard and Copestake 1993, pp. 225–238.

Savory, Allan. 1988. Holistic Resource Management. Island Press, Washington, D.C.

Schneider, Bertrand (ed.). 1987. Africa Facing its Priorities. Co-Operation for Development Series Vol. 7. Published for the Club of Rome by Cassell Tycooly, London.

Schneider, Harold K. 1959. "Pakot Resistance to Change." In Bascom and Herskovits 1959, pp. 144–167.

Schoepf, Brooke Grundfest, and Claude Schoepf. 1988. "Land, Gender and Food Security in Eastern Kivu, Zaïre." In Davison 1988c, pp. 106–130.

Schramm, Gunter. 1987. "Managing Urban/Industrial Wood Fuel Supply and Demand in Africa." The Annals of Regional Science, Special Edition: Environmental Management and Economic Development XXI(3):60–79. Western Washington University, Bellingham, Wash., USA.

———, and Jeremy J. Warford (eds.). 1989. Environmental Management and Economic Development. A World Bank Publication. Johns Hopkins University Press, Baltimore. Md.

Schultz, T. Paul. 1993. "Returns to Women's Education." In King and Hill 1993, pp. 51–99.

Schwartz, Lisa A., and Jacob Kampen. 1992. Agricultural Extension in East Africa. World Bank Technical Paper No. 164. World Bank, Washington, D.C.

Seckler, David. 1987. "Economic Costs and Benefits of Degradation and Its Repair." In Blaikie and Brookfield 1987, pp. 84–99.

——— (ed.). 1993. Agricultural Transformation in Africa. Proceedings of the Seminar on Agricultural Transformation in Africa held in Baltimore, Maryland, May 27–29, 1992. Winrock International Institute for Agricultural Development, Arlington, Va., USA.

———, Doug Gollin and Pierre Antoine. 1991. "Agricultural Potential of 'Mid-Africa': A Technological Assessment." In Gnaegy and Anderson 1991, pp. 61–103.

Serageldin, Ismail. 1992. "Saving Africa's Rainforests." In Cleaver and others. 1992, pp. 337–351.

Shaikh, Asif, Eric Arnold, Kjell Christophersen, Roy Hagen, Joseph Tabor, and Peter Warshall. 1988. Opportunities for Sustained Development: Successful Natural Resources Management in the Sahel. Vol. I, Main Report; vol. II, Case Descriptions. Energy/Development International for U.S.AID, Washington, D.C.

Shanmugaratnam, Nadarajah, Trond Vedeld, Anne Mossige, and Mette Bovin. 1992. Resource Management and Pastoral Institution Building in the West African Sahel. World Bank Discussion Paper No. 175, Africa Technical Department Series. World Bank, Washington, D.C.

Sharma, Narendra P. (ed.). 1992. Managing the World's Forests: Looking for Balance Between Conservation and Development. Kendall/Hunt, Dubuque, Iowa, USA.

Shaw, Paul R. 1989. "Rapid Population Growth and Environmental Degradation: Ultimate Versus Proximate Factors." Environmental Conservation 16(3):199–208.

Shaxson, T. F., N. W. Hudson, D. W. Sanders, E. Roose, and W. C. Moldenhauer. 1989. Land Husbandry: A Framework for Soil and Water Conservation. Published in cooperation with the World Association of Soil and Water Conservation. Soil and Water Conservation Society, Ankeny, Iowa, USA.

Simberloff, Daniel. 1986. "Are We on the Verge of a Mass Extinction in Tropical Rain Forests?" In Elliot 1986, pp. 165–180.

Simpson, James R., and Phylo Evangelou (eds.). 1984. Livestock Development in Subsaharan Africa: Constraints, Prospects, Policy. Westview Press, Boulder, Colorado.

Singh, Ram D., and Mathew J. Morey. 1987. "The Value of Work-at-Home and Contributions of Wives' Household Service in Polygynous Families: Evidence from an African LDC." Economic Development and Cultural Change 35(4):743–765.

Singh, Shiv Raj, L. E. N. Jackai, J. H. R. dos Santos and C. B. Adalla. 1990. "Insect Pests of Cowpeas." In S. R. Singh 1990, pp. 43–89.

Singh, Shiv Raj, (ed.). 1990. *Insect Pests of Tropical Food Legumes.* John Wiley and Sons, Chichester, U.K.

Singh, Susheela, and John Casterline. 1985. "The Socio-Economic Determinants of Fertility." In Cleland and Hobcraft 1985, pp. 199–222.

Smale, Melinda. 1985. "Forest Product Use in Mauritania's Brakna Region." *Women in Forestry Newsletter,* Oregon State University, Corvallis, Oregon, USA.

Smith, Graham, and Clell Harral. 1987. "Road Deterioration in Developing Countries: Financial Requirements." In National Research Council, Transportation Research Board, *Road Deterioration in Developing Countries and Low-Volume Road Engineering.* Transportation Research Record 1128. National Research Council, Washington, D.C.; pp. 28–35.

Smock, David R., and Audrey C. Smock. 1972. *Cultural and Political Aspects of Rural Transformation: A Case Study of Eastern Nigeria.* Praeger, New York.

Songsore, Jacob. 1992. "The Co-operative Credit Union Movement in North-Western Ghana: Development Agent or Agent of Incorporation?" In Taylor and Mackenzie 1992, pp. 82–101.

Southgate, Douglas. 1988. *The Economics of Land Degradation in the Third World.* Environment Department Working Paper No. 2. World Bank, Washington, D.C.

————. 1990. "The Causes of Land Degradation along 'Spontaneously' Expanding Agricultural Frontiers in the Third World." *Land Economics* 66(1):93–101.

————, and David Pearce. 1988. *Agricultural Colonization and Environmental Degradation in Frontier Developing Economies.* Environment Department Working Paper No. 9. World Bank, Washington, D.C.

Southgate, Douglas, John Sanders, and Simon Ehui. 1990. "Resource Degradation in Africa and Latin America: Population Pressure, Policies, and Property Arrangements." In Chapman 1990, pp. 1–9.

Spears, John. 1988. *Containing Tropical Deforestation: A Review of Priority Areas for Technological and Policy Research.* Environment Department Working Paper No. 10. World Bank, Washington, D.C.

————, and Edward S. Ayensu. 1985. "Resources, Development, and the New Century: Forestry." In Repetto 1985, pp. 299–335.

Spears, John, and Raymond Rowe. 1991. "Tree-Based Farming Systems." In Garbus, Pritchard, and Knudsen 1991, pp. 129–154.

Speirs, Mike, and Ole Olsen. 1992. *Indigenous Integrated Farming Systems in the Sahel.* World Bank Technical Paper No. 179, Africa Technical Department Series. World Bank, Washington, D.C.

Spiro, Heather M. 1980. "The Role of Women Farming in Oyo State, Nigeria: A Case Study in Two Rural Communities." Agricultural Economics Discussion Paper No. 7/80. International Institute of Tropical Agriculture, Ibadan, Nigeria.

————. 1985. *The Ilora Farm Settlement in Nigeria.* The Population Council. Kumarian Press, West Hartford, Conn., USA.

Spring, Anita. 1988. "Using Male Research and Extension Personnel to Target Women Farmers." In Poats, Schmink and Spring 1988, pp. 407–426.

Srivastava, Jitendra P. 1991. "Crop Technology for the 1990s." In Garbus, Pritchard, and Knudsen 1991, pp. 71–94.

————, Prabhakar Mahedeo Tamboli, John C. English, Rattan Lal and Bobby Alton Stewart. 1993. *Conserving Soil Moisture and Fertility in the Warm Seasonally Dry Tropics.* World Bank Technical Paper No. 221. World Bank, Washington, D.C.

Starkey, Paul. 1991. "Animal Traction: Constraints and Impact Among African Households." In Haswell and Hunt 1991, pp. 77–90.

Staudt, Kathleen. 1985. *Agricultural Policy Implementation: A Case Study from Western Kenya.* The Population Council. Kumarian Press, West Hartford, Conn., USA.

Steady, F. C. (ed.). 1993. *Women and Children First: Environment, Poverty, and Sustainable Development.* Schenkman Books, Rochester, Vermont, USA.

Stephens, Patience W., Eduard Bos, My T. Vu, and Rodolfo Bulatao. 1991. *Africa Region Population Projections, 1990–91 Edition.* PRE Working Paper WPS 598. World Bank, Washington, D.C.

Stevens, Yvette. 1985. "Improved Technologies for Rural Women: Problems and Prospects in Sierra Leone." In Ahmed 1985, pp. 284–326.

Stichter, Sharon. 1975/76. "Women and the Labor Force in Kenya 1895–1964." *Rural Africana*, Winter 1975/76, pp. 45–67. African Studies Center, Michigan State University, East Lansing, Michigan.

Stocking, Mike. 1987. "Measuring Land Degradation." In Blaikie and Brookfield 1987, pp. 49–63.

Stølen, Kristi Anne. 1983. *Peasants and Agricultural Change in Northern Zambia*. Agricultural University of Norway, International Development Programs, Zambian Soil Productivity Research Programme Studies, Occasional Paper No. 4. Landsbruksbokhandelen, As, Norway.

Stone, C. D. 1984. "Household Variability and Inequality in Kofyar Subsistence and Cash-Cropping Economies." *Journal of Anthropological Research* 40(1).

Streeten, Paul. 1987. *What Price Food? Agricultural Price Policies in Developing Countries*. MacMillan, Basingstoke, Hampshire and London.

Stryker, J. Dirck, with the assistance of Emmanuel Dumeau, Jennifer Wohl, Peter Hammond, Andrew Cook, and Katherine Coon. 1990. *Trade, Exchange Rate, and Agricultural Pricing Policies in Ghana*. World Bank Comparative Studies: The Political Economy of Agricultural Pricing Policy. World Bank, Washington, D.C.

Sutherland, Alistair J. 1988. "The Gender Factor and Technology Options for Zambia's Subsistence Farming Systems." In Poats, Schmink and Spring 1988, pp. 389–406.

Svedberg, Peter. 1991. *Poverty and Undernutrition in Sub-Saharan Africa: Theory, Evidence, Policy*. Monograph Series No. 19, Institute for International Economic Studies. Stockholm University, Stockholm, Sweden.

Swift, Jeremy. 1991. "Local Customary Institutions as the Basis for Natural Resource Management Among Boran Pastoralists in Northern Kenya." *IDS Bulletin* 22(4):34–37.

Swindell, Kenneth. 1982. "From Migrant Farmer to Permanent Settler: The Strange Farmers of The Gambia." In Clarke and Kosinski 1982, pp. 96–101.

Taylor, D. R. Fraser. 1992. "Development from Within and Survival in Rural Africa: A Synthesis of Theory and Practice." In Taylor and Mackenzie 1992, pp. 214–258.

——, and Fiona Mackenzie (eds.). 1992. *Development from Within: Survival in Rural Africa*. Routledge, London and New York.

Tembo, Mary N., and Elizabeth Chola Phiri. 1988. "The Impact of Modern Changes in the Chitemene Farming System in the Northern Province of Zambia." In Poats, Schmink and Spring 1988, pp. 361–372.

Teplitz-Sembitzky, Witold, and Gunter Schramm. 1989. *Woodfuel Supply and Environmental Management*. Industry and Energy Department Working Paper, Energy Series Paper No. 19. World Bank, Washington, D.C.

——, and Gerhard Zieroth. 1990. *The Malawi Charcoal Project: Experience and Lessons*. Industry and Energy Department Working Paper, Energy Series Paper No. 20. World Bank, Washington, D.C.

Thottappilly, G., H. W. Rossel, D. V. R. Reddy, F. J. Morales, S. K. Green and K. M. Makkouk. 1990. "Vectors of Virus and Mycoplasma Diseases: An Overview." In S. R. Singh 1990, pp. 323–342.

Tiffen, Mary, Michael Mortimore, and Francis Gichuki. 1994. *More People, Less Erosion: Environmental Recovery in Kenya*. John Wiley and Sons, Chichester, U.K.

Timberlake, Lloyd (Jon Tinker, ed.). 1985. *Africa in Crisis: The Causes, the Cures of Environmental Bankruptcy*. International Institute of Environment and Development. Earthscan, London and Washington.

—— (ed.). 1986. *The Encroaching Desert: The Consequences of Human Failure*. A Report for the Independent Commission on International Humanitarian Issues, Zed Books, London.

Tinker, Irene. 1981. "New Technologies for Food-Related Activities: An Equity Strategy." In Dauber and Cain 1981, pp. 51–88.

——. 1987. "The Real Rural Energy Crisis: Women's Time." *The Energy Journal* 8:125–146.

Tobisson, Eva, and Anders Rudqvist. 1992. "Popular Participation in Natural Resource Management for Development." In World Bank 1992a, pp. 111–133.

Todaro, Michael P. 1976. *Internal Migration in Developing Countries: A Review of Theory, Evidence, Methodology and Research Priorities*. International Labour Office, Geneva.

Trager, Lillian. 1988. "Rural-Urban Linkages: The Role of Small Urban Centers in Nigeria." *African Studies Review* 31(3):29–38.

Trussell, James, and Anne R. Pebley. 1984. *The Potential Impact of Changes in Fertility on Infant, Child, and Maternal Mortality*. World Bank Staff Working Paper No. 698, Population and Development Series No. 23. World Bank, Washington, D.C.

Tsui, Amy Ong. 1985. "The Rise of Modern Contraception." In Cleland and Hobcraft 1985, pp. 115–138.

Tucker, Compton J., Harold E. Dregne, Wilbur W. Newcomb. 1991. "Expansion and Contraction of the Sahara Desert from 1980 to 1990." *Science* 253:299–301.

Turner II, B. L. (Billie Lee), Goran Hyden, and Robert William Kates (eds.). 1993. *Population Growth and Agricultural Change in Africa*. University Press of Florida, Gainesville, Florida.

Turnham, David. 1992. "Education and Sustainable Rural Development." In World Bank 1992a, pp. 179–184.

Udo, Reuben K. 1975. *Migrant Tenant Farmers of Nigeria: A Geographical Study of Rural Migrations in Nigeria*. African Universities Press/Ibadan University Press, Lagos/Ibadan, Nigeria.

———. 1990. *Land Use Policy and Land Ownership in Nigeria*. Ebieakwa Ventures, Lagos, Nigeria.

Umali, Dina L., Gershon Feder, Cornelis de Haan. 1992. *The Balance Between Public and Private Sector Activities in the Delivery of Livestock Services*. World Bank Discussion Paper No. 163. World Bank, Washington, D.C.

United Nations Children's Fund (UNICEF). 1989. *The State of the World's Children 1989*. Oxford University Press, Oxford, U.K.

United Nations Development Fund for Women (UNIFEM). 1987. *Oil Extraction*. Food Cycle Technology Source Book 1. UNIFEM, New York.

———. 1988a. *Fruit and Vegetable Processing*. Food Cycle Technology Source Book 2. UNIFEM, New York.

———. 1988b. *Cereal Processing*. Food Cycle Technology Source Book 3. UNIFEM, New York.

———. 1988c. *Fish Processing*. Food Cycle Technology Source Book 4. UNIFEM, New York.

———. 1989a. *Root Crop Processing*. Food Cycle Technology Source Book 5. UNIFEM, New York.

———. 1989b. *Women and the Food Cycle*. Intermediate Technology Publications, London.

United Nations Development Programme (UNDP), United Nations Enviornment Programme (UNEP), and World Bank. 1994. *Global Environment Facility: Independent Evaluation of the Pilot Phase*. Washington, D.C.

United Nations Development Programme (UNDP) and World Bank. 1989. *African Economic and Financial Data*. New York and Washington, D.C.

———. 1992. *African Development Indicators*. New York and Washington, D.C.

United Nations Development Programme/World Bank Energy Sector Management Assistance Program (ESMAP). 1988. *Proceedings of the ESMAP Eastern and Southern Africa Household Energy Planning Seminar*. Harare, Zimbabwe, 1–5 February 1988.

United Nations Environment Programme (UNEP). 1981. *Environment and Development in Africa*. A Study Prepared by the Environmental Development Action (ENDA) for the United Nations Environment Programme. UNEP Studies, Vol. 2. Pergamon Press, Oxford, U.K.

U.S. Congress, Office of Technology Assessment (OTA). 1984. *Africa Tomorrow: Issues in Technology, Agriculture, and U.S. Foreign Aid — A Technical Memorandum*. OTA-TM-F-31. US Government Printing Office, Washington, D.C.

———. 1986. *Continuing the Commitment: Agricultural Development in the Sahel*. Special Report OTA-F-308. US Government Printing Office, Washington, D.C.

———. 1988. *Enhancing Agriculture in Africa: A Role for U.S. Development Assistance*. OTA-F-356. US Government Printing Office, Washington, D.C.

U.S. Department of Agriculture. 1981. *Food Problems and Prospects in Sub-Saharan Africa: The Decade of the 1980's*. Foreign Agricultural Economic Report No. 166, Economic Research Service. U.S. Department of Agriculture, Washington, D.C.

Vedeld, Trond. 1983. *Social-Economic and Ecological Constraints on Increased Productivity among Large Circle Chitemene Cultivators in Zambia*. Agricultural University of Norway,

International Development Programs, Zambian Soil Productivity Research Programme Studies, Occasional Paper No. 2. Landsbruksbokhandelen, As, Norway.

Veen, J. J. de. 1980. *The Rural Access Roads Program: Appropriate Technology in Kenya*. International Labour Office, Geneva.

Venema, Bernhard. 1986. "The Changing Role of Women in Sahelian Agriculture." In Creevey 1986, pp. 81–94.

Ventura-Dias, Vivianne. 1985. "Modernisation, Production Organisation and Rural Women in Kenya." In Ahmed 1985, pp. 157–210.

Vermeij, Geerat J. 1986. "Survival During Biotic Crises: The Properties and Evolutionary Significance of Refuges." In Elliott 1986, pp. 231–246.

Vierich, Helga. 1986. "Agricultural Production, Social Status, and Intra-Compound Relationships." In Moock 1986, pp. 155–165.

Walker, Brian W. 1985. *Authentic Development in Africa*. Foreign Policy Association Headline Series, No. 274, New York.

Walker, S. Tjip. 1987. "Making Agricultural Extension Work With Women: The Efforts of MIDENO in Cameroon." International Development Management Center, Division of Agricultural and Life Sciences. University of Maryland, College Park, Md., USA.

Walle, Etienne van de, and Andrew Foster. 1990. *Fertility Decline in Africa: Assessment and Prospects*. World Bank Technical Paper No. 125, Africa Technical Department Series. World Bank, Washington, D.C.

Wardman, Anna, and Lucio G. Salas. 1991. "The Implementation of Anti-Erosion Techniques in the Sahel: A Case Study from Kaya, Burkina Faso." *The Journal of Developing Areas* 26(1):65–80.

Warren, D. Michael. 1991. *Using Indigenous Knowledge in Agricultural Development*. World Bank Discussion Paper No. 127. World Bank, Washington, D.C.

Watts, Michael. 1983. "'Good Try, Mr. Paul': Populism and the Politics of African Land Use." *The African Studies Review* 26(2):73–83.

———. 1987. "Drought, Environment and Food Security: Some Reflections on Peasants, Pastoralists and Commoditization in Dryland West Africa." In Glantz 1987, pp. 171–211.

Webb, Patrick. 1989. *Intrahousehold Decisionmaking and Resource Control: The Effects of Rice Commercialization in West Africa*. Working Papers on Commercialization of Agriculture and Nutrition No. 3. International Food Policy Research Institute, Washington, D.C.

Wellard, Kate, and James G. Copestake (eds.). 1993. *Non-Governmental Organizations and the State in Africa: Rethinking Roles in Sustainable Agricultural Development*. Routledge, London and New York.

Wells, Michael, and Katrina Brandon, with Lee Hannah. 1992. *People and Parks: Linking Protected Area Management with Local Communities*. World Bank, World Wildlife Fund, U.S. Agency for International Development, Washington, D.C.

Were, Gideon S. (ed.). 1985. *Women and Development in Africa*. Journal of Eastern African Research and Development, Vol. 15. Gideon S. Were Press, Nairobi, Kenya.

West, Patrick C., and Steven R. Brechin (eds.). 1991. *Resident Peoples and National Parks: Social Dilemmas and Strategies in International Conservation*. University of Arizona Press, Tucson, Arizona.

Westoff, Charles F., and Luis H. Ochoa. 1991. *Unmet Need and the Demand for Family Planning*. DHS Comparative Studies No. 5. Institute for Resource Development, Columbia, Md., USA.

Whitney, J. B. R. 1987. "Impact of Fuelwood Use on Environmental Degradation in the Sudan." In Little and Horowitz 1987, pp. 115–143.

Williams, Paula J. 1992a. *Women's Participation in Forestry Activities in Africa: Project Summary and Policy Recommendations*. Environment Liaison Centre International, Nairobi.

———. 1992b. *Women, Trees and Forests in Africa: A Resource Guide*. Environment Liaison Centre International, Nairobi.

Winterbottom, Robert. 1992. "Tropical Forestry Action Plans and Indigenous People: The Case of Cameroon." In Cleaver *et al.* 1992, pp. 222–228.

———, and Peter T. Hazlewood. 1987. "Agroforestry and Sustainable Development: Making the Connection." *Ambio* 16(2–3): 100–110. Royal Swedish Academy of Sciences, Stockholm.

Wolfe, Alvin W. 1959. "The Dynamics of the Ngombe Segmentary System." In Bascom and Herskovits 1959, pp. 168–186.

Wolman, M. G., and F. G. A. Fournier (eds.). 1987. *Land Transformation in Agriculture*. Scope 32. Published on Behalf of the Scientific Committee on Problems of the Environment (SCOPE) of the International Council of Scientific Unions (ICSU) by John Wiley and Sons, Chichester, U.K.

World Bank. 1984. *Toward Sustainable Development in Sub-Saharan Africa: A Joint Program of Action*. World Bank, Washington, D.C.

————. 1986. *Population Growth and Policies in Sub-Saharan Africa*. World Bank, Washington, D.C.

————. 1987a. *Ethiopia: Agriculture — A Strategy for Growth; Sector Review*. Eastern Africa Department. World Bank, Washington, D.C.

————. 1987b. *Ghana: Forestry Sector Review*. West Africa Region. World Bank, Washington, D.C.

————. 1987c. *Eastern and Southern Africa Agricultural Research Review*. Eastern and Southern Africa Projects Department. World Bank, Washington, D.C.

————. 1987d. *West Africa Agricultural Research Review*. Western Africa Projects Department. World Bank, Washington, D.C.

————. 1988. *Education in Sub-Saharan Africa: Policies for Adjustment, Revitalization, and Expansion*. World Bank, Washington, D.C.

————. 1989a. *Côte d'Ivoire: Agriculture Sector Adjustment Operation*. President's Report. Occidental Africa Department. World Bank, Washington, D.C.

————. 1989b. *Kenya: The Role of Women in Economic Development*. World Bank, Washington, D.C.

————. 1989c. *Renewable Resource Management in Agriculture*. Operations Evaluation Department. World Bank, Washington, D.C.

————. 1989d. *Sub-Saharan Africa: From Crisis to Sustainable Growth (A Long-Term Perspective Study)*. World Bank, Washington, D.C.

————. 1989e. *Successful Development in Africa: Case Studies of Projects, Programs, and Policies*. EDI Development Policy Case Series, Analytical Case Studies No. 1, Economic Development Institute. World Bank, Washington, D.C.

————. 1990a. *Côte d'Ivoire: Forestry Sector Project*. Staff Appraisal Report. Occidental Africa Department. World Bank, Washington, D.C.

————. 1990b. *Wildlife Resource Management with Local Participation in Africa*. Africa Technical Department, Environment Division. World Bank, Washington, D.C.

————. 1990c. *Republic of Ghana: Second Transport Rehabilitation Project*. Staff Appraisal Report. Western Africa Department. World Bank, Washington, D.C.

————. 1991a. *Forestry Development: A Review of Bank Experience*. Operations Evaluation Department. World Bank, Washington, D.C.

————. 1991b. *Forestry Policy Paper*. Agriculture and Rural Development Department. World Bank, Washington, D.C.

————. 1991c. *World Development Report 1991: The Challenge of Development*. Oxford University Press, Oxford, U.K.

————. 1991d. *The World Bank and the Environment — A Progress Report: Fiscal 1991*. World Bank, Washington, D.C.

————. 1991e. *Population and the World Bank: A Review of Activities and Impacts from Eight Case Studies*. Operations Evaluation Department. World Bank, Washington, D.C.

————. 1991f. *National Environmental Action Plans in Africa*. Proceedings from a Workshop organized by the Government of Ireland, the Environmental Institute, University College, Dublin, and the World Bank (EDIAR and (AFTEN), Dublin, Ireland, December 12–14, 1990. Africa Technical Department, Environment Division. World Bank, Washington, D.C.

————. 1991g. *Issues Facing National Environmental Action Plans in Africa*. Report from a Club of Dublin Workshop, Mauritius, June 17–19, 1991. Africa Technical Department, Environment Division. World Bank, Washington, D.C.

————. 1992a. *Integrated Natural Resource Management*. Report from a Workshop, Francistown, Botswana, December 1–7, 1991. AFTEN Working Paper No. 4, Africa Technical Department, Environment Division. World Bank, Washington, D.C.

————. 1992b. *World Development Report 1992: Development and the Environment.* The Johns Hopkins University Press, Baltimore and London.

————. 1993a. *Social Indicators of Development 1993.* The Johns Hopkins University Press, Baltimore and London.

————. 1993b. *World Tables 1993.* The Johns Hopkins University Press, Baltimore and London.

————. 1993c. *World Development Report 1993: Investing In Health.* The Johns Hopkins University Press, Baltimore and London.

World Resources Institute (WRI). 1992. *World Resources 1992–93 — Toward Sustainable Development.* A Report by the World Resources Institute, in collaboration with the United Nations Environment Programme and the United Nations Development Programme. Oxford University Press, Oxford and New York.

———— and International Institute for Environment and Development (IIED). 1987. *World Resources 1987: An Assessment of the Resource Base that Supports the Global Economy.* Basic Books, New York.

————. 1988. *World Resources 1988–89: An Assessment of the Resource Base that Supports the Global Economy.* Basic Books, New York.

World Resources Institute (WRI), World Bank and U.N. Development Programme. 1985. *Tropical Forests: A Call for Action.* Report of a Task Force convened by the World Resources Institute, the World Bank, and the U.N. Development Programme, World Resources Institute, Washington, D.C.

Yotopoulos, Pan A. 1978. "The Population Problem and the Development Solution," *(Population and Agricultural Development: Selected Relationships and Possible Planning Uses,* Technical Paper No. 2). Policy Analysis Division. Food and Agriculture Organization of the United Nations, Rome.

Youssef, Nadia H. 1982. "The Interrelationship Between the Division of Labour in the Household, Women's Roles and Their Impact on Fertility." In Anker, Buvinic and Youssef 1982, pp. 173–201.

Zachariah, K. C., Julien Condé, N. K. Nair, Chike S. Okoye, Eugene K. Campbell, M. L. Srivastava, and Kenneth Swindell. 1980a. *Demographic Aspects of Migration in West Africa—Vol. 1.* World Bank Staff Working Paper No. 414. World Bank, Washington, D.C.

Zachariah, K. C., Julien Condé, N. K. Nair. 1980b. *Demographic Aspects of Migration in West Africa—Vol. 2.* World Bank Staff Working Paper No. 415. World Bank, Washington, D.C.

Zeidenstein, Sondra (ed.). 1979. *Learning About Rural Women. Studies in Family Planning* 10(11/12). The Population Council, New York.

Zethner, Ole (ed.). 1989. *Pest Management and the African Farmer.* Proceedings of an ICIPE/World Bank Conference on Integrated Pest Management in Africa, Nairobi, Kenya, May 22–26, 1989. International Centre of Insect Physiology and Ecology. ICIPE Science Press, Nairobi, Kenya.

Zinanga, Alex F. 1992. *Development of the Zimbabwe Family Planning Program.* Policy Research Working Paper WPS 1053, Population and Human Resources Department. World Bank, Washington, D.C.

Zinyama, Lovemore M. 1992. "Local Farmer Organizations and Rural Development in Zimbabwe." In Taylor and Mackenzie 1992, pp. 33–57.

The Authors

Kevin M. Cleaver, Director of the World Bank's Africa Technical Department, is a specialist on agricultural issues in Sub-Saharan Africa. He holds a Ph.D. in economics from the Fletcher School of Law and Diplomacy, Tufts University. Mr. Cleaver's previous publications include *A Strategy to Develop Agriculture in Sub-Saharan Africa and a Focus for the World Bank* (1993), *An Agricultural Growth and Rural Environment Strategy for the Coastal and Central African Francophone Countries* (1992), and *Conservation of West and Coastal African Rainforests* (1992), as well as articles on African agriculture.

Götz A. Schreiber is Principal Economist in the World Bank's West Central Africa Department. He studied at Bonn, Yale, and Johns Hopkins universities and holds a Ph.D. from Johns Hopkins. Mr. Schreiber has worked in the areas of macroeconomic policy, agricultural and rural development, human resources, and natural resource management. His previous publications have dealt with rural development and natural resource management issues.